BRANCH CONTROL GROUP

Jump

JMP adr	C3
JNZ adr	C2
JZ adr	CA
JNC adr	D2
JC adr	DA
JPO adr	E2
JPE adr	EA
JP adr	F2
JM adr	FA
PCHL	E9

Call

CALL adr	CD
CNZ adr	C4
CZ adr	CC
CNC adr	D4
CC adr	DC
CPO adr	E4
CPE adr	EC
CP adr	F4
CM adr	FC

Return

RET	C9
RNZ	C0
RZ	C8
RNC	D0
RC	D8
RPO	E0
RPE	E8
RP	F0
RM	F8

Restart

RST	0	C7
	1	CF
	2	D7
	3	DF
	4	E7
	5	EF
	6	F7
	7	FF

I/O AND MACHINE CONTROL

Stack Ops

PUSH	B	C5
	D	D5
	H	E5
	PSW	F5

POP	B	C1
	D	D1
	H	E1
	PSW*	F1

XTHL	E3
SPHL	F9

Input/Output

OUT byte	D3
IN byte	DB

Control

DI	F3
EI	FB
NOP	00
HLT	76

New Instructions (8085 Only)

RIM	20
SIM	30

RESTART TABLE

Name	Code	Restart Address
RST 0	C7	0000_{16}
RST 1	CF	0008_{16}
RST 2	D7	0010_{16}
RST 3	DF	0018_{16}
RST 4	E7	0020_{16}
TRAP	Hardware* Function	0024_{16}
RST 5	EF	0028_{16}
RST 5.5	Hardware* Function	$002C_{16}$
RST 6	F7	0030_{16}
RST 6.5	Hardware* Function	0034_{16}
RST 7	FF	0038_{16}
RST 7.5	Hardware* Function	$003C_{16}$

*NOTE: The hardware functions refer to the on-chip Interrupt feature of the 8085 only

USE OF THE A REGISTER BY RIM AND SIM INSTRUCTIONS (8085 ONLY)

A REGISTER AFTER EXECUTING RIM

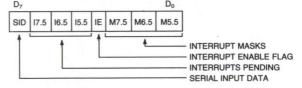

- INTERRUPT MASKS
- INTERRUPT ENABLE FLAG
- INTERRUPTS PENDING
- SERIAL INPUT DATA

A REGISTER BEFORE EXECUTING SIM

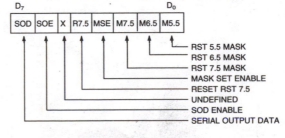

- RST 5.5 MASK
- RST 6.5 MASK
- RST 7.5 MASK
- MASK SET ENABLE
- RESET RST 7.5
- UNDEFINED
- SOD ENABLE
- SERIAL OUTPUT DATA

Microprocessor and Microcontroller Fundamentals

The 8085 and 8051 Hardware and Software

WILLIAM KLEITZ

Tompkins Cortland Community College

Prentice Hall
Upper Saddle River, New Jersey   *Columbus, Ohio*

Library of Congress Cataloging-in-Publication Data

Kleitz, William.
    Microprocessor and microcontroller fundamentals : the 8085 and
8051 hardware and software / William Kleitz.
        p.   cm.
    Includes bibliographical references and index.
    ISBN 0-13-262825-2 (alk. paper)
    1. Microprocessors.   2. Programmable controllers.   3. Intel 8085.
(Microprocessor)   4. Embedded computer systems.   I. Title.
TJ223.M53K5S   1998
004.6'16—dc21   97-24124
                                                        CIP

Cover photo: ©SuperStock
Editor: Charles E. Stewart, Jr.
Production Editor: Alexandrina Benedicto Wolf
Design Coordinator: Julia Zonneveld Van Hook
Cover Designer: Proof Positive/Farrowlyne Assoc., Inc.
Production Manager: Deidra M. Schwartz
Marketing Manager: Debbie Yarnell

This book was set in Times Roman by York Graphic Services, Inc. and was
printed and bound by Courier/Kendallville, Inc. The cover was printed by
Phoenix Color Corp.

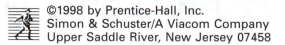
Printed in the United States of America
10 9 8 7 6 5 4 3 2 1

ISBN   0-13-262825-2

Prentice-Hall International (UK) Limited, *London*
Prentice-Hall of Australia Pty. Limited, *Sydney*
Prentice-Hall of Canada, Inc., *Toronto*
Prentice-Hall Hispanoamericana, S. A., *Mexico*
Prentice-Hall of India Private Limited, *New Delhi*
Prentice-Hall of Japan, Inc., *Tokyo*
Simon & Schuster Asia Pte. Ltd., *Singapore*
Editora Prentice-Hall do Brasil, Ltda., *Rio de Janeiro*

To *Patty,* for her constant encouragement and affirmation;
and to my daughters, *Shirelle* and *Hayley*

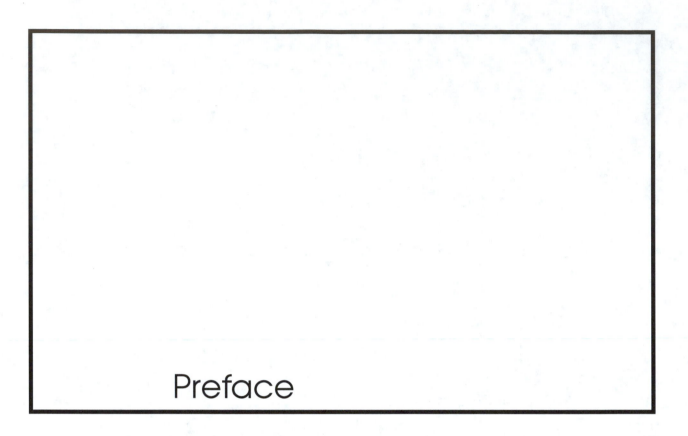

Preface

Eight-bit microprocessors and microcontrollers have become the workhorses of embedded system applications. Embedded systems have the microprocessor contained within the final product, which is used for a specific, dedicated process. Examples are office copy machines, fax machines, automated bank teller machines, and automobile computer control modules. Software applications like word processing and spreadsheets run on a personal computer need the wider data paths provided by 32- and 64-bit processors like the 80486 and Pentium,[1] but the peripheral devices (printers, scanners, and so on) require an embedded microcontroller like the 8051 because it is specifically designed for data acquisition and control functions.

This text uses the 8085A microprocessor and 8051 microcontroller to explain the fundamentals of microprocessor architecture, programming, and hardware. It is intended to be used for an introduction to microprocessors course for students of technology or engineering who have a background in digital electronics. After reading this text, students will be prepared to go on to advanced microprocessor topics such as 16-, 32-, and 64-bit processors; system bus standards; and high-level-language program development.

The microprocessor coverage is approximately 50 percent software and 50 percent hardware. Most of the examples and applications involve some kind of input/output (I/O) with electronic devices such as switches, sensors, analog converters, and displays. This coverage helps tie together digital electronic theory with the hardware/software requirements needed to interface with the outside world via the most commonly used microprocessor support ICs. Solutions to practical design applications illustrate I/O protocol requirements and timing analysis. The software instruction set is not given all at once, but instead the instructions are introduced as needed to solve a particular design application. Only practical, workable designs are used so that the reader can develop a *complete* understanding of the application with no frustrating gaps in the explanations.

All of the programming and hardware interfacing for the 8085A chapters were done on the SDK-85 trainer (see Appendix N), but the explanations and addressing

---

[1]Pentium is a registered trademark of Intel Corporation.

schemes were specifically developed so that any 8080/8085A trainer can be used. The 8051 programs were all written for the student-built 8051 system given in Appendix I. All the programs and system design applications are presented as a complete package, meaning that they are explained, with all required hardware and software, so that they can be duplicated in the lab.

A worthy goal for students learning from this text is to develop a solution to a complete application of a microprocessor-based system performing a task that is both practical and visually stimulating. That is the object of the last two chapters: Interfacing and Applications (Chapter 5), and The 8051 Microcontroller (Chapter 6). Chapter 5 draws on the knowledge gained in the previous four chapters to solve some interesting applications, including generating waveforms with a DAC, measuring temperature with an ADC, driving a multiplexed display, reading a keyboard, and driving a stepper motor.

Chapter 6 introduces the student to the real workhorse in modern automotive and consumer electronics, the *microcontroller*. The beauty of the 8051 microcontroller family is that it was specifically designed to provide a simple solution to the typical data acquisition and control applications faced by today's technology graduates. Assuming that students have a thorough understanding of 8085A hardware and software, this chapter provides the additional information necessary to understand the basic features of the 8051. The chapter concludes with the solutions to applications, including time delays, switch and LED I/O, reading a keyboard, and ADC interfacing. Appendix I (8051 Application Notes) is included as a supplement to Chapter 6. This appendix gives the complete details for building your own 8051-based acquisition and control system for measuring temperature and light and for driving a variable-speed motor.

TO THE STUDENT

As a student of microprocessor electronics, you are in the unique position of becoming proficient at both the hardware *and* software aspects of microprocessor-based systems. This text will provide you with the tools and thought processes required to understand basic microprocessor-based systems, and will provide the foundation required to extend your education to more advanced topics.

You will see that the teaching style of this book is to provide first all the theory required to understand a particular piece of hardware circuitry or software instruction, and then give a completely explained example of its use. By studying the theory and then reworking the examples with the solutions hidden, you can prepare yourself to solve all the problems presented at the end of the chapters. You'll find the answers to selected chapter-end problems in Appendix G.

Each chapter ends with a summary, a glossary, hardware/software problems, and schematic interpretation problems. Use the summary to refresh your memory of the important topics covered in the chapter. The glossary at the end of each chapter can be used to review the key terms presented in that chapter. The problems will be similar to the examples provided in the chapter and will test your understanding of the material. The schematic interpretation problems will give you experience in troubleshooting and tracing signals through complex schematic diagrams similar to those you will find on the job.

If you have written computer software in a high-level language such as BASIC or C, you already know how exciting it is to write a successful program. Microprocessor-level software is even more exciting because of its ability to interact directly with electronic devices. However, it can be frustrating at times because each operation will require you to provide much more detailed instructions. As a beginner, one of the best ways to get started is to copy a program exactly as presented in this text, then modify it to suit your specific needs. Also, skim through the 8085A Instruction Set Reference Encyclopedia in Appendix D again and again. Even though you won't know what each instruction does, you'll learn what instructions are available and how to look them up.

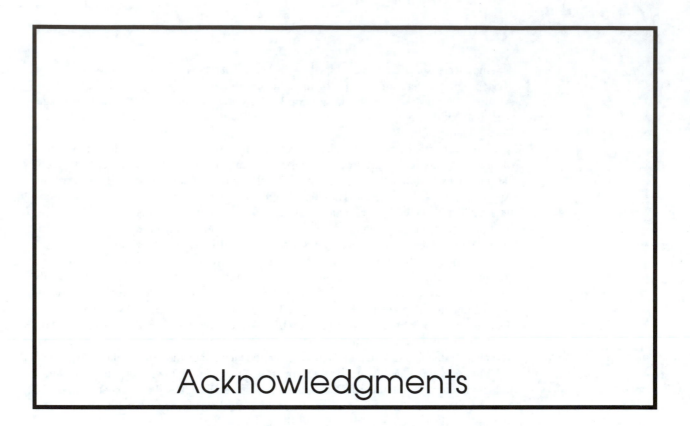

Acknowledgments

I would like to thank Intel Corporation, Advanced Micro Devices Inc., and Philips Semiconductor Corporation for allowing the reproduction of their data sheets, and to URDA Inc. for the illustrations of the SDK-85 trainer in Appendix N. I am grateful to Precision Filters Inc., DQ Systems, and AT&T Corporation for the use of their schematic diagrams. I would also like to thank the editorial and production staff at Prentice Hall for their professional expertise in producing this book.

Contents

CHAPTER 3   *INTRODUCTION TO 8085A SYSTEM HARDWARE*   *35*

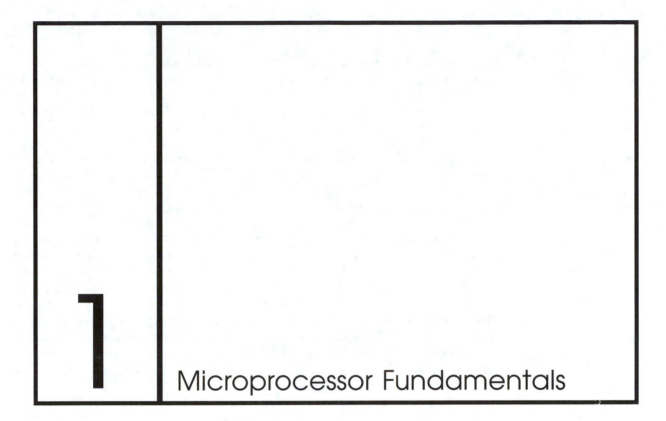

1

Microprocessor Fundamentals

OBJECTIVES

Upon completion of this chapter you should be able to:

- Describe the benefits that microprocessor design has over hard-wired IC logic design.
- Discuss the functional blocks of a microprocessor-based system having basic input/output capability.
- Describe the function of the address, data, and control buses.
- Discuss the timing sequence on the three buses required to perform a simple input/output operation.
- Explain the role of software program instructions in a microprocessor-based system.
- Understand the software program used to read data from an input port and write it to an output port.
- Discuss the basic function of each of the internal blocks of the 8085A microprocessor.
- Follow the flow of data as it passes through the internal parts of the 8085A microprocessor.

INTRODUCTION

Circuit applications designed in the early days of digital electronics were based on combinational logic gates and sequential logic ICs. One example is a traffic light controller that goes through the sequence green–yellow–red. To implement the circuit using combinational and sequential logic, we would use some counter ICs for the timing, a shift reg-

1

ister for sequencing the lights, and a *D* flip-flop if we want to interrupt the sequence with a pedestrian cross-walk pushbutton. A complete design solution is easily within the realm of SSI and MSI ICs.

On the other hand, think about the complexity of electronic control of a modern automobile. There are several analog quantities to monitor, such as engine speed, manifold pressure, and coolant temperature; and there are several digital control functions to perform, such as spark plug timing, fuel mixture control, and radiator circulation control. The operation is further complicated by the calculations and decisions that have to be made on a continuing basis. This is definitely an application for a *microprocessor-based system.*

A system designer should consider a microprocessor-based solution whenever an application involves making calculations, making decisions based on external stimuli, and maintaining memory of past events. A microprocessor offers several advantages over the "hard-wired" SSI/MSI IC approach. First of all, the microprocessor itself is a general-purpose device. It takes on a unique personality by the software program instructions given by the designer. If you want it to count, you tell it to do so, with software. If you want to shift its output level left, there's an instruction for that. And if you want to add a new quantity to a previous one, there's another instruction for that. Its capacity to perform arithmetic, make comparisons, and update memory make it a very powerful digital problem solver. Making changes to an application can usually be done by changing a few program instructions, unlike the hard-wired system that may have to be totally redesigned and reconstructed.

New microprocessors are introduced every year to fill the needs of the design engineer. However, the theory behind microprocessor technology remains basically the same. It is a general-purpose digital device driven by software instructions and it communicates with several external "support" chips to perform the necessary input/output of a specific task. Once you have a general understanding of one of the earlier microprocessors that came on the market, such as the Intel 8080/8085, the Motorola 6800, or the Zilog Z80, it is an easy task to teach yourself the necessary information to upgrade to the new microprocessors as they are introduced. Typically, when a new microprocessor (like the 8051) is introduced, it will have a few new software instructions available and will have some of the I/O features, previously handled by external support chips, integrated right into the microprocessor chip. Learning the basics on these new microprocessor upgrades is more difficult, however, because some of their advanced features tend to hide the actual operation of the microprocessor and may hinder your complete understanding of the system.

This book covers the Intel 8085A microprocessor and the 8051 microcontroller[1] software, hardware, and support circuitry. A thorough understanding of their architecture and operation will allow you to design and troubleshoot most 8-bit microprocessor-based systems and provide the background for learning the operations of the more highly integrated microprocessors as they are introduced.

1–1   INTRODUCTION TO SYSTEM COMPONENTS AND BUSES

Figure 1–1 shows a microprocessor with the necessary support circuitry to perform basic input and output functions. We will use that figure to illustrate how the microprocessor acts like a general-purpose device, driven by software, to perform a specific task related to the input data switches and output data LEDs. First, let's discuss the components of the system.

---

[1]A *microcontroller* is sometimes called a "computer on a chip" because it integrates the most commonly used circuitry of a complete microprocessor-based system into a single integrated circuit package. It contains the "brains" of a microprocessor along with RAM/ROM memory, several I/O ports, and other useful support circuitry, making it well suited for data acquisition and control functions.

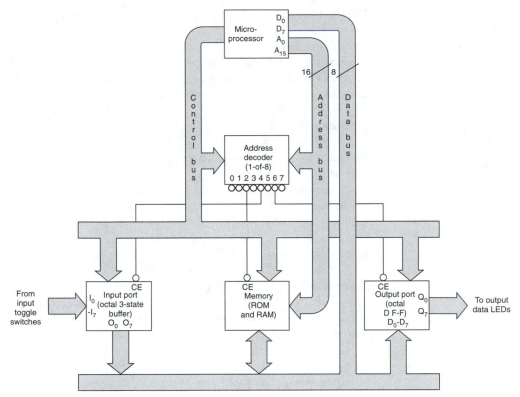

Figure 1–1 An example of a microprocessor-based system used for simple input/output operations.

Microprocessor

The heart of the system is an 8-bit microprocessor. It could be any of the popular 8-bit microprocessors such as the Intel 8085, the Motorola 6800, or the Zilog Z80. They are called 8-bit microprocessors because external and internal data movement is performed on 8 bits at a time. It will read *program instructions* from memory and execute those instructions that drive the three *external buses* with the proper levels and timing to make the connected devices perform specific operations. The buses are simply groups of conductors routed throughout the system and tapped into by various devices (or ICs) that need to share the information traveling on them.

Address Bus

The address bus is 16 bits wide and is generated by the microprocessor to select a particular location or IC to be active. In the case of a selected memory IC, the low-order bits on the address bus select a particular location within the IC. Since the address bus is 16 bits wide, it can actually specify 65,536 (2^{16}) different addresses. The input port is one address, the output port is one address, and the memory in a system of this size may be 4K (4096) addresses. This leaves about 60K addresses available for future expansion.

Data Bus

Once the address bus is set up with the particular address that the microprocessor wants to access, the microprocessor then sends or receives 8 bits of data to or from that address via the *bidirectional* (two-way) data bus.

Control Bus

The control bus is of varying width, depending on the microprocessor being used. It carries control signals that are tapped into by the other ICs to tell what type of operation is being performed. From these signals, the ICs can tell if the operation is a read, a write, an I/O, a memory access, or some other operation.

Address Decoder

The address decoder is usually an octal decoder like the 74LS138. Its function is to provide active-LOW Chip Enables ($\overline{CE}$) to the external ICs based on information it receives from the microprocessor via the control and address buses. Since there are multiple ICs on the data bus, the address decoder ensures that only one IC is active at a time to avoid a bus conflict caused by two ICs writing different data to the same bus.

Memory

There will be at least two memory ICs: ROM or EPROM and a RAM. The ROM will contain the "initialization" instructions, telling the microprocessor what to do when power is first turned on. This includes tasks like reading the keyboard and driving the CRT display. It will also contain several subroutines that can be called by the microprocessor to perform such tasks as time delays or input/output data translation. These instructions, which are permanently stored in ROM, are referred to as the "monitor program" or "operating system." The RAM part of memory is volatile, meaning that it loses its contents when power is turned off, and is therefore used only for temporary data storage.

Input Port

The input port provides data to the microprocessor via the data bus. In this case, it is an octal buffer with three-stated outputs. The input to the buffer will be provided by some input device like a keyboard or, as in this case, from eight HIGH–LOW toggle switches. The input port will dump its information to the data bus when it receives a Chip Enable ($\overline{CE}$) from the address decoder and a Read command ($\overline{RD}$) from the control bus.

Output Port

The output port provides a way for the microprocessor to talk to the outside world. It could be sending data to an output device like a printer, or as in this case, it could send data to eight LEDs. An octal D flip-flop is used as the interface because, after the microprocessor sends data to it, the flip-flop will latch onto the data, allowing the microprocessor to continue with its other tasks.

To load the D flip-flop, the microprocessor must first set up the data bus with the data to be output. Then it sets up the address of the output port so that the address decoder will issue a LOW $\overline{CE}$ to it. Finally, it issues a pulse on its $\overline{WR}$ (write) line that travels the control bus to the clock input of the D flip-flop. When the D flip-flop receives the clock trigger pulse, it latches onto the data that are on the data bus at that time, and drives the LEDs.

1–2 SOFTWARE CONTROL OF MICROPROCESSOR SYSTEMS

The nice thing about microprocessor-based systems is that once you have a working prototype, you can put away the soldering iron because all operational changes can then be made with software. The student of electronics has a big advantage when writing microprocessor software because he or she understands the hardware at work as well as the implications that software will have on the hardware. Areas such as address decoding, chip enables, instruction timing, and hardware interfacing become important when programming microprocessors.

As a brief introduction to microprocessor software, let's refer back to Figure 1–1 and learn the statements required to perform some basic input/output operations. To route the data from the input switches to the output LEDs, the data from the input port must first be read into the microprocessor before they can be sent to the output port. The microprocessor has an 8-bit internal register called the *accumulator* that can be used for that purpose.

The software used to drive microprocessor-based systems is called *assembly language*. The Intel 8080/8085 assembly language statement to load the contents of the input port into the accumulator is LDA *addr*. LDA is called a *mnemonic*, an abbreviation of the operation being performed, which in this case is "Load Accumulator." The suffix *addr* will be replaced with a 16-bit address (4 hex digits) specifying the address of the input port.

After the execution of LDA *addr*, the accumulator will contain the digital value that was on the input switches. Now, to write those data to the output port, we use the command STA *addr*. STA is the mnemonic for "Store Accumulator" and *addr* is the 16-bit address where you want the data stored.

Execution of those two statements is all that is necessary to load the value of the switches into the accumulator and then transfer those data to the output LEDs. The microprocessor takes care of the timing on the three buses, and the address decoder takes care of providing chip enables to the appropriate ICs.

If the system is based on Motorola or Zilog technology, the software in this case will be almost the same. Table 1–1 makes a comparison of the three assembly languages.

TABLE 1–1

Comparison of Input/Output Software on Three Different Microprocessors

Operation	Intel 8080/8085	Motorola 6800	Zilog Z80
Load accumulator with contents of location *addr*	LDA *addr*	LDAA *addr*	LD A, (*addr*)
Store accumulator to location *addr*	STA *addr*	STAA *addr*	LD (*addr*), A

1-3 INTERNAL ARCHITECTURE OF THE 8085A MICROPROCESSOR

The design for the Intel 8085A microprocessor was derived from its predecessor, the 8080A. The 8085A is *software compatible* with the 8080A, meaning that software programs written for the 8080A can run on the 8085A without modification. The 8085A has a few additional features not available on the 8080A. The 8085A also has a higher level of hardware integration, allowing the designer to develop complete microprocessor-based systems with fewer external support ICs than were required by the 8080A. Studying the internal architecture of the 8085A in Figure 1–2 and its pin configuration, Figure 1–3, will give us a better understanding of its operation.

The 8085A is an 8-bit parallel *central processing unit* (CPU). The accumulator discussed in the previous section is connected to an 8-bit *internal data bus*. Six other *general-purpose registers* labeled *B, C, D, E, H,* and *L* are also connected to the same bus.

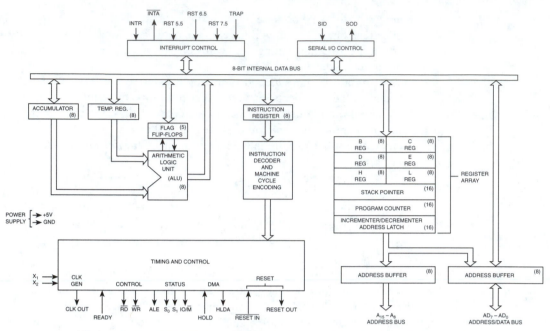

Figure 1–2   8085A CPU functional block diagram. (Courtesy of Intel Corporation)

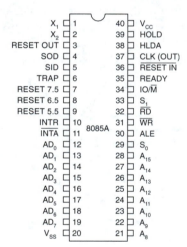

Figure 1–3   8085A pin configuration. (Courtesy of Intel Corporation)

All arithmetic operations take place in the *arithmetic logic unit* (ALU). The accumulator, along with a temporary register, are used as inputs to all arithmetic operations. The output of the operations is sent to the internal data bus and to five *flag flip-flops* that record the status of the arithmetic operation.

The *instruction register* and *decoder* receive the software instructions from external memory, interpret what is to be done, and then create the necessary timing and control signals required to execute the instruction.

The block diagram also shows *interrupt control,* which provides a way for an external digital signal to interrupt a software program while it is executing. This is accomplished by applying the proper digital signal on one of the interrupt inputs: INTR, RSTx.x, or TRAP. *Serial communication* capabilities are provided via the SID (Serial Input Data) and SOD (Serial Output Data) I/O pins.

The *register array* contains the six general-purpose 8-bit registers and three 16-bit registers. Sixteen-bit registers are required whenever you need to store addresses. The *stack pointer* stores the address of the last entry on the stack. The stack is a data storage area in RAM used by certain microprocessor operations, which will be covered in a later chapter. The *program counter* contains the 16-bit address of the next software instruction to be executed. The third 16-bit register is the *address latch,* which contains the current 16-bit address that is being sent to the address bus.

The six general-purpose 8-bit registers can also be used in pairs (*B–C, D–E, H–L*) to store addresses or 16-bit data.

1–4 INSTRUCTION EXECUTION WITHIN THE 8085A

Now, referring back to the basic I/O system diagram of Figure 1–1, let's follow the flow of the LDA and STA instructions as they execute in the block diagram of the 8085A. Figure 1–4 shows the 8085A block diagram with numbers indicating the succession of events that occur when executing the LDA instruction.

Remember, LDA *addr* and STA *addr* are assembly language instructions, stored in an external memory IC, that tell the 8085A CPU what to do. LDA *addr* tells the CPU to load its accumulator with the data value at address *addr.* STA *addr* tells the CPU to store (or send) the 8-bit value in the accumulator to the output port at address *addr.*

The mnemonics LDA and STA cannot be understood by the CPU as they are; they have to be *assembled,* or converted, into a binary string called *machine code.* Binary, or hexadecimal, machine code is what is actually read by the CPU and passed to the instruction register and decoder to be executed. The Intel 8085A Users Manual gives the machine code translation for LDA as $3A_{16}$ (or 3AH), and for STA as 32H.

Before studying the flow of execution in Figure 1–4, we need to make a few assumptions. Let's assume that the input port is at address 4000H and the output port is at

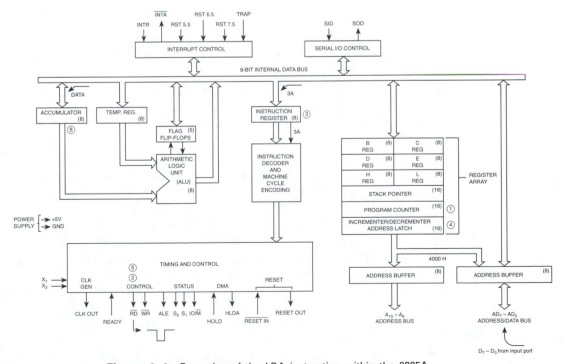

Figure 1–4 Execution of the LDA instruction within the 8085A.

address 6000H. Let's also assume that the machine code program LDA 4000H, STA 6000H is stored in RAM starting at address 2000H.

Load Accumulator

The sequence of execution of LDA 4000H in Figure 1–4 will be as follows:

1. The program counter will put the address 2000H on the address bus.
2. The timing and control unit will issue a LOW pulse on the $\overline{RD}$ line. This will cause the contents of RAM location 2000H to be put onto the external data bus. RAM (2000H) has the machine code 3AH, which will travel across the internal data bus to the instruction register.
3. The instruction register passes the 3AH to the instruction decoder, which determines that 3AH is the code for LDA and that a 16-bit (2-byte) address must follow. Because the entire instruction is 3 bytes (one for the 3AH and two for the address 4000H), the instruction decoder increments the program counter two more times so that the address latch register can read and store byte 2 and byte 3 of the instruction.
4. The address latch and address bus now have 4000H on them, which is the address of the input port.
5. The timing and control unit again issues a LOW pulse on the $\overline{RD}$ line. The data at the input port (4000H) will be put onto the external data bus.
6. That data will travel across the internal data bus to the accumulator where it is now stored. The instruction is complete.

Store Accumulator

Figure 1–5 shows the flow of execution of the STA 6000H instruction.

1. After the execution of the 3-byte LDA 4000H instruction, the program counter will have 2003H in it. (Instruction LDA 4000H resided in locations 2000H, 2001H, 2002H.)
2. The timing and control unit will issue a LOW pulse on the $\overline{RD}$ line. This will cause the contents of RAM location 2003H to be put onto the external data bus. RAM (2003H) has the machine code 32H, which will travel up the internal data bus to the instruction register.
3. The instruction register passes the 32H to the instruction decoder, which determines that 32H is the code for STA and that a 2-byte address must follow. The program counter gets incremented two more times, reading and storing byte 2 and byte 3 of the instruction into the address latch.
4. The address latch and address bus now have 6000H on them, which is the address of the output port.
5. The instruction decoder now issues the command to place the contents of the accumulator onto the data bus.
6. The timing and control unit issues a LOW pulse on the $\overline{WR}$ line. Since the $\overline{WR}$ line is used as a clock input to the D flip-flop of Figure 1–1, the data from the data bus will be stored and displayed on the LEDs.

The complete assembly language and machine code program for the preceding input/output example is given in Table 1–2.

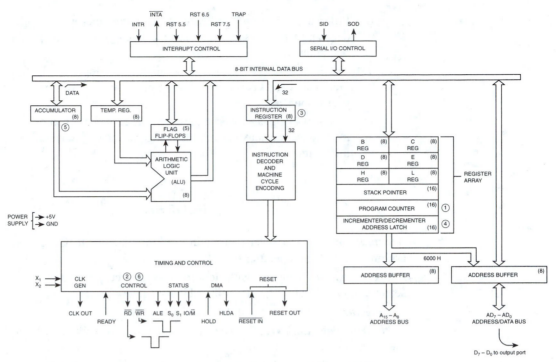

Figure 1–5 Execution of the STA instruction within the 8085A.

TABLE 1–2

Assembly Language and Machine Code Listing for the LDA–STA Program

Memeory location	Assembly language	Machine code	
2000H	LDA 4000H	3A	Three-byte instruction to load
2001H		00	accumulator with contents from
2002H		40	address 4000H
2003H	STA 6000H	32	Three-byte instruction to store
2004H		00	accumulator out to address 6000H
2005H		60	

SUMMARY

In this chapter we have learned that

1. A system designer should consider using a microprocessor instead of logic circuitry whenever an application involves making calculations, making decisions based on external stimuli, and maintaining memory of past events.

2. A microprocessor is the heart of a computer system. It reads and acts on program instructions given to it by a programmer.

3. A microprocessor system has three buses: address, data, and control.

4. Microprocessors operate on instructions given to them in the form of machine code (1's and 0's). The machine code is generated by a higher-level language, like C or Assembly language.

5. The Intel 8085A is an 8-bit microprocessor. It has 7 internal registers, an 8-bit data bus, an arithmetic/logic unit and several input/output functions.

6. Program instructions are executed inside the microprocessor by the instruction decoder, which issues the machine cycle timing and initiates input/output operations.

7. The microprocessor provides the appropriate logic levels on the data and address buses and takes care of the timing of all control signals output to the connected interface circuitry.

8. Assembly language instructions are written using mnemonic abbreviations and then converted into machine language so that they can be interpreted by the microprocessor.

GLOSSARY

Accumulator: The parallel register in a microprocessor that is the focal point for all arithmetic and logic operations.

Address bus: A group of conductors routed throughout a computer system and used to select a unique location based on their binary value.

Architecture: The layout and design of a system.

Arithmetic logic unit (ALU):   The part of a microprocessor that performs all of the arithmetic and digital logic functions.

Assembly language: A low-level programming language unique to each microprocessor. It is converted, or assembled, into machine code before it can be executed.

Bidirectional: Systems capable of transferring digital information in two directions.

Central processing unit (CPU):   The "brains" of a computer system. The term is used interchangeably with *microprocessor.*

Control bus: A group of conductors routed throughout a computer system and used to signify special control functions, such as Read, Write, I/O, Memory, and Ready.

Data bus: A group of conductors routed throughout a computer system and containing the binary data used for all arithmetic and I/O operations.

Hardware: The integrated circuits and electronic devices that make up a computer system.

Instruction decoder: The circuitry inside a microprocessor that interprets the machine code and produces the internal control signals required to execute the instruction.

Instruction register: A parallel register in a microprocessor that receives the machine code.

Interrupt: A digital control signal input to a microprocessor IC pin that suspends current software execution and performs another predefined task.

Machine code: The binary codes that make up a microprocessor's program instructions.

Microprocessor: An LSI or VLSI integrated circuit that is the fundamental building block of a digital computer. It is controlled by software programs that allow it to do all digital arithmetic, logic, and I/O operations.

Mnemonic: The abbreviated spelling of instructions used in assembly language.

Monitor program: The computer software program initiated at power-up that supervises system operating tasks, such as reading the keyboard and driving the CRT.

Operating system: *See* Monitor program.

Program counter: A 16-bit internal register that contains the address of the next program instruction to be executed.

Software: Computer program statements that give step-by-step instructions to a computer to solve a problem.

Stack pointer: A 16-bit internal register that contains the address of the last entry on the RAM stack.

Support circuitry: The integrated circuits and electronic devices that assist the microprocessor in performing I/O and other external tasks.

PROBLEMS

1–1. Describe the circumstances that would prompt you to use a microprocessor-based design solution instead of a hard-wired IC logic design.

1–2. In an 8-bit microprocessor system, how many lines are in the data bus? The address bus?

1–3. What is the function of the address bus?

1–4. Use a TTL data manual to find an IC that you could use for the *output port* in Figure 1–1. Draw its logic diagram and external connections.

1–5. Repeat Problem 1–4 for the *input port*.

1–6. Repeat Problem 1–4 for the *address decoder.* Assume that the input port is at address 4000H, the output port is at address 6000H, and memory is at address 2000H.

1–7. Why must the input port in Figure 1–1 have three-stated outputs?

1–8. What two control signals are applied to the input port in Figure 1–1 to cause it to transfer the switch data to the data bus?

1–9. How many different addresses can be accessed using a 16-bit address bus?

1–10. In the assembly language instruction LDA 4000H, what does the LDA signify and what does the 4000H signify?

1–11. Describe what the statement STA 6000H does.

1–12. What are the names of the six internal 8085A general-purpose registers?

1–13. What is the function of the 8085A's instruction register and instruction decoder?

1–14. Why is the program counter register 16 bits instead of 8?

1–15. During the execution of the LDA 4000 instruction in Figure 1–4, the $\overline{\text{RD}}$ line goes LOW four times. Describe the activity initiated by each LOW pulse.

1–16. What action does the LOW $\overline{\text{WR}}$ pulse initiate during the STA 6000H instruction in Figure 1–5?

SCHEMATIC INTERPRETATION PROBLEMS

Note: Appendix H contains four schematic diagrams of actual digital systems. At the end of each chapter you will have the opportunity to work with these diagrams to gain experience with real-world circuitry and observe the application of the digital logic that was presented in the chapter.

1–17. Find the two 4-bit magnitude comparators, U7 and U8, in the Watchdog Timer schematic. Which IC receives the high-order binary data, U7 or U8? [*Hint:* The bold lines in that schematic represent a *bus,* which is a group of conductors shared by several ICs. It simplifies the diagram by showing a single bold line instead of several separate lines. When the individual lines are taken off the bus, they are labeled appropriately (0-1-2-3 and 4-5-6-7 in this application).]

1–18. Where is the final output of the comparison made by U7, U8 used in the Watchdog Timer schematic?

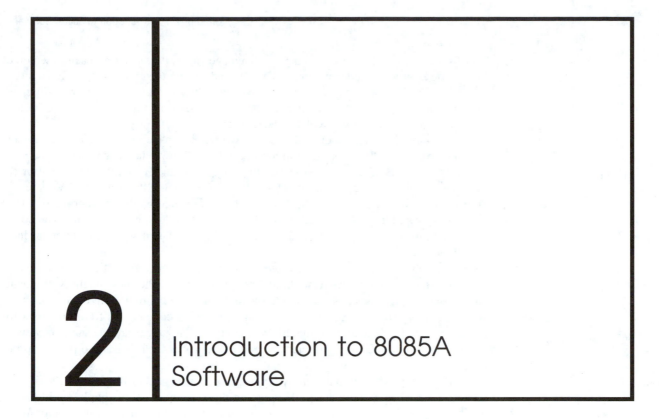

2 Introduction to 8085A Software

OBJECTIVES

Upon completion of this chapter you should be able to:

- Make comparisons between assembly language, machine language, and high-level languages.
- Discuss the fundamental circuitry and timing sequence for external microprocessor I/O.
- Hand assemble assembly language programs into machine language code.
- Write a program for a MOD-*n* counter.
- Draw flowcharts and write programs containing compares and conditional branching.
- Move data into, and between, the internal data registers.
- Use the internal register pairs.
- Write time-delay routines using nested loops.
- Calculate program execution time using instruction T states.
- Write programs that utilize subroutine calls.
- Write programs that perform external I/O to switches and LEDs.

INTRODUCTION

Chapter 1 gave us a look at how a microprocessor can replace hard-wired logic. The microprocessor is driven by software instructions to perform specific tasks. The instructions are first written in assembly language using mnemonic abbreviations and then converted to machine language so that they can be interpreted by the microprocessor. The conversion from assembly language to machine language involves translating each mnemonic into the appropriate hexadecimal machine code and storing the codes in specific memory addresses. This can be done by a software package called an "assembler," provided by the microprocessor manufacturer, or it can be done by the programmer by looking up the codes and memory addresses (called "hand assembly").

Assembly language is classified as a low-level language because the programmer has to take care of all of the most minute details. High-level languages such as C++, FORTRAN, and BASIC are much easier to write but are not as memory efficient or as fast as assembly language. All languages, whether C++, BASIC, or FORTRAN, are reduced to machine language code before they can be executed by the microprocessor. The conversion from high-level languages to machine code is done by a *compiler*. The compiler makes memory assignments and converts the English-language-type instructions into executable machine code.

Assembly language translates *directly* into machine code without using a compiler. This allows the programmer to write the most streamlined, the most memory-efficient, and the fastest programs possible on the specific hardware configuration being used.

Assembly language and its corresponding machine code differs from processor to processor. The fundamentals of the different assembly languages are the same, however, and once you have become proficient on one microprocessor, it is easy to pick it up on another.

The best way to learn assembly language is by studying examples and modifying them to meet your specific needs. Throughout the remainder of this book, we'll do exactly that. The 8085A software instructions will be introduced by writing solutions to specific applications and then covering the advanced instructions by expanding on those solutions.

2–1 HARDWARE REQUIREMENTS FOR BASIC I/O PROGRAMMING

A good way to start out in microprocessor programming is to illustrate program execution by communicating to the outside world. In Chapter 1 we read input switches at memory location 4000H using the LDA instruction and wrote their value to output LEDs at location 6000H using the STA instruction. That was an example of *memory-mapped I/O*. Using that method, the input and output devices were accessed *as if they were memory locations,* by specifying their unique 16-bit address (4000H or 6000H).

The other technique used by the 8085A microprocessor for I/O mapping is called "standard I/O" or "I/O-mapped I/O." *I/O-mapped systems* identify their input and output devices by giving them an 8-bit *port number*. The microprocessor then accesses the I/O ports by using the instructions: OUT *port* and IN *port,* where *port* is 00H to FFH.

Special hardware external to the 8085A is required to provide the source for the IN instruction and the destination for the OUT instruction. Figure 2–1 shows a basic hardware configuration, using standard SSI and MSI ICs, that could be built to input data from eight switches and to output data to eight LEDs using I/O-mapped I/O.

Figure 2–1 is set up to decode the input switches as port FFH and the output LEDs as port FEH. The IO/$\overline{\text{M}}$ line from the microprocessor goes HIGH whenever an IN or OUT instruction is being executed (I/O-mapped I/O). All instructions that access memory, and memory-mapped devices, will cause the IO/$\overline{\text{M}}$ line to go LOW. The $\overline{\text{RD}}$ line from the microprocessor will be pulsed LOW when executing the IN instruction, and the $\overline{\text{WR}}$ line will be pulsed LOW when executing the OUT instruction.

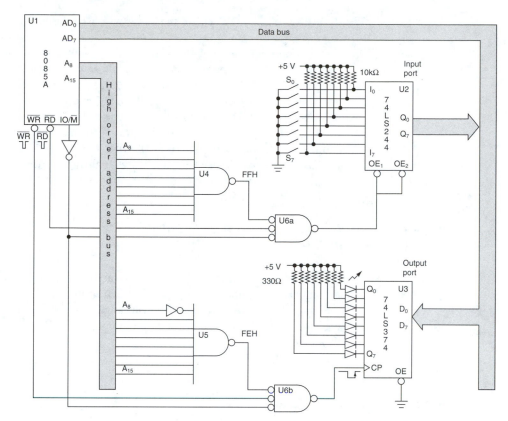

Figure 2–1   Hardware requirements for the IN FFH and OUT FEH instructions.

IN FFH

The 74LS244 is an octal three-state buffer (see Appendix M) that is set up to pass the binary value of the input switches over to the data bus as soon as $\overline{OE}_1$ and $\overline{OE}_2$ are brought LOW. To get that LOW, U6a, the inverted-input NAND gate (OR gate), must receive three LOWs at its input. We know that the IN instruction will cause the *inverted* $IO/\overline{M}$ line to go LOW and the $\overline{RD}$ line to go LOW. The other input is dependent on the output from the eight-input NAND gate (U4). Gate U4 *will* output a LOW because the binary value of the port number (1111 1111) used in the IN instruction is put onto the high-order address bus during the execution of the IN FFH instruction.

All conditions are now met, and U6a will output a LOW pulse (the same width as the LOW $\overline{RD}$ pulse), which will enable the outputs of U2 to pass to the data bus. After the microprocessor drops the $\overline{RD}$ line LOW, it waits a short time for external devices (U2 in this case) to respond, then it reads the data bus and raises the $\overline{RD}$ line back HIGH. The data from the input switches are now stored in the accumulator.

OUT FEH

The 74LS374 is an octal *D* flip-flop (see Appendix M) set up to sink current to illuminate individual LEDs based on the binary value it receives from the data bus. The outputs at Q_0–Q_7 will latch onto the binary values at D_0–D_7 at the LOW-to-HIGH edge of C_p. U5 and U6b are set up similar to U4 and U6a, except U5's output goes LOW when FEH (1111 1110) is input. Therefore, during the execution of OUT FEH,

U6b will output a LOW pulse, the same width as the $\overline{WR}$ pulse issued by the micro-processor.

The setup time of the 74LS374 latch is accounted for by the microprocessor timing specifications. The microprocessor issues a HIGH-to-LOW edge at $\overline{WR}$ that makes its way to C_p. At the same time, the microprocessor also sends the value of the accumulator to the data bus. After a time period greater than the setup time for U3, $\overline{WR}$ goes back HIGH, which applies the LOW-to-HIGH trigger edge for U3, latching the data at Q_0–Q_7.

To summarize, the instruction IN FFH reads the binary value at port FFH into the accumulator. The instruction OUT FEH writes the binary value in the accumulator out to port FEH. Port selection is taken care of by eight-input NAND gates attached to the high-order address bus and by use of the $\overline{RD}$, $\overline{WR}$, and IO/M lines.

2–2   WRITING ASSEMBLY LANGUAGE AND MACHINE LANGUAGE PROGRAMS

Let's start off our software training by studying a completed assembly language program and comparing it to the same program written in the BASIC computer language. BASIC is a high-level language that uses English-language-type commands that are fairly easy to figure out, even by the inexperienced programmer.

Program Definition

Write a program that will function as a down-counter, counting 9 to 0 repeatedly. First, draw a flowchart, then write the program statements in the BASIC language, assembly language, and machine language.

Solution

The flowchart in Figure 2–2 is used to show the sequence of program execution, including the branching and looping that takes place.

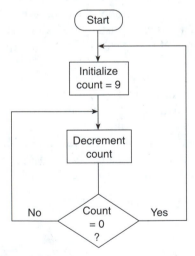

Figure 2–2   Flowchart for Table 2–1.

According to the flowchart, the counter will be decremented repeatedly until zero is reached, at which time the counter is reinitialized to nine, and the cycle repeats. The instructions used to implement the program are given in Table 2–1.

TABLE 2-1

Down-Counter Program in Three Languages

BASIC language		8085A Assembly language		8085A Machine language	
Line	Instruction	Label	Instruction	Address	Contents
10	COUNT=9	START:	MVI A,09H	2000	3E (opcode)
				2001	09 (data)
20	COUNT=COUNT-1	LOOP:	DCR A	2002	3D (opcode)
30	IF COUNT=0		JZ START	2003	CA (opcode)
	THEN GO TO 10			2004	00 }(address)
				2005	20
40	GO TO 20		JMP LOOP	2006	C3 (opcode)
				2007	02 }(address)
				2008	20

BASIC

BASIC uses the variable "COUNT" to hold the counter value. Line 30 checks the count. If COUNT is equal to zero, then the program goes back to the beginning. Otherwise it goes back to subtract 1 from COUNT and checks COUNT again.

The 8085A version of the program is first written in assembly language and then it is either hand assembled into machine language or it is computer assembled using a personal computer with an assembler software package. Throughout this book we will be hand assembling our programs to create machine language.

Assembly Language

Assembly language is written using *mnemonics:* MVI, DCR, JZ, etc. The term *mnemonics* is defined as "abbreviations used to assist the memory." The first mnemonic, MVI, stands for "Move Immediate." The instruction MVI A,09H will move the data value 09H into register *A* (register *A* and the accumulator are the same). The next instruction, DCR A, decrements register *A* by 1.

The third instruction, JZ START is called a *conditional jump.* The condition that it is checking for is the *zero* condition. As the *A* register is decremented, if *A* reaches 0, then a flag bit, called the *zero flag,* gets set (a "set" flag is equal to 1). The instruction JZ START is interpreted as "jump to label START if the zero flag is set."

If the condition is not met (zero flag is not set), then control passes to the next instruction, JMP LOOP, which is an *unconditional jump.* This instruction is interpreted as "jump to label LOOP regardless of any condition flags."

At this point you should see how the assembly language program functions exactly as the BASIC language program.

Machine Language

Machine language is the final step in creating an executable program for the microprocessor. In this step we must determine the actual hexadecimal codes that will be stored in memory to be read by the microprocessor. First, we have to determine what memory locations will be used for our program. These locations depend on the memory map assignments made in the system hardware design. We have 64K of addressable memory locations (0000H to FFFFH). We'll make an assumption here, and use it throughout the rest of the book, that the user program area was set up in the hardware design to start at location 2000H. The length of the program memory area depends on the size of the ROM or RAM memory IC being used. A 256×8 RAM memory is usually sufficient for introductory programming assignments and is commonly used on educational microprocessor trainers. The machine language program listed in Table 2–1 fills up 9 bytes of memory (2000H to 2008H).

The first step in the hand assembly is to determine the code for MVI A. This is known as the opcode (operation code) and is found in the 8085A Assembly Language Reference Chart given in Appendix C. The opcode for MVI A is 3E. The programmer will store the binary equivalent for 3E (0011 1110) into memory location 2000H. Instructions for storing your program into memory are given by the manufacturer of the microprocessor trainer that you are using. If you are using an assembler software package, then the machine code that is generated will usually be saved on a computer disk or used to program an EPROM to be placed in a custom microprocessor hardware design.

The machine language instruction MVI A,09H in Table 2–1 requires 2 bytes to complete. The first byte is the opcode, 3E, which identifies the instruction for the microprocessor. The second byte is the data value, 09H, which is to be moved into register A.

The second instruction, DCR A, is a 1-byte instruction. It requires just its opcode, 3D, which is found in the reference chart.

The opcode for the JZ instruction is CA. It must be followed by the 16-bit (2-byte) address to jump to if the condition (zero) is met. This makes it a 3-byte instruction. Byte 2 of the instruction (location 2004H) is the low-order byte of the address, and byte 3 is the high-order byte of the address to jump to. (Be careful to always enter addresses as low-order first, then high-order).

The opcode for JMP is C3 and must also be followed by a 16-bit (2-byte) address specifying the location to jump to. Therefore, this is also a 3-byte instruction where byte 2–byte 3 give a jump address of 2002H.

2–3 COMPARES AND CONDITIONAL BRANCHING

In the previous down-counter program, we watched for the end of the count by checking the zero flag. Let's say that we want to count *up* 0 to 9 instead. In this case we would have to check for a 9 as the terminal count instead of a 0.

CPI *data*

If we are using the accumulator (*A* register) as our counter, then we can use the CPI *data* (compare) instruction. CPI *data* is a 2-byte instruction that compares the value in the accumulator to the value entered as byte 2 (*data*) of the instruction. Byte 1 of the instruction is the opcode for CPI, which is FE. The function of the CPI instruction is to set the zero flag if the accumulator is equal to byte 2 of the instruction. It is also used to set another flag, called the *carry flag,* if the accumulator is *less than* byte 2. Example 2–1 illustrates the use of the CPI *data* instruction.

EXAMPLE 2–1

Write a program that will function as an up-counter to count 0 to 9 repeatedly.

Solution:

Machine language		Assembly language		
Address	Contents	Label	Instruction	Comments
2000	3E	START:	MVI A,00H	; Move 00H into
2001	00			; register A
2002	3C	LOOP:	INR A	; Increment register A
2003	FE		CPI 09H	; Compare reg.A to 09H,
2004	09			; set Z flag if A=9
2005	CA		JZ START	; Jump to START
2006	00			; if Z flag
2007	20			; is set
2008	C3		JMP LOOP	; Else jump
2009	02			; to LOOP
200A	20			;

Explanation: This program will loop back continuously to address 2002H, increment-ing the accumulator, until the accumulator reaches 9. When A=9, the CPI in-struction will set the zero flag. Now the zero condition of the JZ instruction will be met and control will pass to address 2000H, which reinitializes A to 00H. The cycle repeats.

EXAMPLE 2–2

Write a program that will function as a hexadecimal (MOD-16) up-counter. Dis-play the count on the output LEDs provided in the output port design given in Figure 2–1.

Solution:

Machine language		Assembly language		
Address	Contents	Label	Instruction	Comments
2000	3E	START:	MVI A,00H	; LOAD accumulator
2001	00			; with 00H
2002	2F	LOOP:	CMA	; Complement accumulator
2003	D3		OUT FEH	; Output accumulator
2004	FE			; to port FEH
2005	2F		CMA	; Complement accumulator back
2006	3C		INR A	; Increment accumulator
2007	FE		CPI 10H	; Compare accumulator to 16_{10},
2008	10			; set Z flag if equal
2009	CA		JZ START	; Jump to START
200A	00			; if accumulator
200B	20			; reached 16_{10}
200C	C3		JMP LOOP	; Else jump
200D	02			; to LOOP
200E	20			;

Explanation: This program is very similar to Example 2–1 but with the inclusion of two new instructions: CMA and OUT *port*. In Figure 2–1 we developed decod-ing hardware for port FEH. Notice that the output port was driving *active-LOW* LEDs, which is why we had to complement the accumulator before the OUT FEH instruction. Of course the accumulator must be complemented back to its original value before continuing in the counter loop.

Also notice that the CPI instruction is checking for a value that is *one greater* than the terminal count because the INR A instruction comes *after* the OUT FEH instruction. If you want to see the terminal count of 15 (0FH), then you have to wait until 16 (10H) before restarting the loop.

2–4 USING THE INTERNAL DATA REGISTERS

As mentioned before, the 8085A has six internal data registers besides the *A* register (accumulator). They are referred to as the *B, C, D, E, H,* and *L* registers. Each register is 8 bits wide, but by using certain instructions, they can be grouped together to form *register pairs* (see Figure 2–3). As a register pair they become 16 bits wide, which makes them useful for storing addresses or large numbers.

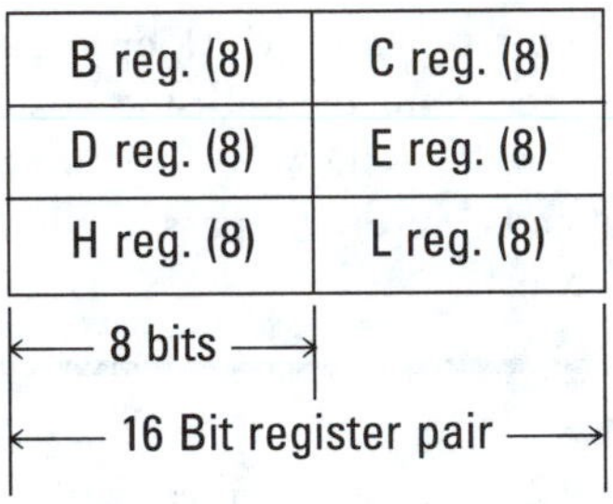

B reg. (8)	C reg. (8)
D reg. (8)	E reg. (8)
H reg. (8)	L reg. (8)

← 8 bits →

← 16 Bit register pair →

Figure 2–3 The internal data registers.

MVI *r,data*

The easiest way to store data into a register is to use the move immediate command: MVI *r,data*. The *r* is replaced with one of the registers *A, B, C, D, E, H,* or *L* and *data* is replaced with a 1-byte data value. In machine language, MVI is a 2-byte instruction. Byte 1 is the opcode, which depends on the register being used, and byte 2 is the data. Table 2–2 lists all of the MVI instructions and their opcodes.

TABLE 2–2

MVI Instructions for Internal Registers

Instruction	Opcode
MVI A,*data*	3E
MVI B,*data*	06
MVI C,*data*	0E
MVI D,*data*	16
MVI E,*data*	1E
MVI H,*data*	26
MVI L,*data*	2E

EXAMPLE 2–3

List the instructions in assembly language and machine language to meet the following requirements:
(a) Load the *B* register with 20H.
(b) Load the *D* register with 100_{10} (64H).

Solution:

	Assembly language	Machine language	Comments
(a) MVI B,20H		06 20	B ← 20H
(b) MVI D,64H		16 64	D ← 64H

MOV *r1,r2*

To move data from register to register, we'll use the move register command: MOV *r1,r2*. Register *r2* is the *source* and *r1* is the *destination* of the data. In other words, to move the data from register *E* into register *C*, we would use the instruction MOV C,E. Data from any register can be moved to any other register. The data in the source register (*r2*) remains unchanged. Because there is no data value to be specified as part of the instruction, they are only 1-byte instructions (opcode only). Rather than list all of the opcodes here, take a moment to be sure that you can find the opcodes in the Assembly Language Reference Chart in Appendix C.

EXAMPLE 2–4

List the instructions in assembly language and machine language to meet the following requirements:

  (a) Move the contents of the *D* register into the *H* register.

  (b) Load the number 44H into both the *C* and *E* registers using only 3 bytes of machine language code.

Solution: The opcodes are found in the Assembly Language Reference Chart in Appendix C.

	Assembly language	Machine code	Comments
(a)	MOV H,D	62	H ← D
(b)	MVI C,44H	0E 44	C ← 44H
	MOV E,C	59	E ← C

(*Note:* MOV E,C copies register *C* into register *E* and leaves register *C* unchanged. Using MVI E,44H would have made the program 4 bytes long instead of 3.)

LXI *rp,data16*

The LXI *rp,data16* instruction allows us to load all 16 bits of a register pair with one instruction. The *rp* is replaced by a single letter signifying which register pair to be loaded. Use *B* for register pair *B–C*, *D* for register pair *D–E*, and *H* for register pair *H–L*. The *data16* operand is replaced with the 16 bits of data to be loaded into the register pair. This makes LXI a 3-byte instruction: byte 1 is the opcode, byte 2 is the low-order byte of data that goes to the low-order register in the register pair, and byte 3 is the high-order byte of data that goes to the high-order register in the register pair (see Example 2–5).

EXAMPLE 2–5

List the instructions that will perform the following operations:
  (a) Load the B register with D5 and the C register with D8.
  (b) Redo part (a) using an LXI instruction.
  (c) Load the D–E register pair with 3800H.

Solution:

Assembly language	Machine language	Comments
(a) MVI B,D5H	06 D5	B ← D5
MVI C,D8H	0E D8	C ← D8
(b) LXI B,D5D8H	01 D8 D5	C ← D8 B ← D5
(c) LXI D,3800H	11 00 38	E ← 00 D ← 38

INR *r*, DCR *r* and INX *rp*, DCX *rp*

As you may have guessed, there are commands for incrementing and decrementing registers and register pairs. When working with an 8-bit register, the INR or DCR instruction acts like it is incrementing or decrementing an 8-bit counter. The register pair commands INX and DCX are similar, except that they work as a 16-bit counter. (You'll notice that all register pair instructions have an X in their mnemonic.)

If you increment a single register that has an FFH in it, it will "roll over" to 00H. If you decrement a register that has a 00H in it, it will "roll over" to FFH. The same happens to register pairs when they are incremented past FFFFH or decremented below 0000H.

EXAMPLE 2–6

Determine the contents of the B and C registers after the execution of each of the following programs.
  (a) LXI B,24FFH
      INX B
  (b) LXI B,46FFH
      INR C
  (c) LXI B,4F88H
      DCR B
  (d) MVI B,C7H
      MVI C,00H
      DCX B

Solution:

  (a) $B = 25H$, $C = 00H$. INX B increments the 16-bit quantity of the B–C register pair.

(b) $B = 46H$, $C = 00H$. INR C increments the 8-bit C register only. C rolls over to 00H without affecting the quantity in the B register.

(c) $B = 4EH$, $C = 88H$. DCR B decrements the B register only.

(d) $B = C6H$, $C = FFH$. Even though B and C were loaded using MVIs, the DCX B command treats them like a 16-bit register pair. To decrement, the C register borrows 1 from the B register.

2-5 WRITING TIME-DELAY ROUTINES

Time delays are used in microprocessor applications to insert delays that are required between processes. One good application is the hexadecimal counter that we designed in Example 2–2 to drive output LEDs. In that program, the counter is incrementing and driving the LEDs from 0 to 15 at microprocessor speeds. This is much too fast for a human to see. A time delay, implemented with software, could be inserted within the loop to slow the process down to any speed that we want.

One simple way to create a time delay is to set a register to FFH and count down until it reaches 0, as shown in Table 2–3.

TABLE 2–3

Short Delay Routine Using a Single Register

Address	Contents	Label	Instruction	Comments
2050	0E	DELAY:	MVI C,FFH	; C ← FFH
2051	FF			;
2052	0D	LOOP1:	DCR C	; C = C−1
2053	C2		JNZ LOOP1	; Keep looping
2054	52			; until
2055	20			; C = 0

This program will continue to loop back to address 2052 until register C finally reaches 0. After that, the program will continue to the statement following the JNZ instruction.

To determine how long this delay will be in seconds, we need to refer to the Instruction Set Timing Index in Appendix E. This index gives the number of T states for each instruction. One T state is the length of one microprocessor clock period. The internal clock frequency of the microprocessor is one-half the frequency of the crystal used to drive the 8085A. Therefore, if the 8085A is using a 4-MHz crystal, then one T state will be 0.5 μs. [One T state = $1/(0.5 \times 4$ MHz$) = 0.5$ μs.]

The MVI C,FFH instruction takes seven T states, DCR C takes four, and JNZ LOOP1 takes 7/10. The 7/10 means that the JNZ instruction takes 10 T states *if the condition is met* (if C is not 0), and 7 T states *if the condition is not met*. It takes the extra time if the condition *is* met because it has to read byte 2–byte 3 of the instruction to determine where to jump to.

Now you add up all of the T states required to complete the delay, as shown in Table 2–4. Since C starts out at FFH (255), then it must be decremented 255 times before setting the zero flag. The 255th time it is decremented, C will be 0 so the JNZ instruction will take only seven T states. For the first 254 times in the loop, it will take $(4 + 10)$ T states for each pass. The last time it will take $(4 + 7)$ T states. This gives us a total of 3574 T states, and a delay time of 1.787 ms (0.5 μs $\times$ 3574 T states).

TABLE 2–4

Determining the *T* States of a Delay Routine

	Instruction	*T* states
DELAY:	MVI C,FFH	7
LOOP1:	DCR C	4 ← Loop (254 + 1) times
	JNZ LOOP1	7/10
T states = 7 + 254 × (4 + 10) + 1 × (4 + 7) = 3574		

EXAMPLE 2–7

Determine the length of time of the following delay loop. Assume that the 8085A is driven with a 5-MHz crystal.

$$\text{DELAY:} \quad \text{MVI} \quad \text{A,00H}$$

$$\text{LOOP:} \quad \text{INR} \quad \text{A}$$

$$\text{CPI} \quad \text{6DH}$$

$$\text{JNZ} \quad \text{LOOP}$$

Solution: The microprocessor clock period (1 *T* state) = $1/(0.5 \times 5 \text{ MHz})$ = 0.4 μs. The *T* states per instruction (found in the Instruction Set Timing Index) are as follows:

$$\text{MVI A} = 7 \text{ } T \text{ states}$$

$$\text{INR A} = 4 \text{ } T \text{ states}$$

$$\text{CPI} = 7 \text{ } T \text{ states}$$

$$\text{JNZ} = 7/10 \text{ } T \text{ states}$$

The number of times around the loop is 6DH or 109 times. Therefore, the total number of *T* states is:

$$T \text{ states} = 7 + 108 \times (4 + 7 + 10) + 1 \times (4 + 7 + 7)$$

$$= 2293$$

And the time delay is

$$T = \text{clock period} \times T \text{ states}$$

$$T = 0.4 \text{ } \mu\text{s} \times 2293 = 917.2 \text{ } \mu\text{s}$$

Nested Loops

The previous delay of 1.787 ms (Table 2–3) would not be long enough to use as a pause between counts on an LED display for us to see the count changing. We need at least one-quarter of a second (250 ms) between counts.

One way to get a 250-ms delay is to execute the previous delay instructions (Table 2–3) 140 times (140 × 1.787 ms ≈ 250 ms). This is called a *nested loop*. It is implemented using the flowchart shown in Figure 2–4 and the program statements in Table 2–5.

The flowchart is a good means of visualizing the flow of the program. It is recommended that one be drawn before writing any program that has branching or looping. The program instructions in Table 2–5 correspond directly to the flowchart. The inner loop (LOOP1) is the same as the previous delay program. It will decrement register *E* 255 times before setting the zero flag and dropping out. Then, when the DCR D in-

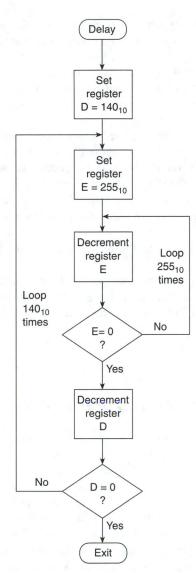

Figure 2–4 Flowchart for a nested loop delay.

TABLE 2–5

A Nested-Loop Program to Create a Delay of $\approx$ 250 ms

Address	Contents	Label	Instruction	Comments
2050	16	DELAY:	MVI D,8CH	; D ← 8CH (140)
2051	8C			;
2052	1E	LOOP2:	MVI E,FFH	; E ← FFH (255)
2053	FF			;
2054	1D	LOOP1:	DCR E	; E ← E-1
2055	C2		JNZ LOOP1	; Jump to
2056	54			; LOOP1
2057	20			; 255 times
2058	15		DCR D	; D ← D-1
2059	C2		JNZ LOOP2	; Jump to
205A	52			; LOOP2
205B	20			; 140 times

struction is executed, register *D* becomes 139 and the zero flag is *reset*. The outer loop (LOOP2) causes the inner loop to be executed repeatedly as register *D* is decremented from 140 down to 0.

For even longer delays you could insert dummy instructions within the loop or you could form a third level of nesting by using a third register. A commonly used dummy or "do nothing" instruction is the NOP (no-operation) instruction, which takes four *T* states.

Register pairs can also be used as our loop counter, giving us a maximum count of FFFFH instead of just FFH provided by single registers. The problem with register pairs, however, is that the DCX *rp* instruction does not set the zero flag when the register pair reaches 0000H. In the previous delays, we were using the zero flag to get us out of the loop. You must be careful when writing programs that depend on the condition of the flags, that the particular instruction *does* affect the flags. For example, DCR *r* will set the zero flag, whereas DCX *rp* will not. This information is provided for each instruction in the 8085A Instruction Set Reference Encyclopedia in Appendix D.

There *are* ways to use register pairs as loop counters, however. To utilize them, we need to use other instructions to set the zero flag when the terminal count is reached. The CMP *r* or the ORA *r* instructions, which are covered in a later chapter, can be used for that purpose.

2–6   USING A TIME-DELAY SUBROUTINE WITH I/O OPERATIONS

Now that we have a one-quarter second delay routine, we can set it up as a *subroutine* and "call" it whenever we need a delay. Subroutines are covered in more detail in a later chapter, but for now all we need to know is that the delay program will be a stand-alone module that will be called by the main program whenever a delay is needed.

To make the delay program of Table 2–5 a subroutine, all we need to do is to put a *return statement* (RET) at the end of it. Then, whenever another program calls it by using a CALL *addr* instruction, it will be executed. When execution of the delay subroutine is complete, the program control returns to the instruction following the CALL *addr* instruction. The operand, *addr,* is the address in memory of the subroutine, which in this case will be 2050H.

Now let's insert a delay within the hexadecimal counter loop of Example 2–2 to slow the count down so that we can see the count change on the output LEDs (see Figure 2–5 and Table 2–6).

The program in Table 2–6 uses the LED circuit that was designed back in Figure 2–1, which was addressed at port FEH. After sending the count to the LEDs, the delay subroutine is called. The opcode for CALL is CD, which is followed by the 2-byte address of the delay subroutine (2050H). Notice that the address is entered low-order (50) first, then high-order (20), the same as with jump addresses.

After the execution of the CALL instruction, program control passes to the delay subroutine at address 2050H. At the end of the delay subroutine, we have added a RETURN that will pass control back to the main program at the next instruction past the CALL instruction.

The delay subroutine was stored, starting at address 2050H, but actually could have started at any memory address past the end of the main program. The addresses between 2011H and 2050H are never executed, and therefore can contain any data without affecting our program.

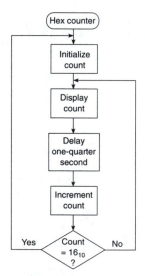

Figure 2–5 Flowchart for a hex counter with a delay.

TABLE 2-6

Hexadecimal Counter Program with a Delay Subroutine[*] Called Between Counts

Address	Contents	Label	Instruction	Comments
2000	3E	START:	MVI A,00H	; Initialize A to 0
2001	00			;
2002	2F	DISPLAY:	CMA	; Complement A
2003	D3		OUT FEH	; Output to LEDs
2004	FE			; at port FEH
2005	2F		CMA	; Complement A back
2006	CD		CALL DELAY	; Call the DELAY
2007	50			; subroutine
2008	20			; at 2050H
2009	3C		INR A	; Increment A
200A	FE		CPI 10H	; Compare A to 10H,
200B	10			; set Z flag if equal
200C	CA		JZ START	; Jump to start
200D	00			; if Z flag
200E	20			; set
200F	C3		JMP DISPLAY	; Else jump
2010	02			; to
2011	20			; DISPLAY
—				
—				
—				
2050	16	DELAY:	MVI D,8CH	; D ← 8CH (140)
2051	8C			;
2052	1E	LOOP2:	MVI E,FFH	; E ← FFH (255)
2053	FF			;
2054	1D	LOOP1:	DCR E	; E ← E-1
2055	C2		JNZ LOOP1	; Jump to
2056	54			; LOOP1
2057	20			; 255 times
2058	15		DCR D	; D ← D-1
2059	C2		JNZ LOOP2	; Jump to
205A	52			; LOOP2
205B	20			; 140 times
205C	C9		RET	; Return to main
				; program

[*] This program assumes that the stack pointer has been initialized (see Section 4-4).

Now that we know how to use the output port at address FEH, let's concentrate on using the *input port* at address FFH. Executing the instruction IN FFH will load the accumulator with the value of the HIGH/LOW toggle switches shown in Figure 2-1. The following examples illustrate the use of the input port.

EXAMPLE 2-8

Assume that the switches at input port FFH are connected to eight temperature limit sensors in an industrial process facility. Write a program that will produce a continuous warning flash on the output LEDs if any of the temperature limits go HIGH.

Solution:

Address	Contents	Label	Instruction	Comments
2000	DB	READIN:	IN FFH	; Read input switches
2001	FF			: into accumulator
2002	FE		CPI 00H	; Compare A to 00H,
2003	00			; set Z if equal
2004	CA		JZ READIN	; Keep rereading as
2005	00			; long as all
2006	20			; switches are LOW
2007	3E	FLASH:	MVI A,00H	; Active-LOW LEDs
2008	00			; will come on with 00H
2009	D3	LOOP:	OUT FEH	; Activate
200A	FE			; LEDs
200B	CD		CALL DELAY	; Wait one-
200C	50			; quarter
200D	20			; second
200E	2F		CMA	; Complement accumulator
200F	C3		JMP LOOP	; Loop continuously
2010	09			;
2011	20			;

Explanation: The program will continuously loop around the first three instructions as long as all input switches are LOW. As soon as one temperature limit switch goes HIGH, the CPI 00H instruction will *reset* the zero flag to 0, allowing program flow to drop down to the MVI A,00H instruction.

The first time that the OUT FEH instruction is executed, the active-LOW LEDs will turn on because *A* was set to 00H. We then use the same delay subroutine that we wrote before (at address 2050H) to hold the LEDs on for one-quarter second. The CMA instruction then complements the accumulator to FFH before looping back to the OUT FEH instruction. Sending FFH to the LEDs will turn them all off. The delay will then hold them off for one-quarter second. The effect of this loop is to cause the LEDs to flash. This is used for a warning that a high temperature exists somewhere in the process facility.

EXAMPLE 2–9

Assume that the binary value on the input switches represents a trouble code in an automobile's electronic control. Write a program that flashes the LEDs the number of times equivalent to the trouble code.

Solution:

Address	Contents	Label	Instruction	Comments
2000	DB	READCD:	IN FFH	; Read trouble
2001	FF			; code
2002	47		MOV B,A	; Move code to reg. B
2003	3E	LOOP:	MVI A,00H	; A ← 00H
2004	00			;
2005	D3		OUT FEH	; Turn LEDs on
2006	FE			;
2007	CD		CALL DELAY	; Delay one-
2008	50			; quarter
2009	20			; second
200A	2F		CMA	; A ← $\overline{A}$
200B	D3		OUT FEH	; Turn LEDs off

Solution: (continued)

Address	Contents	Label	Instruction	Comments
200C	FE			;
200D	CD		CALL DELAY	; Delay one-
200E	50			; quarter
200F	20			; second
2010	05		DCR B	; B ← B-1
2011	C2		JNZ LOOP	; Flash again
2012	03			; until B=0
2013	20			;
2014	76		HLT	; Halt

Explanation: We first read in the trouble code and then transfer it to register *B*. We have to transfer it to register *B* because register *A* is about to be used to flash the LEDs, and we need to remember what the trouble code is. After flashing the LEDs on, then off once, we then decrement the trouble code (register *B*) once and check to see if it is zero. If not, then repeat the on/off sequence. This continues until register *B* is decremented to zero. The LEDs will flash the number of times equivalent to the trouble code, then drop to the last statement, HLT, which halts microprocessor execution.

SUMMARY OF INSTRUCTIONS

LDA addr: (Load Accumulator Direct) Load the accumulator with the contents of memory whose address (*addr*) is specified in byte 2–byte 3 of the instruction.

STA addr: (Store Accumulator Direct) Store the contents of the accumulator to memory whose address (*addr*) is specified in byte 2–byte 3 of the instruction.

IN port: (Input) Load the accumulator with the contents of the specified port.

OUT port: (Output) Move the contents of the accumulator to the specified port.

MVI r,data: (Move Immediate) Move into register *r,* the data specified in byte 2 of the instruction.

DCR r: (Decrement Register) Decrement the value in register *r* by one.

INR r: Increment the value in register *r* by one.

JMP addr: (Jump) Transfer control to address *addr,* specified in byte 2–byte 3 of the instruction.

JZ addr: (Jump If Zero) Transfer control to address *addr* if the zero flag is set.

JNZ addr: (Jump If Not Zero) Transfer control to address *addr* if the zero flag is not set.

CPI data: (Compare Immediate) Compare the accumulator to the data in byte 2 of the instruction. The zero flag is set if A = byte 2. The carry flag is set if A < byte 2.

CMA: (Complement Accumulator) Complement the contents of the accumulator.

MOV r1,r2:   (Move Register) Copy the contents of register *r2* into register *r1.*

LXI rp,data16:   (Load Register Pair Immediate) Load register pair *rp* with the contents of byte 2–byte 3 of the instruction.

INX rp: (Increment Register Pair) Increment the 16-bit value in register pair *rp* by one.

DCX rp: (Decrement Register Pair) Decrement the 16-bit value in register pair *rp* by one.

CALL addr: (Call) Transfer control to address *addr,* specified in byte 2–byte 3 of the instruction.

RET: (Return) Transfer control back to the "calling" program, to the instruction following the last CALL instruction.

HLT: (HALT) Stop the microprocessor.

SUMMARY

In this chapter we have learned that

1. Assembly language converts directly into machine code using a software program called an *assembler.* It can also be converted by hand if the programmer looks up all of the opcodes and addresses required for the machine code translation.

2. Memory-mapped I/O treats every input and output location as if it were a memory address. I/O-mapped I/O (or standard I/O) accesses every input and output location by an assigned port number.

3. I/O-mapped I/O uses the assembly language instructions IN *port* and OUT *port* to read and write data.

4. A flowchart is a useful means of documenting the sequence of program execution.

5. Assembly language is written using mnemonics that are later converted into machine code before being used by the microprocessor.

6. A single microprocessor program instruction occupies 1, 2, or 3 bytes of memory. It always starts with a 1-byte opcode and can be followed by 1 byte of data or a 2-byte address.

7. The looping in a down-counter is redirected to the start when zero is reached by using the JZ instruction. The looping in an up-counter is redirected to the start when the accumulator reaches a certain count by using the CPI and the JZ instructions.

8. Besides the accumulator, there are 6 other registers labeled: *B, C, D, E, H* and *L.* Register-pairs are formed by combining two 8-bit registers.

9. Data can be loaded into a register by using the MVI instruction and into a register-pair by using the LXI instruction. Data movement between registers is done by using the MOV instruction.

10. Incrementing and decrementing registers and register-pairs is done with the INR, DCR, INX, and DCX instructions.

11. Time delay routines are used by microprocessors to introduce a time delay between operations. The length of the delay can be determined by adding up the *T* states of all of the instructions executed in the delay and multiplying that times the microprocessor clock period.

12. Subroutines are used to define a program module that is to be executed several times within the main program. The subroutine is executed by using a CALL statement and is ended when a RET statement is encountered.

GLOSSARY

Assembler: A software package used to convert assembly language into machine language.

Basic language: A high-level computer programming language that uses English-language-type instructions that are converted to executable machine code.

Compiler: A software package that converts a high-level language program into machine language code.

Flowchart: A diagram used by the programmer to map out the looping and conditional branching that a program must make. It becomes the "blueprint" for the program.

Hand assembly: The act of converting assembly language instructions into machine language codes by hand, using a reference chart.

I/O-mapped I/O: A method of input/output that addresses each I/O device as a port selected by an 8-bit port number.

Memory-mapped I/O: A method of input/output that addresses each I/O device as a memory location selected by a 16-bit address.

Nested loop: A loop embedded within another loop.

Opcode: Operation code. It is the unique 1-byte code given to identify each instruction to the microprocessor.

Operand: The parameters that follow the assembly language mnemonic to complete the specification of the instruction.

Port number: An 8-bit number used to select a particular I/O port.

Register pair: In the 8085A microprocessor, six of the internal data registers are paired up to form three register pairs. They are useful for storing 16-bit quantities like addresses and large data values.

Statement label: A meaningful name given to certain assembly language program lines so that they can be referred to from different parts of the program, using statements like JUMP or CALL.

Subroutine: A reusable group of instructions, ending with a return instruction (RET) and called from another part of the program using a CALL instruction.

Time delay: A program segment written using repetitive loops to waste time or to slow down a process.

T state: Timing state. It is the length of time of one microprocessor clock period.

Zero flag: A bit internal to the microprocessor that, when set (1), signifies that the last arithmetic or logic operation had a result of zero.

PROBLEMS

2–1.   Describe one advantage and one disadvantage of writing programs in a high-level language instead of assembly language.

2–2.   Are the following instructions used for memory-mapped I/O or for I/O-mapped I/O?
(a) LDA *addr*
(b) STA *addr*
(c) IN *port*
(d) OUT *port*

2–3.   What is the digital level on the microprocessor's IO/$\overline{\text{M}}$ line for each of the following instructions?
(a) LDA *addr*
(b) STA *addr*
(c) IN *port*
(d) OUT *port*

2–4.   List the new IN and OUT instructions that would be used to I/O to the switches and LEDs if the following changes to U4 and U5 were made to Figure 2–1.
(a) Add inverters to inputs A_8 and A_9 of U4 and to A_9 and A_{10} of U5.
(b) Add inverters to inputs A_{14} and A_{15} of U4 and to A_{14} and A_{15} of U5.

2–5.   U6a and U6b in Figure 2–1 are OR gates. Why are they drawn as inverted-input NAND gates?

2–6.   Are the LEDs in Figure 2–1 active-HIGH or active-LOW?

2–7.   Is the $\overline{\text{RD}}$ line or the $\overline{\text{WR}}$ line pulsed LOW by the microprocessor during the:
(a) IN instruction?
(b) OUT instruction?

2–8. What three conditions must be met to satisfy the output enables of U2 in Figure 2–1?

2–9. What three conditions must be met to provide a pulse to the C_p input of U3 in Figure 2–1?

2–10. Which internal data register is used for the IN and OUT instructions?

2–11. Write the assembly language instruction that would initialize the accumulator to 4FH.

2–12. Describe in words what the instruction JZ LOOP does.

2–13. Look up the opcodes for the following instructions:
   (a) MVI D,*data*
   (b) INR C
   (c) JNZ *addr*
   (d) DCR B

2–14. For each of the instructions in Problem 2–13, determine if they are 1-, 2-, or 3-byte instructions.

2–15. (a) Write the machine language code for the following assembly language program. (Start the machine code at address 2010H.)

   INIT: MVI A,04H
     X1:   DCR A
           JZ INIT
           JMP X1

   (b) Rewrite the program using a JNZ instruction in place of the JZ instruction. However, keep the function of the program the same.

2–16. Draw a flowchart and write the assembly language and machine language code for a MOD-12 down-counter program. (Start the machine code at address 2000H.)

2–17. Describe in words what the instruction CPI 0DH does.

2–18. Draw a flowchart and write the assembly language and machine language code for a MOD-12 up-counter. (Start the machine language code at address 2030H.)

2–19. Why are there *two* CMA instructions required in Example 2–2?

2–20. Modify your program in Problem 2–18 to output its count to the output LEDs at port FEH.

2–21. List the six internal data registers and the three register pairs inside the 8085A.

2–22. List the instructions in assembly language and machine language to meet the following requirements:
   (a) Load the *E* register with 4FH.
   (b) Load the *C* register with 12_{10}.
   (c) Load the *H–L* register pair with the address 2051H.
   (d) Load the *B–C* register pair with 1000_{10}.

2–23. What is the source register and what is the destination register for the instruction: MOV B,D?

2–24. Use the 8085A Instruction Set Reference Encyclopedia in Appendix D to determine which of the following instructions are capable of changing the zero flag:
   (a) INR *r*
   (b) INX *rp*
   (c) DCR *r*
   (d) DCX *rp*

2–25. Determine the contents of the *D* and *E* registers after the execution of each of the following programs.
   (a) MVI D,FFH
       INR D
       MVI E,00H
       DCR E
   (b) LXI D,4050H
       INX D
   (c) LXI D,40FFH
       INX D
   (d) LXI D,40FFH
       INR E

(e) LXI D,A000H
DCX D
(f) LXI D,E000H
DCR D

2–26. Determine the length of time of the following time-delay routines. (Assume that the 8085A is using a 4-MHz crystal.)

(a) DELAY: MVI B,05H
LOOP: DCR B
JNZ LOOP

(b) DELAY: MVI B,C0H
LOOP: DCR B
JNZ LOOP

(c) DELAY: MVI A,00H
LOOP: INR A
CPI 05H
JNZ LOOP

(d) DELAY: MVI B,00H
LOOP: INR B
MOV A,B
CPI D0H
JNZ LOOP

2–27. Modify the first instruction in the nested-loop program shown in Table 2–5 to yield a delay of approximately one-tenth of a second.

2–28. Modify one instruction in the counter program given in Table 2–6 to change it to a MOD-12 counter.

2–29. Add the instructions to the DELAY subroutine in Table 2–6 for a third level of nesting to provide a time delay of approximately 1 s.

2–30. Is the CPI 00H instruction in Example 2–8 really necessary for the temperature limit program to work? Why?

2–31. What modification to the temperature limit program in Example 2–8 could be made so that it will flash only the LED that corresponds to the temperature limit that went HIGH?

2–32. Rewrite the program in Example 2–8 so that it will flash all LEDs 10 times and then halt as soon as any of the temperature limit switches go HIGH. (*Hint:* Use the *B* register as a counter.)

2–33. There is a potential problem with the automobile electronic control program in Example 2–9. That is, how many times will the LEDs flash if the trouble code is 00H? Fix the program so that a trouble code 00H will mean "no trouble" and keep rereading until there is a nonzero trouble code.

SCHEMATIC INTERPRETATION PROBLEMS

2–34. Find U9 in the HC11D0 schematic. LCD_SL and KEY_SL are active-LOW outputs that signify that either the LCD or the keyboard is selected. Add a logic gate to this schematic that outputs a LOW level called I/O_SEL whenever either the LCD or the keyboard is selected.

2–35. U5 and U6 are octal D flip-flops in the Watchdog Timer schematic. They provide two stages of latching for the 8-bit data bus labeled D(7:0).
(a) How are they initially Reset? (*Hint:* CLR is the abbreviation for CLEAR, which is the same as Master Reset.)
(b) What has to happen for the Q-outputs of U5 to receive the value of the data bus?
(c) What has to happen for the Q-outputs of U6 to receive the value of the U5 outputs?

2–36. S2 in grid location B-1 in the HC11D0 schematic is a set of seven 10kΩ pull-up resistors contained in a single DIP. They all have a common connection to V_{cc} as shown. Explain their purpose as they relate to the U12 DIP-switch package and the MODA, MODB inputs to the 68HC11 microcontroller.

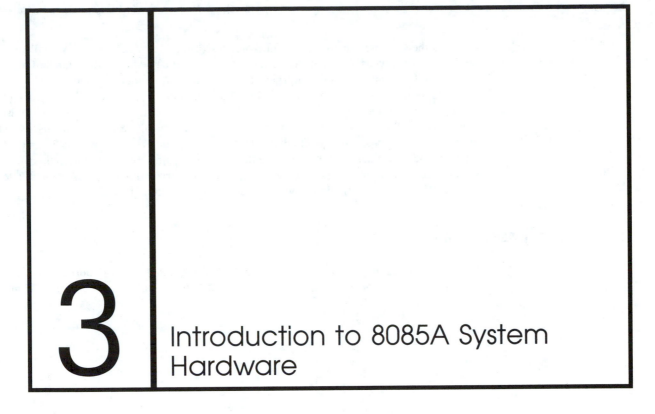

3

Introduction to 8085A System Hardware

OBJECTIVES

Upon completion of this chapter you should be able to:

- Describe the differences between memory-mapped I/O and standard I/O.
- Understand the function of each pin on the 8085A microprocessor.
- Describe how the ALE signal is used to demultiplex the address/data bus.
- Discuss Read and Write machine cycle timing.
- Interface octal buffers and latches to microprocessor buses for performing I/O operations.
- Discuss the hardware design and timing of a complete 8085A system using memory-mapped I/O and standard memories.
- Discuss the hardware design and timing of a complete 8085A system using I/O-mapped I/O with 8085A-compatible support chips.
- Develop a memory map for a microprocessor-based system.
- Explain microprocessor instruction cycle and machine cycle timing.
- Draw Read cycle and Write cycle timing waveforms.
- Set up the 8355/8755A support chip for I/O and write the instructions to use its ports for inputting and outputting data.
- Write the instructions to use the I/O ports on the 8155/8156 IC and to use its timer section for timing and waveform generation.

INTRODUCTION

We saw a little bit of microprocessor hardware in Chapter 1 and we were introduced to software in Chapter 2. In this chapter we will study the 8085A hardware and timing waveforms as they are used in a complete microprocessor-based system design. We will focus on the two basic types of system configuration: memory-mapped I/O using standard memory ICs and I/O-mapped I/O using special 8085A-compatible memory and I/O ICs.

Using the 8085A-compatible ICs (like the 8155 and 8355) makes life very easy for the hardware designer, but it hides many of the intricacies of the microprocessor chip that are important for the beginner to understand. For that reason, we'll start our discussion by using general-purpose ICs like the 2716 EPROM, static RAMs, octal buffers, and *D* latches. Once we understand the hardware interface and timing considerations in this mode, we'll switch over to the simplified design that uses memory and I/O chips specifically designed for interface compatibility with the 8085A (the 8155 and 8355).

3–1 8085A PIN DEFINITIONS

Figure 3–1 gives the pin configuration for the 8085A, and Table 3–1 defines the function of each pin, as presented in the Intel publication *Embedded Controller Handbook, 1988.*

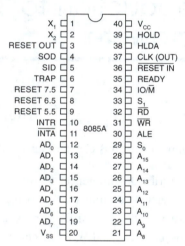

Figure 3–1 8085A pin configuration.

3–2 THE MULTIPLEXED BUS AND READ/WRITE TIMING

To keep the IC pin count to a minimum and thus reduce printed-circuit-board area, most manufacturers have used a *multiplexing* scheme on their address/data bus to allow two functions to "share" the same group of pins.

Pins 12 through 19 on the 8085A are multiplexed, using the same pins for both the low-order address lines (A_0–A_7) and the eight data lines (D_0–D_7). A special output control signal, ALE (Address Latch Enable), provides a signal to the external hardware to tell it when the multiplexed lines, AD_0–AD_7, contain addresses and when they contain data.

If we are using standard memories such as the 2716 EPROM and the 2114 RAM, and using standard octal devices like the 74LS244 buffer and the 74LS374 latch, then we must *demultiplex* the AD_0–AD_7 lines before they can be used. Figure 3–2 shows the most common method for doing that.

The A_8–A_{15} high-order address lines in Figure 3–2 are always valid, and are routed directly to the address bus. For example, the instruction STA 38FFH will place 38H on the A_8–A_{15} lines. The low-order part of the address, FFH, will appear on the AD_0–AD_7 lines early in the instruction cycle, and then disappear to allow the data for the STA instruction to pass out to the data bus via the same AD_0–AD_7 lines.

TABLE 3–1

8085A Functional Pin Definitions

Symbol	Type	Name and function
$A_8–A_{15}$	O	**Address bus:** The most significant 8 bits of memory address or the 8 bits of the I/O address, 3-stated during Hold and Halt modes and during Reset.
AD_{0-7}	I/O	**Multiplexed address/data bus:** Lower 8 bits of the memory address (or I/O address) appear on the bus during the first clock cycle (T state) of a machine cycle. It then becomes the data bus during the second and third clock cycles.
ALE	O	**Address latch enable:** It occurs during the first clock state of a machine cycle and enables the address to get latched into the on-chip latch of peripherals. The falling edge of ALE is set to guarantee setup and hold times for the address information. The falling edge of ALE can also be used to strobe the status information. ALE is never 3-stated.
S_0, S_1, and $IO/\overline{M}$	O	**Machine cycle status:**

$IO/\overline{M}$	S_1	S_0	Status
0	0	1	Memory write
0	1	0	Memory read
1	0	1	I/O write
1	1	0	I/O read
0	1	1	Opcode fetch
1	1	1	Interrupt Acknowledge
*	0	0	Halt
*	X	X	Hold
*	X	X	Reset

* = 3-state (high impedance)

X = unspecified

S_1 can be used as an advanced $R/\overline{W}$ status. $IO/\overline{M}$, S_0, and S_1 become valid at the beginning of a machine cycle and remain stable throughout the cycle. The falling edge of ALE may be used to latch the state of these lines.

Symbol	Type	Name and function
$\overline{RD}$	O	**Read control:** A low level of $\overline{RD}$ indicates the selected memory or I/O device is to be read and that the data bus is available for the data transfer, 3-stated during Hold and Halt modes and during RESET.
$\overline{WR}$	O	**Write control:** A low level on $\overline{WR}$ indicates the data on the data bus are to be written into the selected memory or I/O location. Data are set up at the trailing edge of $\overline{WR}$. 3-stated during Hold and Halt modes and during RESET.
READY	I	**Ready:** If READY is high during a Read or Write cycle, it indicates that the memory or peripheral is ready to send or receive data. If READY is low, the CPU will wait an integral number of clock cycles for READY to go high before completing the Read or Write cycle. READY must conform to specified setup and hold times.
HOLD	I	**Hold:** Indicates that another master is requesting the use of the address and data buses. The CPU, upon receiving the Hold request, will relinquish the use of the bus as soon as the current bus transfer is completed. Internal processing can continue. The processor can regain the bus only after the HOLD is removed. when the HOLD is acknowledged, the address, data $\overline{RD}$, $\overline{WR}$, and IO/M lines are 3-stated.
HLDA	O	**Hold acknowledge:** Indicates that the CPU has received the HOLD request and that it will relinquish the bus in the next clock cycle. HLDA goes low after the HOLD request is removed. The CPU takes the bus one half clock cycle after HLDA goes low.

(continued)

TABLE 3–1

8085A Functional Pin Definitions (continued)

Symbol	Type	Name and function
INTR	I	**Interrupt request:** Is used as a general-purpose interrupt. It is sampled only during the next to the last clock cycle of an instruction and during Hold and Halt states. If it is active, the Program Counter (PC) will be inhibited from incrementing and an INTA will be issued. During this cycle a RESTART or CALL instruction can be inserted to jump to the interrupt service routine. The INTR is enabled and disabled by software. It is disabled by Reset and immediately after an interrupt is accepted.
$\overline{\text{INTA}}$	O	**Interrupt acknowledge:** Is used instead of (and has the same timing as) RD during the Instruction cycle after an INTR is accepted. It can be used to activate an 8259A Interrupt chip or some other interrupt port.
RST 5.5 RST 6.5 RST 7.5	I	**Restart interrupts:** These three inputs have the same timing as INTR except they cause an internal RESTART to be automatically inserted. These interrupts have a higher priority than INTR. In addition, they may be masked out individually using the SIM instruction.
TRAP	I	**Trap:** Trap interrupt is a nonmaskable RESTART interrupt. It is recognized at the same time as INTR or RST 5.5–7.5. It is unaffected by any mask or Interrupt Enable. It has the highest priority of any interrupt.
$\overline{\text{RESET IN}}$	I	**Reset In:** Sets the Program Counter to zero and resets the Interrupt Enable and HLDA flip-flops. The data and address buses and the control lines are 3-stated during RESET and, because of the asynchronous nature of RESET, the processor's internal registers and flags may be altered by RESET with unpredictable results. RESET IN is a Schmitt-triggered input, allowing connection to an *RC* network for power-on RESET delay. Upon power-up, RESET IN must remain low for at least 10 ms after minimum V_{CC} has been reached. For proper reset operation after the power-up duration, RESET IN should be kept low a minimum of three clock periods. The CPU is held in the reset condition as long as RESET IN is applied.
RESET OUT	O	**Reset Out:** Reset Out indicate CPU is being reset. Can be used as a system reset. The signal is synchronized to the processor clock and lasts an integral number of clock periods.
X_1, X_2	I	**X_1 and X_2:** Are connected to a crystal, *LC*, or *RC* network to drive the internal clock generator. X_1 can also be an external clock input from a logic gate. The input frequency is divided by 2 to give the processor's internal operating frequency.
CLK	O	**Clock:** Clock output for use as a system clock. The period of CLK is twice the X_1, X_2 input period.
SID	I	**Serial input data line:** The data on this line are loaded into accumulator bit 7 whenever a RIM instruction is executed.
SOD	O	**Serial output data line:** The output SOD is set or reset as specified by the SIM instruction.
V_{CC}		**Power:** +5-V supply.
V_{SS}		**Ground:** Reference.

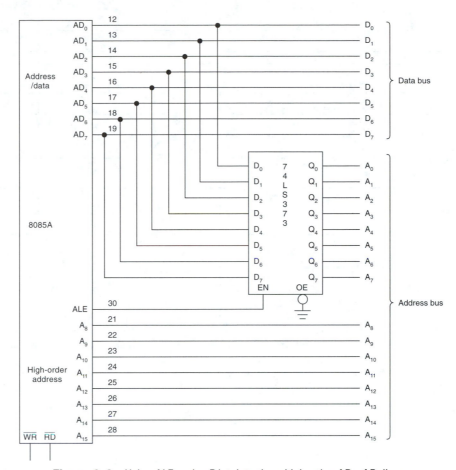

Figure 3-2   Using ALE and a *D* latch to demultiplex the AD_0–AD_7 lines.

ALE

The function of the 74LS373 transparent *D* latch is to "grab" hold of the low-order address information before it disappears. The ALE signal shown in the microprocessor timing diagram in Figure 3–3 is the key to the demultiplexing process.

In the beginning of the Read cycle or Write cycle, the 8085A sends out all 16 bits of the address. It also issues a HIGH on the ALE line. The HIGH ALE enables the 74LS373 to pass the low-order addresses through to the A_0–A_7 lines (① and ②). When the ALE line goes back LOW, the A_0–A_7 information *remains latched* in the 74LS373. (See Appendix M if you need to review *D* latches.)

Read Cycle

Later in the Read cycle, the low-order address is removed from AD_0–AD_7, and the lines go to a high-impedance state (float), as indicated by the dashed lines. Next, the microprocessor issues a LOW on the $\overline{RD}$ line. This LOW is used to drive an active-LOW output enable on the IC that is used to input data to the microprocessor's data bus. This IC now provides the Data In to the microprocessor via the AD_0–AD_7 lines (③). The microprocessor waits for the enabled input IC to respond, then it raises $\overline{RD}$ back HIGH, and at the same time it reads the Data In (④). This so-called input IC is any IC used to input data to the microprocessor, like a ROM, RAM, or input buffer. (See Figure 3–4.)

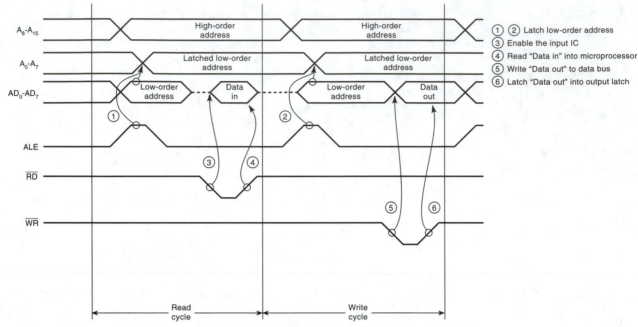

Figure 3–3   ALE and Read/Write cycle timing for the 8085A.

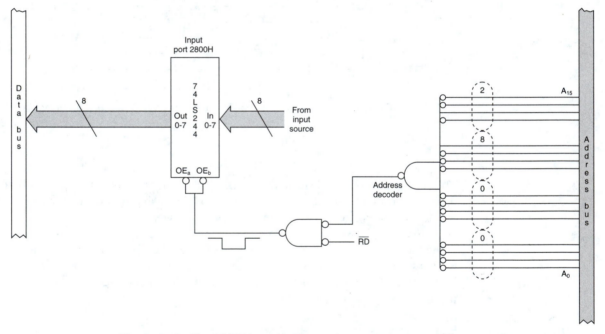

Figure 3–4   The 74LS244 octal buffer used as a memory-mapped input at address 2800H.

An example of a software instruction that reads from a memory-mapped input is LDA 2800H (Load accumulator from 2800H). After the 3-byte LDA instruction is read in and decoded by the microprocessor, the microprocessor performs a fourth Read cycle to read from the addressed input port. For this Read cycle, the microprocessor puts 28H on the high-order address bus and 00H on the AD_0–AD_7 lines. An ALE pulse immediately follows, which latches 00H out to the A_0–A_7 low-order address bus. An address decoder connected to the address bus sees the 2800H and provides a chip select (or $\overline{OE}$ in Figure 3–4) to port 2800H. Later in the Read cycle, the microprocessor floats the AD_0–AD_7 lines

(A_0–A_7 is still latched), and issues a $\overline{RD}$ pulse. This enables the selected port at address 2800H to output its data to the data bus, which is read into the microprocessor on the rising edge of $\overline{RD}$.

Write Cycle

In Figure 3–3 you can see that the Write cycle starts out the same way as the Read cycle does. It sends out 16 address bits and an ALE, but then, instead of floating the AD_0–AD_7 lines, it immediately puts the Data Out onto them. The microprocessor drops the $\overline{WR}$ line LOW at the same time that it sends the data out on AD_0–AD_7 (⑤). The LOW $\overline{WR}$ tells the addressed output or memory that data are available for it on the data bus. Often the output device being written to is a positive edge-triggered D flip-flop (as shown in Figure 3–5), which is triggered when $\overline{WR}$ returns LOW to HIGH (⑥).

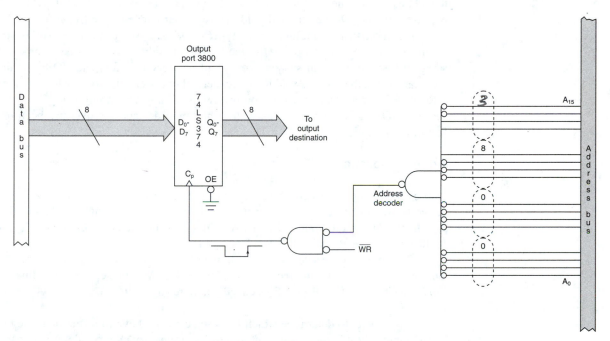

Figure 3–5   The 74LS374 octal D flip-flop used as a memory-mapped output at address 3800H.

An example of a software instruction that writes to a memory-mapped output is STA 3800H (Store accumulator to 3800H). The Write cycle for this instruction sets up A_8–A_{15} with 38H, AD_0–AD_7 with 00H, and drives ALE HIGH. A_0–A_7 latches onto 00H, which together with the 38H, selects the output at 3800H. The microprocessor next places the data from the accumulator on the AD_0–AD_7 lines (data bus) and pulses the $\overline{WR}$ line. The LOW-to-HIGH edge of the $\overline{WR}$ pulse is used as a clock trigger to the D flip-flop connected at address 3800H (see Figure 3–5). At the end of this cycle, the Q outputs of the D flip-flop contain the value that was in the accumulator.

3–3 MICROPROCESSOR SYSTEM DESIGN USING MEMORY-MAPPED I/O AND STANDARD MEMORIES

Now, if we put together the pieces from the previous section and add memory ICs, we can develop a complete system design. We'll design a memory-mapped I/O system, which means that each I/O and memory is treated as a unique 16-bit memory location. Using this mapping scheme, we can read and write to the I/O ICs as if they were memory locations. This allows us to use all of the software instructions related to memory operations to perform input and output operations.

The fact that we are using *standard memories* means that they are general-purpose, universal memories used by any type of microprocessor. Intel also has a family of memory and I/O chips designed to interface directly to the 8085A's multiplexed bus, eliminating the need for an address latch. We'll use those in the next section after we have a better understanding of demultiplexing and memory-mapped I/O. The complete system with I/O and memory is shown in Figure 3–6.

Address Latch—U2

Starting at the top of the diagram, you should recognize the 74LS373 octal latch used as the address latch. The multiplexed AD_0–AD_7 lines are input at D_0–D_7. When the ALE line is pulsed, the Q_0–Q_7 outputs will hold the low-order address byte (A_0–A_7).

Also note that the multiplexed AD_0–AD_7 lines are used as the *data bus*. We must be careful to use the data bus only *after* the low-order address byte has been removed. This safeguard is built into our system because all memory transfers and I/O to the data bus are enabled via the 74LS138 address decoder, which is enabled only when we are doing a Read ($\overline{RD}$) or a Write ($\overline{WR}$). If you review the timing waveform in Figure 3–3, you'll see that $\overline{RD}$ and $\overline{WR}$ are active *only* after the low-order address byte has been removed from the multiplexed bus.

Address Decoder—U3

Address decoding is provided by using the 74LS138 octal decoder. The '138 provides an active-LOW at one of its eight outputs, based on the binary input at A, B, and C (where A = LSB). The one output that is active will select the memory IC, input IC, or output IC that is to have access to the data bus.

Before any IC is selected, the '138 enables (E1, $\overline{E2}$, and $\overline{E3}$) have to be satisfied. This means that it must be receiving a LOW $\overline{RD}$ or $\overline{WR}$ pulse; the $IO/\overline{M}$ line must be LOW (which it is for all memory-related software instructions); and A_{15}–A_{14} must both be LOW.

From there, to determine which IC is selected, we have to further analyze the A, B, and C inputs. At this point, we want to develop a *memory map* of address allocations, as shown in Table 3–2 and Figure 3–7.

Using the procedure outlined in Table 3–2, we're able to develop a pictorial "map" of the placement of I/O and memory as shown in Figure 3–7. As the memory map shows, the decoder has placed each IC at a unique set of addresses.

EPROM—U4

The EPROM will be selected whenever the microprocessor reads from any address from 0000H to 07FFH. Address bits A_{11}, A_{12}, A_{13}, A_{14}, and A_{15} were used to select the EPROM, which leaves bits A_0–A_{10} to select the specific address within the EPROM. Having those 11 address lines allows us to specify 2048 (2^{11}) unique addresses, which happens to be the size of the 2716 EPROM. The selected address will place its 8-bit contents out to the data bus via O_0–O_7. The $\overline{OE}$ line is connected to $\overline{RD}$ to prevent a bus conflict if the programmer mistakenly tries to write to the EPROM's output.

When the 8085A is first powered up and reset, its program counter register points to address 0000H and starts executing from there. Therefore, in our system we'll store the main application's program in EPROM starting at 0000H. This way, when we power up, the software program that we write will automatically take over and perform whatever task we define.

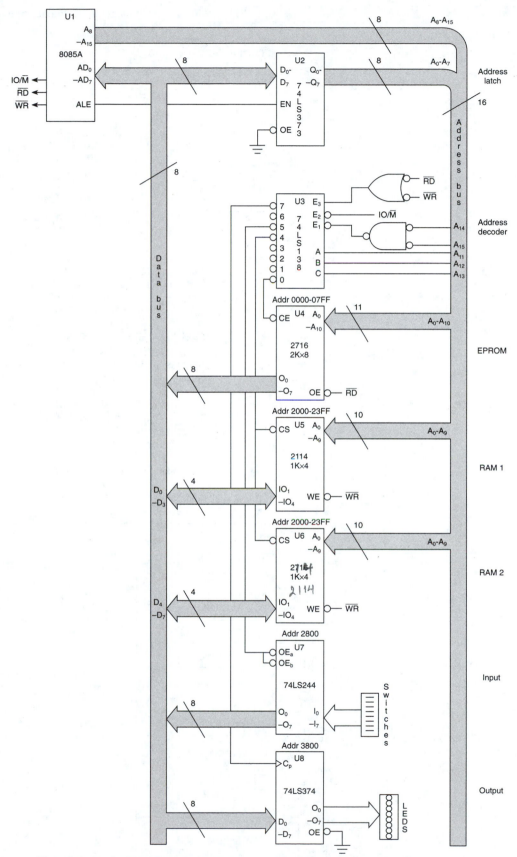

Figure 3–6 An 8085A system design using memory-mapped I/O and standard memories.

TABLE 3–2

Developing a Memory Map for Figure 3–6

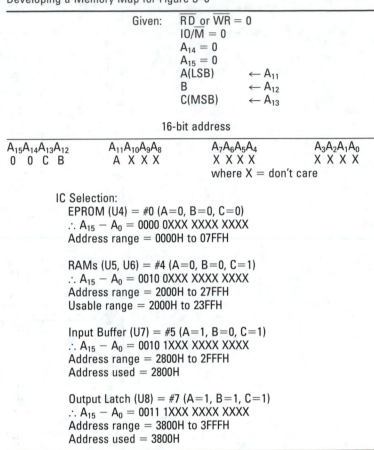

	Given:	$\overline{RD}$ or $\overline{WR} = 0$
		$IO/\overline{M} = 0$
		$A_{14} = 0$
		$A_{15} = 0$
		A(LSB) $\leftarrow A_{11}$
		B $\leftarrow A_{12}$
		C(MSB) $\leftarrow A_{13}$

16-bit address

$A_{15}A_{14}A_{13}A_{12}$	$A_{11}A_{10}A_9A_8$	$A_7A_6A_5A_4$	$A_3A_2A_1A_0$
0 0 C B	A X X X	X X X X	X X X X

where X = don't care

IC Selection:

EPROM (U4) = #0 (A=0, B=0, C=0)

∴ $A_{15} - A_0$ = 0000 0XXX XXXX XXXX

Address range = 0000H to 07FFH

RAMs (U5, U6) = #4 (A=0, B=0, C=1)

∴ $A_{15} - A_0$ = 0010 0XXX XXXX XXXX

Address range = 2000H to 27FFH

Usable range = 2000H to 23FFH

Input Buffer (U7) = #5 (A=1, B=0, C=1)

∴ $A_{15} - A_0$ = 0010 1XXX XXXX XXXX

Address range = 2800H to 2FFFH

Address used = 2800H

Output Latch (U8) = #7 (A=1, B=1, C=1)

∴ $A_{15} - A_0$ = 0011 1XXX XXXX XXXX

Address range = 3800H to 3FFFH

Address used = 3800H

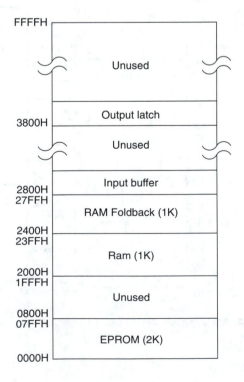

FFFFH

Unused

3800H   Output latch

Unused

2800H   Input buffer

27FFH

RAM Foldback (1K)

2400H

23FFH

Ram (1K)

2000H

1FFFH

Unused

0800H

07FFH

EPROM (2K)

0000H

Figure 3–7   Memory map for Figure 3–6.

RAMs—U5, U6

Two RAMs are required in our design because we need 8 bits at each location and one RAM location is only 4 bits wide. Notice that both RAMs use the same address bits (A_0–A_9) for internal memory selection. Therefore, if you read from location zero, both RAMs will place 4 bits from their own location zero onto the data bus. RAM1 provides D_0–D_3 and RAM2 provides D_4–D_7. Together they give us a full byte of data. If we were using 1K × 1 RAM, we would set up eight RAMs to provide 1 byte at each location.

The pair of RAMs are selected whenever reading or writing to address 2000H to 23FFH or 2400H to 27FFH. Address bits A_{11}–A_{15} are used to select the RAMs, and bits A_0–A_9 are used to select the specific location within the RAMs. With 10 address location bits (A_0–A_9) we can pinpoint 1024 (2^{10}) unique locations. This will take us from location 2000H to 23FFH.

After that, you would think that we are beyond the bounds of the RAMs, but we are not. Address bit A_{10} is not used by the address decoder, nor by the RAMs. Therefore, it is a don't care. If we try to read from address 2400H, A_{10} will be HIGH, but it makes no difference to the RAMs. The RAMs receive all zeros on A_0–A_9 and will output its first memory location. As you try to read locations 2400H through 27FFH, the RAMs are still selected, and you will access all 1024 locations all over again. This is called the *fold-back* area. The RAMs are intended to be accessed at locations 2000H to 23FFH, but the same locations can be accessed at locations 2400H to 27FFH. If you need 2K of RAM, you would put the additional 1K at location 2400H to 27FFH by using the A_{10} bit to select between the two pairs of RAMs.

The Write Enable ($\overline{WE}$) input is used by the RAM to determine which direction the data will flow. We use the $\overline{WR}$ line from the microprocessor to drive it. If $\overline{WE}$ is driven LOW, the addressed RAM location will be written to (Write). If $\overline{WE}$ is driven HIGH, the addressed RAM location will be sent to the data bus (Read).

Input Buffer—U7

The input buffer is accessed at any address from 2800H to 2FFFH because only A_{11}–A_{15} are used in its selection. If we wanted to narrow it down to a single location, we could use a decoding scheme that checks all 16 address bits like the one shown in Figure 3–4. But why bother? We have plenty of address spaces to waste, and using the method given in Figure 3–6 is simpler. We'll assume that the input buffer is at address 2800H, and read from it using the instruction LDA 2800H.

Output Latch—U8

The output latch also has a *range* of addresses that access it (3800H–3FFFH). It could have been narrowed down to a single address using a decoding scheme such as the one shown in Figure 3–5. But instead, we'll use the circuit of Figure 3–6 and write to the LEDs using STA 3800H.

The fact that U8 is a *latch* allows us to write data to the LEDs and then go perform other program instructions while the LEDs remain latched.

3-4 CPU INSTRUCTION TIMING

All software instructions used by the 8085A are made up of a sequence of *Read* and *Write* operations. Each *Read* or *Write* is called a *machine cycle*. A machine cycle takes between three to six CPU clock periods (*T* states) to complete. We have already seen that the total number of *T* states varies, depending on the complexity of the instruction.

Now we'll see that the number of *T* states required for an instruction depends on the number of Read and Write operations it takes to complete. Take, for example, the instruction STA 3800H. The function of STA is to "store the accumulator to memory whose address is specified in byte 2–byte 3 of the instruction." It takes four machine cycles to execute STA 3800H.

The 8085A Instruction Set Timing Index in Appendix E lists the machine cycles and number of *T* states for each instruction. For the STA instruction it shows machine cycles: *F, R, R,* W. Machine cycle *F* is defined as a four *T*-state *opcode fetch, R* is defined as a three *T*-state *memory read,* and *W* is defined as a three *T*-state *memory write.* Figure 3–8 shows the four machine cycles required for the STA 3800 instruction. (ALE is omitted for clarity but would pulse HIGH at the beginning of each machine cycle.)

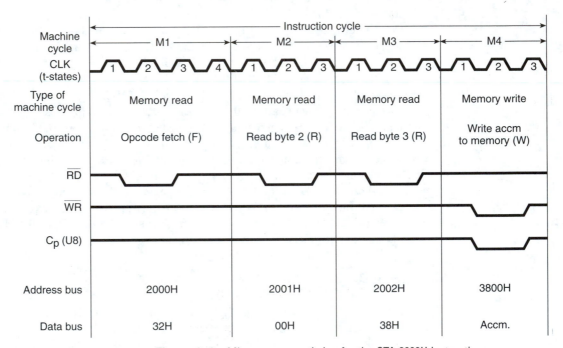

Figure 3–8   Microprocessor timing for the STA 3800H instruction.

During machine cycle M1, the microprocessor performs a four *T*-state *opcode fetch* to determine what instruction to perform. (The M1 cycle is *always* an *opcode fetch.*) To do this, the processor must first set up the address bus with the address of the machine language code (we'll assume 2000H). It then issues a LOW pulse on $\overline{\text{RD}}$, which allows the accessed memory at address 2000H to put the opcode, 32H, onto the data bus. The microprocessor's instruction decoder determines that a 32H is the opcode for STA and that two more bytes for the instruction must follow.

Machine cycle M2 is a *memory read* for byte 2 of the instruction. The program counter is incremented by one (2001H) and put on the address bus. The $\overline{\text{RD}}$ pulse causes the accessed memory at 2001H to be put on the data bus (00H). Then machine cycle M3 is a *memory read* for the third byte of the instruction (38H).

The microprocessor now has read the complete instruction and must act on it. The M4 machine cycle is a *memory write,* which completes the instruction by storing the accumulator to the specified address. During M4, the processor sets up the address bus with the specified address (3800H), puts the accumulator's contents on the data bus, and then pulses the $\overline{\text{WR}}$ line. Referring back to the memory-mapped design of Figure 3–6, you'll see that the $\overline{\text{WR}}$ pulse will be duplicated on the C_p input to U8. This provides the positive trigger to the 74LS374, which latches the accumulator contents from the data bus into the latch and drives the LEDs.

EXAMPLE 3–1

Sketch the timing waveforms at $\overline{RD}$, $\overline{WR}$, C_p (U8), and $\overline{OE}$ (U7) for the following program, which is executing on the microprocessor circuit of Figure 3–6. [Assume that the microprocessor clock frequency is 2 MHz (4-MHz crystal).]

Address	Contents	Label	Instruction	Comments
2000	3A	LOOP:	LDA 2800H	; A ← Memory(2800H)
2001	00			;
2002	28			;
2003	32		STA 3800H	; Memory(3800H) ← A
2004	00			;
2005	38			;
2006	C3		JMP LOOP	; Jump to LOOP
2007	00			;
2008	20			;

Solution: The waveforms that are generated will repeat each time around the loop and could be observed on a logic analyzer or a four-trace oscilloscope. The machine cycles and T states from the Instruction Set Timing Index in Appendix E are as follows:

$$LDA = FRRR \ (13 \ T \text{ states})$$

$$STA = FRRW \ (13 \ T \text{ states})$$

$$JMP = FRR \ (10 \ T \text{ states})$$

The waveforms are shown in Figure 3–9.

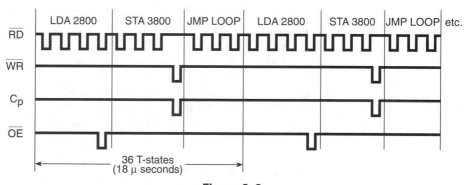

Figure 3–9

Explanation: The individual CLK T states are not drawn out but would total 36. The time for a complete loop is: $36 \times [1/(2 \text{ MHz})] = 18 \ \mu s$.

The LDA instruction requires four machine cycles: opcode fetch, memory read (byte 2), memory read (byte 3), and memory read (from 2800H). During the last machine cycle, the address bus is set up with 2800H so that when $\overline{RD}$ goes LOW, $\overline{OE}$ also goes LOW, passing the input data from the switches to the data bus.

The STA instruction requires four machine cycles: opcode fetch, memory read (byte 2), memory read (byte 3), and memory write (to 3800H). During the last machine cycle, the address bus is set up with 3800H so that when $\overline{WR}$ is pulsed LOW, C_p receives a pulse, latching the accumulator output data from the data bus to the LEDs.

The JMP instruction requires three machine cycles: opcode fetch, memory read (byte 2), and memory read (byte 3). During the third machine cycle, the program counter is loaded with the address specified in byte 2–byte 3, and control passes to that location (2000H).

3–5   A MINIMUM COMPONENT 8085A-BASED SYSTEM USING I/O-MAPPED I/O

Intel Corporation has made it possible to reduce the chip count of an 8085A-based system to three ICs. Using specifically designed 8085A-compatible memory and I/O chips enables us to eliminate several of the ICs that were needed to fulfill the design requirements of the system shown in Figure 3–6. These 8085A-compatible *support chips* accept the multiplexed AD_0–AD_7 lines directly, and use the ALE signal to demultiplex the address internally, eliminating the need for the address latch IC. They also integrate input/output ports on the same chip with RAM or ROM memory. Figure 3–10 shows a three-chip microprocessor system made possible by the 8156 and 8355/8755A support ICs.

The 8355/8755A is the read-only memory for the system. The 8355 is the mask-ROM version, and the 8755A is the EPROM version. The 8755A is used in the early stages of system development and then the pin-compatible 8355 would be used for final mass production. They are both organized as 2K × 8, and each have two 8-bit I/O ports built in.

The 8156 provides the random-access (Read/Write) memory for the system. It is organized as 256 × 8 and has two 8-bit I/O ports, one 6-bit I/O port, and a 14-bit timer/counter.

Memory Mapping Versus I/O Mapping

The circuit connections for Figure 3–10 can be made to form a memory-mapped I/O system or an I/O-mapped I/O system.

For a *memory-mapped I/O* system the A_{15} address line has to be used to drive the $\overline{\text{IO/M}}$ line on the support chips. (Use the connection indicated by the dashed line.) To access the I/O ports on the support chips, A_{15} must be HIGH. To access memory, A_{15} must be LOW. This is done by specifying A_{15} as 1 or 0 in the address field of the software instruction. Since A_{15} is dedicated to driving the $\overline{\text{IO/M}}$ line, it cannot be used as the sixteenth bit of an address, limiting the total addressable memory to 32K instead of 64K.

For *I/O-mapped I/O* (standard I/O) the $\overline{\text{IO/M}}$ line is connected directly to the $\overline{\text{IO/M}}$ line of the microprocessor as shown in Figure 3–10. This way, the A_{15} line is free to be used on the address bus. The only limitation with standard I/O, however, is that all input and output to the ports must be made with the IN *port* or OUT *port* instructions; whereas with memory-mapped I/O, you can use any of the memory-directed instructions such as STA, LDA, MOV, and MVI. For most of our applications we'll use the standard I/O method for input/output.

Chip Decoding

The chip decoding (or selection) used in Figure 3–10 couldn't be any simpler. If A_{13} is HIGH, the 8156 in enabled; if A_{13} is LOW, the 8355/8755A is enabled. Also, because the 8355/8755A has 2048 memory locations, it needs 11 lines to pinpoint each internal location. Therefore, to enable the 8355/8755A we'll make A_{11} through A_{15} all LOW, and use AD_0–AD_7 and A_8–A_{10} to select specific memory locations. The range of addresses for the 8355/8755A will therefore be 0000H to 07FFH.

The 8156 RAM is accessed when A_{13} is HIGH; and memory is pinpointed by AD_0–AD_7 (256 locations). The range of addresses for the 8156 memory will therefore be 2000H to 20FFH.

The other control signals, $\overline{\text{IO/M}}$, $\overline{\text{RD}}$, and $\overline{\text{WR}}$, brought into both chips, tell whether it is an I/O port Read or Write or whether it is a memory Read or Write.

I/O Ports

Because we will be using the standard I/O mapped system, we'll use the IN *port* and OUT *port* instructions for I/O operations. When using IN or OUT, the 8-bit port number is duplicated on the high-order, and the low-order, address bus.

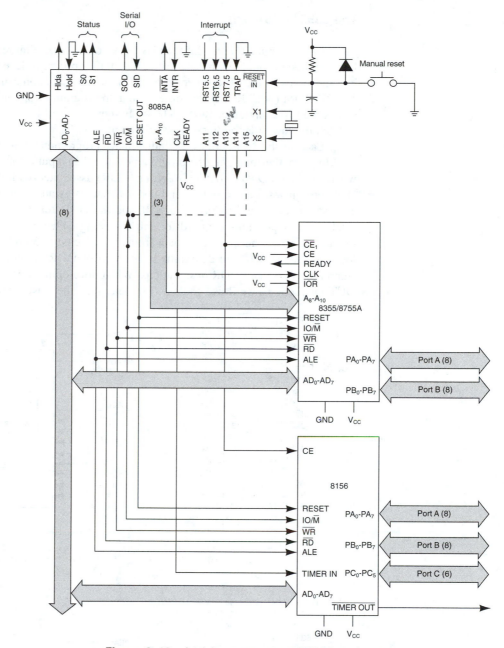

Figure 3–10 A minimum component 8085A-based system.

For example, IN 23H will set up the address bus with 2323H. With 2323H on the address bus, bit A_{13} will be HIGH, enabling the 8156. The three low-order bits of the port number are used to determine which port to use. The 3 in the number 23H specifies port C in the 8156 (more on that in Section 3–6).

To access the I/O ports on the 8355/8755A you need to make A_{13} LOW. To read port A you would use IN 00H. To read port B you would use IN 01H. (See Section 3–6.)

3–6 THE 8355/8755A AND 8155/8156 PROGRAMMABLE SUPPORT ICs

As mentioned earlier, the 8355/8755A and 8155/8156 ICs are specifically designed to simplify system design with the 8085A microprocessor (and also the 8088 microprocessor). These memory chips accept the multiplexed address/data bus directly and have built-in I/O ports.

The 8355/8755A

The block diagrams for the 8355 and 8755A are given in Figure 3–11a and b. The two ICs are pin compatible with each other so that after program development and debugging is complete using the EPROM version, the mask-ROM version can be directly substituted. The 2K ROM (or EPROM) section will contain program or operating system instructions and is read like any other ROM. The ALE signal is used in conjunction with AD_0–AD_7 to latch the low-order address, A_0–A_7, internally.

Each of the 16 I/O lines are individually programmable as input or output. To use the I/O ports, they must first be programmed as either input or output. Each 8-bit port has what is called a *Data Direction Register* (DDR) associated with it. Outputting 1's to the DDR designates it as an output and 0's designate it as an input. The DDR for port *A* is accessed as port number XXXX XX10, and the DDR for port *B* is accessed as XXXX XX11. The X positions are used for chip decoding (selection). An IN *port* or OUT *port* instruction will send or receive data from the selected 8355/8755. The 8355/8755 then looks at AD_1 and AD_0 to determine which port or DDR is being referred to. Table 3–3 summarizes port and DDR designations. When developing a port number for the IN and OUT instructions, we'll use Table 3–3 to determine the least significant bits (AD_1, AD_0).

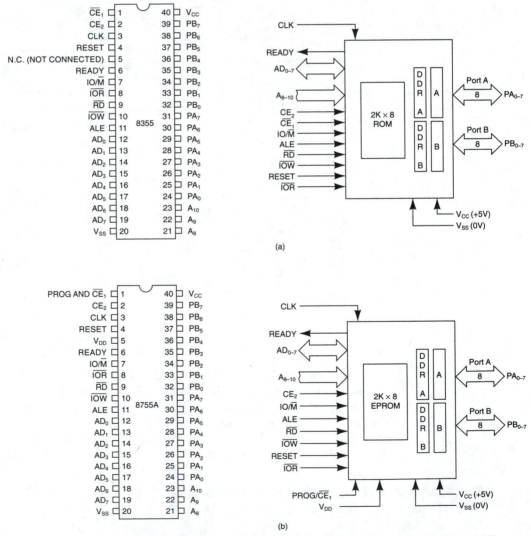

Figure 3–11 Pin configurations and block diagrams: (a) 8355 ROM with I/O; (b) 8755A EPROM with I/O. (Courtesy of Intel Corporation)

TABLE 3–3

Summary of Port and DDR Designations

AD_1	AD_0	Selection
0	0	Port A
0	1	Port B
1	0	Port A Data Direction Register (DDR A)
1	1	Port B Data Direction Register (DDR B)

We need to refer back to Figure 3–10 to determine the other six bits. To provide a Chip Enable to the 8355 (or 8755A), A_{13} must be LOW. Remember that the low-order address byte is duplicated on the high-order address byte. Therefore a LOW on AD_5 will show up on A_{13}, providing an active-LOW for $\overline{CE_1}$. Now we can build Table 3–4, which will show the actual port numbers to be used to access the ports and DDRs for the 8355/8755A in Figure 3–10.

TABLE 3–4

Port Numbers Used for the 8355/8755A in Figure 3–10

AD_7–AD_0 7 6 5 4 3 2 1 0	Selection	Port numbers used
X X 0 X X X 0 0	Port A	00H
X X 0 X X X 0 1	Port B	01H
X X 0 X X X 1 0	DDR A	02H
X X 0 X X X 1 1	DDR B	03H

The following examples will illustrate the use of the I/O ports on the 8355/8755A.

EXAMPLE 3–2

Write the instructions that would be used to designate port A of the 8355 in Figure 3–10 as input and port B as output.

Solution:

```
MVI A,00H    ; Send 0s to DDR A
OUT 02H      ;   to designate "Input"
MVI A,FFH    ; Send 1s to DDR B
OUT 03H      ;   to designate "Output"
```

EXAMPLE 3–3

Write the instructions that would be used to designate port A's least significant 4 bits as input, and its most significant 4 bits as output, for the 8355 in Figure 3–10.

Solution:

```
MVI A,F0H    ; LSBs = IN, MSBs = OUT
OUT 02H      ; DDR A ← Acc
```

EXAMPLE 3–4

In Figure 3–10, assume that input switches are connected to port A of the 8355, and output LEDs are connected to port B. Write a program to read the input switches and write their value to the output LEDs.

Solution:

MVI A,00H	; Define Port A
OUT 02H	; as input
MVI A,FFH	; Define Port B
OUT 03H	; as output
IN 00H	; Read Port A into Acc
OUT 01H	; Write Acc to Port B

The 8155/8156

The 8155/8156 is a RAM with I/O ports and a timer. It is used in a minimum-component 8085A-based system. The difference between the two versions is that the 8155 uses an active-LOW Chip Enable ($\overline{CE}$), while the 8156 uses an active-HIGH Chip Enable (CE). The pin configuration and block diagram for the 8155/8156 are given in Figure 3–12.

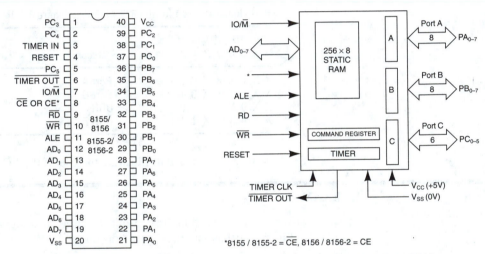

Figure 3–12 Pin configuration and block diagram for the 8155/8156 RAM with I/O ports and timer. (Courtesy of Intel Corporation)

The RAM section provides 256 bytes of volatile program or data storage. Ports *A* and *B* each provide 8 bits, and port *C* provides 6 bits, of I/O capability. The IO/$\overline{M}$ line is used to select either the I/O ports or the RAM memory. The ALE line is used to internally demultiplex the AD_0–AD_7 lines.

Programming the Command Register

Before using the I/O and timer features, we must program an 8-bit latch called the *command register*. The command register, shown in Figure 3–13, defines how the ports and timer section are to be used. Bits 0 and 1 define the 8 bits of ports *A* and *B* as input or output. (You do not have the capability to define individual bits within the port as you can with the 8355/8755A.)

Bits 2 and 3 define the 6-bit port *C* as input (ALT 1), output (ALT 2), or control (ALT 3, ALT 4). The "Control" feature of port *C* provides special handshaking capability for 8085A-based systems. For our purposes, we'll use only ALT 1 and 2.

Command register bits 4 and 5 are used when in the ALT 3 and 4 mode, and bits 6 and 7 are used to start/stop the internal timer.

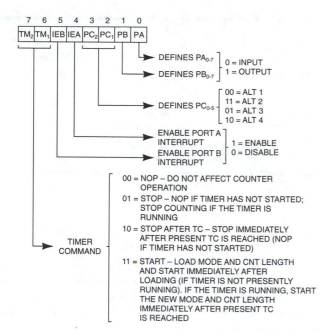

Figure 3–13 Command Register bit assignment. (Courtesy of Intel Corporation)

To program the command register, you must first load the accumulator with the bit string that you want sent to the command register, and then use the OUT *port* instruction. The *port* number for the command registers, I/O ports, and timer are determined based on the information presented in Table 3–5.

TABLE 3–5

I/O and Timer Port Numbers

AD_7–AD_0 7 6 5 4 3 2 1 0	Selection	Port number used[a]
X X 1 X X 0 0 0	Command/Status Register	20
X X 1 X X 0 0 1	Port A	21
X X 1 X X 0 1 0	Port B	22
X X 1 X X 0 1 1	Port C	23
X X 1 X X 1 0 0	Low-order timer	24
X X 1 X X 1 0 1	High-order timer, timer mode	25

X: Don't care.

[a] *Port number* is based on bit AD_5 being HIGH to enable the 8156 in the system design of Figure 3–10.

EXAMPLE 3–5

Write the assembly language to program the command register of the 8156 in Figure 3–10 so that port *A* is defined as input, port *B* as output, and port *C* as input.

Solution:

```
MVI    A,02H    ; A ← 0000 0010
                ;  (see Figure 3–13)
OUT    20H      ; Output to Command Register
                ;  (see Table 3–5)
```

EXAMPLE 3-6

Write the assembly language to program the command register of the 8156 in Figure 3–10 so that all 22 I/O port bits are defined as outputs.

Solution:

```
MVI   A,0FH    ; A ← 0000 1111
               ;  (see Figure 3–13)
OUT   20H      ; Output to Command Register
               ;  (see Table 3–5)
```

Timer Operation

The timer section of the 8155/8156 is a 14-bit down-counter that can be used to produce varying frequency square waves or timing pulses at a time period determined by the initial count preloaded into the counter. Because it is 14 bits, the counter length can be as high as 3FFFH. The CLK output pin from the 8085A microprocessor is usually used to drive the clock input (TIMER IN) to the counter. The nice thing about using an external counter/timer like this is that once you have programmed and started it, the microprocessor is then free to return to performing other tasks as the counter ticks away. Figure 3–14 shows the format of the timer register. The initial starting value for the down-counter is loaded in two steps. The least significant 8 bits of the count length are output to port 24, as was determined in Table 3–5. The most significant 6 bits of the count length are output to port 25 along with the 2-bit *timer mode*, as shown in Figure 3–14.

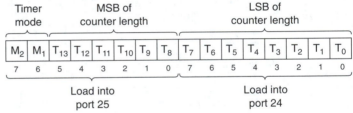

Figure 3–14 Timer register format.

Figure 3–15 lists the four timer modes and the resultant waveform produced at the TIMER OUT pin of the 8155/8156. There are four possible waveforms output at the TIMER OUT pin: a single square wave, a continuous square wave, a single pulse, and continuous pulses.

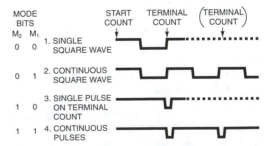

Figure 3–15 TIMER OUT operation modes and waveforms. (Courtesy of Intel Corporation)

The length of time from the point labeled "START COUNT" to the point labeled "TERMINAL COUNT" is the length of time it takes for the counter to count from its initial value down to zero. If we call this time the "TIMER OUT period," we can write the following equation:

$$\overline{\text{TIMER OUT}} \text{ period} = \text{TIMER IN period} \times \text{count length}$$

For example, if the microprocessor clock, connected to TIMER IN, has a period of 0.5 μs (2 MHz), and the initial counter value is 00FFH, then the period of a single square wave would be

$$\overline{\text{TIMER OUT}}\ \text{period} = \text{TIMER IN period} \times \text{count length}$$

$$= 0.5\ \mu s \times 255$$

$$= 127.5\ \mu s$$

Once we have loaded the initial count and timer mode into the timer register, we then have to start the counter. If you refer back to Figure 3–13, you'll see that bit 6 and bit 7 of the command register are used to start and stop the counter (1–1 starts the counter). The following examples illustrate the use of the timer section.

EXAMPLE 3–7

Write the assembly language instructions that would program the 8156 to continuously output LOW pulses at $\overline{\text{TIMER OUT}}$ every 100 μs. Use the port assignments developed in Table 3–5, which were based on the microprocessor system shown in Figure 3–10. (Assume a microprocessor CLK period of 0.5 μs.)

Solution: To find the count length:

$$\overline{\text{TIMER OUT}}\ \text{period} = \text{TIMER IN period} \times \text{count length}$$

$$100\ \mu s = 0.5\ \mu s \times \text{count length}$$

$$\text{Count length} = 200\ \text{or}\ 00\text{C8H}$$

Timer register:

```
        1100    0000          1100      1000
        └┬┘ └──┬──┘          └───┬───┘
       Timer  MSB of             LSB of
       mode   count              count
              length             length
           └──────┬──────┘    └─────┬─────┘
                 To                 To
               port 25            port 24
```

Command register:

```
              11XX    XXXX
              └┬┘ └───┬───┘
             Start   Don't
             count   care
              └────────┬────────┘
                      To
                    port 20
```

Assembly language:

```
MVI A,C0H    ; Load Timer Mode
OUT 25H      ;   and MSB of Count
MVI A,C8H    ; Load
OUT 24H      ;   LSB of Count
MVI A,C0H    ; Start timer
OUT 20H      ;   running
HLT          ; End
```

EXAMPLE 3–8

Write a program that will produce a continuous 50-kHz square wave.

Solution: To find the count length:

$$\overline{\text{TIMER OUT}} \text{ period} = 1/50 \text{ kHz}$$

$$= 20 \ \mu s$$

$$\text{Count length} = \overline{\text{TIMER OUT}} \text{ period/TIMER IN period}$$

$$= 20 \ \mu s/0.5 \ \mu s$$

$$= 40 \text{ or } 0028H$$

Timer register:

```
    0100  0000              0010  1000
```

```
Timer  MSB of               LSB of
mode   count                count
       length               length

        To                   To
      port 25              port 24
```

Command register:

```
              11XX  XXXX
```

```
              Start  Don't
              count  care

                 To
               port 20
```

Assembly language:

```
MVI A,40H    ; Load Timer Mode
OUT 25H      ;   and MSB of Count
MVI A,28H    ; Load
OUT 24H      ;   LSB of Count
MVI A,C0H    ; Start timer
OUT 20H      ;   running
HLT          ; End
```

SUMMARY

In this chapter we have learned that

1. The low-order address bus is multiplexed with the data bus to reduce the pin count on the 8085A.
2. The 8085A pulses the address latch enable (ALE) line HIGH when there is a valid address on the multiplexed address/data bus.
3. The address/data bus can be demultiplexed by a D latch like the 74LS373.
4. During the READ cycle, data to be input is placed on the data bus by an external device and the $\overline{RD}$ line is pulsed LOW.
5. During the WRITE cycle, the microprocessor places data on the data bus and then pulses the $\overline{WR}$ line LOW.

6. The 74LS138 is a common address decoder found in microprocessor systems. Its outputs are used to enable a single device to be active on the data bus.

7. The 74LS244 octal buffer is commonly used as the interface chip for input devices. The 74LS374 octal D flip-flop is commonly used as the interface chip to provide latched outputs.

8. Each machine cycle is made up of a READ or a WRITE cycle and can take from three to six CPU clock periods.

9. The first machine cycle in every instruction is an opcode fetch (READ) to determine what instruction is to be executed.

10. A minimum-component microprocessor system can be constructed with an 8085A, an 8355/8755 ROM, and an 8156 RAM.

11. The 8355 (ROM) and the 8755 (EPROM) contain a 2K × 8 memory and two I/O ports, and were designed to interface directly to the 8085A.

12. The data direction registers (DDR A and DDR B) of the 8355/8755 must be loaded with an input or output designation before the two I/O ports can be used.

13. The 8155/8156 interface chip has RAM, I/O ports, and a timer. Its command register must be loaded before using its I/O ports or timer.

GLOSSARY

Address Latch Enable (ALE):   A signal output by the microprocessor to demultiplex the data bus and low-order address bus. A HIGH ALE signifies that the multiplexed bus currently contains address information.

Command register: A register inside a microprocessor support IC programmed to designate the function and operation of the IC.

Data direction register (DDR):   A register inside a microprocessor support IC programmed to designate the direction of data flow (in or out).

Fold-back: An area of memory that duplicates a memory area at a different address. This occurs when an address decoding scheme has don't care address bits. By changing the state of the don't care bits, you will access the same memory using different addresses.

Instruction cycle: The instruction cycle is made up of the number of Read or Write machine cycles required to complete the execution of a single microprocessor instruction.

IO/$\overline{M}$:   A control signal issued by the microprocessor to signify whether the I/O of data is to a memory device (LOW) or an I/O port (HIGH).

Machine cycle: The execution of each microprocessor instruction consists of several Read or Write operations to external devices. Each Read or Write operation is a machine cycle.

Memory map: A table developed for each microprocessor system design listing the range of addresses that access each device or IC in the system.

Multiplexed bus: Two or more signals sharing the same bus. The data bus and the low-order address bus share the same pins on the 8085A microprocessor.

Read cycle: The microprocessor machine cycle that issues a LOW $\overline{RD}$ pulse and reads 8 bits from the addressed memory or I/O port.

Support chips: ICs that interface to microprocessor buses to perform the specific tasks required of a microprocessor-based system.

Write cycle: The microprocessor machine cycle that issues a LOW $\overline{WR}$ pulse and writes 8 bits to the addressed memory or I/O port.

PROBLEMS

3–1. For what are the SID and SOD pins on the 8085A used?

3–2. Which pins on the 8085A are multiplexed?

3–3. Does the IO/$\overline{\text{M}}$ line go HIGH or LOW during:
(a) An opcode fetch?
(b) A memory write?
(c) An I/O read?

3–4. Describe the relationship between the X1–X2 pins and the CLK pin of the 8085A microprocessor.

3–5. What is one advantage and one disadvantage of the multiplexed bus?

3–6. When the ALE line goes HIGH, does AD_0–AD_7 contain an address or data?

3–7. Within a Read cycle or a Write cycle, what information is output to the AD_0–AD_7 lines first: address or data?

3–8. Assume that the waveforms in Figure P3–8 are observed in the circuit of Figure 3–2. Sketch the waveform that will result at A_0.

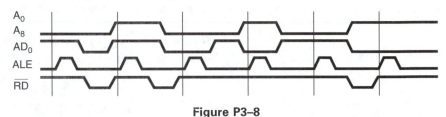

Figure P3–8

3–9. During what transition on the $\overline{\text{RD}}$ line does the microprocessor read data from the data bus (positive edge or negative edge)?

3–10. During what transition on the $\overline{\text{WR}}$ line does the microprocessor write data to the data bus (positive edge or negative edge)?

3–11. Modify the 16-input NAND gate in Figure 3–4 so that it decodes the address 6400H instead of 2800H.

3–12. Our 8085A system design in Figure 3–6 uses AD_0–AD_7 as the data bus, D_0–D_7. What safeguard is built into the circuit to ensure that we use the data bus only *after* the low-order address is removed?

3–13. List the conditions that must be met to *enable* the 74LS138 in Figure 3–6.

3–14. Develop a new memory map for Figure 3–6 using the new 74LS138 connections shown in Figure P3–14.

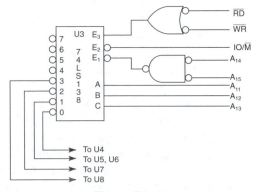

Figure P3–14

3–15. How many address locations does the 2114 RAM have? How many data bits are at each location?

3–16. Why does the design in Figure 3–6 use a *pair* of 2114's?

3–17. What is the range of addresses of the *fold-back* area for the 2114's in Figure 3–6? Why does the fold-back area exist?

3–18. Use the 8085A Instruction Set Timing Index in Appendix E to list the machine cycles for the following instructions:
(a) JMP *label*
(b) IN *port*
(c) MVI A,*data*
(d) RET

3–19. How long does each instruction in Problem 3–18 take if you are using a 4-MHz crystal?

3–20. The first machine cycle in *every* instruction is an opcode fetch. (True or false?)

3–21. Briefly describe the action taking place during each of the four machine cycles of the instruction LDA 2800H.

3–22. The following program is being executed on the microprocessor circuit of Figure 3–6. Sketch the waveforms at $\overline{RD}$, $\overline{WR}$, C_p (U8), and $\overline{OE}$ (U7) for two executions of the loop. (Assume that a 4-MHz crystal is being used.)

```
LOOP:   LDA 2800H
        CMA
        STA 3800H
        JMP LOOP
```

3–23. What is the length of time from the first LOW pulse on $\overline{OE}$ to the second LOW pulse on $\overline{OE}$ in Problem 3–22?

3–24. Why is there no need for an address latch IC when using the 8355 and 8155 support ICs?

3–25. At what point would the 8755A IC be used in place of the 8355 in Figure 3–10?

3–26. The I/O-mapped microprocessor circuit of Figure 3–10 can be changed to memory-mapped I/O by changing the switch connection to A_{15}. List one advantage and one disadvantage of doing this.

3–27. What range of addresses would access the 8156 RAM in Figure 3–10 if CE were connected to A_{11} instead of A_{13}?

3–28. (a) Write the assembly language instructions to set up port A of the 8355 in Figure 3–10 as an output port and port B as an input port.
(b) Write the instructions to read the input port and write those data to the output port.

3–29. What is the port address of the command register in the 8156 of Figure 3–10?

3–30. Rebuild Table 3–5 with the new port numbers that would be used if CE were connected to A_{11} instead of A_{13} in Figure 3–10.

3–31. Write the assembly language to program the command register of the 8156 in Figure 3–10 so that port A is output, port B is output, and port C is input.

3–32. Write the assembly language program that will generate a pulse every 20 μs at $\overline{\text{TIMER OUT}}$ in Figure 3–10. Use a 4-MHz crystal.

3–33. Write the assembly language program that will create a continuous 10-KHz square wave at $\overline{\text{TIMER OUT}}$ of Figure 3–10. Use a 4-MHz crystal.

SCHEMATIC INTERPRETATION PROBLEMS

3–34. Locate the output pins labeled E and R/W on U1 of the HC11D0 schematic. During certain operations line E goes HIGH, and line R/W is then used to signify a READ operation if it is HIGH or a WRITE operation if it is LOW. For a READ operation, which line goes LOW: WE_B or OE_B?

3–35. Find the octal decoder U5 in the HC11D0 schematic. Determine the levels on AS, AD_{13}, AD_{14}, and AD_{15} required to provide an active-LOW signal on the line labeled MON_SL.

3–36. The octal decoder U9 in the HC11D0 schematic is used to determine if the LCD (LCD_SL) or the keyboard (KEY_SL) is to be active.
(a) Determine the levels of AD_{3-5}, AD_{11-15}, and AS required to select the LCD.
(b) Repeat for selecting the keyboard.

3–37. Locate the 68HC11 microcontroller in the HC11D0 schematic. (A microcontroller is a microprocessor with built-in RAM, ROM and I/O ports). Pins 31–38 are the low-order address bus (A_0–A_7) multiplexed (shared) with the data bus (D_0–D_7). Pins 9–16 are the high-order address bus (A_8–A_{15}). The low-order address bus is demultiplexed (selected and latched)

from the shared address/data lines by U2 and the AS (Address Strobe) line.
   (a) Which ICs are connected to the data bus (DB_0–DB_7)?
   (b) Which ICs are connected to the address bus (AD_0–AD_{15})?

3–38. U9 and U5 in the HC11D0 schematic are used for address decoding. Determine the levels on AD_{11}–AD_{15} and AD_3–AD_5 to select:
   (a) The LCD (LCD_SL).
   (b) The keyboard (KEY_SL).

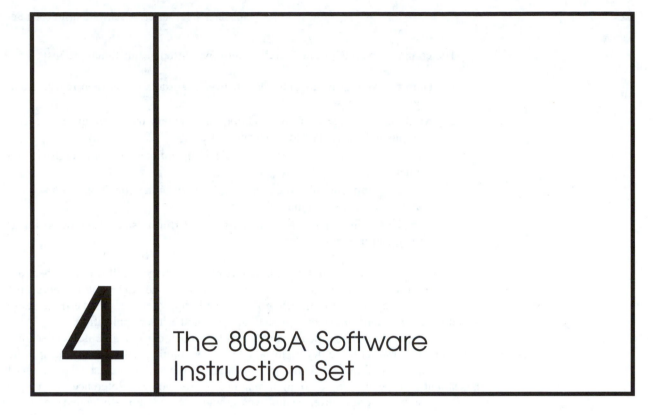

4

The 8085A Software Instruction Set

OBJECTIVES

Upon completion of this chapter you should be able to:

- Write intermediate-level applications programs.
- Use the indirect-addressing instructions for data transfer.
- Use logic instructions to perform Boolean operations.
- Perform multidigit BCD addition.
- Determine the status of the flag byte after the execution of arithmetic and logical instructions.
- Use logical instructions for masking off unwanted data.
- Write structured programs using subroutine modules.
- Describe stack operations associated with the CALL, RETurn, PUSH, and POP instructions.
- Use the interrupt capability of the 8085A microprocessor.

INTRODUCTION

A microprocessor does only what it is told to do by the program instructions. We have covered several of the 8085A instructions in the previous chapter and will now proceed to cover most of the remaining instructions in this chapter.

The 8085A microprocessor has 80 different instructions, totaling 246 different opcodes when all of the instruction variations are included. For example, the instruction MOV *r1,r2* has 49 unique opcodes, depending on which destination register (*r1*) and which source register (*r2*) are used.

The complete instruction set is divided into five different functional groups:

1. **Data transfer group:** Copies data between registers or between registers and memory locations.
2. **Arithmetic group:** Performs addition, subtraction, incrementing, and decrementing with registers and memory locations.
3. **Logical group:** Performs logical (Boolean) operations on data in registers and memory.
4. **Branch group:** Modifies program flow by performing conditional or unconditional jumps, calls, or returns.
5. **Stack, I/O, and machine control group:** Performs stack operations, input/output, and interrupt control.

As you become more familiar with 8085A programming, you'll find that there are usually several different ways to get the same job done. Some ways may be more time efficient, others may be more memory efficient, and still others may make more sense logically and be easier to transfer as a "module" to another user application.

As a beginning programmer, you will find that much of your time is spent searching through the instruction set trying to find an instruction that will perform the specific task that you have in mind, not knowing if such an instruction even exists! That's why I suggest that you spend time skimming through the Instruction Set Reference Encyclopedia in Appendix D over and over again. Even though you won't totally understand what you are reading, you will become familiar with the various operations that are available and the format of the reference encyclopedia.

A key to learning assembly and machine language is to write and "debug" your programs on a microprocessor trainer. There are several of these trainers available, the Intel SDK-85 being one of the more popular ones. The SDK-85, and most other trainers, use support ICs like the 8355 and 8156, and have other circuitry to ease program development and testing. Operating instructions for the SDK-85 trainer are provided in Appendix N.

The programs in this book can be tested on any 8085A or 8080-based trainer. Several of the programs read an input port and write to an output port. We will assume that we are using an 8085A-based system similar to the circuit presented back in Figure 3–10. That circuit has a 256-byte RAM area for program and data storage at 2000H to 20FFH, and I/O ports at 00H, 01H, 21H, 22H, and 23H. If you are familiar with the SDK-85 trainer, you will notice a great deal of similarities.

4–1 THE DATA TRANSFER INSTRUCTION GROUP

The instructions in this group are used to *transfer*, or to *move*, data around the system. Data can be moved into a register (MVI), into a register pair (LXI), from register to register (MOV), to and from memory directly (LDA,STA), and to and from memory indirectly. All of the data transfer instructions have been covered in previous chapters except for the *indirect* memory transfers.

Indirect Addressing of Memory

The LDA *addr* and STA *addr* instructions were examples of *direct* addressing of memory. For example, the instruction STA 20A0H will store the accumulator data to memory location 20A0H. Direct memory addressing is limited to data transfers to and from memory and the accumulator. If you want to move one of the other registers, or a data byte, to memory, then you must use *indirect memory addressing*.

Indirect addressing uses the *H–L* register pair as a *memory address pointer.* Before using one of the indirect-addressing instructions, you must first load the *H–L* register pair with the 16-bit address of the memory location that you want to access. You can then use one of the MVI or MOV instructions that refer to memory moves (instructions having a capital letter *M* in the operand field).

MVI M,*data*

For example, to move the data byte F8H to memory location 20A0H, you would use the program given in Table 4–1.

TABLE 4–1

Using Indirect Addressing to Load F8H into Memory Location 20A0H

Address	Contents	Label	Instruction	Comments
2000	21	START:	LXI H,20A0H	; HL ← 20A0H
2001	A0			;
2002	20			;
2003	36		MVI M,F8H	; M(20A0H) ← F8H
2004	F8			;

The instruction MVI M,*data,* used in Table 4–1, is interpreted as follows: "Move the *data* given in byte 2 of the instruction to memory (M) whose address is pointed to by the *H–L* register pair." Figure 4–1 illustrates this data transfer.

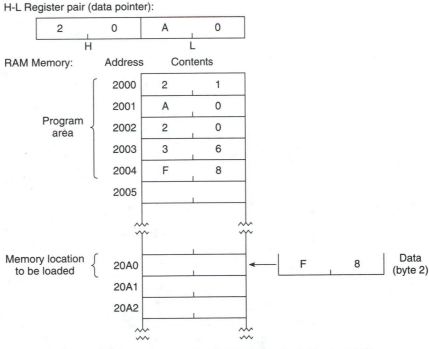

Figure 4–1   Illustration of the MVI M,F8H where *H–L* is 20A0H.

MOV M,*r* and MOV *r*,M

To use indirect memory addressing with the registers, we use the instructions MOV M,*r* and MOV *r*,M, where *r* is one of the registers *A, B, C, D, E, H,* or *L.* Again, we use the *H–L* register pair as the memory pointer. For example, to move the contents of memory location 20B0H into register *D* and then transfer it to location 20C0H, we would use the program given in Table 4–2.

TABLE 4–2

Program Using Indirect Addressing to Move Data from 20B0H, to Register *D*, to 20C0H

Address	Contents	Label	Instruction	Comments
2000	21	START:	LXI H,20B0H	; HL ← 20B0H
2001	B0			;
2002	20			;
2003	56		MOV D,M	; D ← M(20B0H)
2004	21		LXI H,20C0H	; HL ← 20C0H
2005	C0			;
2006	20			;
2007	72		MOV M,D	; M(20C0H) ← D

If you skim through the data transfer instructions in Appendix D, you won't find a move instruction that allows you to move memory to memory. That is why we had to use the *D* register in Table 4–2 as a temporary holding area, before moving the data to memory location 20C0H.

The following examples further illustrate the use of indirect addressing for data movement.

EXAMPLE 4–1

Write a program that will load memory locations 20C0H to 20CFH with even numbers, starting with the number 00H.

Solution:

Address	Contents	Label	Instruction	Comments
2000	06	START:	MVI B,00H	; Initialize
2001	00			; B ← 00H
2002	21		LXI H,20C0H	; Initialize
2003	C0			; HL ← 20C0H
2004	20			;
2005	70	LOOP:	MOV M,B	; M(HL) ←B
2006	04		INR B	; B ← B+1
2007	04		INR B	; B ← B+1
2008	23		INX H	; HL ← HL+1
2009	3E		MVI A,D0H	; ⎫ Set Z flag
200A	D0			; ⎬ if L has
200B	BD		CMP L	; ⎭ reach D0H
200C	C2		JNZ LOOP	; If not, loop back
200D	05			; to load next
200E	20			; even number
200F	76		HLT	; Stop

Explanation: We initialize the *B* register to zero and use it for the even-number counter. The *H–L* memory pointer is initialized to 20C0H. Each time through the loop, register *B* is incremented twice, keeping it even, and *H–L* is incremented once, pointing to the next memory location. Program lines 2009 through 200B are used to determine if the low-order part of the *H–L* pointer has gone past the last location to be loaded (20CFH).

EXAMPLE 4–2

The 8355/8755A ROM/EPROM IC in the microprocessor system of Figure 3–10 is to be used for I/O operations. Figure 4–2 shows the connections for reading switches at port 00 and writing to LEDs at port 01. Use indirect memory addressing to send the contents of memory locations 20C0H through 20CFH to the LEDs, repeatedly. Use the one-quarter second time-delay program given in Table 2–6 to slow the display down.

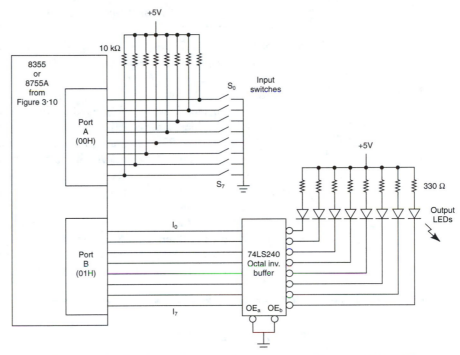

Figure 4–2   Interfacing input switches and output LEDs to an 8355/8755A microprocessor support IC.

Solution:

Address	Contents	Label	Instruction	Comments
2000	3E	START:	MVI A,FFH	; Designate port B
2001	FF			; as output
2002	D3		OUT 03H	; Program
2003	03			; DDR B
2004	21	LOOPA:	LXI H,20C0H	; Starting address
2005	C0			; of data
2006	20			; for display
2007	7E	LOOPB:	MOV A,M	; A ← M(HL)
2008	D3		OUT 01H	; Send contents of A
2009	01			; to output LEDs
200A	CD		CALL DELAY	; Delay
200B	50			; one-quarter
200C	20			; second at 2050H
200D	23		INX H	; Increment HL
200E	3E		MVI A,D0H	; ⎫ Set Z flag
200F	D0			; ⎬ if L has
2010	BD		CMP L	; ⎭ reached D0H
2011	C2		JNZ LOOPB	; Display next

Solution: (continued)

Address	Contents	Label	Instruction	Comments
2012	07			; memory
2013	20			; location
2014	C3		JMP LOOPA	; Restart at
2015	04			; beginning of
2016	20			; display memory
.				
.				
.				
2050		DELAY: (See Table 2–6)		

Explanation: The 74LS240 buffer in Figure 4–2 is required because the 8355/8755A cannot sink the 10 mA required to illuminate an LED. An *inverting* buffer was chosen so that placing a 1 at pin I_0 through I_7 will turn the corresponding LED ON.

In Chapter 3 we determined that the data direction register for port *B* (DDR B) is at port number 03H, and to access port *B* we use port number 01H. Lines 2000H to 2003H program port *B* as *output.* Line 2008H writes the accumulator to port *B* (LEDs). The DELAY subroutine that we wrote in Chapter 2 is called to slow the display down so that we can see it. The output ports on the 8355/8755A are *latches,* so the LEDs will remain ON while we are in the DELAY subroutine.

Once we have displayed the data from all memory locations, 20C0H through 20CFH, then the CMP L instruction sets the zero flag, which forces us back to LOOPA to repeat the same displays again. (If this program is run *after* Example 4–1, then the data displayed will be the even numbers starting with 00H.)

Load/Store Data Transfer

Another way to move data is by using the LDA *addr* and STA *addr* instructions. You should remember from previous examples that LDA *addr* will "load the accumulator with the contents of memory at address *addr.*" Also from previous examples, STA *addr* will "store the accumulator to memory at address *addr.*" The operand *addr* is a 16-bit address given in byte 2–byte 3 of the instruction.

Another form of Load/Store data transfer is available using indirect addressing. The LDAX B, LDAX D, STAX B, and STAX D instructions use the 16-bit address stored in the *B–C* or *D–E* register pairs as the memory pointer. For example, the instruction LDAX D is interpreted as "load the accumulator with the contents of memory pointed to by *D–E.*"

EXAMPLE 4–3

The following program is used to transfer data from one place in memory to another:

Instruction	Comments
LDA 20A0H	; A ← M(20A0H)
STA 20B0H	; M(20B0H) ← A

Rewrite that program using LDAX B and STAX D instructions.

Solution:

Instruction	Comments
LXI B,20A0H	; BC ← 20A0H (SOURCE)
LXI D,20B0H	; DE ← 20B0H (DESTINATION)
LDAX B	; A ← M(BC)
STAX D	; M(DE) ← A

Explanation: To use the LDAX B instruction, we must first load the *B–C* register pair with the address 20A0H. (This is the address of the data *source*.) The LDAX B instruction will load the accumulator with the contents of memory location 20A0H. The *D–E* register pair is loaded with the *destination* address, 20B0H, and the STAX D instruction stores the accumulator to that location.

To use LDAX and STAX instead of LDA and STA is that the memory address becomes a *variable* that can be changed during program execution by changing the contents of the *B–C* or *D–E* register pairs.

4–2 THE ARITHMETIC INSTRUCTION GROUP

The arithmetic group includes instructions to increment, decrement, add, and subtract. We have used the increment and decrement instructions with registers and register pairs in previous examples. Instructions in the arithmetic group have an effect on the various flags used by the 8085A.

The Flag Byte

When a register is decremented to 00H, a flag bit, called the zero flag, is set to 1. There are several other flag bits besides the zero flag that can be affected as a result of arithmetic and logical instructions. These flags are useful for determining the status of a register after an arithmetic or logical instruction. These flags can then be used by the "conditional branching" instructions to Jump, Call, or Return, only if a specific flag bit is set or reset. (A "set" flag equals 1; a "reset" flag equals 0.)

The five flags used by the 8085A are stored in the flag byte shown in Figure 4–3. You must read the definition given in the Instruction Set Reference Encyclopedia in Appendix D for each instruction used to determine what effect that instruction has on each flag bit. If an instruction states that a particular flag is affected, then that flag will be forced to a 0 (reset) or a 1 (set) after completion of that instruction.

The *carry flag* is set when the result of an addition is greater than FFH. Subtraction operations use the carry bit to indicate a "borrow." It is also affected by the logical instructions.

The *parity flag* is set if the number of 1 bits in the result of the operation is even (i.e., if the result has even parity). It is reset if the number of 1 bits is odd.

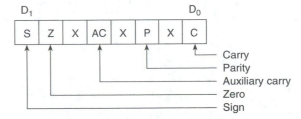

Figure 4–3 The 8085A flag byte.

The *auxiliary carry flag* is set when there is a carry (overflow) from bit 3 to bit 4, as a result of the operation. This flag is used by the DAA instruction to form BCD numbers.

The *zero flag* is set when the result of certain instructions is zero.

The *sign flag* is used to indicate a negative result from an arithmetic or logical operation. It assumes that two's-complement notation is being used, and sets the sign flag if bit 7 of the accumulator is 1 (negative).

EXAMPLE 4–4

Determine the value of the flag byte upon completion of the following groups of instructions. (Assume that all flag bits are initially reset.)

   (a)   MVI A,55H
            INR A

Solution:

$$
\begin{aligned}
A &= 0101\ 0101 \\
&\underline{+\ 1} \\
A &= 0101\ 0110
\end{aligned}
$$

C = Unaffected by INR A
P = 1
AC = 0
Z = 0
S = 0
Flag Byte = 00X0 X1X0 = 04H

   (b)   MVI C,FFH
            INR C

Solution:

$$
\begin{aligned}
C &= 1111\ 1111 \\
&\underline{+\ 1} \\
C &= 0000\ 0000
\end{aligned}
$$

C = Unaffected by INR C
P = 1
AC = 1
Z = 1
S = 0
Flag Byte = 01X1 X1X0 = 54H

ADD *r*, ADI *data*, SUB *r*, and SUI *data*

These instructions are used to add or subtract a register, a memory location, or a data byte to or from the accumulator. The result of all arithmetic operations is placed in the accumulator.

For example, instruction ADD *r* adds the value in register *r* to the accumulator and places the result in the accumulator. (SUB *r* is a similar instruction used to subtract a register value from the accumulator.) The instruction ADI *data* adds the data value entered in byte 2 of the instruction to the accumulator. (SUI *data* is a similar instruction used to subtract a data value from the accumulator.) When performing multibyte addition and subtraction, there are four other instructions: ADC *r*, SBB *r*, ACI *data*, and SBI *data* that use the carry (or borrow) flag within the arithmetic operation. The following examples illustrate the use of the arithmetic instructions.

EXAMPLE 4–5

Determine the contents of the accumulator after completion of the following program instructions.

(a)

Instruction	Comments
MVI A,52H	; A ← 52H
MVI B,28H	; B ← 28H
ADD B	; A ← A+B
Answer: A = 7AH	

(b)

Instruction	Comments
MVI A,74H	; A ← 74H
MVI D,6BH	; D ← 6BH
SUB D	; A ← A−D
Answer: A = 09H	

(c)

Instruction	Comments
MVI A,0CH	; A ← 0CH
ADI 22H	; A ← A + 22H
Answer: A = 2EH	

(d)

Instruction	Comments
MVI A,6DH	; A ← 6DH
SUI 1FH	; A ← A − 1FH
Answer: A = 4EH	

(e)

Instruction	Comments
LXI H,20C0H	; HL ← 20C0H
MVI M,20H	; M(HL) ← 20H
MVI A,2AH	; A ← 2AH
ADD M	; A ← A + M(HL)
Answer: A = 4AH	

EXAMPLE 4–6

Write the assembly language instructions to store 10 numbers in RAM starting at address 20B0H. Use the ADI instruction to make each number stored 5 larger than the previous. The first location should contain the data byte 00H.

Solution:

	Instruction	Comments
	LXI H,20B0H	; Starting location of RAM
	MVI B,0AH	; B=counter for ten numbers
	MVI A,00H	; A holds numbers to be stored
LOOP:	MOV M,A	; Move number to memory
	ADI 05H	; Add 5 to A
	INX H	; Next memory location
	DCR B	; Decrement counter
	JNZ LOOP	; Loop back to store next number
	HLT	; End

DAA

The DAA (decimal adjust accumulator) instruction is required whenever you are using BCD numbers in arithmetic operations. The reason for this is that the microprocessor naturally performs all arithmetic in binary. You would get incorrect answers if you enter and add BCD numbers and expect to get BCD answers.

For example, if we want to add the base 10 decimal numbers 44 + 28, we would enter them as BCD, and the operation would look as follows:

$$
\begin{array}{r}
44 = 0100\ 0100 \\
+\ 28 = 0010\ 1000 \\
\hline
72 \neq 0110\ 1100\ (6CH)
\end{array}
$$

The microprocessor adds the two BCD numbers and gets 6CH for an answer. We wanted to get the answer 72 (0111 0010), however. To correct the problem, we need to execute the DAA instruction. The DAA instruction uses the following rules to form the correct BCD result.

1. If the value of the least significant 4 bits of the accumulator is greater than 9 *or* if the AC flag is set, 6 is added to the accumulator.
2. If the value of the most significant 4 bits of the accumulator is now greater than 9 *or* if the CY flag is set, 6 is added to the most significant 4 bits of the accumulator.

Applying those rules to the previous addition will result in the following operations:

$$
\begin{array}{r}
44 = 0100\ 0100 \\
+\ 28 = 0010\ 1000 \\
\hline
0110\ 1100 \\
*+\qquad\quad 0110 \\
\hline
0111\ 0010 = 72\ (\text{correct})
\end{array}
$$

EXAMPLE 4–7

Add the decimal numbers 39 + 29 and adjust the result to a valid BCD answer by applying the rules of the DAA instruction.

Solution:

$$
\begin{array}{r}
39 = 0011\ 1001 \quad \text{BCD} \\
+\ 29 = 0010\ 1001 \quad \text{BCD} \\
\hline
0110\ 0010 \\
\smile \\
\text{AC}
\end{array}
$$

Add 6
$$
\begin{array}{r}
+\ 0110 \\
\hline
0110\ 1000\ \text{BCD} = 68 \quad \textit{Answer}
\end{array}
$$

EXAMPLE 4–8

Write an assembly language program to store the following five decimal numbers in RAM, in BCD form, starting at location 20B0H: 42, 51, 77, 32, and 63. Add the numbers and store the three-digit BCD answer in the *B–C* register pair (*B* = hundreds digit, *C* = tens digit and ones digit).

---

*The least significant 4 bits are greater than 9, so add 6.

Solution:

	Instruction	Comments
MAIN:	CALL STORE	; Store the numbers
	CALL ADD	; Add the numbers
	MOV C,A	; Transfer tens and ones to C
	HLT	; End
		;
		; Subroutine to store 5 numbers
STORE:	MVI A,42H	; A ← 42H
	STA 20B0H	; Store 1st number
	MVI A,51H	; A ← 51H
	STA 20B1H	; Store 2nd number
	MVI A,77H	; A ← 77H
	STA 20B2H	; Store 3rd number
	MVI A,32H	; A ← 32H
	STA 20B3H	; Store 4th number
	MVI A,63H	; A ← 63H
	STA 20B4H	; Store 5th number
	RET	; Return to MAIN
		;
		; Subroutine to add 5 numbers
ADD:	LXI H,20B0H	; Address of 1st number
	MVI B,00H	; Initialize hundreds digit to zero
	MVI D,04H	; Numbers counter
	MOV A,M	; Move 1st number to A
	INX H	; Increment address to 2nd number
LOOP:	ADD M	; Add each successive number to A
	DAA	; Adjust A to valid BCD
	CC HNDRDS	; Call HNDRDS if carry set
	DCR D	; Decrement numbers counter
	RZ	; Return if zero
	INX H	; Increment address to next number
	JMP LOOP	; Loop back
		;
		; Subroutine to increment hundreds counter
HNDRDS:	INR B	; Increment hundreds counter
	RET	; Return to ADD subroutine

Explanation: This program is a good example of using a *structured programming* technique. The program is broken up into three *modules,* or subroutines. Each module has a specific function and can be written and tested on its own. This is very helpful for program development and debugging. Each module would be entered in a different block of memory. For example, MAIN could start at address 2000H, STORE could start at 2010H, ADD could start at 2030H, and HNDRDS could start at 2050H.

The MAIN program does nothing but CALL two subroutines and perform a move. The STORE subroutine uses MVI and STA instructions to store the five numbers to be added. These numbers are entered in hexadecimal, which when translated to binary for the microprocessor will be the same as BCD.

The ADD subroutine has two new instructions in it: a conditional call (CC HNDRDS) and a conditional return (RZ). Calls and returns (as well as jumps) can be based on the condition of any of the following flags: *Z, C, P,* or *S.* The CC HNDRDS instruction is necessary to increment the hundreds counter if there is an overflow (carry) due to the ADD M or DAA instruction (result > 99). The RZ instruction returns control to the MAIN program when *D* is decremented to zero.

4–3   THE LOGICAL INSTRUCTION GROUP

The logical group provides a way to perform the Boolean operations AND, OR, and exclusive-OR between registers or between memory and a register. This group also provides instructions to rotate (shift) the bits in the accumulator, compare data, and complement data. The compares (CPI, CMP) and complement (CMA) have been explained in previous examples.

ANA *r*, ANI *data*, XRA *r*, XRI *data*, ORA *r*, and ORI *data*

These instructions perform Boolean operations between the accumulator and a register or memory. The result of the operation is placed in the accumulator. For example, Figure 4–4 illustrates the operation that takes place when executing the instruction ANA B (A ← A AND B). Bit A_0 is ANDed with bit B_0, and the result is put back into A_0. This process is repeated for all 8 bits. The XRA and ORA instructions operate the same way except exclusive-OR gates or OR gates are used in place of the AND gates.

The logic instructions ending with an *I* (ANI, XRI, and ORI) operate with an *immediate* data byte entered as byte 2 of the instruction. For example, ORI 35H would OR the accumulator with the bit string 0011 0101.

EXAMPLE 4–7

Determine the contents of the accumulator after the completion of each of the following groups of instructions.

    (a) MVI A,42H
           MVI D,15H
           ORA D

Solution:

                A = 0100 0010
                D = 0001 0101
       A OR D = 0101 0111 = 57H   *Answer*

    (b) MVI A,5CH
           XRI FEH

Solution:

                A = 0101 1100
             data = 1111 1110
     A ex-OR *data* = 1010 0010 = A2H   *Answer*

    (c) MVI A,F0H
           XRA A

Solution:

                A = 1111 0000
                A = 1111 0000
     A ex-OR A = 0000 0000 = 00H   *Answer*

Note: XRA A is often used as a 1-byte instruction to zero the accumulator.

    (d) MVI A,3CH
           ANI 87H

Solution:

                A = 0011 1100
            data = 1000 0111
    A AND *data* = 0000 0100 = 04H   *Answer*

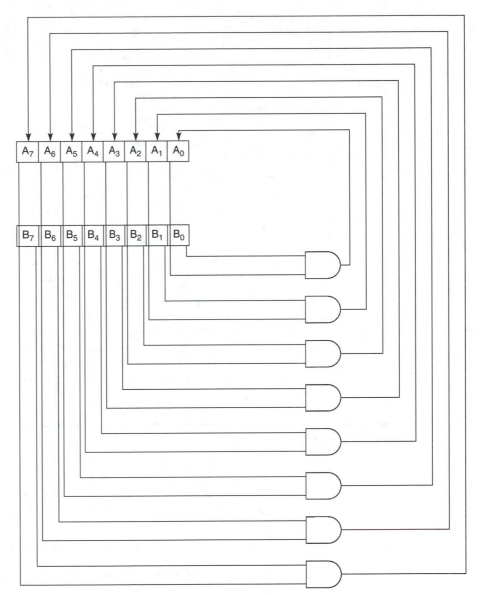

Figure 4–4   Illustration of the instruction ANA B.

Masking

In your application program you have an occasional need to read the status of a single bit. Let's say, for example, that you have eight level-sensing switches connected to input port 00H as shown in Figure 4–5. When the temperature or pressure exceeds a certain limit, the digital level on that switch goes HIGH. Let's say that temperature *A* and pressure *A* are critical monitoring points in a chemical processing plant. The other temperatures and pressures are just "nice to know" levels, not critical to the operation.

Your job is to flash the warning LEDs if temperature *A* or pressure *A* go HIGH, ignoring the other temperatures and pressures. Unfortunately you cannot read just bit 0 and bit 4. When you execute the instruction IN 00H, the accumulator is loaded with the status of *all eight* switches. If you then want to check whether bit 0 or bit 4 is HIGH, you would have to have several CPI *data* compares to check for all of the accumulator values that could arise from varying digital levels on the don't-care inputs.

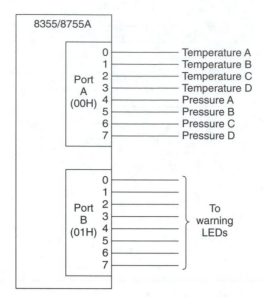

Figure 4–5 Level-sensing switches and warning LEDs connected to the I/O ports of an 8355/8755A.

You want to ignore all of the don't-care inputs. This is where *masking* is very helpful. After you read the input switches into the accumulator (IN 00H), you then AND the accumulator with 0001 0001 (ANI 11H). This is called "masking off" bits 1, 2, 3, 5, 6, and 7. They are forced to zero while preserving the level of bits 0 and 4. Now if the accumulator is not zero, then bit 0 or bit 4 must be HIGH; flash the LEDs (see Example 4–10).

EXAMPLE 4–10

Assume that the connections shown in Figure 4–5 are used for monitoring temperatures and pressures in a chemical processing plant. Write an assembly language program that will flash the warning LEDs continuously if temperature *A* or pressure *A* goes HIGH, regardless of the other inputs.

Solution:

	Instruction	Comments
START:	MVI A,00H	; Send 0s to DDR A to
	OUT 02H	; designate "Input" (Ch. 3)
	MVI A,FFH	; Send 1s to DDR B to
	OUT 03H	; designate "Output" (Ch. 3)
READSW:	IN 00H	; Read limit switches
	ANI 11H	; Mask OFF all but bits 0 and 4
	CNZ FLASH	; If A is not 0, then CALL FLASH
	JMP READSW	; Else keep reading
		;
		; Subroutine FLASH
FLASH:	MVI A,FFH	; LEDs ON
LOOPA:	OUT 01H	; Output to LEDs
	CALL DELAY	; Use Delay from Table 2–6
	CMA	; Complement A
	JMP LOOPA	; Repeat

EXAMPLE 4–11

Modify the program in Example 4–10 to flash the LEDs if *all temperatures* are HIGH, regardless of the pressures.

Solution:

Modified instruction	Comments
READSW: IN 00H	; Read limit switches
ANI 0FH	; Mask OFF all pressure switches
CPI 0FH	; Set Z flag if all temperatures HIGH
CZ FLASH	; If zero, call FLASH
JMP READSW	; Else keep reading

Rotates: RLC, RRC, RAL, and RAR

These instructions treat the accumulator like a recirculating shift register. Each bit can be shifted left or right, and the carry flag can be included as part of the shift register. Figure 4–6 illustrates the effect that each instruction has on the accumulator and carry flag.

As the illustration shows, RLC and RRC are 8-bit rotates, and RAL and RAR are 9-bit rotates. The following example will help you understand the effect that the rotates have on the accumulator and carry flag.

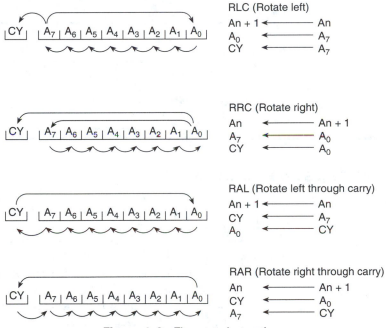

Figure 4–6 The rotate instructions.

EXAMPLE 4–12

Determine the contents of the accumulator and carry flag after each of the following groups of instructions is executed. (Assume CY = 0 initially.)

(a) MVI A,C3H
    RLC

Solution:

	CY	A_7–A_0 7 6 5 4 3 2 1 0	
Before RLC	0	1 1 0 0 0 0 1 1	
After RLC	1	1 0 0 0 0 1 1 1	*Answer*

(b) MVI A,73H
    RRC
    RRC
    RRC

Solution:

	CY	A_7–A_0 7 6 5 4 3 2 1 0	
Before RRC	0	0 1 1 1 0 0 1 1	
1st RRC	1	1 0 1 1 1 0 0 1	
2nd RRC	1	1 1 0 1 1 1 0 0	
3rd RRC	0	0 1 1 0 1 1 1 0	Answer

(c) MVI A,FFH
    RAR
    RAR
    RAR

Solution:

	CY	A_7–A_0 7 6 5 4 3 2 1 0	
Before RAR	0	1 1 1 1 1 1 1 1	
1st RAR	1	0 1 1 1 1 1 1 1	
2nd RAR	1	1 0 1 1 1 1 1 1	
3rd RAR	1	1 1 0 1 1 1 1 1	Answer

4–4 SUBROUTINES AND THE STACK

We have seen that using subroutines allows us to develop a modular approach to solving program applications. Programs that need to execute the same group of instructions more than once can reduce program size by using that group of instructions as a subroutine and CALLing it whenever it is required. Another use for subroutines is to divide large applications programs into several modules, each module performing a specific function that can be developed and tested on its own.

An example of a structured (modular) program application might be for a microprocessor-based energy management system. The program has to read several area temperature sensors, convert the readings to centigrade degrees, and provide ON/OFF control to the area heating units. The flowchart for that application is shown in Figure 4–7.

Each subroutine can be written and tested by a different programmer and then linked together to form a complete application solution. The machine language and assembly language for the main program is given in Table 4–3.

The Stack

Each subroutine must end with a return or a conditional return. In Table 4–3, upon completion of the READTEMP routine, we want program control to pass to the instruction following the call, which is at address 2003H. This is where the *stack* becomes important. The stack is an area in RAM used by certain program instructions to automatically store addresses and data. In the case of the CALL and RETurn instructions, when a CALL is executed, the 2-byte address of the instruction following the CALL (2003H) is placed on the stack. Then, when the subroutine encounters a RETurn, the microprocessor takes

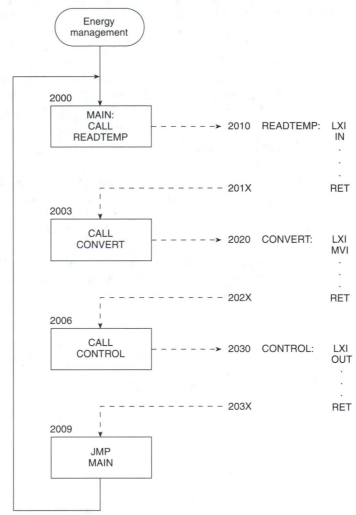

Figure 4–7 A modular approach to solving a microprocessor-based energy management application.

TABLE 4–3

Listing for the Main Program of the Energy Management Application

Address	Contents	Label	Instruction	Comments
2000	CD	MAIN:	CALL READTEMP	; Read area temperatures
2001	10			;
2002	20			;
2003	CD		CALL CONVERT	; Convert to centigrade
2004	20			;
2005	20			;
2006	CD		CALL CONTROL	; Control heating units
2007	30			;
2008	20			;
2009	C3		JMP MAIN	; Repeat
200A	00			;
200B	20			;

the address on the stack, and places it into the program counter, which forces control to return to that location (2003H). This storage and retrieval of the return address is taken care of automatically by the CALL and RET instructions.

The default location of the stack is usually at the very end of the available RAM area. It can also be specified by loading the 16-bit *stack pointer* (SP) with the address of the top of the stack. If we want the top of the stack to be at 20C0H, then we would start our program with the instruction: LXI SP,20C0H.

When an address is put on the stack, the stack pointer is decremented by 2 to point to the new top of the stack. Figure 4–8 shows the stack operations that take place due to the CALL READTEMP and RET instructions, assuming the stack pointer starts at 20C0H.

PUSH *rp* and POP *rp*

Another use for the stack is for the temporary storage of the registers and flags. As your programs become more complex, you may need to use certain registers for more than one purpose. For instance, the accumulator must be used for the IN and OUT instructions, but it is also used to receive the results of all arithmetic operations. Therefore, if the accumulator has some important data in it, you can temporarily save it out on the stack before executing an IN instruction. After you are done working with the data received from the IN instruction, you can retrieve the accumulator data back from the stack.

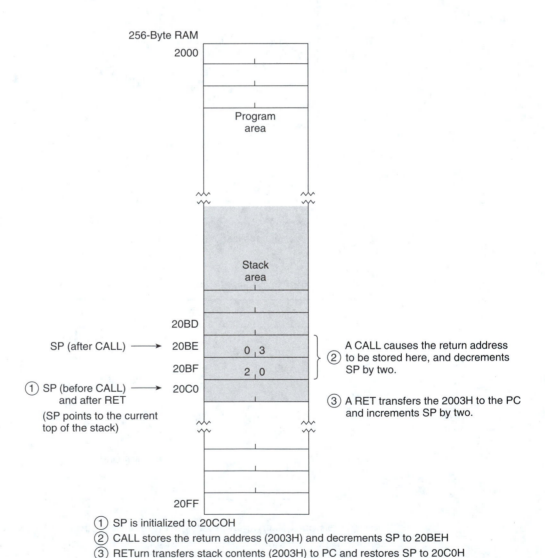

Figure 4–8   Stack operations due to CALL READTEMP and RET.

The saving and retrieval of registers from the stack is accomplished by using the PUSH *rp* and POP *rp* instructions. The PUSH *rp* instruction saves the register pair *rp* on the top of the stack, and POP *rp* retrieves the register pair. The high-order register of the register pair is saved at stack address SP-1, and the low-order register is saved at address SP-2.

The register pairs are *B–C, D–E, H–L,* and a new pair called PSW. PSW stands for *Program Status Word,* and is made up of the accumulator byte, followed by the flag byte.

More than one register pair can be saved on the stack by using successive PUSH instructions. However, when doing so, you must remember to POP the registers back off the stack in the reverse order (last on, first off). For each PUSH the SP is decremented by 2, and for each POP the SP is incremented by 2. Table 4–4 and Figure 4–9 illustrate a program that uses the stack for both PUSH/POPs and CALL/RETs. The 2-byte stack pointer shown in Figure 4–9 is initialized at 20C0H and then decremented by 2 for the CALL and each PUSH instruction. (SP always points to the top of the stack.) Then SP is incremented by 2 for each POP and the RET instruction. Upon returning to the INR instruction in the MAIN program, SP is back to its original value, 20C0H. Even though the subroutine "CONTROL" may have altered the registers, they are restored to their original values before returning to MAIN.

The values temporarily stored on the stack remain there, but you don't have access to them unless you alter the stack pointer, which is now 20C0H. The next time that you use the stack, those values will be overwritten by the new ones.

TABLE 4–4

Program Using the Stack for the Instructions CALL, RET, PUSH, and POP

	Instruction	*Comments*
MAIN:	LXI SP,20C0H	; Initialize SP to top of stack
	MVI	; ⎤ Program instructions
	ADD	; ⎟ which use all
	DCR	; ⎟ registers.
	etc.	; ⎦
	.	
	.	
	.	
	CALL CONTROL	; Sub CONTROL needs registers for other
		; purposes.
	INR	; ⎤ Remainder of MAIN
	MOV	; ⎟ program which needs
	RAR	; ⎟ to use previously
	etc.	; ⎦ defined data registers.
	.	
	.	
	.	
	HLT	; End
CONTROL:	PUSH B	; ⎤ Save register
	PUSH D	; ⎟ values
	PUSH H	; ⎦ defined
	PUSH PSW	; ⎤ in MAIN program.
	MVI	; ⎟ Use
	IN	; ⎟ registers for
	RAR	; ⎦ other
	etc.	; purposes.
	.	
	.	
	.	
	POP PSW	; ⎤ Retrieve previous
	POP H	; ⎟ register values (in
	POP D	; ⎦ reverse order)
	POP B	; before returning.
	RET	; Return to MAIN (INR instruction)

Notice that when loading the stack, the addresses are heading toward your program area. You must be careful to leave room for both. Also, all PUSHes need corresponding POPs, and CALLs need RETurns to restore the stack pointer to its initial value. When you become an advanced programmer, there are some fancy ways to work around these conventions by using instructions such as INX SP, XTHL, and SPHL. Those instructions will also allow you to return to a location other than the instruction following the CALL. It *is* okay to use nested CALLs as long as each subroutine has an equal number of PUSHes and POPs and ends with a RETurn (or conditional return).

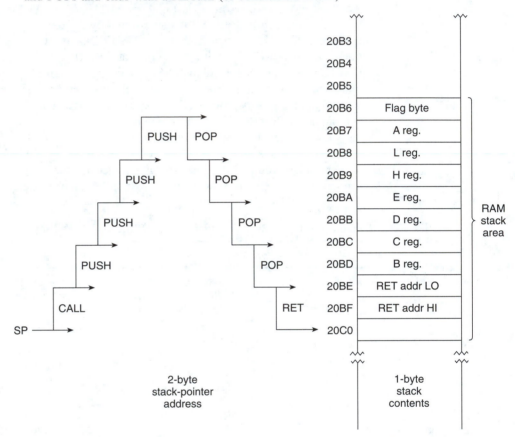

Figure 4–9   Stack operations resulting from the program in Table 4–4.

EXAMPLE 4–13

Draw a diagram of the stack contents upon completion of the following program.

Address	Contents	Label	Instruction	Comments
2000	31	MAIN:	LXI SP,20C0H	; Initialize stack pointer
2001	C0			;
2002	20			;
2003	01		LXI B,44FFH	; B ← 44H, C ← FFH
2004	FF			;
2005	44			;
2006	11		LXI D,AA77	; D ← AAH, E ← 77H
2007	77			;
2008	AA			;
2009	CD		CALL X1	; CALL subroutine X1
200A	10			;
200B	20			;
200C	76		HLT	; End
200D	00		NOP	; No operation

(continued)

Address	Contents	Label	Instruction	Comments
200E	00		NOP	; No operation
200F	00		NOP	; No operation
2010	C5	X1:	PUSH B	; Save BC on stack
2011	D5		PUSH D	; Save DE on stack
2012	1E		MVI E,00H	; E ← 00H
2013	00			;
2014	DB		IN 00H	; A ← port 00H
2015	00			;
2016	67		MOV H,A	; H ← A
2017	D1		POP D	; Retrieve DE
2018	C1		POP B	; Retrieve BC
2019	C9		RET	; Return to MAIN

Solution:

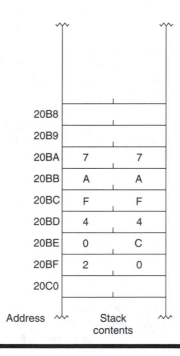

Address	Stack contents	
20B8		
20B9		
20BA	7	7
20BB	A	A
20BC	F	F
20BD	4	4
20BE	0	C
20BF	2	0
20C0		

Figure 4–10   Solution to Example 4–13.

4–5   INTERRUPTS

The 8085A microprocessor provides several ways to *interrupt* program execution by means of an external digital signal. This interruption allows you to break into the execution of your main applications program to perform some special operation that is required whenever the interrupt signal is provided. Depending on which interrupt input pin is used on the 8085A, the interrupt is initiated by providing either a rising edge or a HIGH-level input signal or both. Acknowledgment of the interrupt signal can be either enabled or disabled by software instructions. If a particular interrupt pin is enabled and it receives the proper input trigger, program execution will branch to a new address just as if a CALL were made. The five interrupt inputs and resulting branch addresses are given in Table 4–5.

For the purposes of this book, we'll use the RST 7.5 pin for interrupts. We will initiate an interrupt by pressing a pushbutton to simulate an interrupt signal from an external device. The circuit in Figure 4–11 could be used to provide the rising-edge trigger signal required at the RST 7.5 interrupt input. (*Note:* Due to switch bounce, this circuit will provide multiple rising edges when the pushbutton is pressed *and* released.)

TABLE 4–5

The 8085A Interrupts

Name	Priority	Address[a] branched to when interrupt occurs	Type trigger
TRAP	1	0024H	Rising edge AND high level until sampled
RST 7.5	2	003CH	Rising edge (latched)
RST 6.5	3	0034H	High level until sampled
RST 5.5	4	002CH	High level until sampled
INTR	5	[b]	High level until sampled

[a]In the case of TRAP and RST 5.5–7.5, the contents of the Program Counter are pushed onto the stack before the branch occurs.
[b]Depends on the instruction provided to the 8085A by the 8259 or other circuitry when the interrupt is acknowledged.

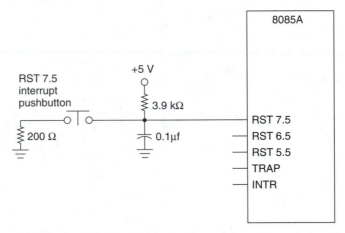

Figure 4–11   A pushbutton circuit used to provide an interrupt signal for the RST 7.5 input.

For example, if the 8085A receives a rising-edge signal on its pin labeled RST 7.5, then the microprocessor will go through the steps of executing a CALL 003CH. Address 003CH is within the system ROM (or EPROM) and must contain the instructions for the action to be taken upon receiving an interrupt.

All five interrupt branch addresses chosen by Intel are packed into a small area (0024H to 003CH), leaving only eight addresses between each one for interrupt instructions. We have room at each of these branch addresses only to put in a JMP *addr* instruction to jump to another location that has more room for us to write our *Interrupt Service Routine* (ISR). The interrupt service routine is a subroutine that performs the action required whenever the interrupt condition is initiated.

Before applying an interrupt signal, we have to define which interrupts will be used, and then enable the interrupts to be acknowledged. This requires two new instructions, SIM and EI.

SIM and EI

The SIM (Set Interrupt Mask) instruction is used to tell which interrupts RST 5.5, 6.5, and 7.5 are to be enabled by the execution of the EI (Enable Interrupt) instruction. Before executing SIM, you must load the accumulator with the data for the interrupt mask. The definition of the accumulator bits required before execution of SIM is shown in Figure 4–12.

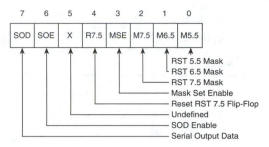

Figure 4–12 Accumulator contents before executing SIM.

Bits 6 and 7 are used for outputting serial data to the SOD pin on the microprocessor. Because we are not using SIM for serial I/O, make bits 6 and 7 equal to 0. Bit 5 is a don't care. Making bit 4 of the accumulator a 1 before executing SIM will reset the RST 7.5 edge-triggered flip-flop.

To set up the interrupt masks, you first set bit 3 of the accumulator to 1 and put a 0 in bits 2, 1, and 0 to enable interrupts RST 7.5, 6.5, and 5.5, respectively. You then execute SIM.

The interrupts are not actually enabled to be acknowledged by the microprocessor until the EI instruction is executed. When executing the EI instruction, the microprocessor uses the interrupt mask defined by the SIM instruction to determine which interrupts to enable. Each time an interrupt signal is applied and acknowledged by the microprocessor, the interrupts are *disabled* and must be reenabled by another EI instruction if they are to be acknowledged again later in the program.

EXAMPLE 4–14

Write the program instructions to enable the RST 6.5 interrupt.

Solution:

```
MVI A,0DH    ; A ← 0000 1101
SIM          ; Set Interrupt Mask
EI           ; Enable Interrupts
```

EXAMPLE 4–15

Write the program instructions to enable the RST 7.5 and the RST 6.5 interrupts.

Solution:

```
MVI A,09H    ; A ← 0000 1001
SIM          ; Set Interrupt Mask
EI           ; Enable Interrupts
```

If we want to use the interrupt pushbutton circuit of Figure 4–11, we need to first enable the RST 7.5 interrupt within our MAIN program. Then as the MAIN program is executing other tasks, if the pushbutton is pressed, the microprocessor will execute a CALL 003CH.

Location 003CH is within the monitor ROM (operating system). The contents at 003CH must be predetermined before manufacturing the ROM or before programming the EPROM. Because we want to be in an area where we can write an interrupt service routine, let's assume that the instruction JMP 20CEH is at location 003CH. We then jump to 2080H because that is a location in RAM that provides room for us to write our ISR to service our interrupt request. The program in Table 4–6 lists the program instructions required to turn on the LEDs at port 01 if the RST 7.5 pushbutton is pressed.

TABLE 4–6

Program Execution Using the RST 7.5 Interrupt Pushbutton to Turn on the LEDs

Address	Label	Instruction	Comments
			; Pressing the RST 7.5 pushbutton
			; executes a "CALL 003CH"
003C	RST7.5:	JMP 20CEH	; Jump to ISR in RAM
.			
.			
.			
2000	MAIN:	LXI SP,20A0H	; Initialize stack pointer
		MVI A,FFH	; Define port 01
		OUT 03H	; DDR B = output
		MVI A,0BH	; RST7.5 to be enabled
		SIM	; Set interrupt mask
		EI	; Enable interrupt
	LOOP:	NOP	; Endless loop
		JMP LOOP	; awaiting interrupt
.			
.			
.			
2080	ISR:	MVI A,FFH	; A ← 1111 1111
		OUT 01H	; Turn ON the LEDs
		RET	; Return to LOOP
.			
.			
.			
20CE		JMP 2080H	; Jump to different RAM area

The main program contains an endless loop that is executed continuously until the RST 7.5 pushbutton is pressed. The RST 7.5 interrupt causes the microprocessor to execute "CALL 003CH." At 003CH is a jump to 20CEH, the location of our interrupt service routine. The ISR turns on the LEDs and executes a return (RET). RET causes program control to return to the instruction that was just about to be executed before the interrupt occurred. Now we are back in the loop and the LEDs remain latched on. Since the microprocessor has acknowledged an interrupt, all interrupts are disabled. We will remain within the loop, even if RST 7.5 is pressed again.

EXAMPLE 4–16

Write a program that will rotate a single LED at port 01 continuously to the left if the RST 7.5 interrupt is pressed.

Solution:

Address	Label	Instruction	Comments
003C	RST7.5:	JMP 20CEH	; Jump to ISR in RAM*
.			
.			
2000	MAIN:	LXI SP,20A0H	; Initialize stack pointer
		MVI A,FFH	; Define port 01

*Note: To determine the jump address for the RST 7.5 interrupt, a programmer must look at the ROM listing for the particular microprocessor trainer being used. This example assumes that we are using the SDK-85 trainer, which uses 20CEH for the jump address of the RST 7.5 interrupt. Also, the SDK-85 reserves only 3 bytes of memory at that location, so we need to jump immediately to another area of RAM that has enough room for our ISR.

Solution (continued)

Address	Label	Instruction	Comments
		OUT 03H	; DDR B = output
		MVI A,0BH	; RST7.5 to be enabled
		SIM	; Set interrupt mask
		EI	; Enable interrupt
	LOOP:	NOP	; Endless loop
		JMP LOOP	; awaiting interrupt·
2050	DELAY:	MVI D,8CH	; Delay one-quarter second
	LOOP2:	MVI E,FFH	; (from Table 2–6)
	LOOP1:	DCR E	;
		JNZ LOOP1	;
		DCR D	;
		JNZ LOOP2	;
		RET	;
2080	ISR:	MVI A,01H	; Make LSB HIGH
	DISP:	OUT 01H	; Turn ON rightmost LED
		CALL DELAY	; Wait one-quarter second
		RLC	; Rotate the ON bit
		JMP DISP	; Do it again
20CE		JMP 2080H	; Jump to different RAM area

Explanation: The MAIN program enables the RST 7.5 interrupt and then waits in an endless loop for the RST 7.5 pushbutton to be pressed. When it is pressed, the microprocessor executes a CALL 003CH. Location 003CH instructs the microprocessor to jump to location 20CEH. Since there are only 3 bytes available at 20CEH, we need to jump to another area of RAM (2080H) that will have enough room for our Interrupt Service Route (ISR). The ISR turns on the rightmost LED and then rotates it slowly to the left, continuously.

EXAMPLE 4–17

Write a program that will flash the LEDs at port 01H ON then OFF the number of times indicated on the binary input switches at port 00H as soon as the RST 7.5 interrupt is pressed.

Solution:

Address	Label	Instruction	Comments
003C	RST7.5:	JMP 20CEH	; Jump to ISR in RAM
2000	MAIN:	LXI SP,20A0H	; Initialize stack pointer
		MVI A,00H	; Define port 00
		OUT 02H	; DDR A = input
		MVI A,FFH	; Define port 01
		OUT 03H	; DDR B = output
		MVI A,0BH	; RST7.5 to be enabled
		SIM	; Set interrupt mask
		EI	; Enable interrupt
	LOOP:	NOP	; Endless loop
		JMP LOOP	; awaiting interrupt

Solution (continued)

Address	Label	Instruction	Comments
.			
.			
.			
2050	DELAY:	MVI D,8CH	; Delay one-quarter second
	LOOP2:	MVI E,FFH	; (from Table 2–6)
	LOOP1:	DCR E	;
		JNZ LOOP1	;
		DCR D	;
		JNZ LOOP2	;
		RET	;
.			
.			
.			
2080	ISR:	IN 00H	; Read the binary input switches
		MOV B,A	; Move switch value to Reg B
	FLASH:	MVI A,00H	; Turn LEDs
		OUT 01H	; OFF
		CALL DELAY	; Delay one-quarter second
		CMA	; Turn LEDS
		OUT 01H	; ON
		CALL DELAY	; Delay one-quarter second
		DCR B	; Decrement switch counter
		JNZ FLASH	; Keep looping until B = 0
		RET	; Return
.			
.			
20CE		JMP 2080H	; Jump to different RAM area

Explanation: The MAIN program defines both I/O ports, enables the RST 7.5 interrupt, and then waits in an endless loop for the RST 7.5 pushbutton to be pressed. The ISR is placed in RAM starting at 2080H because there is room for only 3 bytes at 20CEH (again, assuming we are using the SDK-85 trainer). The first statement in the ISR is to read the binary input switches into the accumulator. This value is then moved to the *B* register because the accumulator will later be used to flash the LEDs. The LEDs are flashed OFF then ON once. The *B* register is then decremented and checked for zero. If it is not zero, the LEDs are flashed again and again until *B* is decremented to zero.

SUMMARY OF INSTRUCTIONS

CMP r: (Compare register) Compare the accumulator to register *r*. The Z flag is set if A = *r*. The CY flag is set if A < *r*.

MVI M,data: (Move to memory immediate) Move the *data* in byte 2 of the instruction to the memory location whose address is pointed to by *H–L*.

MOV r,M: (Move from memory) Move the data in the memory location whose address is pointed to by *H–L* to register *r*.

LDAX rp: (Load accumulator indirect) Load the accumulator with the contents of the memory location whose address is pointed to by register pair *rp*.

STAX rp: (Store accumulator indirect) Store the contents of the accumulator to the memory location whose address is pointed to by register pair *rp*.

ADD r: (Add register) Add the contents of register *r* to the accumulator.

ADI data: (Add immediate) Add the contents of byte 2 of the instruction to the accumulator.

SUB r: (Subtract register) Subtract register *r* from the accumulator.

SUI data: (Subtract immediate) Subtract the contents of byte 2 of the instruction from the accumulator.

DAA: (Decimal adjust accumulator) Adjust the 8-bit number in the accumulator to form two BCD digits.

CC addr: (Call if carry set) Transfer control to the program statement whose address, *addr*, is specified in byte 2–byte 3 of the instruction, if the carry flag is set.

RZ: (Return if zero) Return to the calling program if the zero flag is set.

ANA r: (AND register) Logically AND the contents of register *r* with the accumulator.

ANI data: (AND immediate) Logically AND the *data* in byte 2 of the instruction with the accumulator.

XRA r: (Ex-OR register) Exclusive-OR the contents of register *r* with the accumulator.

XRI data: (Ex-OR immediate) Exclusive-OR the *data* in byte 2 of the instruction with the accumulator.

ORA r: (OR register) Logically OR the contents of register *r* with the accumulator.

ORI data: (OR immediate) Logically OR the *data* in byte 2 of the instruction with the accumulator.

RLC: (Rotate left) Rotate the 8 bits of the accumulator one position to the left.

RRC: (Rotate right) Rotate the 8 bits of the accumulator one position to the right.

RAL: (Rotate left through carry) Rotate the 9 bits of the accumulator plus carry, one position to the left.

RAR: (Rotate right through carry) Rotate the 9 bits of the accumulator plus carry, one position to the right.

PUSH rp: (Push register pair) Store the 16-bit contents of register pair *rp* on the top of the stack.

POP rp: (Pop register pair) Move the 16 bits in the two top positions of the stack into register pair *rp*.

SIM: (Set interrupt mask) Program the interrupt mask for the RST 7.5, 6.5, and 5.5 hardware interrupts.

EI: (Enable Interrupt) Enable the interrupt system.

SUMMARY

In this chapter we have learned that

1. The move instructions (MOV, MVI) allow the programmer to move data from register to register, register to memory, and memory to register.

2. Indirect addressing gives the programmer access to the data stored in the memory location specified in byte 2–byte 3 of the instruction.

3. The *H–L* register pair is often used as the memory address pointer by indirect address instructions.

4. The I/O ports on the 8355/8755A can be used to read data switches and to write to LED indicators using the IN *port* and OUT *port* instructions.

5. The LDA *addr* and STA *addr* instructions are like the IN *port* and OUT *port* except they use indirect addresses (*addr*) to specify the source and destination of the data.

6. The flag byte can be examined to tell whether the following flags are set or reset: sign, zero, auxiliary carry, parity, and carry.

7. Flags are set or reset based on the result of particular program instructions. Conditional branching is often dictated by the status of these flags.

8. Several different addition and subtraction instructions are available. The accumulator is used to receive the results of all additions and subtractions.

9. The DAA instruction is used after performing arithmetic operations on BCD numbers. This ensures that the resulting number is always a valid BCD number.

10. Several logical instructions are available to perform AND, OR, complement and Exclusive-OR operations.

11. Masking is a technique used to force unwanted bits in the accumulator to the 1-state or the 0-state.

12. Four different rotate instructions are available for shifting bits to the left or right. The value in the carry flag can be included or excluded in the rotation.

13. A subroutine is a group of instructions used to form a *module* that can be executed whenever it is called by the main program.

14. The stack is an area set aside in RAM and used by certain program instructions to temporarily store addresses and data.

15. The PUSH and POP instructions are used to store and retrieve register pairs to and from the stack.

16. The *Program Status Work* (PSW) is a 16-bit register-pair that consists of the accumulator plus the flag byte.

17. As the stack is being loaded and unloaded with data and addresses, the *stack pointer* keeps track of the address of the current top of the stack.

18. Interrupt inputs are provided by the 8085A as a means to interrupt normal program execution by inputting an external electrical pulse.

19. An interrupt is like a CALL. When the interrupt signal is acknowledged, program control passes to a subroutine that was previously defined to service that interrupt request.

GLOSSARY

Auxiliary carry flag: Tells if there was a carry from bit 3 to bit 4 as a result of the previous arithmetic or logical operation.

Carry flag: Tells if there was a carry or borrow out of bit 7 due to the previous arithmetic or logical operation.

Conditional branching: Program branching, or rerouting, due to CALLs, RETurns, and JMPs can be made based on the "condition" of any one of the flag bits.

Flag byte: The status of the five 8085A flags are stored in the "flag byte."

Immediate data: The data that make up byte 2 of the instructions and that end with the letter *I*. The data are used in the execution of the instruction.

Indirect addressing: A means of addressing a memory location by using the contents of a register pair (usually *H–L*) as a memory pointer to specify the memory location.

Interrupt: A way to use an external digital signal to break into normal program execution to initiate a branch to a special service subroutine.

Interrupt mask: A data string used to determine which interrupts are to be enabled and which are to be disabled.

Interrupt Service Routine (ISR):   The subroutine executed when the microprocessor receives an interrupt.

Logical instructions: Microprocessor instructions that deal with the Boolean functions: AND, OR and exclusive-OR.

Masking: Covering up or nullifying unwanted bits in a data byte.

Parity flag: Tells if the result of the previous arithmetic or logical operation has even or odd parity.

Program Status Word (PSW):   The 16 bits composed of the accumulator plus the flag byte.

Sign flag: Tells whether the result of the previous arithmetic or logical operation is positive or negative.

Stack: An area set aside in RAM and used by certain instructions for the temporary storage of data and addresses.

Stack pointer: A 16-bit register containing an address used to point to the top of the stack.

Structured programming: A programming method that emphasizes breaking the application into several subroutine modules, each performing a specific function.

Top of stack: The address of the last entry on the stack.

PROBLEMS

4–1.   Rewrite the following instructions using indirect addressing to perform the same function.

LDA 20B0H

STA 20B1H

4–2.   Write the instructions that use indirect addressing to load memory location 20B0H with the contents of register *C*.

4–3.   Write the instructions that use indirect addressing to move the contents of memory location 20C5H to location 20C6H.

4–4.   Rewrite the solution to Problem 4–3 using the LDA and STA instructions.

4–5.   Write a program that transfers the contents of memory address 20XXH to the output LEDs at port 01. (Use the I/O interface circuit in Figure 4–2.) The low-order address, XX, will be read in from the input switches.

4–6.   Why is the 74LS240 buffer required in Figure 4–2? Why use an *inverting* buffer?

4–7.   Change one statement in the solution to Example 4–2 so that LEDs will display memory contents 20C0H to 20DFH instead of 20C0H to 20CFH.

4–8.   Most indirect-addressing instructions use the *H–L* register pair as a pointer. What register pairs do the LDAX and STAX instructions use?

4–9.   Expand the solution to Example 4–3 so that the memory contents at 20A0H through 20AFH are transferred to locations 20B0H through 20BFH.

4–10.   Determine which flag bits (S, Z, AC, P, C) are set if the flag byte equals:
(a) 44H
(b) 95H

4–11.   Use the Instruction Set Reference Encyclopedia in Appendix D to determine which flags are affected by the following instructions.
(a) INR *r*   (b) ANA *r*
(c) DCX *rp*   (d) CMA
(e) STC   (f) RLC
(g) MVI *r*   (h) CMP *r*

4–12.   Determine the value of the registers and flag byte (F) upon completion of the following instructions. (Assume all flag bits are initially reset.)
(a) MVI A,4FH
   INR A

   A = _____
   F = _____

(b) LXI B,027EH
   INR C
   INX B

   B = _____
   C = _____
   F = _____

    (c) LXI B,05FFH
       INR C
       MVI C,2AH

                B = _____
                C = _____
                F = _____

4–13. Repeat Problem 4–12 for the following instructions:
    (a) LXI B,253AH
       MVI A,52H
       ADD B
       MOV B,A
       ORA C

                A = _____
                B = _____
                F = _____

    (b) MVI A,4FH
       ADI 1AH

                A = _____
                F = _____

    (c) MVI A,2FH
       XRI A2H

                A = _____
                F = _____

    (d) MVI A,29H
       ADI 38H
       DAA

                A = _____
                F = _____

    (e) XRA A
       LXI B,7267H
       ADD B
       ADD C
       DAA

                A = _____
                F = _____

4–14. The solution to Example 4–8 is an example of structured programming. Why is it important to write large programs using this technique?

4–15. Assume that you are reading temperatures and pressures at input port 00, as shown in Figure 4–5. You are interested only in the pressures. What instruction could be used to mask off (ignore) all temperatures?

4–16. Modify the solution to Example 4–10 to flash the LEDs only if all temperatures are HIGH and all pressures are LOW by using an XRI *data* instruction.

4–17. Determine the contents of the accumulator and carry flag after the completion of the following instructions. (Assume CY = 0 initially.)
    (a) MVI A,0FH
       RAR
       RAR

                CY = _____
                A = _____

    (b) MVI A,FFH
       INR A
       RAL

                CY = _____
                A = _____

(c) MVI A,AFH
    RRC
    RRC

$$CY = \underline{\hspace{1cm}}$$
$$A = \underline{\hspace{1cm}}$$

4–18. Write a program that will continuously rotate a single ON LED at port 01, left to right, with a one-quarter second stop at each position.

4–19. Write a program that will continuously bounce a single ON LED left to right (all the way D_7 to D_0), then right to left, then left to right, etc., at one-quarter second for each position. (*Hint:* Use a conditional branch on carry.)

4–20. How is the stack used when making a subroutine CALL and RETurn?

4–21. The stack pointer should be initially set at the (beginning, middle, or end) of the available RAM area.

4–22. What does the instruction PUSH PSW do? What happens to the stack pointer due to that instruction?

4–23. When using multiple PUSH instructions in a subroutine, the registers must be POPped in the *same* order. (True or false?)

4–24. What would happen if a RETurn instruction were encountered before all registers are POPped off the stack?

4–25. The one-quarter second DELAY subroutine that we have been using uses the *D* and *E* registers for counters. Modify the subroutine so that it is transparent, which means that it has no effect on the other programs that also need to use the *D* and *E* registers.

4–26. Draw a diagram of the stack contents upon completion of the following program.

Address	Label	Instruction
2000	MAIN:	LXI SP,20B0H
2003		LXI B,3344H
2006		PUSH B
2007		CALL SUB1
200A		POP B
200B		HLT
200C	SUB1:	PUSH B
200D		NOP
200E		POP B
200F		RET

4–27. How is an 8085A interrupt like a subroutine? How is it different?

4–28. When an interrupt is made, program control first branches to (ROM or RAM).

4–29. Write the program instructions to enable the RST 6.5 and RST 5.5 interrupts.

4–30. Why is a second EI instruction sometimes required at the end of the interrupt service routine?

4–31. Write a program that will display the status of the temperature and pressure limit switches of Figure 4–5 each time the RST 7.5 interrupt pushbutton is pressed.

4–32. Write a program that will display the number of times that the RST 7.5 interrupt pushbutton is pressed. (Each time the pushbutton is pressed, increase the count on the LEDs.) Assume the LEDs are connected at port 01.

SCHEMATIC INTERPRETATION PROBLEMS

4–33. Describe the operation of U6 in the 4096/4196 schematic. Use the names of the input/output labels provided on the IC for your discussion.

4–34. Refer to sheet 2 of the 4096/4196 schematic. Describe the sequence of operations that must take place to load the 8-bit data string labeled IA_0–IA_7 and the 8-bit data string labeled ID_0–ID_7. Include reference to U30, U32, U23, U13:A, U1:F, and U33.

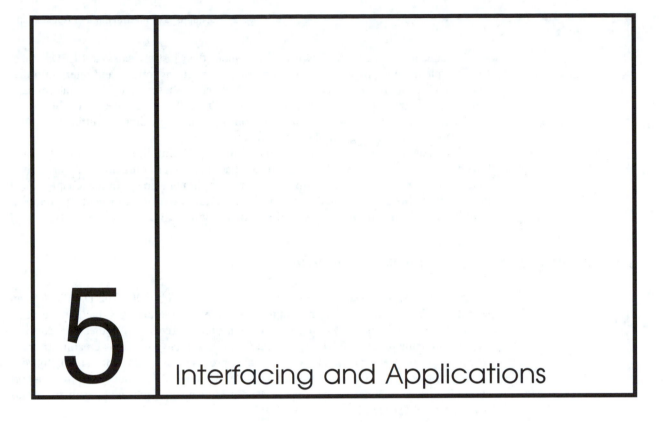

5

Interfacing and Applications

OBJECTIVES

Upon completion of this chapter you should be able to:

- Interface a digital-to-analog converter (DAC) to the I/O ports of an 8085A microprocessor system.
- Write software to use a DAC as a programmable voltage source and waveform generator.
- Interface an analog-to-digital converter (ADC) to the I/O ports of an 8085A microprocessor system.
- Write the software for handshaking between an ADC and the microprocessor.
- Describe the operation of the hardware and software required for a digital thermometer application.
- Understand how a look-up table is used for data translation.
- Describe the operation of the hardware and software required to drive a multiplexed display.
- Understand the software required to read a matrix keyboard.
- Describe the construction and operation of a stepper motor.
- Write the software to drive a stepper motor at a particular speed and number of revolutions.

INTRODUCTION

So far we've covered 90% of the instructions that you'll ever need to solve most 8085A-based system applications. Up to now our I/O has dealt with reading 8 input switches and writing to 8 output LEDs.

Practical I/O interfacing involves much more than just switches and LEDs. Take, for example, a microprocessor-based microwave oven. It has to read and interpret a matrix keypad, control a high-wattage microwave element, sense analog temperatures, and drive a multidigit display. Sounds complex, doesn't it? Well, we have all of the fundamental building blocks involved in such an application: multiplexing, demultiplexing, A/D conversion, load buffering, and D/A conversion.

The complete solution to a comprehensive application like a microwave oven is beyond the scope of this book. However, the hardware interfacing and software driver routines for each component within the system *is* within our grasp. In this chapter we'll draw on the knowledge gained in previous chapters so that we can develop practical interfaces to the analog world, as well as expand on our digital I/O capability.

5–1 INTERFACING TO A DIGITAL-TO-ANALOG CONVERTER

For microprocessor D/A applications, we can use the DAC0808 IC. The DAC0808 is an 8-bit DAC that produces a current output proportional to the binary value applied at its inputs. Using a microprocessor to drive the binary inputs gives us a tremendous capability for producing *programmable current and voltage sources* as well as creating *specialized waveforms*. Interfacing the DAC to the microprocessor system is done simply by connecting to any of the 8-bit output ports provided by one of the microprocessor support chips. Figure 5–1 shows the connections and calculated V_{out} that will result from outputting a C5H (1100 0101) to the DAC0808.

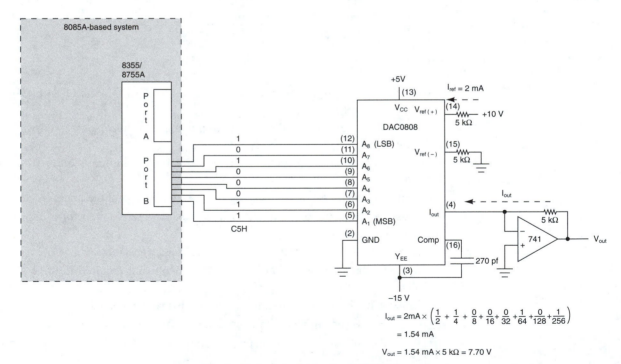

$$I_{out} = 2mA \times \left(\frac{1}{2} + \frac{1}{4} + \frac{0}{8} + \frac{0}{16} + \frac{0}{32} + \frac{1}{64} + \frac{0}{128} + \frac{1}{256} \right)$$

$$= 1.54 \text{ mA}$$

$$V_{out} = 1.54 \text{ mA} \times 5 \text{ k}\Omega = 7.70 \text{ V}$$

Figure 5–1   Interfacing the DAC0808 to a microprocessor system.

EXAMPLE 5–1

Write an assembly language program for the DAC circuit of Figure 5–1 to produce an output voltage of 4.50 V.

Solution: V_{out} is proportional to the binary input. The largest binary input, 1111 1111, produces an output voltage of 9.96 V. The following algebraic ratio can be set up to solve for the required binary input (Req B_{in}):

$$\frac{\text{Max } B_{in}}{\text{Max } V_{out}} = \frac{\text{Req } B_{in}}{\text{Req } V_{out}}$$

$$\frac{1111\ 1111}{9.96} = \frac{\text{Req } B_{in}}{4.50}$$

$$255 \times 4.50 = 9.96 \times \text{Req } B_{in}$$

$$\text{Req } B_{in} = 115_{10}\ (73\text{H or } 0111\ 0011_2)$$

Assembly language program:

Label	Instruction	Comments
Start:	MVI A,FFH	; Program DDR B for
	OUT 03H	; Port B = Output
	MVI A,73H	; Output 0111 0011
	OUT 01H	; to Port B
	HLT	; End

5-2 USING A DAC FOR WAVEFORM GENERATION

Besides using the DAC as a programmable voltage or current source, it can also be used to produce specialized waveforms. You can create a *square wave* by outputting a high voltage, then a low voltage, repeatedly. The frequency and duty cycle can be set by inserting appropriate delays within the loop.

A 256-step *sawtooth wave* can be created by counting 00H to FFH repeatedly. Its frequency can be adjusted by adding a small delay to each step.

More exotic repetitive waveforms can also be created. For example, to create a *sine wave* with, let's say, 24 steps, we would have to determine the binary value that will yield the correct output voltage at each of the 15° increments along the sine wave. These values would then be stored in a data table (a look-up table) and then used as input to the DAC to reproduce the sine wave. The resolution, or smoothness, of the sine wave will improve as you increase the number of data points in the table. The following examples illustrate the capability of the DAC as a waveform generator.

EXAMPLE 5-2

The following program is used to create a square wave at V_{out} in Figure 5–1. Sketch the resultant waveform and label the voltage levels and times. (Assume that a 6.144-MHz crystal is used.)

Label	Instruction	Comments	T states
	MVI A,FFH	; Program	7
	OUT 03H	; DDR B = Output	10
LOOP:	MVI A,80H	; Output 1000 0000	7
	OUT 01H	; to Port B DAC	10
	NOP	; No operation*	4
	MVI A,00H	; Output 0000 0000	7
	OUT 01H	; to Port B DAC	10
	NOP	; No operation*	4
	JMP LOOP	; Repeat	10

* *Note:* The NOPs were added to increase the pulse widths slightly. The HIGH pulse width could be increased to 10.1 μs (50% duty cycle) by inserting a 10 *T* state "dummy" instruction like LXI after the first NOP.

Solution: Voltage levels:

$$V_{\text{out}} \text{ for 80H:}$$

$$V_{\text{out}} = 10 \text{ V} \times (\tfrac{1}{2}) = 5.0 \text{ V}$$

$$V_{\text{out}} \text{ for 00H:}$$

$$V_{\text{out}} = 10 \text{ V} \times (0) = 0.0 \text{ V}$$

Time periods:

$$1\ T \text{ state} = 2 \times \text{crystal period}$$

$$= 2 \times 1/6.144 \text{ MHz}$$

$$= 0.326\ \mu s$$

$V_{out} = +5\ V$ from the end of the first OUT 01H to the end of the second OUT 01H.

$$T \text{ states} = 4 + 7 + 10 = 21$$

$$T_{\text{HIGH}} = 21 \times 0.326\ \mu s = 6.84\ \mu s$$

$V_{out} = 0\ V$ from the end of the second OUT 01H to the end of the first OUT 01H.

$$T \text{ states} = 4 + 10 + 7 + 10 = 31$$

$$T_{\text{LOW}} = 31 \times 0.326\ \mu s = 10.1\ \mu s$$

$$\text{Frequency} = 1/(6.84\ \mu s + 10.1\ \mu s) = 59 \text{ kHz}$$

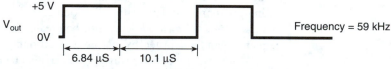

Figure 5–2   Solution to Example 5–2.

EXAMPLE 5–3

The following program is used to create a sawtooth waveform at V_{out} in Figure 5–1. Sketch the resultant waveform and label the voltage levels and times. (Assume that a 6.144-MHz crystal is used.)

Label	Instructions	Comments	T states
	MVI A,FFH	; Program Port B	7
	OUT 03H	; DDR B = Output	10
	MVI A,00H	; Start V_{out} at zero	7
LOOP:	OUT 01H	; Output to DAC	10
	INR A	; Increase one step	4
	JMP LOOP	; Next step	10

Solution: Voltage level ranges from 0 V (0000 0000) to 9.96 V (1111 1111).

$$1\ T \text{ state} = 2 \times 1/6.144 \text{ MHz} = 0.326\ \mu s$$

$$\text{Each step} = 4 + 10 + 10 = 24\ T \text{ states}$$

$$\text{Time per step} = 24\ T \text{ states} \times 0.326\ \mu s = 7.82\ \mu s$$

$$\text{Total time} = 256 \text{ steps} \times 7.82\ \mu s = 2.00 \text{ ms}$$

$$\text{Frequency} = 1/(2 \text{ ms}) = 500 \text{ Hz}$$

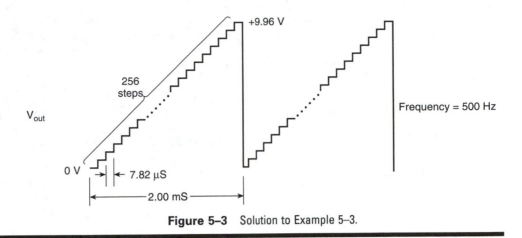

Figure 5–3   Solution to Example 5–3.

5–3 INTERFACING TO AN ANALOG-TO-DIGITAL CONVERTER

Analog quantities such as temperature, pressure, and strain need to be converted to an equivalent digital value if they are to be interpreted by a microprocessor system. To perform an analog-to-digital conversion, we can use the ADC0801 IC. We can modify the ADC circuit to interface to our 8085A system by connecting the 8-bit digital output of the ADC0801 to an input port on our ROM IC and connecting start-conversion/end-conversion control signals to a second I/O port on our ROM. Figure 5–4 shows the connections that we'll use to interface the ADC0801 to our 8085A-based microprocessor system.

Port *A* will be programmed as an input port to receive the 8 bits of data from the ADC. The conversion process is initiated when bit 0 of port *B* outputs the LOW pulse for the start-conversion ($\overline{SC}$) signal. The microprocessor will now continuously read bit 7 of port *B*, waiting for the end-of-conversion ($\overline{EOC}$) line to drop LOW. When $\overline{EOC}$ does drop LOW, the conversion is complete, and the microprocessor reads the 8 bits of data on port *A*. The program listed in Table 5–1 shows the "handshaking" that takes place between the I/O ports and the ADC when making an A/D conversion.

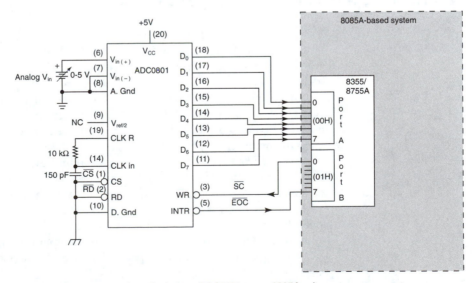

Figure 5–4   Interfacing an ADC0801 to an 8085A microprocessor system.

TABLE 5–1

Software Handshaking Required to Perform an A/D Conversion in Figure 5–4

Label	Instruction	Comments
INIT:	MVI A,00H	; Program Port A
	OUT 02H	; DDR A = Input
	MVI A,01H	; Program Port B
	OUT 03H	; Bit 7 = Input, Bit 0 = Output
SC:	MVI A,00H	; Output a LOW on Bit 0
	OUT 01H	; for start conversion ($\overline{SC}$)
	MVI A,01H	; Output a HIGH on Bit 0
	OUT 01H	; to return line HIGH
WAIT:	IN 01H	; Read Port B
	ANI 80H	; Mask off all but Bit 7
	JNZ WAIT	; Reread until $\overline{EOC}$ goes LOW
DONE:	IN 00H	; Read digital result into accumulator
	HLT	; End

The first four lines of the program define the data direction registers for port *A* and port *B* (DDR A and DDR B). Port B is to be used for both input (bit 7) *and* output (bit 0).

The start-conversion signal, $\overline{SC}$, is generated by the instructions following the "SC:" label. The A/D conversion starts when pin 3 ($\overline{WR}$) on the ADC receives a LOW-to-HIGH signal. That LOW to HIGH is made by outputting a LOW on bit 0, followed by a HIGH.

After starting the conversion, we have to wait several clock periods for the conversion to be complete (66 to 73 clock periods according to manufacturer specifications). There are several ways to do this. One way is to insert a time delay that is longer than 73 clock periods. Another way is to connect the $\overline{EOC}$ line into an interrupt pin on the microprocessor and wait for an interrupt. The method used in this program uses the three instructions following the "WAIT:" label. In this method, we keep reading port *B* and check to see if bit 7 is LOW. A LOW on bit 7 tells us that $\overline{EOC}$ is LOW and the digital data are available at $D_0–D_7$.

The last two instructions read the 8-bit result into the accumulator (IN 00H) and halt (HLT).

5–4 DESIGNING A DIGITAL THERMOMETER USING AN ADC

A good way to illustrate the versatility of a microprocessor in A/D applications is by working through the design of a *digital thermometer*. The binary output of the ADC in Figure 5–5 will increase in linear steps numerically equal to the temperature in degrees centigrade.

To display the temperature as a two-digit decimal number, we need to convert the 8-bit binary output to two BCD digits and output them to a pair of seven-segment LED displays. Figure 5–5 shows the complete circuit required for a two-digit microprocessor-based thermometer.

The thermometer circuit is centered around the three-chip minimum-component 8085A microprocessor system introduced in Figure 3–10. We'll use the two I/O ports on the 8355/8755A for the A/D handshaking as we did before.

The 8-bit port *A* on the 8156 will be used to drive the two-digit display. The decoder/driver circuitry accepts BCD data, converts them to seven-segment code, and turns on the appropriate segments. Port *A* (21H) will output two digits worth of BCD data. The least significant BCD data are output on bits 0–3 and the most significant BCD data are output on bits 4–7.

The binary data that the microprocessor receives from the ADC are not in a form

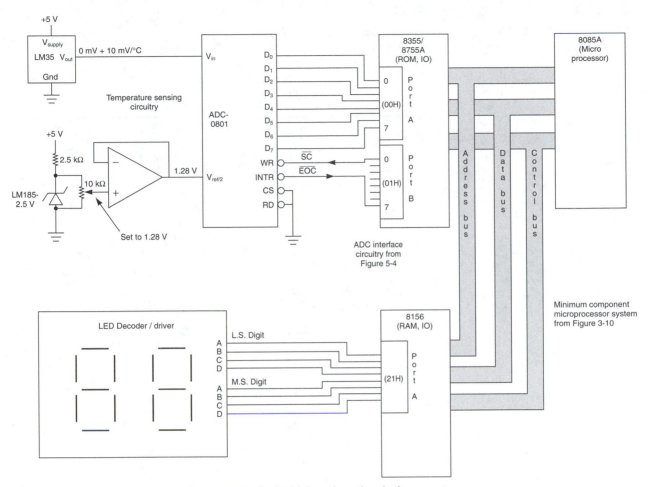

Figure 5–5   An 8085A-based centigrade thermometer.

that can be used by the two-digit display. For example, if the temperature is 20°, the ADC will output $0001\ 0100_2$. This has to be converted to $0010\ 0000_{BCD}$ before being output to the display.

This conversion can be done with MSI ICs specifically designed for binary-to-BCD conversion. Another way (the method that we'll use) is to write a software subroutine to perform the conversion. A third way is to use a *look-up table*.

To use a look-up table for this application, we would need 100 additional RAM locations to hold the table values. A second 8156 could be placed in the fold-back area, 2100H to 21FFH, to provide the required memory space. Indirect memory addressing would be used to access the BCD data to be output. The *H* register would contain 21H to point to the HIGH-order address in the look-up table. The *L* register would hold the binary output of the ADC.

For example, if the temperature is 20°, the ADC will output $0001\ 0100_2$ (14H), making the *H–L* register pair 2114H. The content of RAM location 2114H is $0010\ 0000_{BCD}$. (See Table 5–2.) This value can be output directly to the LED display. In a sense, we have "looked up" the BCD value to be output by using the binary value placed in the *L* register as a pointer to the RAM table.

The table look-up technique is very useful for nonlinear and other complex data conversion. Its disadvantage is that it uses a lot of valuable memory to hold the table entries.

Because the results in our temperature application are linear and have a one-to-one correlation, a simple *software algorithm* can be written to do the conversion. A DAA in-

TABLE 5–2
Look-up Table for Binary-to-BCD Conversion
Register H = 21 H
Register $L = D_7–D_0$ from ADC

Memory address (H–L)	Memory contents	
2100	0000 0000	(0)
2101	0000 0001	(1)
2102	0000 0010	(2)
2103	0000 0011	(3)
.	.	
.	.	
.	.	
2109	0000 1001	(9)
210A	0001 0000	(10)
210B	0001 0001	(11)
.	.	
.	.	
.	.	
2110	0001 0110	(16)
2111	0001 0111	(17)
2112	0001 1000	(18)
2113	0001 1001	(19)
2114	0010 0000	(20)
.	.	
.	.	
.	.	
215F	1001 0101	(95)
2160	1001 0110	(96)
2161	1001 0111	(97)
2162	1001 1000	(98)
2163	1001 1001	(99)

$D_7–D_0$ from ADC ⟶   Equivalent BCD (63H = 99_{10})

struction by itself is not enough to convert binary to BCD. (It would have no effect on the binary string 0001 0100, for instance.) What we could do, however, is count from zero up to the numeric value that was read from the ADC. We will execute a DAA instruction for each count, keeping the result a valid BCD number for each increment. The end result will be the two-digit BCD equivalent of the binary ADC output. Table 5–3 lists the complete program solution for the thermometer application.

This program is another example of a *structured, modular* program. The MAIN program does nothing but CALL the three subroutines, which do all of the work. The first subroutine, INIT, programs the data direction registers of the 8355/8755A, and the command register of the 8156, for I/O.

The second subroutine, ADC, is the same as the A/D program listed in Table 5–1. At the completion of this subroutine, the accumulator contains the binary equivalent of the temperature.

The last subroutine, CONVRT, converts the binary value into an equivalent two-digit BCD result. The BCD answer is then sent to output port 21H, which drives the seven-segment LED display circuitry.

5–5 DRIVING A MULTIPLEXED DISPLAY

Multidigit LED or LCD displays are commonly used in microprocessor systems. To drive each digit of a six-digit display using separate, dedicated drivers would require six 8-bit I/O ports. Instead, a *multiplexing* scheme is usually used. Using the multiplexing tech-

TABLE 5–3

Program Listing for the 0–99°C Thermometer Circuit of Figure 5–5

Label	Instruction	Comments
MAIN:	LXI SP,20C0H	; Initialize stack pointer
	CALL INIT	; Initialize I/O ports
LOOP:	CALL ADC	; Perform A/D conversion
	CALL CONVRT	; Convert bin-to-BCD and display
	JMP LOOP	; Repeat continuously
		;
		;
		;
INIT:	MVI A,00H	; Program Port A
	OUT 02H	; DDR A = Input
	MVI A,01H	; Program Port B
	OUT 03H	; Bit 7 = Input, Bit 0 = Output
	MVI A,01H	; Program Port A of the 8156
	OUT 20H	; as an Output port
	RET	; Return to MAIN
		;
		;
ADC:	MVI A,00H	; Output a
	OUT 01H	; LOW-then-HIGH
	MVI A,01H	; on Bit 0 to
	OUT 01H	; Start conversion ($\overline{SC}$)
WAIT:	IN 01H	; Keep rereading Bit 7 of
	ANI 80H	; Port B ($\overline{EOC}$) until
	JNZ WAIT	; it goes LOW
	IN 00H	; Read digital result into accumulator
	RET	; Return to MAIN
		;
		;
CONVRT:	MOV D,A	; Move binary value to D
	XRA A	; Zero out A
COUNT:	INR A	; Count up
	DAA	; in BCD
	DCR D	; Decrement binary value
	JNZ COUNT	; Keep counting until D = 0
	OUT 21H	; Output BCD to seven segment display
	RET	; Return to MAIN

nique, up to eight digits can be driven by using only two output ports. One output port is used to select which digit is to be active, while the other port is used to drive the appropriate *segments* within the selected digit. Figure 5–6 shows how the two I/O ports of an 8355/8755A can be used to drive a six-digit multiplexed display.

The displays used in Figure 5–6 are common-cathode LEDs. To enable a digit to work, the connection labeled COM must be grounded. The individual segments are then illuminated by supplying + 5 V, via a 150-Ω limiting resistor, to the appropriate segment.

It takes about 10 mA to illuminate a single segment. If all segments in one digit are on, as with the number 8, the current in the COM line will be 70 mA. The output ports of the 8355/8755A can sink only 2 mA. This is why we need the *PNP* transistors set up as current buffers. When port A outputs a 0 on bit 0, the first *PNP* turns on, shorting the emitter to collector. This allows current to flow from the + 5-V supply through the 150-Ω limiting resistor, to the *a* segments. None of the *a* segments will illuminate unless one of the digits' COM lines is brought LOW. To enable the LSD, port B will output a 0 on bit 0, which shorts the emitter to collector of that transistor. The short provides a path for current to flow from the COM on the LSD, to ground. Figure 5–7 shows the bit as-

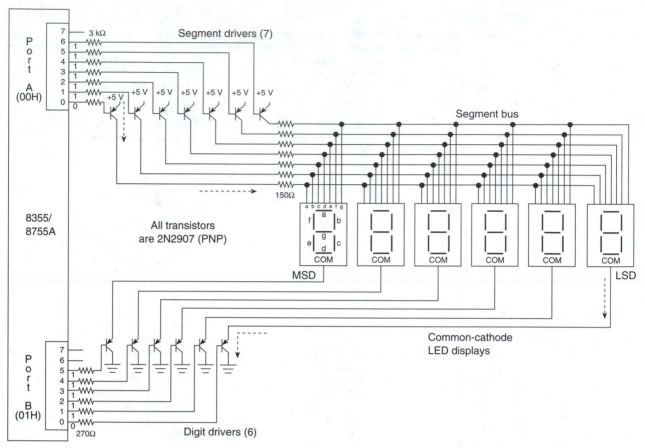

Figure 5–6   A multiplexed six-digit display with the *a* segment of the LSD illuminated.

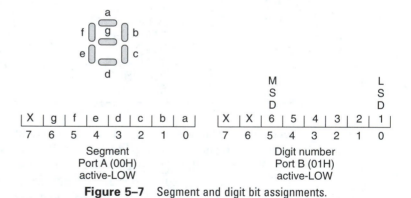

Figure 5–7   Segment and digit bit assignments.

signments for each of the segments and each of the digits.

Notice that enabling both the segment and the digit requires an active-LOW signal. To drive all six digits, we have to *scan* the entire display repeatedly with the appropriate numbers to be displayed. For example, to display the number 123456, we need to turn on the segments for the number 1 (*b* and *c*), then turn on the MSD. We then turn off all digits, turn on the segments for the number 2 (*a*, *b*, *g*, *e*, and *d*) and turn on the next digit. We then turn off all digits, turn on the segments for the number 3, and turn on the next digit. This process repeats until all six digits have been flashed on once. At that point, the MSD is cycled back on, followed by each of the next digits. By repeating this cycle over and over again, the number 123456 appears to be on all the time. The following example shows the instructions required to carry out this task.

EXAMPLE 5–4

Write a program to display the number 123456 in the multiplexed display of Figure 5–6.

Solution:

Label	Instructions	Comments
MAIN:	LXI SP,20C0H	; Initialize stack pointer
	MVI A,FFH	; Program Ports A and B
	OUT 02H	; DDR A = Output
	OUT 03H	; DDR B = Output
LOOP:	MVI B,F9H	; B← #1 segments
	MVI C,DFH	; C←6th digit (MSD)
	CALL DISP	; Display #1
	MVI B,A4H	; B← #2 segments
	MVI C,EFH	; C←5th digit
	CALL DISP	; Display #2
	MVI B,B0H	; B← #3 segments
	MVI C,F7H	; C←4th digit
	CALL DISP	; Display #3
	MVI B,99H	; B← #4 segments
	MVI C,FBH	; C←3rd digit
	CALL DISP	; Display #4
	MVI B,92H	; B← #5 segments
	MVI C,FDH	; C←2nd digit
	CALL DISP	; Display #5
	MVI B,82H	: B← #6 segments
	MVI C,FEH	; C←1st digit (LSD)
	CALL DISP	; Display #6
	JMP LOOP	; Repeat
DISP:	MVI A,FFH	; Turn off
	OUT 01H	; all digits
	MOV A,B	; Move segment data to A
	OUT 00H	; Output A to segment bus
	MOV A,C	; Move digit data to A
	OUT 01H	; Turn on selected digit
	RET	; Return for next digit

Explanation: Figures 5–8 and 5–9 give the segment assignments and digit position assignments used in our program. The LOOP instructions load the *B* register with the data required for the active-LOW segment port, and load the *C* register with the data required for the active-LOW digit port. With *B* and *C* loaded with the data for the MSD, the subroutine DISP is called.

DISP starts by turning off all digits. This is necessary because the next step is to drive the segment bus, not knowing which digit is to be turned on. OUT 00H drives the appropriate lines on the segment bus LOW. Because all digits are

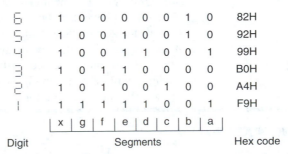

Digit	x	g	f	e	d	c	b	a	Hex code
6	1	0	0	0	0	0	1	0	82H
5	1	0	0	1	0	0	1	0	92H
4	1	0	0	1	1	0	0	1	99H
3	1	0	1	1	0	0	0	0	B0H
2	1	0	1	0	0	1	0	0	A4H
1	1	1	1	1	1	0	0	1	F9H

Digit   Segments   Hex code

Figure 5–8   Segment assignments for numbers 1, 2, 3, 4, 5, and 6 in Example 5–4.

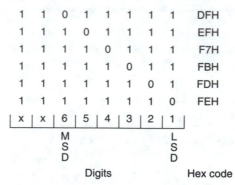

1	1	0	1	1	1	1	1	DFH
1	1	1	0	1	1	1	1	EFH
1	1	1	1	0	1	1	1	F7H
1	1	1	1	1	0	1	1	FBH
1	1	1	1	1	1	0	1	FDH
1	1	1	1	1	1	1	0	FEH

x | x | 6 | 5 | 4 | 3 | 2 | 1

MSD   LSD

Digits   Hex code

Figure 5–9 Digit assignments for all six-digit positions in Example 5–4.

disabled, no segments are illuminated yet. The last two instructions in DISP turn on the digit that goes with the segment data currently on the segment bus.

The first digit to be illuminated is the MSD. The next group of three instructions in LOOP turns on digit 5, the next group turns on digit 4, and so on, down to the LSD. This cycle repeats continuously, illuminating each digit one-sixth of the time.

EXAMPLE 5–5

Write a program that will continuously rotate the number zero left to right in the six-digit display given in Figure 5–6. Pause at each digit position for one-quarter second.

Solution:

Label	Instruction	Comments
MAIN:	LXI SP,20C0H	; Initialize stack pointer
	MVI A,FFH	; Program Ports A and B
	OUT 02H	; DDR A = Output
	OUT 03H	; DDR B = Output
	MVI A,C0H	; Load segment bus with
	OUT 00H	; data for number 0
MSD:	MVI A,DFH	; Data string to enable MSD
LOOP:	OUT 01H	; Drive digit bus
	CALL DELAY	; One-quarter second delay (Table 2–5)
	RRC	; Rotate right
	JNC MSD	; If CY now equals 0 then restart at MSD
	JMP LOOP	; Else display next position

Explanation: After programming ports *A* and *B* as outputs, we send the segment code (C0H) for 0 to the segment bus. This information is latched in port *A* (00H) and will remain constant on the segment bus. Next, the MSD is enabled by sending DFH (1101 1111) to the digits. The 0 now appears on the MSD. The delay will cause the display to stay on for one-quarter second. The RRC instruction is used to rotate the accumulator, which has a single zero in it, to enable just one of the digits at a time. The display–delay–rotate continues to the LSD. The next rotate sends the zero bit of the accumulator into the carry bit, resetting CY. The JNC condition will be met, forcing program control back to label MSD, which sets up the accumulator to point to the leftmost digit (MSD). The cycle repeats.

5–6 SCANNING A KEYBOARD

A keyboard is one of the most common means of entering data into a microprocessor or computer system. With the large number of different keys on a typical keyboard, it is impossible to assign a separate input pin for each key. A 64-key keyboard would require 64 separate input pins, or eight, 8-bit input ports.

Instead, most keyboards are connected up as an *X-Y matrix*. For example, a 64-key keyboard would be wired up with eight rows and eight columns. A software program is then written to drive each of the rows active, one at a time, while reading the columns to see if any of the keys in the active row are depressed. When a key is pressed, the program decodes the particular key by knowing which row and which column are active.

The software for decoding an 8-by-8 keyboard is fairly complex, but we can get the general idea of the decoding process by studying the hardware and software solution to the hexadecimal keyboard shown in Figure 5–10.

Instead of using 16 individual lines for the 16 keys, a 4-by-4 matrix is set up. When a key is pressed, the adjacent row and column are connected electrically. To determine which key is pressed, the program must know which row is active-LOW when a LOW is encountered on one of the columns.

The scanning process is initiated by outputting a 0 on row 0, and 1's on the other three rows (port 00H). Next, the microprocessor reads the columns (port 01H). If one of the keys in row 0 (0, 1, 2, or 3) is depressed at the time, then the data read at port 01H will have a zero in bit 0, 1, 2, or 3. If so, the program will be able to pinpoint which key was pressed.

If none of the columns are LOW when row 0 is active, then row 1 is made LOW. Again, the program reads the columns (port 01H) and checks for a LOW bit. The program continues to loop around all four rows, checking the columns each time, until one of the column bits is LOW.

To convert the row–column value into an actual hexadecimal number, refer to Table 5–4. Table 5–4 shows that if row 1 were made LOW and column 2 were read as a LOW, then the number 6 key is being pressed. This holds true if you trace through the schematic

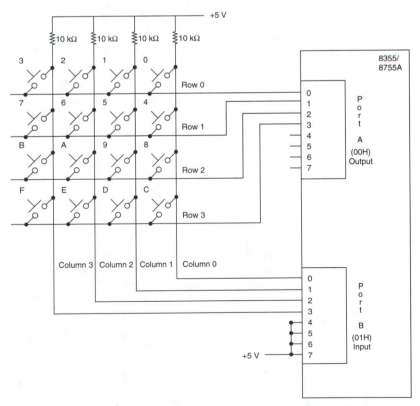

Figure 5–10 Hardware requirements for decoding a 4-by-4 hexadecimal keyboard.

TABLE 5–4

Determining the Key Pressed by Applying Weighting
Factors to the Active-LOW Row and Column Indicators

Row 3 2 1 0	Column 3 2 1 0	Key pressed
1 1 1 0	1 1 1 0	0
1 1 1 0	1 1 0 1	1
1 1 1 0	1 0 1 1	2
1 1 1 0	0 1 1 1	3
1 1 0 1	1 1 1 0	4
1 1 0 1	1 1 0 1	5
1 1 0 1	1 0 1 1	6
1 1 0 1	0 1 1 1	7
1 0 1 1	1 1 1 0	8
1 0 1 1	1 1 0 1	9
1 0 1 1	1 0 1 1	A
1 0 1 1	0 1 1 1	B
0 1 1 1	1 1 1 0	C
0 1 1 1	1 1 0 1	D
0 1 1 1	1 0 1 1	E
0 1 1 1	0 1 1 1	F

```
Add 12 ──────────┐↑↑↑            ↑↑↑↑─────── Add 0
Add 8  ──────────┘↑↑              │↑│└─────── Add 1
Add 4  ───────────┘↑              ││└──────── Add 2
Add 0  ────────────┘              │└───────── Add 3
```

given in Figure 5–10. Trace through several other keys, just to be sure that you can see how Table 5–4 is built from Figure 5–10.

The weighting factors given at the bottom of the table are used to establish the value of the key pressed. For example, whenever row 1 is LOW, we are looking for the numbers 4, 5, 6, or 7. If a column position goes LOW, we add 4 to the column number to get the key value. In the case of the number 6 key, we are in row 1 and column 2, so we add 4 plus 2 and get a value of 6. Try adding the weighting factors for several of the other row–column combinations to prove to yourself that this technique works.

A final note on keyboard scanning. As with any other mechanical switch, there will be *switch bounce* that has to be accounted for. One simple way to avoid erroneous results is to wait for one-quarter second after encountering a key closure, to give the user time to release the key and for the key to stop bouncing.

Table 5–5 lists a program that will scan the keyboard until a key is pressed, and then place the numeric value of that key into the accumulator.

TABLE 5–5

Program Used to Scan and Decode the Hex Keyboard of Figure 5–10

Label	Instruction	Comments
INIT:	MVI A,FFH	; Program Port A
	OUT 02H	; DDR A = Output
	CMA	; Program Port B
	OUT 03H	; DDR B = Input
		;
ROW0:	MVI B,00H	; B = Row weighting = 0
	MVI A,FEH	; A←1111 1110
	OUT 00H	; Drive Row 0 LOW
	IN 01H	; Read columns
	CPI FFH	; Set Z flag if all columns HIGH

TABLE 5–5 (continued)

Label	Instruction	Comments
	JNZ COL	; Jump to COL if any column LOW
		;
ROW1:	MVI B,04H	; Row weighting = 4
	MVI A,FDH	; A←1111 1101
	OUT 00H	; Drive Row 1 LOW
	IN 01H	; Read columns
	CPI FFH	; Check for a
	JNZ COL	; LOW column
		;
ROW2:	MVI B,08H	; Row weighting = 8
	MVI A,FBH	; A←1111 1011
	OUT 00H	; Drive Row 2 LOW
	IN 01H	; Read columns
	CPI FFH	; Check for a
	JNZ COL	; LOW column
ROW3:	MVI B,0CH	; Row weighting = 12
	MVI A,F7H	; A←1111 0111
	OUT 00H	; Drive Row 3 LOW
	IN 01H	; Read columns
	CPI FFH	; Check for a
	JNZ COL	; LOW column
	JMP ROW0	; No key pressed, scan again
		;
COL:	MVI C,00H	; C = column counter = 0
	RRC	; Rotate LOW column
	JNC DONE	; If LOW is now in CY, then done
	INR C	; C = 1
	RRC	; Rotate LOW column again
	JNC DONE	; If LOW is now in CY, then done
	INR C	; C = 2
	RRC	; Rotate LOW column again
	JNC DONE	; If LOW is now in CY, then done
	INR C	; Else C = 3
		;
DONE:	XRA A	; Clear A
	ADD B	; Add row weighting plus
	ADD C	; column weighting to A
	HLT	; A = Value of key pressed

5–7 DRIVING A STEPPER MOTOR

A stepper motor makes its rotation in steps instead of a smooth, continuous motion, as with conventional motors. Typical stepping angles are 15° or 7.5° per step, requiring 24 or 48 steps, respectively, to complete one revolution. The stepping action is controlled by digital levels that energize magnetic coils within the motor.

Because they are driven by digital signals, they are well suited for microprocessor-based control applications. For example, a program could be written to cause the stepper motor to rotate at 100 rpm, for 32 revolutions, and then stop. This is useful for applications requiring exact positioning control without the use of closed-loop feedback circuitry to monitor the position. Typical applications are floppy disk Read/Write head positioning, printer type head and line feed control, and robotics.

There are several ways to construct a motor to achieve this digitally controlled stepping action. One such way is illustrated in Figure 5–11.

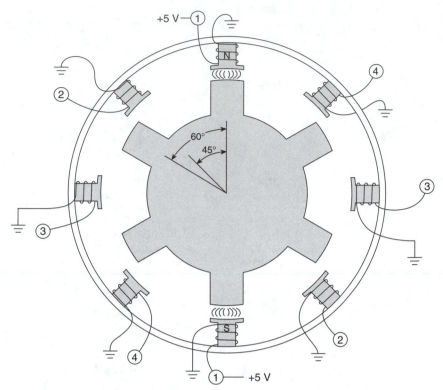

Figure 5–11   A four-coil stepper motor with stator coil 1 energized.

This particular stepper motor construction uses four *stator* (stationary) *coils* set up as four pole-pairs. Each stator pole is offset from the previous one by 45°. The directions of the windings are such that energizing any one coil will develop a "north" field at one pole and a "south" field at the opposite pole. The north and south poles created by energizing coil 1 are shown in Figure 5–11. The rotating part of the motor (the *rotor*) is designed with three ferromagnetic pairs, spaced 60° apart from each other. (A ferromagnetic material is one that is attracted to magnetic fields.) Since the stator poles are spaced 45° apart, this makes the next stator-to-rotor 15° out of alignment.

In Figure 5–11 the rotor has aligned itself with the flux lines created by the north–south stator poles of coil 1. To step the rotor 15° clockwise, coil 1 is deenergized and coil 2 is energized. The rotor pair closest to coil 2 will now line up with stator pole pair 2's flux lines. The next 15° steps are made by energizing coil 3, then 4, then 1, then 2, etc., for as many steps as you require. Figure 5–12 shows the stepping action achieved by energizing each successive coil six times. Table 5–6 shows the digital codes applied to the stator coils for 15° clockwise and 15° counterclockwise rotation.

The amount of current required to energize a coil pair is much higher than the capability of a parallel I/O port, so we will need some current-buffering circuitry similar to that shown in Figure 5–13.

The output of the upper 7406 inverting buffer in Figure 5–13 is LOW, forward biasing the base–emitter of the MJ2955 *PNP* power transistor. This causes the collec-

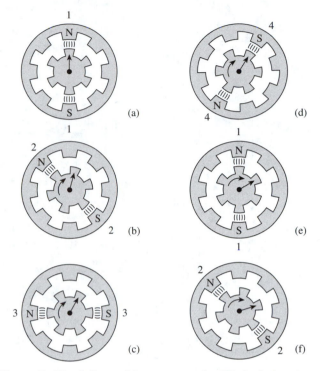

Figure 5–12 Coil energizing sequence for 15° clockwise steps.

TABLE 5–6

Digital Codes for 15° Clockwise and Counterclockwise Rotation

Clockwise coil 1 2 3 4	Counterclockwise coil 1 2 3 4
1 0 0 0	0 0 0 1
0 1 0 0	0 0 1 0
0 0 1 0	0 1 0 0
0 0 0 1	1 0 0 0
1 0 0 0	0 0 0 1
0 1 0 0	0 0 1 0
etc.	etc.

tor–emitter to short, allowing the large current to flow through the number 1 coils to ground. The IN4001 diodes protect the coils from arcing over when the current is stopped.

The software program to drive the stepper motor involves rotating a single ON bit left to right, or right to left, repeatedly. The speed of rotation will be dictated by the delay period that is inserted between rotates. One complete revolution will be made by executing the RRC or RLC instruction 24 times (15° per step). The following examples illustrate the software requirements for driving a stepper motor.

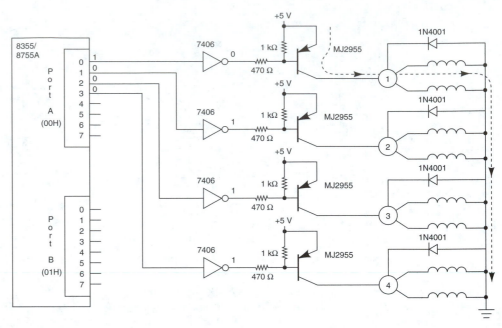

Figure 5–13   Drive circuitry for a four-coil stepper motor showing the number 1 coils energized.

EXAMPLE 5–6

Connect eight input switches to port *B* of the stepper motor circuit in Figure 5–13. Rotate the stepper motor clockwise, continuously, at a speed dictated by the value read in on the input switches (00H = fastest, FFH = slowest).

Solution:

Label	Instruction	Comments
INIT:	LXI SP,20C0H	; Initialize stack pointer
	MVI A,FFH	; Program Port A
	OUT 02H	; DDR A = Output
	CMA	; Program Port B
	OUT 03H	; DDR B = Input
	MVI A,11H	; A←0001 0001
STEP:	OUT 00H	; Send low-order nibble to stepper
	PUSH PSW	; Save A
	CALL DELAY	; Pause at that step
	POP PSW	; Restore A
	RLC	; Rotate A to energize next coil
	JMP STEP	; Repeat
DELAY:	IN 01H	; Read input switches for delay
	MOV B,A	; Move delay value to B
	MVI C,FFH	; C←FFH
LOOP:	DCX B	; Decrement B–C register pair
	MOV A,C	; Set Z flag if
	ORA B	; C = 0 *and* B = 0
	RZ	; Return if B–C reached 0000H
	JMP LOOP	; Else decrement B–C again

Explanation: The stepper motor is connected to the low-order 4 bits (nibble) of port *A*. Because RLC is an 8-bit rotate, we have to repeat the low-order information on the high-order bits so that after the fourth rotate, the A_0 bit will be HIGH again to continue the rotation (A = 0001 0001). The PUSH and POP instructions are required because the DELAY subroutine changes A when it reads the input switches. The DELAY subroutine is used to insert a pause between each step in the rotation. The pause is proportional to the length of time it takes to decrement the B–C register pair from XXFFH, down to zero, where XX is the value read from the input switches. Since the DCX instruction affects *no* flags, the ORA B instruction is used to set the zero flag when both B and C equal zero. The maximum decrement is FFFFH to 0000H (65,536) and the minimum is 00FFH to 0000H (256). This gives us a very broad range of stepper motor speeds.

EXAMPLE 5–7

Write a program to drive the stepper motor five revolutions clockwise, then five revolutions counterclockwise, then five revolutions clockwise, etc., continuously. Use the same subroutine that was developed in Example 5–6 to set the speed of rotation based on the input switch settings.

Solution:

Label	Instruction	Comments
INIT:	LXI SP,20C0H	; Initialize stack pointer
	MVI A,FFH	; Program Port A
	OUT 02H	; DDR A = Output
	CMA	; Program Port B
	OUT 03H	; DDR B = Input
	MVI A,11H	; A←0001 0001
LOOP:	MVI D,78H	; D steps = 5 rev × 24 = 78H
CWISE:	OUT 00H	; Output to stepper coils
	PUSH PSW	; Save A
	CALL DELAY	; Pause at that step (Ex. 5–6)
	POP PSW	; Restore A
	RLC	; Rotate one step clockwise
	DCR D	; Decrement step counter
	JNZ CWISE	; If not zero, step again
	MVI D,78H	; Else reset counter for 5 revs
CCWISE:	OUT 00H	; Output to stepper coils
	PUSH PSW	; Save A
	CALL DELAY	; Pause at that step (Ex. 5–6)
	POP PSW	; Restore A
	RRC	; Rotate one step counterclockwise
	DCR D	; Decrement step counter
	JNZ CCWISE	; If not zero, step again
	JMP LOOP	; Else restart with clockwise

Explanation: This is similar to Example 5–6 except that we have to count the number of revolutions. The step angle of our motor is 15°, requiring 24 steps for one revolution. Five revolutions will therefore require 120 steps (5 × 24 = 120). And 120 converted to hexadecimal is 78H. Clockwise rotation is made by using the RLC instruction, which will energize coil 1, then 2, and 3, etc. Counterclockwise rotation is made by using the RRC instruction, which will energize coil 1, then 4, then 3, then 2, etc.

SUMMARY

In this chapter we have learned that

1. A digital-to-analog converter can be driven by an output port of a microprocessor to create specialized square, sawtooth, and triangle waveforms. The period of the waveform is controlled by a delay inserted between the steps.

2. Two ports are required on a microprocessor system to interface to an analog-to-digital converter. One port is used to receive the digital result and the other port uses one bit to issue a *start-conversion* signal and then monitors another bit for the *end-of-conversion* response.

3. An LM35 linear temperature sensor can be input to an A-to-D converter to provide an accurate means of monitoring temperatures with a microprocessor.

4. A *look-up table* is a simple way to convert between digital codes, but a lot of memory locations can be used up to implement a complete table.

5. Driving multiplexed displays can be accomplished using two ports: one to drive the segments of all digits, and one to select which digit is to be active.

6. Scanning a keyboard is accomplished by setting it up as a row–column matrix and then activating individual rows and seeing which column receives the signal. Once the row–column combination is known, the individual key that is pressed can be determined.

7. Stepper motors revolve by taking small angular steps. Their speed and number of revolutions can be accurately controlled by software. To rotate the motor, one out of the four stator coils is energized, then each adjacent coil is energized in succession.

GLOSSARY

Algorithm: A procedure or formula used to solve a problem.

Closed-loop feedback: A system that sends information about an output device back to the device driving the output device, to keep track of the particular activity.

Common-cathode: A seven-segment display having the cathodes of each segment connected to a common ground point. Individual segments are then illuminated by supplying + 5 V via a series-limiting resistor.

Ferromagnetic: A material in which magnetic flux lines can pass easily (high permeability).

Flux lines: The north-to-south magnetic field set up by magnets is made up of flux lines.

Handshaking: The communication between a data sending device and receiving device that is necessary to determine the status of the transmitted data.

Look-up table: A data table used in software programs to translate a particular binary string into a meaningful binary output. The translation is made by "looking up" the output value by using the input string as an address pointer.

Matrix keyboard: A multikey keyboard whose keys are electrically connected up in an X-Y matrix configuration with each key located by its row–column address.

Multiplexed display: A multidigit display whose digits share a common segment bus and are enabled one at a time.

Pole-pair: Two opposing magnetic poles situated opposite each other in a motor housing and energized concurrently.

Programmable voltage source: A device whose output voltage level is controlled by software program instructions.

Rotor: The rotating part of the stepper motor.

Sawtooth wave: A repetitive waveform characterized by a linearly rising voltage level that reaches a high point and then drops back to its initial value.

Segment bus: A common set of seven conductors (eight if the decimal point is used) shared by each digit of a multiplexed display.

Stator coil: A stationary coil, mounted on the inside of the motor housing.

Step angle: The number of degrees that a stepper motor rotates for each change in the digital input signal (usually 15° or 7.5°).

Stepper motor: A motor whose rotation is made in steps that are controlled by a digital input signal.

PROBLEMS

5–1. Determine the value of V_{out} in the DAC circuit of Figure 5–1 that would result from the execution of the following program segments:
  (a) MVI A,01H
      OUT 01H
  (b) MVI A,80H
      OUT 01H
  (c) MVI A,FFH
      OUT 01H

5–2. Write the programs that will output the following voltage in the DAC circuit in Figure 5–1.
  (a) $V_{out} \cong 1.2$ V
  (b) $V_{out} \cong 5.0$ V
  (c) $V_{out} \cong 0.2$ V

5–3. Sketch and label the voltage and time for the output waveform that will result from executing the following program with the DAC circuit of Figure 5–1. (Assume that a 6.144-MHz crystal is being used.)

```
            MVI A,FFH
            OUT 03H
     LOOP:  MVI A,40H
            OUT 01H
            MVI A,04H
            OUT 01H
            JMP LOOP
```

5–4. What change could be made to the program in Problem 5–3 to make the duty cycle of the output wave 50%?

5–5. Write a program that uses the DAC circuit of Figure 5–1 to create a triangle wave of any frequency and any amplitude.

5–6. Describe the handshaking that takes place between the ADC0801 and the I/O ports in Figure 5–4 when making an A/D conversion.

5–7. Which instructions in Table 5–1 are responsible for issuing the LOW-to-HIGH start-conversion signal to the ADC in Figure 5–4?

5–8. What is the 8-bit binary output of the ADC in Figure 5–5 if the temperature is 25° C?

5–9. In Figure 5–5 what conversion must be made to the 8-bit data string received from the ADC before it can be output to the two-digit display?

5–10. What is one advantage and one disadvantage of using a look-up table for the translation of data values?

5–11. Briefly describe the operation of the multiplexed display circuit of Figure 5–6.

5–12. Why are transistors required for segment drivers and digit drivers in Figure 5–6?

5–13. Why is it necessary to turn off all digits in the beginning of the DISP subroutine in Example 5–4?

5–14. Write a program that will display the number 7 in the least significant digit position in Figure 5–6.

5–15. Modify the program in Example 5–4 so that it displays the word HELP in the four rightmost positions.

5–16. Write a program that will continuously flash the number 4, ON one-quarter second, OFF one-quarter second, in the LSD of Figure 5–6.

5–17. Briefly describe the technique used to decode the matrix keyboard shown in Figure 5–10.

5–18. Assume that an active-LOW LED circuit is connected to bit 7 of port *A* in Figure 5–10. Determine which key must be pressed for the following program to turn on the LED.

```
INIT:     MVI A,FFH
          OUT 02H
          CMA
          OUT 03H
ROW:      MVI A,FBH
          OUT 00H
COL:      IN 01H
          CPI FDH
          JNZ COL
LED:      MVI A,7FH
          OUT 00H
          JMP LED
```

5–19. Rewrite the program given in Problem 5–18 so that it turns on the LED if the number 6 key is pressed.

5–20. Briefly describe how the instructions following label COL: in Table 5–5 convert the key pressed into the actual hexadecimal value.

5–21. Describe how a stepper motor differs from other motors.

5–22. Which direction will the stepper motor rotor turn in Figure 5–11 if the coil sequence is 1–4–3–2–1?

5–23. The stepper motor coils in Figure 5–11 are activated by (a HIGH, or a LOW).

5–24. What is the purpose of the MJ2955 *PNP* transistors in Figure 5–13?

5–25. (a) Why are the PUSH and POP instructions required in the solution to Example 5–6?
(b) Could they be placed *inside* the DELAY subroutine instead of where they are?

5–26. Assume that there are input switches connected to port *B* of the 8355/8755A in Figure 5–13. Write a program that drives the stepper motor counterclockwise at a slow speed. The motor will make XX revolutions, where XX is the value read in from the input switches.

SCHEMATIC INTERPRETATION PROBLEMS

5–27. On a separate piece of paper draw the circuit connections to add a bank of eight LEDs with current limiting resistors to the octal D flip-flop, U5, in the 4096/4196 schematic.

5–28. Identify the following ICs on the 4096/4196 schematic (sheets 1 and 2):
(a) The three-state octal buffers
(b) The three-state octal D flip-flops
(c) The three-state octal transceivers
(d) The three-state octal latches

5–29. Design a "missing pulse detector." It will be used to monitor the DAV input line in the 4096/4196 schematic. Assume that the DAV line is supposed to provide a 2-μS HIGH pulse every 100 μS. Monitor the DAV line with a 74123 monostable multivibrator. Have the 74123 output a HIGH to port 1, bit 7 (P1.7) of the 8031 microcontroller if a missing pulse is detected.

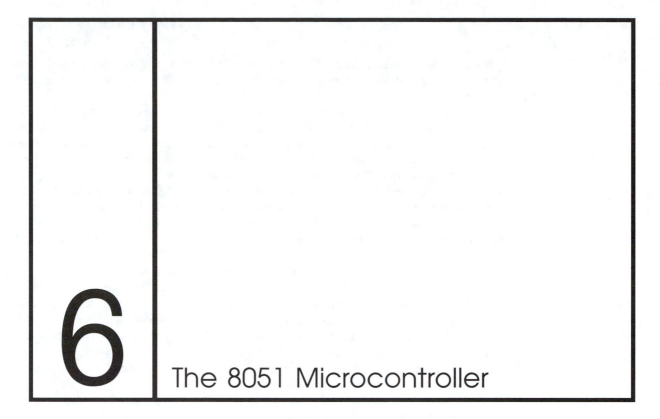

6

The 8051 Microcontroller

OBJECTIVES

Upon completion of this chapter you should be able to:

- Describe the advantages that a microcontroller has over a microprocessor for control applications.
- Describe the functional blocks within the 8051 microcontroller.
- Make comparisons between the different microcontrollers available within the 8051 family.
- Write the software instructions to read and write data to and from the I/O ports.
- Describe the use of the alternate functions on the I/O ports.
- Make the distinction between the internal and external data and code memory spaces.
- Use various addressing modes to access internal data memory and the Special Function Registers (SFRs).
- Interface an external EPROM and a RAM to the 8051.
- Use some of the more commonly used instructions of the 8051 instruction set.
- Write simple 8051 I/O programs.
- Use the bit operations of the 8051.
- Understand program solutions to applications such as a keyboard decoder and analog-to-digital converter.

INTRODUCTION

In the previous chapters you should have recognized several common components incorporated into most microprocessor-based system applications. These are the microprocessor, RAM, ROM (or EPROM), and parallel I/O ports. Intel Corporation has recognized this and over the years, since the introduction of the 8085A, has been developing a new line of microprocessors specifically designed for control applications. They are called *microcontrollers.*

The microcontroller has the CPU, RAM, ROM, timer/counter, and parallel and serial I/O ports fabricated into a single IC. It is often called "a computer on a chip." The CPU's instruction set is improved for control applications and offers bit-oriented data manipulation, branching, and I/O, as well as multiply and divide instructions.

The microcontroller is most efficiently used in systems that have a fixed program for a dedicated application. A microcontroller is used in a keyboard for a personal computer to scan and decode the keys. It is used in an automobile for sensing and controlling engine operation. Other dedicated applications such as a microwave oven, a video cassette recorder, a gas pump, and an automated teller machine use the microcontroller IC also.

The previous chapters have provided a good background for understanding the microcontroller. The theory behind microprocessor buses, external memory, and I/O ports is necessary to utilize the features available on a microcontroller. In this chapter we'll be introduced to one of the most widely used microcontrollers available today: the Intel 8051. You'll see several similarities between it and the 8085A-based systems previously discussed. You should appreciate the way that you were eased into microprocessor operational theory using the 8085A, but now you will see why the 8051 can be a much better solution to dedicated control applications.

Most control applications require extensive I/O and need to work with individual bits. The 8051 addresses both of these needs by having 32 I/O lines and a CPU instruction set that handles single-bit I/O, bit manipulation, and bit checking.

6–1 THE 8051 FAMILY OF MICROCONTROLLERS

The basic architectural structure of the 8051 is given in Figure 6–1. The block diagram gives us a good picture of the hardware included in the 8051 IC. For internal memory it has a 4K × 8 ROM and a 128 × 8 RAM. It has two 16-bit counter/timers and interrupt control for five interrupt sources. Serial I/O is provided by TXD and RXD (transmit and

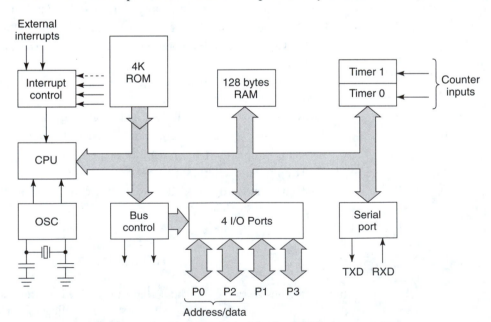

Figure 6–1 Block diagram of the Intel 8051 microcontroller.

receive), and it also has four 8-bit parallel I/O ports (P0, P1, P2, P3). There is also an 8052 series of microcontrollers available that has an 8K ROM, 256 RAM, and three counter/timers.

Other versions of the 8051 are the 8751, which has an internal EPROM for program storage in place of the ROM, and the 8031, which has *no* internal ROM, but instead accesses an external ROM or EPROM for program instructions. Table 6–1 summarizes a partial list of the 8051 family of microcontrollers. Notice that the 8052/8752/8032 series has an extra 4K of program space (except the 8032), double the RAM area, an extra timer/counter, and one additional interrupt source. All parts use the same CPU instruction set. The ROMless versions (8031 and 8032) are the least expensive parts but require an external ROM or EPROM like a 2732 or 2764 for program storage.

TABLE 6–1

The 8051 Family of Microcontrollers

Device number	Internal memory		Timers/ event counters	Interrupt sources
	Program	Data		
8051	4K × 8 ROM	128 × 8 RAM	2 × 16-bit	5
8751H	4K × 8 EPROM	128 × 8 RAM	2 × 16-bit	5
8031	None	128 × 8 RAM	2 × 16-bit	5
8052AH	8K × 8 ROM	256 × 8 RAM	3 × 16-bit	6
8752BH	8K × 8 EPROM	256 × 8 RAM	3 × 16-bit	6
8032AH	None	256 × 8 RAM	3 × 16-bit	6

6–2 8051 ARCHITECTURE

To squeeze so many functions on a single chip, the designers had to develop an architecture that uses the same internal address spaces and external pins for more than one function. This technique is similar to that used by the 8085A for the multiplexed AD_0–AD_7 lines.

The 8051 is a 40-pin IC. Thirty-two pins are needed for the four I/O ports. To provide for the other microcontroller control signals, most of those pins have alternate functions, which will be described in this section. Also in this section, we'll see how the 8051 handles the overlapping address spaces used by internal memory, external memory, and the special function registers.

The pin configuration for the 8051 is given in Figure 6–2.

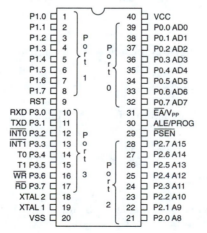

Figure 6–2 The 8051 pin configuration.

Port 0

Port 0 is dual purpose, serving as either an 8-bit bidirectional I/O port (P0.0–P0.7) or the low-order multiplexed address/data bus (AD_0–AD_7). As an I/O port, it can sink up to 8 LS TTL loads in the LOW condition and is a float for the HIGH condition ($I_{OL} = 3.2$ mA). The alternate port designations, AD_0–AD_7, are used to access external memory. They are activated automatically whenever reference is made to external memory. The AD lines are demultiplexed into A_0–A_7 and D_0–D_7 by using the ALE signal, the same way that it was done with the 8085A.

Port 1

Port 1 is an 8-bit bidirectional I/O port that can sink or source up to 4 LS TTL loads. ($I_{OL} = 1.6$ mA, $I_{OH} = -80$ μA.)

Port 2

Port 2 is dual purpose, serving as either an 8-bit bidirectional I/O port (P2.0–P2.7), or as the high-order address bus (A_8–A_{15}) for access to external memory. As an I/O port it can sink or source up to 4 LS TTL loads. The port becomes active as the high-order address bus whenever reference to external memory is made.

Port 3

Port 3 is dual purpose, serving as an 8-bit bidirectional I/O port that can sink or source up to 4 LS TTL loads or as special-purpose I/O to provide the functions listed in Table 6–2.

TABLE 6–2

Alternative Functions of Port 3

Port pin	Alternative function
P3.0	RXD (serial input port)
P3.1	TXD (serial output port)
P3.2	INT0 (external interrupt 0)
P3.3	INT1 (external interrupt 1)
P3.4	T0 (Timer 0 external input)
P3.5	T1 (Timer 1 external input)
P3.6	WR (external data memory write strobe)
P3.7	RD (external data memory read strobe)

RST

Reset input. A HIGH on this pin resets the microcontroller.

ALE/$\overline{PROG}$

Address Latch Enable output pulse for latching the low-order byte of the address during accesses to external memory. This pin is also the program pulse input ($\overline{PROG}$) during programming of the EPROM parts.

$\overline{PSEN}$

Program Store Enable is a read strobe for external program memory. It will be connected to the Output Enable ($\overline{OE}$) of an external ROM or EPROM.

EA/VPP

External Access ($\overline{EA}$) is tied LOW to enable the microcontroller to fetch its program code from an external memory IC. This pin also receives the 21-V programming supply voltage (VPP) for programming the EPROM parts.

XTAL1,XTAL2

Connections for a crystal or an external oscillator.

Address Spaces

The address spaces of the 8051 are divided into four distinct areas: internal data memory, external data memory, internal code memory, and external code memory (see Figure 6–3).

The 8051 allows for up to 64K of external data memory (RAM) and 64K of external code memory (ROM/EPROM). The only disadvantage of external memory, besides the additional circuitry, is that ports 0 and 2 get tied up for the address and data bus. The actual hardware interfacing for external memory will be given later in this chapter.

When the 8051 is first reset, the program counter starts at 0000H. This points to the first program instruction in the *internal code memory* unless $\overline{EA}$ (External Access) is tied LOW. If $\overline{EA}$ is tied LOW, the CPU issues a LOW on $\overline{PSEN}$ (Program Store Enable), enabling the *external code memory* ROM/EPROM instead. $\overline{EA}$ *must* be tied LOW if you are using the ROMless (8031) version.

With $\overline{EA}$ tied HIGH, the first 4K of program instruction fetches are made from the internal code memory. Any fetches from code memory above 4K (1000H to FFFFH) will automatically be made from the external code memory.

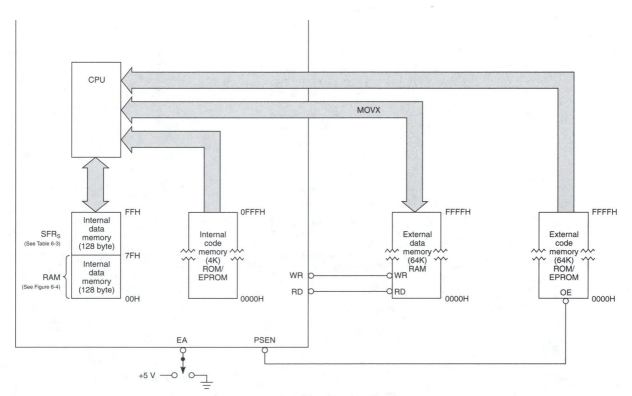

Figure 6–3 8051 address spaces.

If the application has a need for large amounts of data memory, then *external data memory* (RAM) can be used. I/O to external RAM can be made only by using one of the MOVX instructions. When executing a MOVX instruction, the 8051 knows that you are referring to external RAM and issues the appropriate $\overline{WR}$ or $\overline{RD}$ signal.

If 128 bytes (256 for the 8052) of RAM storage is enough, then the *internal data memory* is better to use because it has a much faster response time and a broad spectrum of instructions to access it. Figure 6–3 shows two blocks of internal data memory. The first is the 128-byte RAM at address 00H to 7FH. The second is made up of the Special Function Registers (SFRs) at addresses 80H to FFH. Notice that *all addresses are only 1 byte wide,* which allows for more efficient use of code space and faster access time. The use of the address space in the 128-byte RAM is detailed in Figure 6–4.

The first 32 locations are set aside for four banks of data registers, giving the programmer the use of 32 separate registers. The registers within each bank are labeled R0 through R7. The bank presently in use is defined by the setting of the two "bank select bits" in the PSW (Program Status Word).

RAM addresses 20H through 2FH are designated as bit-addressable memory locations. This meets the needs of control applications for a large number of ON/OFF bit flags, by providing 128 uniquely addressable bit locations.

The last 80 locations are set aside for general-purpose data storage and stack operations.

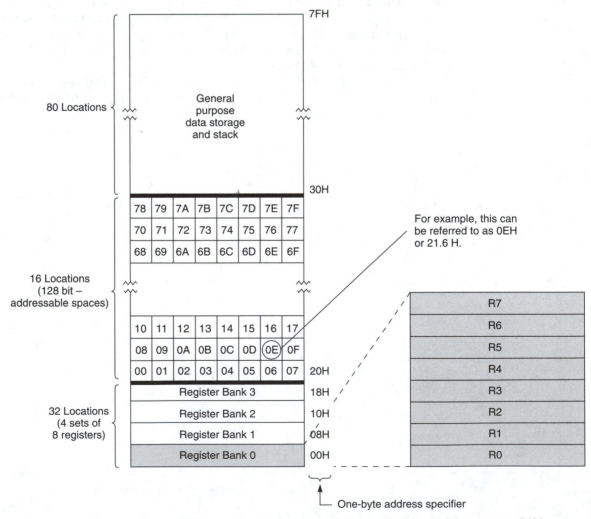

Figure 6–4   Address space in the 128-byte internal data memory RAM.

The Special Function Registers (SFRs) are maintained in the next 128 addresses in the internal data memory of the 8051 (address 80H to FFH). It contains registers required for software instruction execution as well as those used to service the special hardware features built into the 8051. Table 6–3 lists the SFRs and their addresses.

TABLE 6–3

The Special Function Registers (SFRs) [Internal Data Memory (80H to FFH)]

Register	Address	Function
P0	80H[a]	Port 0
SP	81H	Stack Pointer
DPL	82H	Data Pointer (Low)
DPH	83H	Data Pointer (High)
TCON	88H[a]	Timer register
TMOD	89H	Timer Mode register
TL0	8AH	Timer 0 Low byte
TL1	8BH	Timer 1 Low byte
TH0	8CH	Timer 0 High byte
TH1	8DH	Timer 1 High byte
P1	90H[a]	Port 1
SCON	98H[a]	Serial port Control register
SBUF	99H	Serial port data Buffer
P2	A0H[a]	Port 2
IE	A8H[a]	Interrupt Enable register
P3	B0H[a]	Port 3
IP	B8H[a]	Interrupt Priority register
PSW	D0H[a]	Program Status Word
ACC	E0H[a]	Accumulator (direct address)
B	F0H[a]	B register

[a]Bit-addressable register.

The address of an SFR is also only 1 byte wide. However, instead of specifying the 1-byte hex address, you also have the option of addressing any SFR location by simply specifying its register name, like P0 or SP. Several of the SFRs are bit addressable. For example, to address bit 3 of the accumulator, you would use the address E0H.3 (or you could use ACC.3). The PSW is also bit addressable, having the bit addresses listed in Table 6–4. For example, to address the parity bit in the PSW, you would use the address D0H.0 (or you could use PSW.0).

TABLE 6–4

The PSW Bit Addresses

Symbol	Address	Function
CY	D0H.7	Carry flag
AC	D0H.6	Auxiliary carry flag
F0	D0H.5	General-purpose flag
RS1	D0H.4	Register bank select (MSB)
RS0	D0H.3	Register bank select (LSB)
OV	D0H.2	Overflow flag
—	D0H.1	User-definable flag
P	D0H.0	Parity flag

6–3 INTERFACING TO EXTERNAL MEMORY

Up to 64K of code memory (ROM/EPROM) and 64K of data memory (RAM) can be added to any of the 8051 family members. If you are using the 8031 (ROMless) part, then you *have* to use external code memory for storing your program instructions. As mentioned earlier, the alternate function of port 2 is to provide the high-order address byte (A_8–A_{15}), and the alternate function of port 0 is to provide the multiplexed low-order address/data byte (AD_0–AD_7).

If you are interfacing to a general-purpose EPROM like the 2732, then the ALE signal provided by the 8031 is used to demultiplex the AD_0–AD_7 lines via an address latch, as shown in Figure 6–5. (Also see Appendix I for 8051 interfacing.)

As you can see, two of the I/O ports are used up to provide the address and data buses. The AD_0–AD_7 lines output on port 0 are demultiplexed by the ALE signal and the address latch, the same way as they were in the 8085A circuits studied earlier. The PSEN signal is asserted at the end of each instruction fetch cycle to enable the EPROM outputs to put the addressed code byte on the data bus to be read by port 0. The $\overline{EA}$ line is tied LOW so that the 8031 knows to fetch all program code from external memory.

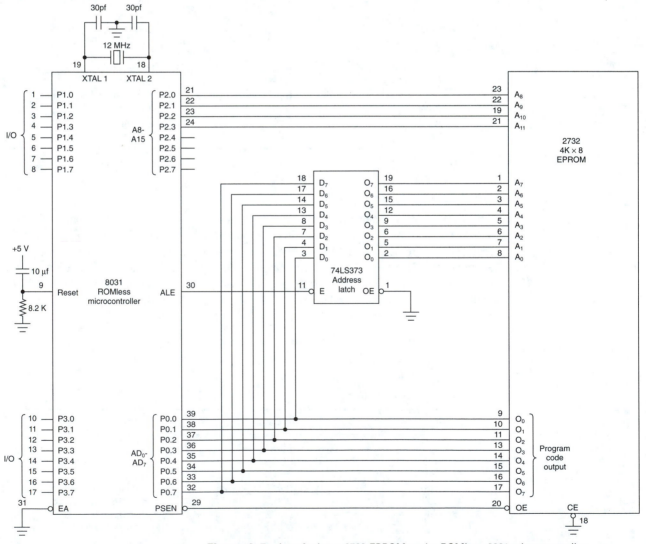

Figure 6–5   Interfacing a 2732 EPROM to the ROMless 8031 microcontroller.

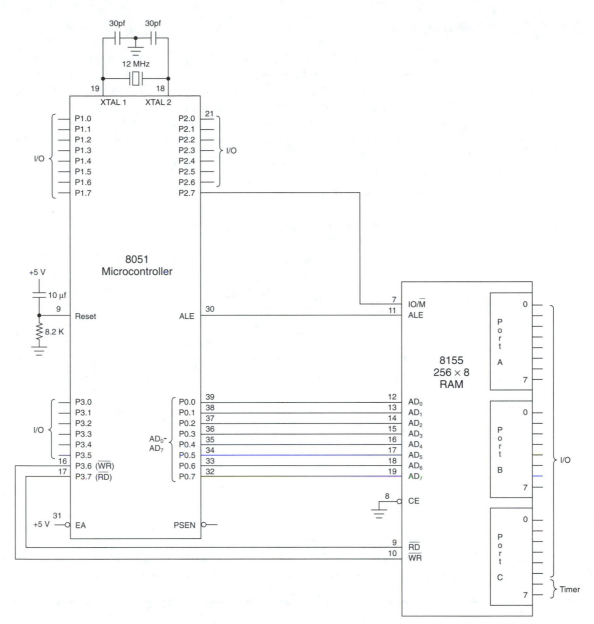

Figure 6–6   Interfacing an 8155 RAM/IO/Timer to the 8051 microcontroller.

If extra *data memory* is needed, then the interface circuit given in Figure 6–6 can be used. The 8155 RAM accepts the AD_0–AD_7 lines directly and uses the ALE signal to internally demultiplex, eliminating the need for an address latch IC. We have to use 11 of the 8051 pins to interface to the 8155, but the 8155 provides an additional 22 I/O lines, giving us a net gain of 11.

The addresses of the external RAM locations are 0000H to 00FFH, overlapping the addresses of the internal data memory. There is no conflict, however, because all I/O to the external data memory is made using the MOVX instruction. The MOVX instruction ignores internal memory and instead, activates the appropriate control signal, $\overline{RD}$ or $\overline{WR}$, via port 3. The LOW $\overline{RD}$ or $\overline{WR}$ signal allows the 8155 to send or receive data to or from port 0 of the 8051.

The I/O ports on the 8155 are accessed by making the $IO/\overline{M}$ line HIGH. This is done by using memory-mapped I/O and specifying an address whose bit A_{15} is HIGH (8000H or higher).

6–4 THE 8051 INSTRUCTION SET

All the members of the 8051 family use the same instruction set. (The complete instruction set is given in the 8051 Instruction Set Summary in Appendix F.) Several new instructions in the 8051 make it especially well suited for control applications. The discussion that follows assumes that you are using a commercial assembler software package like ASM51, available from Intel. Hand assembly of the 8051 instructions into executable machine code is very difficult and misses out on several of the very useful features available to the ASM51 programmer.

Addressing Modes

The instruction set provides several different ways to address data memory locations. We'll use the MOV instruction to illustrate several common addressing modes. For example, to move data into the accumulator, any of the following instructions could be used:

> *MOV A,Rn:* *Register addressing,* the contents of register *Rn* (where $n = 0 - 7$) is moved to the accumulator.
>
> *MOV A,@Ri:* *Indirect addressing,* the contents of memory whose address is in *Ri* (where $i = 0$ or 1) is moved to the accumulator. (*Note:* Only registers R_0 and R_1 can be used to hold addresses for the indirect-addressing instructions.)
>
> *MOV A,20H:* *Direct addressing,* move the contents of RAM location 20H to the accumulator. I/O ports can also be accessed as a direct address, as shown in the following instruction.
>
> *MOV A,P3:* *Direct addressing,* move the contents of port 3 to the accumulator. Direct addressing allows you to specify the address by giving its actual hex address (e.g., B0H) or by giving its abbreviated name (e.g., P3), which is listed in the SFR table (Table 6–3).
>
> *MOV A,#64H:* *Immediate constant,* move the number 64H into the accumulator.

In each of the previous instructions, the *destination* of the move was the accumulator. The destination in any of those instructions could also have been a register, a direct address location, or an indirect address location. You should already be realizing the extended flexibility that this instruction set has over the 8085A.

EXAMPLE 6–1

Write the 8051 instruction to perform each of the following operations.

(a) Move the contents of the accumulator to register 5.
(b) Move the contents of RAM memory location 42H to port 1.
(c) Move the value at port 2 to register 3.
(d) Send FFH to port 0.
(e) Send the contents of RAM memory, whose address is in register 1, to port 3.

Solution: (a) MOV R5,A
(b) MOV P1,42H
(c) MOV R3,P2
(d) MOV P0,#0FFH (Notice the addition of the leading 0 to FFH. This addition is made because the ASM51 assembler requires that the first position of any hexadecimal number be a numeric digit from 0 to 9.)
(e) MOV P3,@R1

Program Branching Instructions

8051 assembly language provides several different ways to branch (jump) to various program segments within the 64K of code memory area. Below are some of the most useful jump instructions.

JMP label (Unconditional jump):   Program control passes to location *label*. The JMP instruction is converted by the ASM51 assembler into an absolute jump, AJMP; a short jump, SJMP; or a long jump, LJMP, depending on the destination pointed to by *label*.

JZ label (Jump if accumulator zero):   Program control passes to location *label* if the accumulator equals zero.

JNZ label (Jump if accumulator not zero):   Program control passes to location *label* if the accumulator is not equal to zero.

JB bit,label (Jump if bit set):   Program control passes to location *label* if the specified bit, *bit,* is set.

JNB bit,label (Jump if bit not set):   Program control passes to location *label* if the specified bit, *bit,* is not set.

DJNZ Rn,label (Decrement register and jump if not zero):   Program control passes to location *label* if, after decrementing register *Rn*, the register is not equal to zero ($n = 0 - 7$).

CJNE Rn,#data,label (Compare immediate data to register and jump if not equal):   Program control passes to location *label* if register *Rn* is not equal to the immediate data *#data*. The compare can also be made to the accumulator by specifying *A* instead of *Rn*.

CALL label (Call subroutine):   Program control passes to location *label*. The return address is stored on the stack. The CALL instruction is converted by the ASM51 assembler into an absolute call, ACALL, or a long call, LCALL, depending on the destination pointed to by *label*.

RET (Return):   Program control is returned back to the instruction following the CALL instruction.

EXAMPLE 6–2

Write a program that continuously reads a byte from port 1 and writes it to port 0 until the byte read equals zero.

Solution:

```
READ:     MOV A,P1        ; A←P1
          MOV P0,A        ; P0←A
          JNZ READ        ; Repeat until A = 0
          NOP             ; Remainder of program
          etc.
```

EXAMPLE 6–3

Repeat Example 6–2, except stop the looping when the number 77H is read.

Solution:

```
READ:     MOV A,P1            ; A←P1
          MOV P0,A            ; P0←A
          CJNE A,#77H,READ    ; Repeat until A = 77H
          NOP                 ; Remainder of program
          etc.
```

EXAMPLE 6–4

Repeat Example 6–2, except stop the looping when bit 3 of port 2 is set.

Solution:

```
READ:     MOV A,P1         ; A←P1
          MOV P0,A         ; P0←A
          JNB P2.3,READ    ; Repeat until bit 3 of port 2 is set
          NOP              ; Remainder of program
          etc.             ;
```

EXAMPLE 6–5

Write a program that will produce an output at port 0 that counts down from 80H to 00H.

Solution:

```
          MOV R0,#80H      ; R0←80H
COUNT:    MOV P0,R0        ; P0←R0
          DJNZ R0,COUNT    ; Decrement R0, jump to COUNT if not 0
          NOP              ; Remainder of program
          etc.             ;
```

Logical and Bit Operations

The 8051 instruction set provides the basic logical operations (OR, AND, Ex-OR, and NOT), rotates (left or right, with or without carry), and bit operations (clear, set, and complement). The following list shows some of the most commonly used of those operations.

ANL A,Rn (AND register to accumulator):   Logically AND register *Rn,* bit by bit, with the accumulator and store the result in the accumulator.

ANL A,#data (AND data byte to accumulator):   Logically AND data byte *#data,* bit by bit, with the accumulator and store the result in the accumulator.

The descriptions of logical ORs and exclusive-ORs are similar to the AND, and use the following instructions:

ORL A,Rn (OR register to accumulator)
ORL A,#data (OR data byte to accumulator)
XRL A,Rn (Ex-OR register to accumulator)
XRL A,#data (Ex-OR data byte to accumulator)

The most commonly used instructions to operate on individual bits are as follows:

CLR bit (Clear bit):   Clear (reset to zero) the value of the bit located at address *bit.*
SETB bit (Set bit):   Set (set to one) the value of the bit located at address *bit.*
CPL bit (Complement bit):   Complement the value of the bit located at address *bit.*

The rotate commands available to the 8051 programmer are as follows:

RL A (Rotate accumulator left):   Rotate the 8 bits of the accumulator one position to the left.

RLC A (Rotate accumulator left through carry): Rotate the 9 bits of the accumulator including carry one position to the left.

RR A (Rotate accumulator right): Rotate the 8 bits of the accumulator one position to the right.

RRC A (Rotate accumulator right through carry): Rotate the 9 bits of the accumulator including carry one position to the right.

The following examples illustrate the use of the logical and bit operations.

EXAMPLE 6–6

Determine the contents of the accumulator after the execution of the following program segments.

(a) MOV A,#3CH ; A←0011 1100
MOV R4,#66H ; R4←0110 0110
ANL A,R4 ; A←A AND R4

Solution:

A = 0011 1100
R4 = 0110 0110
A AND R4 = 0010 0100 = 24H *Answer*

(b) MOV A,#3FH ; A←0011 1111
XRL A,#7CH ; A←A EX-OR 7CH

Solution:

A = 0011 1111
7CH = 0111 1100
A EX-OR 7CH = 0100 0011 = 43H *Answer*

(c) MOV A,#0A3H ; A←1010 0011
RR A ; Rotate right

Solution:

A = 1010 0011
Rotate right
A = 1101 0001 *Answer*

(d) MOV A,#0C3H ; A←1100 0011
RLC A ; Rotate left through carry

Solution:

Assume carry = 0 initially
A = 1100 0011
Rotate left through carry
A = 1000 0110, carry = 1 *Answer*

EXAMPLE 6–7

Use the SETB, CLR, and CPL instructions to do the following operations:

(a) Clear bit 7 of the accumulator.
(b) Output a 1 on bit 0 of port 3.
(c) Complement the parity flag (bit 0 of the PSW).

Solution:

(a) CLR ACC.7 (*Note:* According to Table 6–3, the symbol for the direct address of the accumulator is ACC.)

(b) SETB P3.0

(c) CPL PSW.0

EXAMPLE 6–8

Describe the activity at the output of port 0 during the execution of the following program segment:

```
                MOV R7,#0AH
                MOV P0,#00H
        LOOP:   CPL P0.7
                DJNZ R7,LOOP
```

Solution: Register 7 is used as a loop counter with the initial value of 10 (0AH). Each time that the complement instruction (CPL) is executed, bit 7 will toggle to its opposite state. Toggling bit 7 ten times will create a waveform with five positive pulses.

Arithmetic Operations

The 8051 is capable of all the basic arithmetic functions: addition, subtraction, incrementing, decrementing, multiplication, and division. The following list outlines the most commonly used forms of the arithmetic instructions.

ADD A,Rn (Add register to accumulator):   Add the contents of register *Rn* (where $n = 0 - 7$) to the accumulator and place the result in the accumulator.

ADD A,#data (Add immediate data to accumulator):   Add the value of *#data* to the accumulator and place the result in the accumulator.

SUBB A,Rn (Subtract register from accumulator with borrow):   Subtract the contents of register *Rn* and borrow (carry flag) from the accumulator and place the result in the accumulator.

SUBB A,#data (Subtract immediate data from accumulator with borrow):   Subtract the value of *#data* and borrow (carry flag) from the accumulator and place the result in the accumulator.

INC A (Increment accumulator)

INC Rn (Increment register)

DEC A (Decrement accumulator)

DEC Rn (Decrement register)

MUL AB (Multiply A times B):   Multiply the value in the accumulator times the value in the *B* register. The low-order byte of the 16-bit product is left in the accumulator and the high-order byte is placed in register *B*.

DIV AB (Divide A by B):   Divide the value in the accumulator by the value in the *B* register. The accumulator receives the quotient and register *B* receives the remainder.

DA A (Decimal adjust accumulator):   Adjust the value in the accumulator, resulting from an addition, into two BCD digits.

The following examples illustrate the use of arithmetic instructions.

EXAMPLE 6–9

Add the value being input at port 1 to the value at port 2 and send the result to port 3.

Solution:

```
MOV R0,P1      ; R0←P1
MOV A,P2       ; A←P2
ADD A,R0       ; A←A + R0
MOV P3,A       ; P3←A
```

EXAMPLE 6–10

Multiply the value being input at port 0 times the value at port 1 and send the result to ports 3 and 2 (high order, low order).

Solution:

```
MOV A,P0       ; A←P0
MOV B,P1       ; B←P1
MUL AB         ; A × B
MOV P2,A       ; P2←A (low order)
MOV P3,B       ; P3←B (high order)
```

6–5 8051 APPLICATIONS[1]

Having bit-handling instructions and built-in I/O makes the 8051 a good choice for data acquisition and control applications. In this section we'll look at a few applications that illustrate how we can utilize these new features to simplify our program solutions.

Instruction Timing

The 8051 circuitry that we looked at earlier was driven with a 12-MHz crystal. The 12 MHz is a convenient choice because each instruction machine cycle takes 12 clock periods to complete. This means that one machine cycle takes 1 μs. All 8051 instructions are completed in one or two machine cycles (12 or 24 oscillator periods), except MUL and DIV, which take four. The oscillator periods for each instruction are given in the 8051 Instruction Set Summary in Appendix F. For example, the MOV A,Rn instruction requires 12 oscillator periods to complete, which will take 1 μs [12 × (1/12 MHz)].

Time Delay

Knowing the time duration of each instruction, we can write accurate time delays for our applications programs. Writing counter/loop programs is much easier now, with the introduction of the DJNZ and the CJNE instructions. Table 6–5 and Figure 6–7 show a time-delay program that we could call as a subroutine from an applications program.

TABLE 6–5

Time-Delay Subroutine

DELAY:	MOV R1,#0F3H	; Outer-loop counter (F3H = 243)
	MOV R0,#00H	; Inner-loop counter
LOOP:	DJNZ R0,LOOP	; Loop 256 times
	DJNZ R1,LOOP	; Loop 243 times
	RET	; Return

[1]See Appendix I for additional 8051 applications.

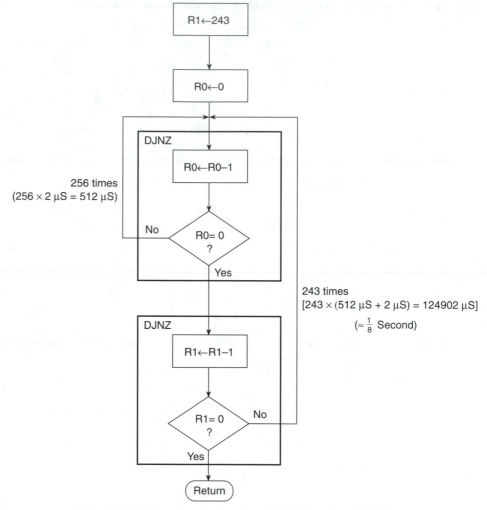

Figure 6–7   Flowchart for the time-delay subroutine of Table 6–5.

The DJNZ instruction takes 24 oscillator periods, or 2 μs. By initializing register 0 at 00H, the first time DJNZ R0,LOOP is executed, R0 will become FFH. The program will loop within that same instruction 255 more times until R0 equals 0. At that point, control drops down to the next DJNZ, which functions as an outer loop, as shown in the flowchart.

The R0 (inner) loop will take 512 μs to complete. The R1 (outer) loop executes the inner loop 243 times for a total time delay of approximately one-eighth second. A third loop, using R2, can be added to increase the time by another factor of 256.

EXAMPLE 6–11

Assume that there are input switches connected to port 0 and output LEDs connected to port 1 of an 8051. Write a program that will flash the LEDs ON one second, OFF one second, the number of times indicated on the input switches.

Solution:

Label	Instruction	Comments
READ:	MOV A,P0	; Keep reading port 0 switches
	JZ READ	; into A until A ≠ 0
	MOV R0,A	; Transfer A to register 0

Solution (continued)

Label	Instruction	Comments
ON:	MOV P1,#0FFH	; Turn ON port 1 LEDs
	CALL DELAY	; Delay 1 second
OFF:	MOV P1,#00H	; Turn OFF port 1 LEDs
	CALL DELAY	; Delay 1 second
	DJNZ R0,ON	; Loop back number of times on switches
STOP:	JMP STOP	; Suspend operation
		;
		; Delay 1 second subroutine
DELAY:	MOV R7,#08H	; Outer loop counter
	MOV R5,#00H	; Inner loop counter
LOOP2:	MOV R6,#0F3H	; Middle loop counter
LOOP1:	DJNZ R5,LOOP1	; LOOP1 delays for
	DJNZ R6,LOOP1	; one-eighth second
	DJNZ R7,LOOP2	; LOOP2 executes LOOP1 eight times
	RET	; Return

EXAMPLE 6–12

Write a program that will decode the hexadecimal keyboard shown in Figure 6–8.

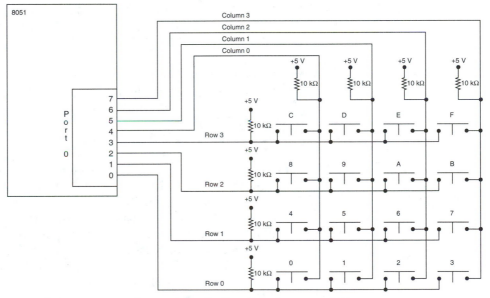

Figure 6–8 Keyboard interface to an 8051.

Solution:

Label	Instruction	Comments
KEYSCAN:	CALL ROWRD	; Determine row of key pressed
	CALL COLRD	; Determine column of key pressed
	CALL CONVRT	; Convert row/column to key value
STOP:	JMP STOP	; Suspend operation
		;
ROWRD:	MOV P0,#0FH	; Output 0s to all columns
	MOV R0,#00H	; Row = 0
	JNB P0.0,RET1	; Return if row 0 is LOW
	MOV R0,#01H	; Row = 1
	JNB P0.1,RET1	; Return if row 1 is LOW
	MOV R0,#02H	; Row = 2

Solution (continued)

Label	Instruction	Comments
	JNB P0.2,RET1	; Return if row 2 is LOW
	MOV R0,#03H	; Row = 3
	JNB P0.3,RET1	; Return if row 3 is LOW
	JMP ROWRD	; Else keep reading
RET1:	RET	; Return
		;
COLRD:	MOV P0,#0F0H	; Output 0s to all rows
	MOV R1,#00H	; Column = 0
	JNB P0.4,RET2	; Return if column 0 is LOW
	MOV R1,#01H	; Column = 1
	JNB P0.5,RET2	; Return if column 1 is LOW
	MOV R1,#02H	; Column = 2
	JNB P0.6,RET2	; Return if column 2 is LOW
	MOV R1,#03H	; Column = 3
	JNB P0.7,RET2	; Return if column 3 is LOW
	JMP COLRD	; Else keep reading
RET2:	RET	; Return
		;
CONVRT:	MOV B,#04H	; B = Multiplication factor
	MOV A,R0	; Move row number to A
	MUL AB	; A = row × 4
	ADD A,R1	; A = row × 4 + column
	RET	; A now contains value of key pressed

Explanation: The keyboard is wired as a 4 × 4 row–column matrix. The low-order nibble of port 0 is connected to the rows, and the high order is connected to the columns. The rows *and* columns are held HIGH with the 10-kΩ pull-up resistors. Since the I/O ports of the 8051 can be both read *and* written to (bidirectional), we can use a different technique to scan a keyboard than we used with the 8085A. To determine the row of a depressed key, we drive all of the columns LOW and all of the rows HIGH by executing the instruction MOV P0,#0FH. The HIGH on the rows is actually a *float* state, allowing the rows to be read. The next series of instructions in the ROWRD subroutine read each row to determine the row number that is LOW, if any. If, for example, key 5 is depressed, then row 1 will be LOW and the other three rows will be HIGH.

Now that we know the row, we must next determine the column. The instruction MOV P0,#0F0H will drive the rows LOW and float the columns. If the number 5 key is still depressed, column 1 will be LOW.

The last subroutine converts the row–column combination to the numeric value of the key pressed. Rows 0, 1, 2, and 3 have weighting factors of 0, 4, 8, and 12, respectively, and columns 0, 1, 2, and 3 have weighting factors of 0, 1, 2, and 3, respectively. Knowing that, the CONVRT subroutine uses the following formula to determine the numeric value of the key pressed:

$$\text{Key pressed} = \text{row} \times 4 + \text{column}$$

EXAMPLE 6–13

Figure 6–9 shows how an ADC0801 is interfaced to an 8051. Write a program that takes care of the handshaking requirements for $\overline{SC}$ and $\overline{EOC}$ to complete an analog-to-digital conversion.

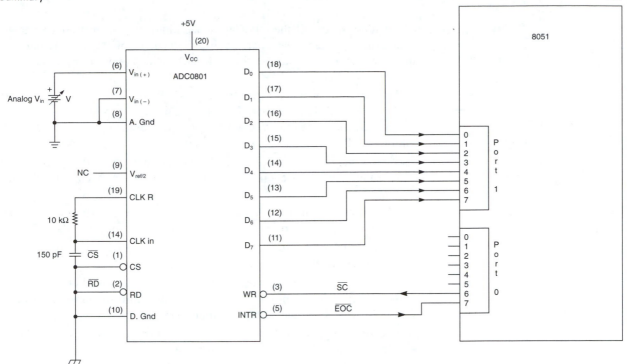

Figure 6–9 Interfacing an analog-to-digital converter to an 8051.

Solution:

Label	Instruction	Comments
FLOAT:	MOV P1,#0FFH	; Write 1s to port 1
	MOV P0,#0FFH	; Write 1s to port 0
SC:	CLR P0.6	; Output LOW-then-HIGH
	SETB P0.6	; on $\overline{SC}$
WAIT:	JB P0.7,WAIT	; Wait here until $\overline{EOC}$ goes LOW
DONE:	MOV R0,P1	; Transfer ADC result to register 0

Explanation: The I/O ports are in the float condition after the initial reset of the 8051. They must be floating to be used as inputs. The first two instructions in this program write 1's to ports 1 and 0, which make them float just in case they had 0's in them from a previous step in the program. To start the conversion process, bit 6 of port 0 ($\overline{SC}$) is pulsed LOW then HIGH using the clear (CLR) and set bit (SETB) instructions. The jump-if-bit-set instruction (JB) then monitors bit 7 of port 0 ($\overline{EOC}$) and remains in a WAIT loop until it goes LOW. Finally, at the end of conversion, port 1 is read into register 0, which is used to hold the ADC result.

SUMMARY

In this chapter we have learned that

1. The 8051 microcontroller is different from a microprocessor because it has the CPU, ROM, RAM, timer/counter and parallel and serial ports fabricated into a single IC.

2. Thirty-two of the forty pins of the 8051 are used for the four 8-bit parallel I/O ports. Three of the ports share their function with the address, data, and control buses.

3. The address spaces of the 8051 are divided into four distinct areas: internal data memory, external data memory, internal code memory, and external code memory. The internal data memory is further divided into user RAM and Special Function Registers (SFRs).

4. To interface to an external EPROM like the 2732, an octal D-latch is required to demultiplex the address/data bus that is shared with port 0. The External Access ($\overline{EA}$) pin is tied LOW and the ($\overline{PSEN}$) output is used to enable the output of the EPROM.

5. Extra data memory and I/O ports can be interfaced by using the 8155 IC. The 8155 demultiplexes the address/data bus internally so an octal D-latch is not required.

6. The MOV instruction is very powerful. It provides the ability to move data almost anywhere internal or external to the microcontroller and to the I/O ports.

7. Program branching is accomplished by use of many different conditional and unconditional jumps and calls.

8. The 8051 instruction set provides the ability to work with individual bits, which makes it very efficient for on/off control operations. Instructions are available for all the logic functions, rotates, and bit manipulations.

9. Instructions are provided for all of the basic arithmetic instructions: addition, subtraction, multiplication, division, incrementing, and decrementing.

10. Each instruction machine cycle takes 12 clock periods to complete. This means that if a 12MHz crystal is used, each machine cycle takes 1 microsecond to complete. One complete instruction takes 1, 2, or 4 machine cycles.

11. A 4 × 4 matrix keyboard can be scanned using bit operations on a single I/O port.

12. Interfacing an 8-bit analog-to-digital converter to an 8051 is accomplished with one port and two bits on a second port. The *start-conversion* LOW pulse is issued with bit-setting instructions, and the *end-of-conversion* signal is monitored with bit-checking instructions.

GLOSSARY

Assembler: A software package used to convert assembly language programs into executable machine code.

Bidirectional: An I/O port that can be used for both input and output.

Bit addressable: Memory spaces in the internal RAM and SFR area that allow for the addressing of individual bits.

External Access ($\overline{EA}$): An active-LOW input that when forced LOW, tells the processor that all program memory is external.

Microcontroller: A computer on a chip. It contains a CPU, ROM, RAM, counter/timers, and I/O ports. It is especially well suited for control applications.

Program Store Enable ($\overline{PSEN}$): An active-LOW output control signal issued by the microcontroller as the read strobe for external program memory.

Register bank: A group of eight registers. The 8051 has four sets of banks that are selected by writing to the two bank-select bits in the PSW.

Special Function Register (SFR): A data register that has a dedicated space within the microcontroller. It is used to maintain the data required for microcontroller operations.

PROBLEMS

6–1. Why is a microcontroller sometimes referred to as a "computer on a chip"?

6–2. Describe the differences among the 8031, 8051, and 8751.

6–3. What additional features does the 8052 have over the 8051?

6–4. Port 2 is dual purpose. One purpose is as a bidirectional I/O port. What is its other purpose?

6–5. If you are using the internal ROM in the 8051 for your program code memory, then $\overline{EA}$ should be tied HIGH or LOW?

6–6. What is the maximum size EPROM and RAM that can be interfaced to the 8051?

6–7. What is the address range of the Special Function Registers (SFRs)?

6–8. What are the SFR addresses of the four I/O ports?

6–9. The 8051 has four register banks with eight registers in each bank. How does the CPU know which bank is currently in use?

6–10. Why is there a need for the 74LS373 address latch when interfacing the 2732 EPROM in Figure 6–5 but not when interfacing the 8155 RAM in Figure 6–6?

6–11. Determine the value of the accumulator after the execution of instructions A:, B:, C:, and D:

```
            MOV 40H,#88H
            MOV R0,#40H
     A:     MOV A,R0        ; A = _____
     B:     MOV A,@R0       ; A = _____
     C:     MOV A,40H       ; A = _____
     D:     MOV A,#40H      ; A = _____
```

6–12. Repeat Problem 6–11 for the following instructions:

```
            MOV 50H,#33H
            MOV 40H,#22H
            MOV R0,#30H
            MOV 30H,50H
            MOV R1,#40H
     A:     MOV A,40H       ; A = _____
     B:     MOV A,@R0       ; A = _____
     C:     MOV A,R1        ; A = _____
     D:     MOV A,30H       ; A = _____
```

6–13. Write the instructions to perform each of the following operations:
(a) Output a C7H to port 3.
(b) Load port 1 into register 7.
(c) Load the accumulator with the number 55H.
(d) Send the contents of RAM memory, whose address is in register 0, to the accumulator.
(e) Output the contents of register 1 to port 0.

6–14. Write a program that continuously reads port 0 until the byte read equals A7H. At that time, turn on the output LEDs connected at port 1.

6–15. Write a program that will produce an output at port 1 that counts up from 20H to 90H repeatedly.

6–16. Determine the value of the accumulator after the execution of instructions A:, B:, and C:

```
            MOV A,#00H
            MOV R0,#36H
     A:     XRL A,R0        ; A = _____
     B:     ORL A,#71H      ; A = _____
     C:     ANL A,#0F6H     ; A = _____
```

6–17. Repeat Problem 6–16 for the following program:

```
         MOV A,#77H
    A:   CLR ACC.1     ; A = _____
    B:   SETB ACC.7    ; A = _____
    C:   RL A          ; A = _____
```

6–18. Modify one instruction in Example 6–8 so that it will output eight pulses at port 0 instead of five.

6–19. Write a program that adds 05H to the number read at port 0 and outputs the result to port 1.

6–20. What is the length of time of the following time-delay subroutine? (Assume that a 12-MHz crystal is used.)

```
    DELAY:   MOV R1,#00H
             MOV R0,#00H
    LOOP:    DJNZ R0,LOOP
             DJNZ R1,LOOP
             RET
```

SCHEMATIC INTERPRETATION PROBLEMS

6–21. Find Port 2 (P2.7–P2.0) of U8 in the 4096/4196 schematic. This port outputs the high-order address bits for the system (A_8–A_{15}). On a separate piece of paper, draw a binary comparator that compares the four bits A_8–A_{11} to the four bits A_{12}–A_{15}. The HIGH output for an equal comparison is to be input to P3.4 (pin 14).

6–22. Locate the microcontroller in the 4096/4196 schematic.
   (a) What is its grid location and part number?
   (b) Its low-order address is multiplexed like the 68HC11 in problem 3–37. What IC and control signal is used to demultiplex the address/data bus (AD_0–AD_7) into the low-order address bus (A_0–A_7)?
   (c) What IC and control signal is used to demultiplex the address/data bus (AD_0–AD_7) into the data bus (D_0–D_7)?

A

Bibliography

ABT Advanced BiCMOS Logic Databook. Sunnyvale, Calif.: Philips Semiconductors, 1994.

Analog Data Manual. Sunnyvale, Calif.: Philips Semiconductors, 1987.

CMOS Databook. Santa Clara, Calif.: National Semiconductor Corporation, 1987.

CMOS HE4000B I.C. Family. Sunnyvale, Calif.: Signetics Corporation, 1990.

Component Data Catalog. Santa Clara, Calif.: Intel Corporation, 1981.

Data Conversion/Acquisition Databook. Santa Clara, Calif.: National Semiconductor Corporation, 1993.

Embedded Controller Handbook. Santa Clara, Calif.: Intel Corporation, 1988.

FAST Logic Databook. Sunnyvale, Calif.: Philips Semiconductors, 1994.

High-Speed CMOS Data Manual. Sunnyvale Calif.: Philips Semiconductors, 1990.

High-Speed CMOS Logic Data Book. Dallas, Tex.: Texas Instruments, Inc., 1984.

Linear Databook. Santa Clara, Calif.: National Semiconductor Corporation, 1988.

Linear LSI Data and Applications Manual. Sunnyvale, Calif.: Philips Semiconductors, 1987.

Low-Voltage Logic. Sunnyvale, Calif.: Philips Semiconductors, 1994.

Low-Voltage Logic. Dallas, Tex.: Texas Instruments, Inc., 1993.

MCS-80/85 Family User's Manual. Santa Clara, Calif.: Intel Corporation, 1983.

Memory Data. Phoenix, Ariz.: Motorola, Inc., 1988.

Memory Databook. Santa Clara, Calif.: National Semiconductor Corporation, 1993.

Memory Data Manual. Sunnyvale, Calif.: Philips Semiconductors, 1994.

PALASM User's Manual. Sunnyvale, Calif.: Advanced Micro Devices, Inc., 1990.

Programmable Logic Devices. Sunnyvale, Calif.: Philips Semiconductors, 1993.

TTL Data Manual. Sunnyvale, Calif.: Philips Semiconductors, 1990.

TTL Logic Data Book. Dallas, Tex.: Texas Instruments, Inc., 1988.

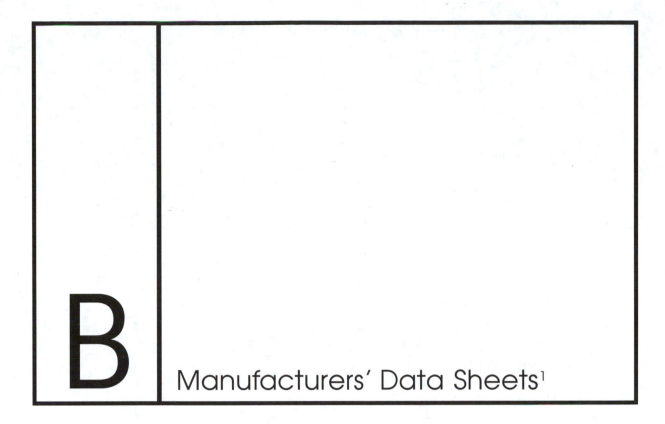

B

Manufacturers' Data Sheets[1]

IC NUMBERS:

7400
ADC0801
MC1508/1408
μA741
2732
74244
74373
74374

[1]Courtesy of Philips Components—Signetics and Intel Corporation.

Quad Two-Input NAND Gate

TYPE	TYPICAL PROPAGATION DELAY	TYPICAL SUPPLY CURRENT (Total)
7400	9ns	8mA
74LS00	9.5ns	1.6mA
74S00	3ns	15mA

ORDERING CODE

PACKAGES	COMMERCIAL RANGES $V_{CC}=5V \pm 5\%$; $T_A=0°C$ to $+70°C$	MILITARY RANGES $V_{CC}=5V \pm 10\%$; $T_A=-55°C$ to $+125°C$
Plastic DIP	N7400N • N74LS00N N74S00N	
Plastic SO	N74LS00D N74S00D	
Ceramic DIP	S5400F • S54S00F	
Flatpack	S5400W • S54LS00W	S54S00W
LLCC		S54LS00G

INPUT AND OUTPUT LOADING AND FAN-OUT TABLE

PINS	DESCRIPTION	54/74	54/74S	54/74LS
A, B	Inputs	1ul	1Sul	1LSul
Y	Output	10ul	10Sul	10LSul

NOTE
Where a 54/74 unit load (ul) is understood to be 40μA I_{IH} and −1.6mA I_{IL}, a 54/74S unit load (Sul) is 50μA I_{IH} and −2.0mA I_{IL}, and 54/74LS unit load (LSul) is 20μA I_{IH} and −0.4mA I_{IL}.

FUNCTION TABLE

INPUTS		OUTPUT
A	B	Y
L	L	H
L	H	H
H	L	H
H	H	L

H = HIGH voltage level
L = LOW voltage level

LOGIC SYMBOL

LOGIC SYMBOL (IEEE/IEC)

PIN CONFIGURATION

DC ELECTRICAL CHARACTERISTICS (Over recommended operating free-air temperature range unless otherwise noted)

PARAMETER		TEST CONDITIONS		54/7400 Min	54/7400 Typ[2]	54/7400 Max	54/74LS00 Min	54/74LS00 Typ[2]	54/74LS00 Max	54/74S00 Min	54/74S00 Typ[2]	54/74S00 Max	UNIT
V_{OH} HIGH-level output voltage	Mil	$V_{CC}=MIN$, $V_{IH}=MIN$, $V_{IL}=MAX$, $I_{OH}=MAX$		2.4	3.4		2.5	3.4		2.5	3.4		V
	Com'l			2.4	3.4		2.7	3.4		2.7	3.4		V
V_{OL} LOW-level output voltage	Mil	$V_{CC}=MIN$, $V_{IH}=MIN$, $I_{OL}=MAX$			0.2	0.4		0.25	0.4			0.5[4]	V
	Com'l				0.2	0.4		0.35	0.5			0.5	V
	74LS	$I_{OL}=4mA$						0.25	0.4				V
V_{IK} Input clamp voltage		$V_{CC}=MIN$, $I_I=I_{IK}$				−1.5			−1.5			−1.2	V
I_I Input current at maximum input voltage		$V_{CC}=MAX$, $V_I=5.5V$				1.0						1.0	mA
		$V_I=7.0V$							0.1				mA
I_{IH} HIGH-level input current		$V_{CC}=MAX$, $V_I=2.4V$				40			20				µA
		$V_I=2.7V$										50	µA
I_{IL} LOW-level input current		$V_{CC}=MAX$, $V_I=0.4V$				−1.6			−0.4				mA
		$V_I=0.5V$										−2.0	mA
I_{OS} Short-circuit output current[3]	Mil	$V_{CC}=MAX$		−20		−55	−20		−100	−40		−100	mA
	Com'l			−18		−55	−20		−100	−40		−100	mA
I_{CC} Supply current (total)		$V_{CC}=MAX$	I_{CCH} Outputs HIGH		4	8		0.8	1.6		10	16	mA
			I_{CCL} Outputs LOW		12	22		2.4	4.4		20	36	mA

NOTES
1. For conditions shown as MIN or MAX, use the appropriate value specified under recommended operating conditions for the applicable type
2. All typical values are at $V_{CC}=5V$, $T_A=25°C$
3. I_{OS} is tested with $V_{OUT}=+0.5V$ and $V_{CC}=V_{CC}$ MAX +0.5V. Not more than one output should be shorted at a time and duration of the short circuit should not exceed one second
4. $V_{OL}=+0.45V$ MAX for 54S at $T_A=+125°C$ only

AC WAVEFORM

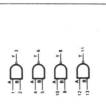

WAVEFORM FOR INVERTING OUTPUTS

$V_M=1.3V$ for 54LS/74LS, $V_M=1.5V$ for all other TTL families

Waveform 1

AC CHARACTERISTICS $T_A=25°C$, $V_{CC}=5.0V$

PARAMETER	TEST CONDITIONS	54/74 $C_L=15pF$, $R_L=400\Omega$ Min	54/74 Max	54/74LS $C_L=15pF$, $R_L=2k\Omega$ Min	54/74LS Max	54/74S $C_L=15pF$, $R_L=280\Omega$ Min	54/74S Max	UNIT
t_{PLH} t_{PHL} Propagation delay	Waveform 1		22		15		4.5	ns
			15		15		5.0	

GATES
54/7400, LS00, S00

ABSOLUTE MAXIMUM RATINGS (Over operating free-air temperature range unless otherwise noted.)

	PARAMETER	54	54LS	54S	74	74LS	74S	UNIT
V_{CC}	Supply voltage	7.0	7.0	7.0	7.0	7.0	7.0	V
V_{IN}	Input voltage	− 0.5 to + 5.5	− 0.5 to + 7.0	− 0.5 to + 5.5	− 0.5 to + 5.5	− 0.5 to + 7.0	− 0.5 to + 5.5	V
I_{IN}	Input current	− 30 to + 5	− 30 to + 1	− 30 to + 5	− 30 to + 5	− 30 to + 1	− 30 to + 5	mA
V_{OUT}	Voltage applied to output in HIGH output state	− 0.5 to + V_{CC}	− 0.5 to + V_{CC}	− 0.5 to + V_{CC}	− 0.5 to + V_{CC}	− 0.5 to + V_{CC}	− 0.5 to + V_{CC}	V
T_A	Operating free-air temperature range	− 55 to + 125			0 to 70			°C

RECOMMENDED OPERATING CONDITIONS

	PARAMETER		54/74 Min	54/74 Nom	54/74 Max	54/74LS Min	54/74LS Nom	54/74LS Max	54/74S Min	54/74S Nom	54/74S Max	UNIT
V_{CC}	Supply voltage	Mil	4.5	5.0	5.5	4.5	5.0	5.5	4.5	5.0	5.5	V
		Com'l	4.75	5.0	5.25	4.75	5.0	5.25	4.75	5.0	5.25	V
V_{IH}	HIGH-level input voltage		2.0			2.0			2.0			V
V_{IL}	LOW-level input voltage	Mil			+ 0.8			+ 0.7			+ 0.8	V
		Com'l			+ 0.8			+ 0.8			+ 0.8	V
I_{IK}	Input clamp current				− 12			− 18			− 18	mA
I_{OH}	HIGH-level output current				− 400			− 400			− 1000	μA
I_{OL}	LOW-level output current	Mil			16			4			20	mA
		Com'l			16			8			20	mA
T_A	Operating free-air temperature	Mil	− 55		+ 125	− 55		+ 125	− 55		+ 125	°C
		Com'l	0		70	0		70	0		70	°C

NOTE
V_{IL} = + 0.7V MAX for 54S at T_A = + 125°C only

TEST CIRCUITS AND WAVEFORMS

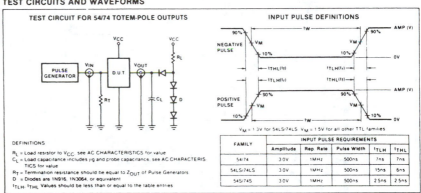

TEST CIRCUIT FOR 54/74 TOTEM-POLE OUTPUTS

INPUT PULSE DEFINITIONS

V_M = 1.3V for 54LS/74LS V_M = 1.5V for all other TTL families

DEFINITIONS

R_L = Load resistor to V_{CC}, see AC CHARACTERISTICS for value
C_L = Load capacitance includes jig and probe capacitance, see AC CHARACTERISTICS for value
R_T = Termination resistance should be equal to Z_{OUT} of Pulse Generators
D = Diodes are 1N916, 1N3064, or equivalent
t_{TLH}, t_{THL} Values should be less than or equal to the table entries

FAMILY	INPUT PULSE REQUIREMENTS				
	Amplitude	Rep. Rate	Pulse Width	t_{TLH}	t_{THL}
54/74	3.0V	1MHz	500ns	7ns	7ns
54LS/74LS	3.0V	1MHz	500ns	15ns	6ns
54S/74S	3.0V	1MHz	500ns	2.5ns	2.5ns

CMOS 8-BIT A/D CONVERTERS

Preliminary

DESCRIPTION

The ADC0801 family is a series of five CMOS 8-bit successive approximation A/D converters using a resistive ladder and capacitive array together with an auto-zero comparator. These converters are designed to operate with microprocessor controlled buses using a minimum of external circuitry. The three-state output data lines can be connected directly to the data bus.

The differential analog voltage input allows for increased common-mode rejection and provides a means to adjust the zero scale offset. Additionally, the voltage reference input provides a means of encoding small analog voltages to the full 8 bits of resolution.

FEATURES

- Compatible with most microprocessors
- Differential inputs
- Three-state outputs
- Logic levels TTL and MOS compatible
- Can be used with internal or external clock
- Analog input range 0V to V_{CC}
- Single 5V supply
- Guaranteed specification with 1MHz clock

APPLICATIONS

- Transducer to microprocessor interface
- Digital thermometer
- Digitally-controlled thermostat
- Microprocessor-based monitoring and control systems

PIN CONFIGURATION

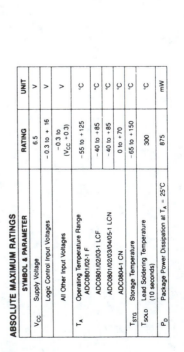

F,N PACKAGE

CS [1]		[20] V_{CC}
RD [2]		[19] CLK R
WR [3]		[18] D0
CLK IN [4]		[17] D1
INTR [5]		[16] D2
$V_{IN}(+)$ [6]		[15] D3
$V_{IN}(-)$ [7]		[14] D4
A GND [8]		[13] D5
V_{ref}/2 [9]		[12] D6
D GND [10]		[11] D7

TOP VIEW

ORDER NUMBERS
ADC0801/02-1 F
ADC0801/02/03-1 LCF
ADC081/02/03/04/05-1 LCN
ADC0804-1 CN

ABSOLUTE MAXIMUM RATINGS

SYMBOL & PARAMETER		RATING	UNIT
V_{CC}	Supply Voltage	6.5	V
	Logic Control Input Voltages	-0.3 to $+16$	V
	All Other Input Voltages	-0.3 to $(V_{CC}+0.3)$	V
T_A	Operating Temperature Range		
	ADC0801/02-1 F	-55 to $+125$	°C
	ADC0801/02/03-1 LCF	-40 to $+85$	°C
	ADC0801/02/03/04/05-1 LCN	-40 to $+85$	°C
	ADC0804-1 CN	0 to $+70$	°C
T_{STG}	Storage Temperature	-65 to $+150$	°C
T_{SOLD}	Lead Soldering Temperature (10 seconds)	300	°C
P_D	Package Power Dissipation at $T_A = 25$°C	875	mW

Preliminary

BLOCK DIAGRAMS

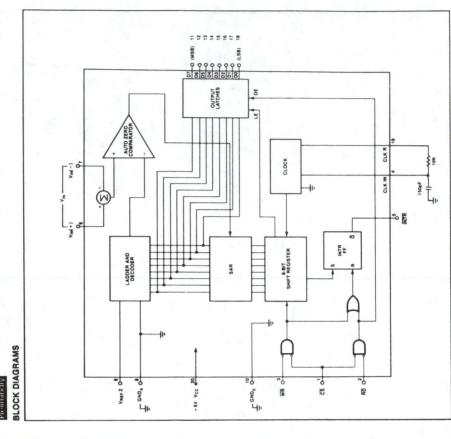

AC ELECTRICAL CHARACTERISTICS

Preliminary

SYMBOL & PARAMETER	TO	FROM	TEST CONDITIONS	ADC0801/2/3/4/5			UNIT
				Min	Typ	Max	
Conversion Time			f_{CLK} = 1MHz[1]	66		73	μS
f_{CLK} Clock Frequency			See Note 1	0.1	1.0	3.0	MHz
Clock Duty Cycle			See Note 1	40		60	%
CR Free-Running Conversion Rate			$\overline{CS}$ = 0, f_{CLK} = 1MHz $\overline{INTR}$ Tied To $\overline{WR}$			13690	conv s
$t_{W(WR)L}$ Start Pulse Width			$\overline{CS}$ = 0	30			ns
t_{ACC} Access Time	Output	$\overline{RD}$	$\overline{CS}$ = 0, C_L = 100 pF		75	100	ns
t_{1H}, t_{0H} Three-State Control	Output	$\overline{RD}$	C_L = 10 pF, R_L = 10K See Three-State Test Circuit		70	100	ns
t_{WI}, t_{RI} $\overline{INTR}$ Delay	$\overline{INTR}$	$\overline{WR}$ or $\overline{RD}$			100	150	ns
C_{IN} Logic Input Capacitance					5	7.5	pF
C_{OUT} Three-State Output Capacitance					5	7.5	pF

NOTE
1. Accuracy is guaranteed at f_{CLK} = 1MHz. Accuracy may degrade at higher clock frequencies

---

DC ELECTRICAL CHARACTERISTICS

V_{CC} = 5.0V, f_{CLK} = 1MHz, $T_{MIN} \leq T_A \leq T_{MAX}$, unless otherwise specified

SYMBOL & PARAMETER	TEST CONDITIONS	ADC0801/2/3/4/5			UNIT
		Min	Typ	Max	
ADC0801 Relative Accuracy Error (Adjusted)	Full Scale Adjusted			0.25	LSB
ADC0802 Relative Accuracy Error (Unadjusted)	$\frac{V_{REF}}{2}$ = 2.500 V_{DC}			0.50	LSB
ADC0803 Relative Accuracy Error (Adjusted)	Full Scale Adjusted			0.50	LSB
ADC0804 Relative Accuracy Error (Unadjusted)	$\frac{V_{REF}}{2}$ = 2.500 V_{DC}			1	LSB
ADC0805 Relative Accuracy Error (Unadjusted)	$\frac{V_{REF}}{2}$ = has no connection			1	LSB
$\frac{V_{REF}}{2}$ Input Resistance		400	640		Ω
Analog Input Voltage Range	Over Analog Input Voltage Range	-0.05		V_{CC} +0.05	V
DC Common Mode Error			1/16	1/8	LSB
Power Supply Sensitivity	V_{CC} = 5V ± 10%[1]				
CONTROL INPUTS					
V_{IH} Logical "1" Input Voltage	V_{CC} = 5.25V_{DC}	2.0		15	V_{DC}
V_{IL} Logical "0" Input Voltage	V_{CC} = 4.75V_{DC}			0.8	V_{DC}
I_{IH} Logical "1" Input Current	V_{IN} = 5V_{DC}		0.005	1	μA$_{DC}$
I_{IL} Logical "0" Input Current	V_{IN} = 0V_{DC}	-1	-0.005		μA$_{DC}$
CLOCK IN AND CLOCK R					
V_{T+} Clk In Positive-Going Threshold Voltage		2.7	3.1	3.5	V_{DC}
V_{T-} Clk In Negative-Going Threshold Voltage		1.5	1.8	2.1	V_{DC}
V_H Clk In Hysteresis (V_{T+}) - (V_{T-})		0.6	1.3	2.0	V_{DC}
V_{OL} Logical "0" Clk R Output Voltage	I_{OL} = 360μA, V_{CC} = 4.75 V_{DC}			0.4	V_{DC}
V_{OH} Logical "1" Clk R Output Voltage	I_{OH} = -360μA, V_{CC} = 4.75 V_{DC}	2.4			V_{DC}
DATA OUTPUT AND INTR					
V_{OL} Logical "0" Output Voltage					
Data Outputs	I_{OL} = 1.6mA, V_{CC} = 4.75 V_{DC}			0.4	V_{DC}
$\overline{INTR}$ Outputs	I_{OL} = 1.0mA, V_{CC} = 4.75 V_{DC}			0.4	V_{DC}
V_{OH} Logical "1" Output Voltage	I_{OH} = -360μA, V_{CC} = 4.75 V_{DC}	2.4			V_{DC}
	I_{OH} = -10μA, V_{CC} = 4.75 V_{DC}	4.5			V_{DC}
I_{OZL} 3-State Output Leakage	V_{OUT} = 0V_{DC}, $\overline{CS}$ = Logical "1"	-3			μA$_{DC}$
I_{OZH} 3-State Output Leakage	V_{OUT} = 5V_{DC}, $\overline{CS}$ = Logical "1"			3	μA$_{DC}$
I_{SC} + Output Short Circuit Current	V_{OUT} = 0V, T_A = 25°C	4.5	6		mA$_{DC}$
I_{SC} - Output Short Circuit Current	V_{OUT} = V_{CC}, T_A = 25°C	9.0	16		mA$_{DC}$
I_{CC} Power Supply Current	f_{CLK} = 1MHz, V_{REF} 2 = Open $\overline{CS}$ = Logical "1", T_A = 25°C	3.0		3.5	mA

NOTE:
1. Analog inputs must remain within the range -0.05 ≤ V_{IN} ≤ V_{CC} + 0.05V

FUNCTIONAL DESCRIPTION

The ADC0801 through ADC0805 series of A/D converters are successive approximation A/D converters with 8-bit resolution and no missing codes. The most significant bit is tested first and after 64 clock cycles a digital 8-bit binary word is transferred to an output latch and the INTR pin goes low, indicating that conversion is complete. A conversion in progress can be interrupted by issuing another start command. The device may be operated in a continuous conversion mode by connecting the INTR and WR pins together and holding the CS pin low. To insure start-up when connected this way, an external WR pulse is required at power-up.

As the WR input goes low, when CS is low, the SAR is cleared and remains so as long as these two inputs are low. Conversion begins between 1 and 8 clock periods after at least one of these inputs goes high. As the conversion begins, the INTR line goes high. Note that the INTR line will remain low until 1 to 8 clock cycles after either the WR or the CS input (or both) goes high.

When the CS and RD inputs are both brought low to read the data, the INTR line will go low and the three-state output latches are enabled.

The digital control lines (CS, RD, and WR) operate with standard TTL levels and have been renamed when compared with standard A/D Start and Output Enable labels. For non-microprocessor based applications, the CS pin can be grounded, the WR pin can be interpreted as a START pulse pin, and the RD pin performs the OE (Output Enable) function.

The $V_{IN}(-)$ input can be used to subtract a fixed voltage from the input voltage. Because there is a time interval between sampling the $V_{IN}(+)$ and the $V_{IN}(-)$ inputs, it is important that these inputs remain constant, during the entire conversion cycle.

THREE-STATE TEST CIRCUITS AND WAVEFORMS

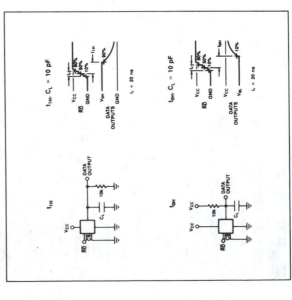

TIMING DIAGRAMS (All timing is measured from the 50% voltage points)

Note: Read strobe must occur 8 clock periods ($8 t_{CLK}$) after assertion of interrupt to guarantee reset of INTR

DESCRIPTION

The MC1508/MC1408 series of 8-bit monolithic digital-to-analog converters provide high speed performance with low cost They are designed for use where the output current is a linear product of an 8-bit digital word and an analog reference voltage

FEATURES

- Fast settling time—70ns (typ)
- Relative accuracy ±0.19% (max error)
- Non-inverting digital inputs are TTL and CMOS compatible
- High speed multiplying rate 4.0mA/μs (input slew)
- Output voltage swing -.5V to -5.0V
- Standard supply voltages + 5.0V and -5.0V to -15V
- Military qualifications pending

APPLICATIONS

- Tracking A-to-D converters
- 2½-digit panel meters and DVM's
- Waveform synthesis
- Sample and hold
- Peak detector
- Programmable gain and attenuation
- CRT character generation
- Audio digitizing and decoding
- Programmable power supplies
- Analog-digital multiplication
- Digital-digital multiplication
- Analog-digital division
- Digital addition and subtraction
- Speech compression and expansion
- Stepping motor drive
- Modems
- Servo motor and pen drivers

CIRCUIT DESCRIPTION

The MC1508/MC1408 consists of a reference current amplifier, an R-2R ladder, and 8 high speed current switches. For many applications, only a reference resistor and reference voltage need be added.

The switches are non-inverting in operation, therefore a high state on the input turns on the specified output current component

The switch uses current steering for high speed, and a termination amplifier consisting of an active load gain stage with unity gain feedback. The termination amplifier holds the parasitic capacitance of the ladder at a constant voltage during switching, and provides a low impedance termination of equal voltage for all legs of the ladder

The R-2R ladder divides the reference amplifier current into binarily-related components, which are fed to the switches Note that there is always a remainder current which is equal to the least significant bit This current is shunted to ground, and the maximum output current is 255/256 of the reference amplifier current or 1 992mA for a 2.0mA reference amplifier current if the NPN current source pair is perfectly matched

PIN CONFIGURATION

F,N PACKAGE

```
           TOP VIEW
   NC    [1]        [16] COMPEN
   GND   [2]        [15] V_REF(-)
   V_EE  [3]        [14] V_REF(+)
(MSB) A_1 [4]       [13] V_CC
   A_2   [5]        [12] A_8 (LSB)
   A_3   [6]        [11] A_7
   A_4   [7]        [10] A_6
   A_5   [8]        [9]  A_5
```

ORDER NUMBERS
MC1508.8F   MC1408.7N
MC1408.7F

D³ PACKAGE

```
           TOP VIEW
   V+       [1]     [16] A_8 (LSB)
   V_REF(+) [2]     [15] A_7
   V_REF(-) [3]     [14] A_6
   COMPEN   [4]     [13] A_5
   NC       [5]     [12] A_4
   GND      [6]     [11] A_3
   V-       [7]     [10] A_2
   I_O      [8]     [9]  A_1 (MSB)
```

ORDER NUMBER
MC1408.8D

NOTES
1 SOL Released in Large SO package only
2 SOL and non-standard pinout
3 SO and non-standard pinouts

BLOCK DIAGRAM

ABSOLUTE MAXIMUM RATINGS T_A = +25°C unless otherwise specified

PARAMETER		RATING	UNIT
Power Supply Voltage			
V_{CC}	Positive	+ 5.5	V
V_{EE}	Negative	- 16.5	V
$V_5 - V_{12}$	Digital Input Voltage	0 to V_{CC}	V
I_O	Applied Output Voltage	- 5.2 to + 18	V
V_{14}, V_{15}	Reference Current	5.0	mA
	Reference Amplifier Inputs	V_{EE} to V_{CC}	
P_D	Power Dissipation (Package Limitation)		
	Ceramic Package	1000	mW
	Plastic Package	800	mW
	Lead Soldering Temperature (60 sec)	300	°C
T_A	Operating Temperature Range		
	MC1508	- 55 to + 125	°C
	MC1408	0 to + 75	°C
T_{stg}	Storage Temperature Range	- 65 to + 150	°C

DC ELECTRICAL CHARACTERISTICS[1]

Pin 3 must be 3V more negative than the potential to which R_{15} is returned

V_{CC} = +5.0Vdc; V_{EE} = -15Vdc: $\frac{V_{ref}}{R_{14}}$ = 2.0mA

unless otherwise specified

MC1508 T_A = -55°C to 125°C MC1408: T_A = 0°C to 75°C

unless otherwise noted

PARAMETER		TEST CONDITIONS	MC1508-8 Min	MC1508-8 Typ	MC1508-8 Max	MC1408-8 Min	MC1408-8 Typ	MC1408-8 Max	MC1408-7 Min	MC1408-7 Typ	MC1408-7 Max	UNIT
E_r	Relative accuracy	Error relative to full scale I_O, Figure 3			±0.19			±0.19			±0.39	%
t_s	Setting time[1]	To within ½ LSB, includes ↑PLH, T_A = +25°C, Figure 4		70			70			70		ns
	Propagation delay time	T_A = +25°C, Figure 4										ns
t_{PLH}	Low-to-high			35			35			35		
t_{PHL}	High-to-low			100			100			100		
TC_{IO}	Output full scale current drift			-20			-20			-20		PPM/°C
	Digital input logic level (MSB)	Figure 5										Vdc
V_{IH}	High		2.0			2.0			2.0			
V_{IL}	Low				0.8			0.8			0.8	
	Digital input current (MSB)	Figure 5										mA
I_{IH}	High	V_{IH} = 5.0V		0	0.04		0	0.04		0	0.04	
I_{IL}	Low	V_{IL} = 0.8V		-0.4	-0.8		-0.4	-0.8		-0.4	-0.8	
I_{15}	Reference input bias current	Pin 15 Figure 5		-10	-5.0		-10	-5.0		-10	-5.0	μA
I_{OR}	Output current range	Figure 5 V_{EE} = -5.0V V_{EE} = -7.0V to -15V	0 0	2.0 2.0	2.1 4.2	0 0	2.0 2.0	2.1 4.2	0 0	2.0 2.0	2.1 4.2	mA
I_O	Output current	Figure 5 V_{ref} = 2.000V, R14 = 1000Ω All bits low	1.9	1.99	2.1	1.9	1.99	2.1	1.9	1.99	2.1	mA
$I_{O(min)}$	Off-state	$E \le 0.19\%$ at T_A = +25°C, Figure 5	0	0	4.0	0	0	4.0	0	0	4.0	μA
V_O	Output voltage compliance	V_{EE} = -5V V_{EE} below -10V		-0.6, +10 -5.5, +10	-0.55, +0.5 -5.0, +0.5		-0.6, +10 -5.5, +10	-0.55, +0.5 -5.0, +0.5		-0.6, +10 -5.5, +10	-0.55, +0.5 -5.0, +0.5	Vdc
SR_{Iref}	Reference current slew rate	Figure 6		8.0			8.0			8.0		mA/μs
$PSRR_{I-}$	Output current power supply sensitivity	I_{ref} = 1mA		0.5	27		0.5	27		0.5	27	μA/V
	Power supply current	All bits low, Figure 5										mA
I_{CC}	Positive			+2.5	+22		+2.5	+22		+2.5	+22	
I_{EE}	Negative			-6.5	-13		-6.5	-13		-6.5	-13	
	Power supply voltage range	T_A = +25°C, Figure 5										Vdc
V_{CCR}	Positive		+4.5	+5.0	+5.5	+4.5	+5.0	+5.5	+4.5	+5.0	+5.5	
V_{EER}	Negative		-4.5	-15	-16.5	-4.5	-15	-16.5	-4.5	-15	-16.5	
P_D	Power dissipation	All bits low, Figure 5 V_{EE} = -5.0Vdc V_{EE} = -15Vdc		34 110	170 305		34 110	170 305		34 110	170 305	mW

NOTES
1 All bits switched

TEST CIRCUITS

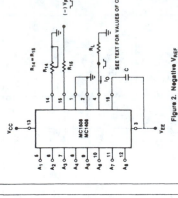

Figure 1. Positive V_{REF}

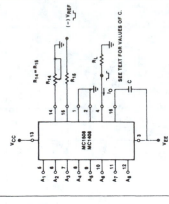

Figure 2. Negative V_{REF}

TYPICAL PERFORMANCE CHARACTERISTICS

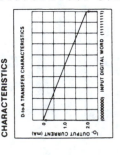

FUNCTIONAL DESCRIPTION

Reference Amplifier Drive and Compensation

The reference amplifier input current must always flow into pin 14 regardless of the setup method or reference supply voltage polarity.

Connections for a positive reference voltage are shown in Figure 1. The reference voltage source supplies the full reference current. For bipolar reference signals, as in the multiplying mode, R_{15} can be tied to a negative voltage corresponding to the minimum input level. R_{15} may be eliminated and pin 15 grounded, with only a small sacrifice in accuracy and temperature drift.

The compensation capacitor value must be increased with increasing values of R_{14} to maintain proper phase margin. For R_{14} values of 1.0, 2.5, and 5.0K ohms, minimum capacitor values are 15, 37, and 75pF. The capacitor may be tied to either V_{EE} or ground, but using V_{EE} increases negative supply rejection. (Fluctuations in the negative supply have more effect on accuracy than do any changes in the positive supply).

A negative reference voltage may be used if R_{14} is grounded and the reference voltage is applied to R_{15}, as shown in Figure 2. A high input impedance is the main advantage of this method. The negative reference voltage must be at least 3.0V above the V_{EE} supply. Bipolar input signals may be handled by connecting R_{14} to a positive reference voltage equal to the peak positive input level at pin 15.

Capacitive bypass to ground is recommended when a DC reference voltage is used. The 5.0V logic supply is not recommended as a reference voltage, but if a

well regulated 5.0V supply which drives logic is to be used as the reference, R_{14} should be formed of two series resistors and the junction of the two resistors bypassed with 0.1μF to ground. For reference voltages greater than 5.0V, a clamp diode is recommended between pin 14 and ground.

If pin 14 is driven by a high impedance such as a transistor current source, none of the above compensation methods apply and the amplifier must be heavily compensated, decreasing the overall bandwidth.

Output Voltage Range

The voltage at pin 4 must always be at least 4.5 volts more positive than the voltage of the negative supply (pin 3) when the reference current is 2mA or less, and at least 8 volts more positive than the negative supply when the reference current is between 2mA and 4mA. This is necessary to avoid saturation of the output transistors, which would cause serious degradation of accuracy.

Signetics' MC1508/MC1408 does not need a range control because the design extends the compliance range down to 4.5 volts (or 8 volts—see above) above the negative supply voltage without significant degradation of accuracy. Signetics' MC1508/MC1408 can be used in sockets designed for other manufacturers' MC1508/MC1408 without circuit modification.

Output Current Range

Any time the full scale current exceeds 2mA, the negative supply must be at least 8 volts more negative than the output voltage. This is due to the increased internal voltage drops between the negative supply and the outputs with higher reference currents.

Accuracy

Absolute accuracy is the measure of each output current level with respect to its intended value, and is dependent upon relative accuracy and full scale current drift. Relative accuracy is the measure of each output current level as a fraction of the full scale current after zero scale current has been nulled out. The relative accuracy of the MC1508/MC1408 is essentially constant over the operating temperature range because of the excellent temperature tracking of the monolithic resistor ladder. The reference current may drift with temperature, causing a change in the absolute accuracy of output current; however, the MC1508/MC1408 has a very low full scale current drift over the operating temperature range.

The MC1508/MC1408 series is guaranteed accurate to within ±1/2 LSB at +25°C at a full scale output current of 1.99mA. The relative accuracy test circuit is shown in Figure 3. The 12-bit converter is calibrated to a full scale output current of 1.99219mA; then the MC1508/MC1408's full scale current is trimmed to the same value with R_{14} so that a zero value appears at the error amplifier output. The counter is activated and the error band may be displayed on the oscilloscope, detected by comparators, or stored in a peak detector.

Two 8-bit D-to-A converters may not be used to construct a 16-bit accurate D-to-A converter. Sixteen-bit accuracy implies a total of ±1/2 part in 65,536, or ±0.00076%, which is much more accurate than the ±0.19% specification of the MC1508/MC1408.

Monotonicity

A monotonic converter is one which always provides an analog output greater than or equal to the preceding value for a corresponding increment in the digital input code. The MC1508/MC1408 is monotonic for all values of reference current above 0.5mA. The recommended range for operation is a DC reference current between 0.5mA and 4.0mA.

Settling Time

The worst case switching condition occurs when all bits are switched on, which corresponds to a low-to-high transition for all input bits. This time is typically 70ns for settling to within 1/2 LSB for 8-bit accuracy. This time applies when $R_L < 500$ ohms and $C_O < 25pF$. The slowest single switch is the least significant bit, which typically turns on and settles in 65ns. In applications where the D-to-A converter functions in a positive going ramp mode, the worst case condition does not occur and settling times less than 70ns may be realized.

Extra care must be taken in board layout since this usually is the dominant factor in satisfactory test results when measuring settling time. Short leads, 100μF supply bypassing for low frequencies, minimum scope lead length, good ground planes and avoidance of ground loops are all mandatory.

TEST CIRCUITS (Cont'd)

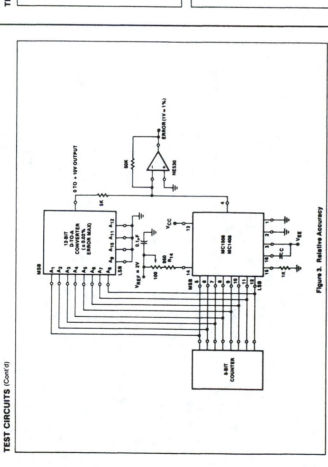

Figure 3. Relative Accuracy

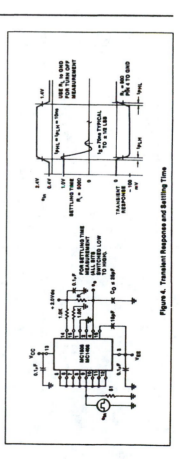

Figure 4. Transient Response and Settling Time

TEST CIRCUITS (Cont'd)

V_I AND I_I APPLY TO INPUTS A_1 THROUGH A_8

THE RESISTOR TIED TO PIN 15 IS TO TEMPERATURE COMPENSATE THE BIAS CURRENT AND MAY NOT BE NECESSARY FOR ALL APPLICATIONS.

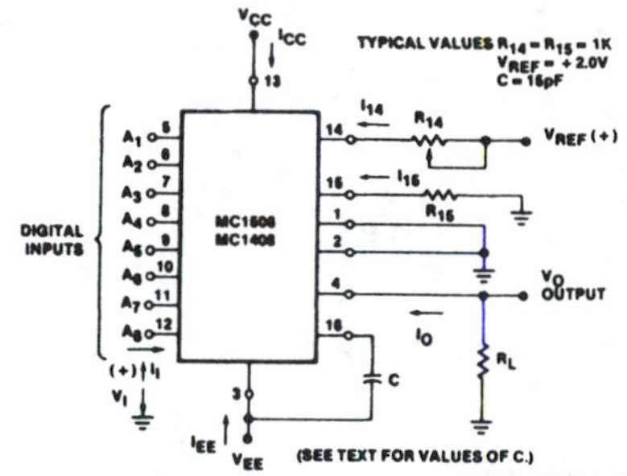

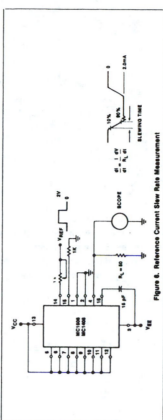

$$I_O = K \left\{ \frac{A_1}{2} + \frac{A_2}{4} + \frac{A_3}{8} + \frac{A_4}{16} + \frac{A_5}{32} + \frac{A_6}{64} + \frac{A_7}{128} + \frac{A_8}{256} \right\}$$

where $K \cong \frac{V_{REF}}{R_{14}}$

and A_N = "1" IF A_N IS AT HIGH LEVEL
A_N = "0" IF A_N IS AT LOW LEVEL

Figure 5. Notation Definitions

Figure 6. Reference Current Slew Rate Measurement

Signetics

µA741/µA741C/SA741C
General Purpose Operational Amplifier

Product Specification

Linear Products

DESCRIPTION

The µA741 is a high performance operational amplifier with high open-loop gain, internal compensation, high common mode range and exceptional temperature stability. The µA741 is short-circuit-protected and allows for nulling of offset voltage.

FEATURES

- **Internal frequency compensation**
- **Short circuit protection**
- **Excellent temperature stability**
- **High input voltage range**

PIN CONFIGURATION

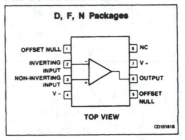

ORDERING INFORMATION

DESCRIPTION	TEMPERATURE RANGE	ORDER CODE
8-Pin Plastic DIP	−55°C to +125°C	µA741N
8-Pin Plastic DIP	0 to +70°C	µA741CN
8-Pin Plastic DIP	−40°C to +85°C	SA741CN
8-Pin Cerdip	−55°C to +125°C	µA741F
8-Pin Cerdip	0 to +70°C	µA741CF
8-Pin SO	0 to +70°C	µA741CD

EQUIVALENT SCHEMATIC

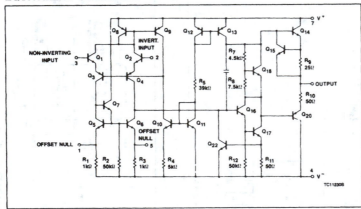

Signetics Linear Products

Product Specification

General Purpose Operational Amplifier μA741/μA741C/SA741C

ABSOLUTE MAXIMUM RATINGS

SYMBOL	PARAMETER	RATING	UNIT
V_S	Supply voltage μA741C μA741	±18 ±22	V V
P_D	Internal power dissipation D package N package F package	500 1000 1000	mW mW mW
V_{IN}	Differential input voltage	±30	V
V_{IN}	Input voltage[1]	±15	V
I_{SC}	Output short-circuit duration	Continuous	
T_A	Operating temperature range μA741C SA741C μA741	0 to +70 −40 to +85 −55 to +125	°C °C °C
T_{STG}	Storage temperature range	−65 to +150	°C
T_{SOLD}	Lead soldering temperature (10sec max)	300	°C

NOTE:
1. For supply voltages less than ±15V, the absolute maximum input voltage is equal to the supply voltage.

DC ELECTRICAL CHARACTERISTICS (μA741, μA741C) $T_A = 25°C$, $V_S = ±15V$, unless otherwise specified.

SYMBOL	PARAMETER	TEST CONDITIONS	μA741			μA741C			UNIT
			Min	Typ	Max	Min	Typ	Max	
V_{OS} $\Delta V_{OS}/\Delta T$	Offset voltage	$R_S = 10k\Omega$ $R_S = 10k\Omega$, over temp.		1.0 1.0 10	5.0 6.0		2.0 10	6.0 7.5	mV mV μV/°C
I_{OS} $\Delta I_{OS}/\Delta T$	Offset current	 Over temp. $T_A = +125°C$ $T_A = -55°C$		20 7.0 20 200	200 200 500		20 200	200 300	nA nA nA nA pA/°C
I_{BIAS} $\Delta I_B/\Delta T$	Input bias current	 Over temp. $T_A = +125°C$ $T_A = -55°C$		80 30 300 1	500 500 1500		80 1	500 800	nA nA nA nA nA/°C
V_{OUT}	Output voltage swing	$R_L = 10k\Omega$ $R_L = 2k\Omega$, over temp.	±12 ±10	±14 ±13		±12 ±10	±14 ±13		V V
A_{VOL}	Large-signal voltage gain	$R_L = 2k\Omega$, $V_O = ±10V$ $R_L = 2k\Omega$, $V_O = ±10V$, over temp.	50 25	200		20 15	200		V/mV V/mV
	Offset voltage adjustment range			±30			±30		mV
PSRR	Supply voltage rejection ratio	$R_S \leq 10k\Omega$ $R_S \leq 10k\Omega$, over temp.		10	150		10	150	μV/V μV/V
CMRR	Common-mode rejection ratio	Over temp.	70	90					dB dB
I_{CC}	Supply current	$T_A = +125°C$ $T_A = -55°C$		1.4 1.5 2.0	2.8 2.5 3.3		1.4	2.8	mA mA mA

General Purpose Operational Amplifier   μA741/μA741C/SA741C

DC ELECTRICAL CHARACTERISTICS (Continued) (μA741, μA741C) $T_A = 25°C$, $V_S = \pm15V$, unless otherwise specified.

SYMBOL	PARAMETER	TEST CONDITIONS	μA741			μA741C			UNIT
			Min	Typ	Max	Min	Typ	Max	
V_{IN} R_{IN}	Input voltage range Input resistance	(μA741, over temp.)	±12 0.3	±13 2.0		±12 0.3	±13 2.0		V MΩ
P_D	Power consumption	$T_A = +125°C$ $T_A = -55°C$		50 45 45	80 75 100		50	85	mW mW mW
R_{OUT}	Output resistance			75			75		Ω
I_{SC}	Output short-circuit current		10	25	60	10	25	60	mA

DC ELECTRICAL CHARACTERISTICS (SA741C) $T_A = 25°C$, $V_S = \pm15V$, unless otherwise specified.

SYMBOL	PARAMETER	TEST CONDITIONS	SA741C			UNIT
			Min	Typ	Max	
V_{OS} $\Delta V_{OS}/\Delta T$	Offset voltage	$R_S = 10k\Omega$ $R_S = 10k\Omega$, over temp.		2.0 10	6.0 7.5	mV mV μV/°C
I_{OS} $\Delta I_{OS}/\Delta T$	Offset current	Over temp.		20 200	200 500	nA nA pA/°C
I_{BIAS} $\Delta I_B/\Delta T$	Input bias current	Over temp.		80 1	500 1500	nA nA nA/°C
V_{OUT}	Output voltage swing	$R_L = 10k\Omega$ $R_L = 2k\Omega$, over temp.	±12 ±10	±14 ±13		V V
A_{VOL}	Large-signal voltage gain	$R_L = 2k\Omega$, $V_O = \pm10V$ $R_L = 2k\Omega$, $V_O = \pm10V$, over temp.	20 15	200		V/mV V/mV
	Offset voltage adjustment range			±30		mV
PSRR	Supply voltage rejection ratio	$R_S \leqslant 10k\Omega$		10	150	μV/V
V_{IN}	Input voltage range	(μA741, over temp.)	±12	±13		V
R_{IN}	Input resistance		0.3	2.0		MΩ
P_d	Power consumption			50	85	mW
R_{OUT}	Output resistance			75		Ω
I_{SC}	Output short-circuit current			25		mA

AC ELECTRICAL CHARACTERISTICS $T_A = 25°C$, $V_S = \pm15V$, unless otherwise specified.

SYMBOL	PARAMETER	TEST CONDITIONS	μA741, μA741C			UNIT
			Min	Typ	Max	
C_{IN}	Parallel input capacitance	Open-loop, f = 20Hz		1.4		pF
	Unity gain crossover frequency	Open-loop		1.0		MHz
t_R SR	Transient response unity gain Rise time Overshoot Slew rate	$V_{IN} = 20mV$, $R_L = 2k\Omega$, $C_L \leqslant 100pF$ $C \leqslant 100pF$, $R_L \geqslant 2k\Omega$, $V_{IN} = \pm10V$		0.3 5.0 0.5		μs % V/μs

2732A
32K (4K x 8) PRODUCTION AND UV ERASABLE PROMS

- **200 ns (2732A-2) Maximum Access Time ... HMOS*-E Technology**
- **Compatible with High-Speed Microcontrollers and Microprocessors ... Zero WAIT State**
- **Two Line Control**
- **10% V$_{CC}$ Tolerance Available**

- **Low Current Requirement**
  - **−100 mA Active**
  - **−35 mA Standby**
- **int$_e$lligent Identifier™ Mode**
  - **−Automatic Programming Operation**
- **Industry Standard Pinout ... JEDEC Approved 24 Pin Ceramic Package**
  (See Packaging Spec. Order #231369)

The Intel 2732A is a 5V-only, 32,768-bit ultraviolet erasable (cerdip) Electrically Programmable Read-Only Memory (EPROM). The standard 2732A access time is 250 ns with speed selection (2732A-2) available at 200 ns. The access time is compatible with high performance microprocessors such as the 8 MHz iAPX 186. In these systems, the 2732A allows the microprocessor to operate without the addition of WAIT states.

An important 2732A feature is Output Enable ($\overline{OE}$) which is separate from the Chip Enable ($\overline{CE}$) control. The $\overline{OE}$ control eliminates bus contention in microprocessor systems. The $\overline{CE}$ is used by the 2732A to place it in a standby mode ($\overline{CE}$ = V$_{IH}$) which reduces power consumption without increasing access time. The standby mode reduces the current requirement by 65%; the maximum active current is reduced from 100 mA to a standby current of 35 mA.

*HMOS is a patented process of Intel Corporation.

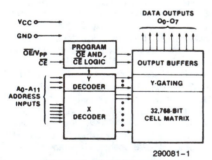

Figure 1. Block Diagram

290081–1

Pin Names

A$_0$–A$_{11}$	Addresses
$\overline{CE}$	Chip Enable
$\overline{OE}$/V$_{PP}$	Output Enable/V$_{PP}$
O$_0$–O$_7$	Outputs

27128 27128A	2764 2764A 27C64 87C64	2716	2732A		2716	2764 2764A 27C64 87C64	27128 27128A
V$_{PP}$	V$_{PP}$					V$_{CC}$ $\overline{PGM}$	V$_{CC}$ $\overline{PGM}$
A$_{12}$	A$_{12}$						
A$_7$	A$_7$	A$_7$	A$_7$ 1 — 24 V$_{CC}$	V$_{CC}$	N.C.	A$_{13}$	
A$_6$	A$_6$	A$_6$	A$_6$ 2 — 23 A$_8$	A$_8$	A$_8$	A$_8$	
A$_5$	A$_5$	A$_5$	A$_5$ 3 — 22 A$_9$	A$_9$	A$_9$	A$_9$	
A$_4$	A$_4$	A$_4$	A$_4$ 4 — 21 A$_{11}$	V$_{PP}$	A$_{11}$	A$_{11}$	
A$_3$	A$_3$	A$_3$	A$_3$ 5 — 20 $\overline{OE}$/V$_{PP}$	$\overline{OE}$	$\overline{OE}$	$\overline{OE}$	
A$_2$	A$_2$	A$_2$	A$_2$ 6 — 19 A$_{10}$	A$_{10}$	A$_{10}$	A$_{10}$	
A$_1$	A$_1$	A$_1$	A$_1$ 7 — 18 $\overline{CE}$	$\overline{CE}$	$\overline{OE}$ ALE/$\overline{CE}$	$\overline{CE}$	
A$_0$	A$_0$	A$_0$	A$_0$ 8 — 17 O$_7$	O$_7$	O$_7$	O$_7$	
O$_0$	O$_0$	O$_0$	O$_0$ 9 — 16 O$_6$	O$_6$	O$_6$	O$_6$	
O$_1$	O$_1$	O$_1$	O$_1$ 10 — 15 O$_5$	O$_5$	O$_5$	O$_5$	
O$_2$	O$_2$	O$_2$	O$_2$ 11 — 14 O$_4$	O$_4$	O$_4$	O$_4$	
GND	GND	GND	GND 12 — 13 O$_3$	O$_3$	O$_3$	O$_3$	

NOTE:
Intel "Universal Site" compatible EPROM configurations are shown in the blocks adjacent to the 2732A pins.

290081–2

Figure 2. Cerdip Pin Configuration

intel   **2732A**

DEVICE OPERATION

The modes of operation of the 2732A are listed in Table 1. A single 5V power supply is required in the read mode. All inputs are TTL levels except for $\overline{OE}/V_{PP}$ during programming and 12V on A_9 for the inteligent Identifier™ mode. In the program mode the $\overline{OE}/V_{PP}$ input is pulsed from a TTL level to 21V.

Table 1. Mode Selection

Pins Mode	$\overline{CE}$	$\overline{OE}/V_{PP}$	A_9	A_0	V_{CC}	Outputs
Read/Program Verify	V_{IL}	V_{IL}	X	X	V_{CC}	D_{OUT}
Output Disable	V_{IL}	V_{IH}	X	X	V_{CC}	High Z
Standby	V_{IH}	X	X	X	V_{CC}	High Z
Program	V_{IL}	V_{PP}	X	X	V_{CC}	D_{IN}
Program Inhibit	V_{IH}	V_{PP}	X	X	V_{CC}	High Z
Inteligent Identifier[3] —Manufacturer —Device	V_{IL} V_{IL}	V_{IL} V_{IL}	V_H V_H	V_{IL} V_{IH}	V_{CC} V_{CC}	89H 01H

NOTES:
1. X can be V_{IH} or V_{IL}.
2. $V_H = 12V \pm 0.5V$.
3. A_1–A_8, A_{10}, $A_{11} = V_{IL}$.

Read Mode

The 2732A has two control functions, both of which must be logically active in order to obtain data at the outputs. Chip Enable ($\overline{CE}$) is the power control and should be used for device selection. Output Enable ($\overline{OE}/V_{PP}$) is the output control and should be used to gate data from the output pins, independent of device selection. Assuming that addresses are stable, address access time (t_{ACC}) is equal to the delay from $\overline{CE}$ to output (t_{CE}). Data is available at the outputs after the falling edge of $\overline{OE}/V_{PP}$, assuming that $\overline{CE}$ has been low and addresses have been stable for at least $t_{ACC}-t_{OE}$.

Standby Mode

EPROMs can be placed in a standby mode which reduces the maximum active current of the device

by applying a TTL-high signal to the $\overline{CE}$ input. When in standby mode, the outputs are in a high impedance state, independent of the $\overline{OE}/V_{PP}$ input.

Two Line Output Control

Because EPROMs are usually used in larger memory arrays, Intel has provided two control lines which accommodate this multiple memory connection. The two control lines allow for:

a) The lowest possible memory power dissipation, and

b) complete assurance that output bus contention will not occur.

To use these two control lines most efficiently, $\overline{CE}$ should be decoded and used as the primary device selecting function, while $\overline{OE}/V_{PP}$ should be made a common connection to all devices in the array and connected to the $\overline{READ}$ line from the system control bus. This assures that all deselected memory devices are in their low power standby mode and that the output pins are active only when data is desired from a particular memory device.

SYSTEM CONSIDERATION

The power switching characteristics of EPROMs require careful decoupling of the devices. The supply current, I_{CC}, has three segments that are of interest to the system designer—the standby current level, the active current level, and the transient current peaks that are produced by the falling and rising edges of Chip Enable. The magnitude of these transient current peaks is dependent on the output capacitive and inductive loading of the device. The associated transient voltage peaks can be suppressed by complying with Intel's two-line control and by use of properly selected decoupling capacitors. It is recommended that a 0.1 μF ceramic capacitor be used on every device between V_{CC} and GND. This should be a high frequency capacitor of low inherent inductance and should be placed as close to the device as possible. In addition, a 4.7 μF bulk electrolytic capacitor should be used between V_{CC} and GND for

int_e_l   2732A

---

every eight devices. The bulk capacitor should be located near where the power supply is connected to the array. The purpose of the bulk capacitor is to overcome the voltage droop caused by the inductive effects of PC board traces.

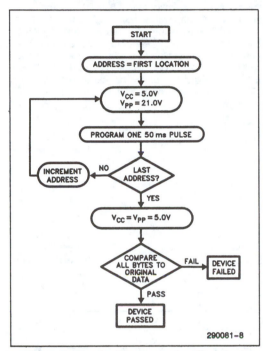

Figure 3. Standard Programming Flowchart

PROGRAMMING MODES

CAUTION: Exceeding 22V on $\overline{OE}/V_{PP}$ will permanently damage the device.

Initially, and after each erasure (cerdip EPROMs), all bits of the EPROM are in the "1" state. Data is introduced by selectively programming "0s" into the bit locations. Although only "0s" will be programmed, both "1s" and "0s" can be present in the data word. The only way to change a "0" to a "1" in cerdip EPROMs is by ultraviolet light erasure.

The device is in the programming mode when the $\overline{OE}/V_{PP}$ input is at 21V. It is required that a 0.1 μF capacitor be placed across $\overline{OE}/V_{PP}$ and ground to suppress spurious voltage transients which may damage the device. The data to be programmed is applied 8 bits in parallel to the data output pins. The levels required for the address and data inputs are TTL.

When the address and data are stable, a 20 ms (50 ms typical) active low, TTL program pulse is ap-

plied to the $\overline{CE}$ input. A program pulse must be applied at each address location to be programmed (see Figure 3). Any location can be programmed at any time—either individually, sequentially, or at random. The program pulse has a maximum width of 55 ms. The EPROM must not be programmed with a DC signal applied to the $\overline{CE}$ input.

Programming of multiple 2732As in parallel with the same data can be easily accomplished due to the simplicity of the programming requirements. Like inputs of the paralleled 2732As may be connected together when they are programmed with the same data. A low level TTL pulse applied to the $\overline{CE}$ input programs the paralleled 2732As.

Program Inhibit

Programming of multiple EPROMs in parallel with different data is easily accomplished by using the Program Inhibit mode. A high level $\overline{CE}$ input inhibits the other EPROMs from being programmed. Except for $\overline{CE}$, all like inputs (including $\overline{OE}/V_{PP}$) of the parallel EPROMs may be common. A TTL low level pulse applied to the $\overline{CE}$ input with $\overline{OE}/V_{PP}$ at 21V will program that selected device.

Program Verify

A verify (Read) should be performed on the programmed bits to determine that they have been correctly programmed. The verify is performed with $\overline{OE}/V_{PP}$ and $\overline{CE}$ at V_{IL}. Data should be verified t_{DV} after the falling edge of $\overline{CE}$.

Int_e_ligent Identifier™ Mode

The int_e_ligent Identifier Mode allows the reading out of a binary code from an EPROM that will identify its manufacturer and type. This mode is intended for use by programming equipment for the purpose of automatically matching the device to be programmed with its corresponding programming algorithm. This mode is functional in the 25°C ±5°C ambient temperature range that is required when programming the device.

To activate this mode, the programming equipment must force 11.5V to 12.5V on address line A9 of the EPROM. Two identifier bytes may then be sequenced from the device outputs by toggling address line A0 from V_{IL} to V_{IH}. All other address lines must be held at V_{IL} during the int_e_ligent Identifier Mode.

Byte 0 (A0 = V_{IL}) represents the manufacturer code and byte 1 (A0 = V_{IH}) the device identifier code. These two identifier bytes are given in Table 1.

intel   2732A

ERASURE CHARACTERISTICS (FOR CERDIP EPROMS)

The erasure characteristics are such that erasure begins to occur upon exposure to light with wavelengths shorter than aproximately 4000 Angstroms (Å). It should be noted that sunlight and certain types of fluorescent lamps have wavelengths in the 3000–4000Å range. Data shows that constant exposure to room level fluorescent lighting could erase the EPROM in approximately 3 years, while it would take approximately 1 week to cause erasure when exposed to direct sunlight. If the device is to be exposed to these types of lighting conditions for extended periods of time, opaque labels should be placed over the window to prevent unintentional erasure.

The recommended erasure procedure is exposure to shortwave ultraviolet light which has a wavelength of 2537 Angstroms (Å). The integrated dose (i.e., UV intensity × exposure time) for erasure should be a minimum of 15 Wsec/cm^2. The erasure time with this dosage is approximately 15 to 20 minutes using an ultraviolet lamp with a 12000 μW/cm^2 power rating. The EPROM should be placed within 1 inch of the lamp tubes during erasure. The maximum integrated dose an EPROM can be exposed to without damage is 7258 Wsec/cm^2 (1 week @ 12000 μW/cm^2). Exposure of the device to high intensity UV light for longer periods may cause permanent damage.

PROGRAMMING

D.C. PROGRAMMING CHARACTERISTICS

$T_A = 25°C \pm 5°C$, $V_{CC} = 5V \pm 5\%$, $V_{PP} = 21V \pm 0.5V$

Symbol	Parameter	Limits			Units	Test Conditions (Note 1)
		Min	Typ[3]	Max		
I_{LI}	Input Current (All Inputs)			10	μA	$V_{IN} = V_{IL}$ or V_{IH}
V_{IL}	Input Low Level (All Inputs)	−0.1		0.8	V	
V_{IH}	Input High Level (All Inputs Except $\overline{OE}/V_{PP}$)	2.0		$V_{CC} + 1$	V	
V_{OL}	Output Low Voltage During Verify			0.45	V	$I_{OL} = 2.1$ mA
V_{OH}	Output High Voltage During Verify	2.4			V	$I_{OH} = -400$ μA
I_{CC2}[4]	V_{CC} Supply Current (Program and Verify)		85	100	mA	
I_{PP2}[4]	V_{PP} Supply Current (Program)			30	mA	$\overline{CE} = V_{IL}$, $\overline{OE}/V_{PP} = V_{PP}$
V_{ID}	A_9 int$_e$ligent Identifier Voltage	11.5		12.5	V	

Signetics

Logic Products

74LS244, S244
Buffers

Octal Buffers (3-State)
Product Specification

TYPE	TYPICAL PROPAGATION DELAY	TYPICAL SUPPLY CURRENT (TOTAL)
74LS244	12ns	25mA
74S244	6ns	112mA

FUNCTION TABLE

INPUTS				OUTPUTS	
$\overline{OE}_a$	I_a	$\overline{OE}_b$	I_b	Y_a	Y_b
L	L	L	L	L	L
L	H	L	H	H	H
H	X	H	X	(Z)	(Z)

H = HIGH voltage level
L = LOW voltage level
X = Don't care
(Z) = HIGH impedance (off) state

ORDERING CODE

PACKAGES	COMMERCIAL RANGE $V_{CC} = 5V \pm 5\%$; $T_A = 0°C$ to $+70°C$
Plastic DIP	N74LS244N, 74S244N
Plastic SOL-20	74LS244D

NOTE:
For information regarding devices processed to Military Specifications, see the Signetics Military Products Data Manual.

INPUT AND OUTPUT LOADING AND FAN-OUT TABLE

PINS	DESCRIPTION	74S	74LS
All	Inputs	1Sul	1LSul
All	Outputs	24Sul	30LSul

NOTE:
A 74S unit load (Sul) is $50\mu A$ I_{IH} and $-2.0mA$ I_{IL}, and a 74LS unit load (LSul) is $20\mu A$ I_{IH} and $-0.4mA$ I_{IL}.

PIN CONFIGURATION

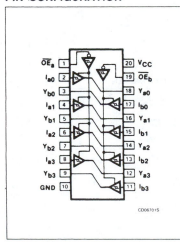

LOGIC SYMBOL

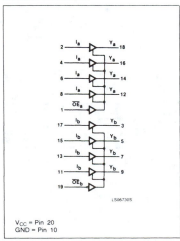

LOGIC SYMBOL (IEEE/IEC)

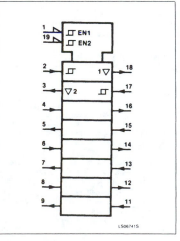

Signetics Logic Products   Product Specification

Buffers   74LS244, S244

ABSOLUTE MAXIMUM RATINGS (Over operating free-air temperature range unless otherwise noted.)

	PARAMETER	74LS	74S	UNIT
V_{CC}	Supply voltage	7.0	7.0	V
V_{IN}	Input voltage	−0.5 to +7.0	−0.5 to +5.5	V
I_{IN}	Input current	−30 to +1	−30 to +5	mA
V_{OUT}	Voltage applied to output in HIGH output state	−0.5 to +V_{CC}	−0.5 to +V_{CC}	V
T_A	Operating free-air temperature range	0 to 70		°C

RECOMMENDED OPERATING CONDITIONS

	PARAMETER	74LS			74S			UNIT
		Min	Nom	Max	Min	Nom	Max	
V_{CC}	Supply voltage	4.75	5.0	5.25	4.75	5.0	5.25	V
V_{IH}	HIGH-level input voltage	2.0			2.0			V
V_{IL}	LOW-level input voltage			+0.8			+0.8	V
I_{IK}	Input clamp current			−18			−18	mA
I_{OH}	HIGH-level output current			−15			−15	mA
I_{OL}	LOW-level output current			24			64	mA
T_A	Operating free-air temperature	0		70	0		70	°C

5

TEST CIRCUITS AND WAVEFORMS

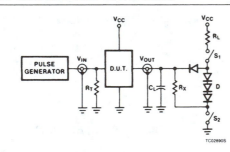

Test Circuit For 3-State Outputs

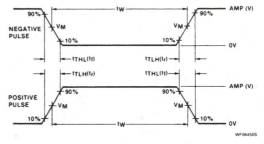

V_M = 1.3V for 74LS; V_M = 1.5V for all other TTL families.

Input Pulse Definition

SWITCH POSITION

TEST	SWITCH 1	SWITCH 2
t_{PZH}	Open	Closed
t_{PZL}	Closed	Open
t_{PHZ}	Closed	Closed
t_{PLZ}	Closed	Closed

FAMILY	INPUT PULSE REQUIREMENTS				
	Amplitude	Rep. Rate	Pulse Width	t_{TLH}	t_{THL}
74	3.0V	1MHz	500ns	7ns	7ns
74LS	3.0V	1MHz	500ns	15ns	6ns
74S	3.0V	1MHz	500ns	2.5ns	2.5ns

DEFINITIONS

R_L = Load resistor to V_{CC}; see AC CHARACTERISTICS for value.

C_L = Load capacitance includes jig and probe capacitance; see AC CHARACTERISTICS for value.

R_T = Termination resistance should be equal to Z_{OUT} of Pulse Generators.

D = Diodes are 1N916, 1N3064, or equivalent.

R_X = 1kΩ for 74, 74S, R_X = 5kΩ for 74LS.

t_{TLH}, t_{THL} Values should be less than or equal to the table entries.

Signetics Logic Products

Product Specification

Buffers

74LS244, S244

DC ELECTRICAL CHARACTERISTICS (Over recommended operating free-air temperature range unless otherwise noted.)

PARAMETER		TEST CONDITIONS[1]		74LS244			74S244			UNIT
				Min	Typ[2]	Max	Min	Typ[2]	Max	
ΔV_T	Hysteresis ($V_{T+} - V_{T-}$)	V_{CC} = MIN		0.2	0.4		0.2	0.4		V
V_{OH}	HIGH-level output voltage	V_{CC} = MIN, V_{IH} = MIN, V_{IL} = 0.5V, I_{OH} = MAX		2.0			2.0			V
		V_{CC} = MIN, V_{IH} = MIN, V_{IL} = MAX, I_{OH} = MAX		2.4	3.4		2.4			V
V_{OL}	LOW-level output voltage	V_{CC} = MIN, V_{IH} = MIN, V_{IL} = MAX	I_{OL} = MAX			0.5			0.55	V
			I_{OL} = 12mA (74LS)			0.4				V
V_{IK}	Input clamp voltage	V_{CC} = MIN, $I_I = I_{IK}$				−1.5			−1.2	V
I_{OZH}	Off-state output current, HIGH-level voltage applied	V_{CC} = MAX, V_{IH} = MIN, V_{IL} = MAX	V_O = 2.7V			20				μA
			V_O = 2.4V						50	μA
I_{OZL}	Off-state output current, LOW-level voltage applied	V_{CC} = MAX, V_{IH} = MIN, V_{IL} = MAX	V_O = 0.4V			−20				μA
			V_O = 0.5V						−50	μA
I_I	Input current at maximum input voltage	V_{CC} = MAX	V_I = 5.5V						1.0	mA
			V_I = 7.0V			0.1				mA
I_{IH}	HIGH-level input current	V_{CC} = MAX, V_I = 2.7V				20			50	μA
I_{IL}	LOW-level input current	V_{CC} = MAX	V_I = 0.4V			−0.2				mA
			V_I = 0.5V $\overline{OE}$ inputs						−2.0	mA
			V_I = 0.5V Other inputs						−0.4	mA
I_{OS}	Short-circuit output current[3]	V_{CC} = MAX		−40		−130	−80		−180	mA
I_{CC}	Supply current[4] (total)	V_{CC} = MAX	I_{CCH} Outputs HIGH		17	27		95	160	mA
			I_{CCL} Outputs LOW		27	46		120	180	mA
			I_{CCZ} Outputs OFF		32	54		120	180	mA

NOTES:
1. For conditions shown as MIN or MAX, use the appropriate value specified under recommended operating conditions for the applicable type.
2. All typical values are at V_{CC} = 5V, T_A = 25°C.
3. I_{OS} is tested with V_{OUT} = + 0.5V and V_{CC} = V_{CC} MAX + 0.5V. Not more than one output should be shorted at a time and duration of the short circuit should not exceed one second.
4. I_{CC} is measured with outputs open.

AC ELECTRICAL CHARACTERISTICS T_A = 25°C, V_{CC} = 5.0V

PARAMETER		TEST CONDITIONS	74LS		74S		UNIT
			C_L = 45pF, R_L = 667Ω		C_L = 50pF, R_L = 90Ω		
			Min	Max	Min	Max	
t_{PLH}	Propagation delay	Waveform 1		18		9	ns
t_{PHL}	Propagation delay	Waveform 1		18		9	ns
t_{PZH}	Enable to HIGH	Waveform 2		23		12	ns
t_{PZL}	Enable to LOW	Waveform 3		30		15	ns
t_{PHZ}	Disable from HIGH	Waveform 2, C_L = 5pF		18		9	ns
t_{PLZ}	Disable from LOW	Waveform 3, C_L = 5pF		25		15	ns

Signetics

Logic Products

FEATURES
- 8-bit transparent latch — '373
- 8-bit positive, edge-triggered register — '374
- 3-State output buffers
- Common 3-State Output Enable
- Independent register and 3-State buffer operation

DESCRIPTION
The '373 is an octal transparent latch coupled to eight 3-State output buffers. The two sections of the device are controlled independently by Latch Enable (E) and Output Enable ($\overline{OE}$) control gates.

74LS373, 74LS374, S373, S374
Latches/Flip-Flops

'373 Octal Transparent Latch With 3-State Outputs
'374 Octal D Flip-Flop With 3-State Outputs
Product Specification

TYPE	TYPICAL PROPAGATION DELAY	TYPICAL SUPPLY CURRENT (TOTAL)
74LS373	19ns	24mA
74S373	10ns	105mA
74LS374	19ns	27mA
74S374	8ns	116mA

ORDERING CODE

PACKAGES	COMMERCIAL RANGE $V_{CC} = 5V \pm 5\%$; $T_A = 0°C$ to $+70°C$
Plastic DIP	N74LS373N, N74S373N, N74LS374N, N74S374N
Plastic SOL-20	N74LS373D, N74S373D, N74LS374D, N74S374D

NOTE:
For information regarding devices processed to Military Specifications, see the Signetics Military Products Data Manual.

INPUT AND OUTPUT LOADING AND FAN-OUT TABLE

PINS	DESCRIPTION	74S	74LS
All	Inputs	1Sul	1LSul
All	Outputs	10Sul	30LSul

NOTE:
Where a 74S unit load (Sul) is 50µA I_{IH} and −2.0mA I_{IL}, and a 74LS unit load (LSul) is 20µA I_{IH} and −0.4mA I_{IL}.

5

PIN CONFIGURATION
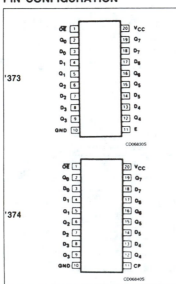

LOGIC SYMBOL
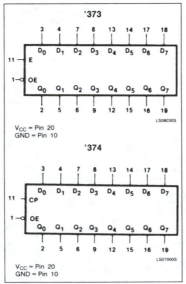

LOGIC SYMBOL (IEEE/EC)
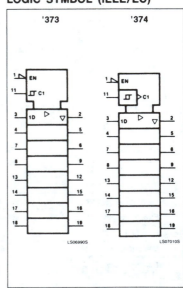

Signetics Logic Products

Product Specification

Latches/Flip-Flops

74LS373, 74LS374, S373, S374

The data on the D inputs are transferred to the latch outputs when the Latch Enable (E) input is HIGH. The latch remains transparent to the data inputs while E is HIGH, and stores the data present one set-up time before the HIGH-to-LOW enable transition. The enable gate has hysteresis built in to help minimize problems that signal and ground noise can cause on the latching operation.

The 3-State output buffers are designed to drive heavily loaded 3-State buses, MOS memories, or MOS microprocessors. The active LOW Output Enable ($\overline{OE}$) controls all eight 3-State buffers independent of the latch

operation. When $\overline{OE}$ is LOW, the latched or transparent data appears at the outputs. When $\overline{OE}$ is HIGH, the outputs are in the HIGH impedance "off" state, which means they will neither drive nor load the bus.

The '374 is an 8-bit, edge-triggered register coupled to eight 3-State output buffers. The two sections of the device are controlled independently by the Clock (CP) and Output Enable ($\overline{OE}$) control gates.

The register is fully edge triggered. The state of each D input, one set-up time before the LOW-to-HIGH clock transition, is transferred

to the corresponding flip-flop's Q output. The clock buffer has hysteresis built in to help minimize problems that signal and ground noise can cause on the clocking operation.

The 3-State output buffers are designed to drive heavily loaded 3-State buses, MOS memories, or MOS microprocessors. The active LOW Output Enable ($\overline{OE}$) controls all eight 3-State buffers independent of the register operation. When $\overline{OE}$ is LOW, the data in the register appears at the outputs. When $\overline{OE}$ is HIGH, the outputs are in the HIGH impedance "off" state, which means they will neither drive nor load the bus.

LOGIC DIAGRAM, '373

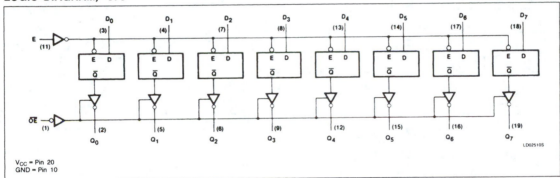

V_{CC} = Pin 20
GND = Pin 10

LOGIC DIAGRAM, '374

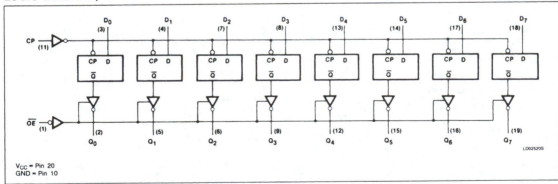

V_{CC} = Pin 20
GND = Pin 10

MODE SELECT — FUNCTION TABLE '373

OPERATING MODES	INPUTS			INTERNAL REGISTER	OUTPUTS
	$\overline{OE}$	E	D_n		$Q_0 - Q_7$
Enable and read register	L	H	L	L	L
	L	H	H	H	H
Latch and read register	L	L	l	L	L
	L	L	h	H	H
Latch register and disable outputs	H	L	l	L	(Z)
	H	L	h	H	(Z)

Signetics Logic Products   Product Specification

Latches/Flip-Flops   74LS373, 74LS374, S373, S374

MODE SELECT — FUNCTION TABLE '374

| OPERATING MODES | INPUTS | | | INTERNAL REGISTER | OUTPUTS |
	$\overline{OE}$	CP	D_n		$Q_0 - Q_7$
Load and read register	L	↑	l	L	L
	L	↑	h	H	H
Load register and disable outputs	H	↑	l	L	(Z)
	H	↑	h	H	(Z)

H = HIGH voltage level
h = HIGH voltage level one set-up time prior to the LOW-to-HIGH clock transition or HIGH-to-LOW $\overline{OE}$ transition
L = LOW voltage level
l = LOW voltage level one set-up time prior to the LOW-to-HIGH clock transition or HIGH-to-LOW $\overline{OE}$ transition
(Z) = HIGH impedance "off" state
↑ = LOW-to-HIGH clock transition

ABSOLUTE MAXIMUM RATINGS (Over operating free-air temperature range unless otherwise noted.)

	PARAMETER	74LS	74S	UNIT
V_{CC}	Supply voltage	7.0	7.0	V
V_{IN}	Input voltage	−0.5 to +7.0	−0.5 to +5.5	V
I_{IN}	Input current	−30 to +1	−30 to +5	mA
V_{OUT}	Voltage applied to output in HIGH output state	−0.5 to +V_{CC}	−0.5 to +V_{CC}	V
T_A	Operating free-air temperature range	0 to 70		°C

RECOMMENDED OPERATING CONDITIONS

| | PARAMETER | 74LS | | | 74S | | | UNIT |
		Min	Nom	Max	Min	Nom	Max	
V_{CC}	Supply voltage	4.75	5.0	5.25	4.75	5.0	5.25	V
V_{IH}	HIGH-level input voltage	2.0			2.0			V
V_{IL}	LOW-level input voltage			+0.8			+0.8	V
I_{IK}	Input clamp current			−18			−18	mA
I_{OH}	HIGH-level output current			−2.6			−6.5	mA
I_{OL}	LOW-level output current			24			20	mA
T_A	Operating free-air temperature	0		70	0		70	°C

5

Signetics Logic Products

Product Specification

Latches/Flip-Flops

74LS373, 74LS374, S373, S374

DC ELECTRICAL CHARACTERISTICS (Over recommended operating free-air temperature range unless otherwise noted.)

PARAMETER		TEST CONDITIONS[1]		74LS373, 374			74S373, 374			UNIT
				Min	Typ[2]	Max	Min	Typ[2]	Max	
V_{OH}	HIGH-level output voltage	V_{CC} = MIN, V_{IH} = MIN, V_{IL} = MAX, I_{OH} = MAX		2.4	3.1		2.4	3.1		V
V_{OL}	LOW-level output voltage	V_{CC} = MIN, V_{IH} = MIN, V_{IL} = MAX	I_{OL} = MAX		0.35	0.5			0.5	V
			I_{OL} = 12mA (74LS)		0.25	0.4				V
V_{IK}	Input clamp voltage	V_{CC} = MIN, I_I = I_{IK}				−1.5			−1.2	V
I_{OZH}	Off-state output current, HIGH-level voltage applied	V_{CC} = MAX, V_{IH} = MIN	V_O = 2.7V			20				µA
			V_O = 2.4V						50	µA
I_{OZL}	Off-state output current, LOW-level voltage applied	V_{CC} = MAX, V_{IH} = MIN	V_O = 0.4V			−20				µA
			V_O = 0.5V						−50	µA
I_I	Input current at maximum input voltage	V_{CC} = MAX	V_I = 7.0V			0.1				mA
			V_I = 5.5V						1.0	mA
I_{IH}	HIGH-level input current	V_{CC} = MAX, V_I = 2.7V				20			50	µA
I_{IL}	LOW-level input current	V_{CC} = MAX	V_I = 0.4V			−0.4				mA
			V_I = 0.5V						−0.25	mA
I_{OS}	Short-circuit output current[3]	V_{CC} = MAX		−30		−130	−40		−100	mA
I_{CC}	Supply current (total)	V_{CC} = MAX	I_{CCZ} $\overline{OE}$ = 4.5V 'LS373		24	40				mA
			I_{CCL} $\overline{OE}$ = 0V 'S373					105	160	mA
			I_{CCZ} $\overline{OE}$ = 4.5V 'LS374		27	40				mA
			I_{CCL} All inputs grounded 'S374					102	140	mA
			I_{CCZ} CP, $\overline{OE}$ = 4.5V D inputs = GND 'S374					131	180	mA

NOTES:
1. For conditions shown as MIN or MAX, use the appropriate value specified under recommended operating conditions for the applicable type.
2. All typical values are at V_{CC} = 5V, T_A = 25°C.
3. I_{OS} is tested with V_{OUT} = +0.5V and V_{CC} = V_{CC} MAX + 0.5V. Not more than one output should be shorted at a time and duration of the short circuit should not exceed one second.

AC ELECTRICAL CHARACTERISTICS T_A = 25°C, V_{CC} = 5.0V

PARAMETER		TEST CONDITIONS	74LS		74S		UNIT
			C_L = 45pF, R_L = 667Ω		C_L = 15pF, R_L = 280Ω		
			Min	Max	Min	Max	
f_{MAX}	Maximum clock frequency	Waveform 6, '374	35		75		MHz
t_{PLH} t_{PHL}	Propagation delay Latch enable to output	Waveform 1, '373		30 30		14 18	ns
t_{PLH} t_{PHL}	Propagation delay Data to output	Waveform 4, '373		18 18		12 12	ns
t_{PLH} t_{PHL}	Propagation delay Clock to output	Waveform 6, '374		28 28		15 17	ns
t_{PZH}	Enable time to HIGH level	Waveform 2		28		15	ns
t_{PZL}	Enable time to LOW level	Waveform 3, '373 '374		36 28		18 18	ns
t_{PHZ}	Disable time from HIGH level	Waveform 2, C_L = 5pF		20		9	ns
t_{PLZ}	Disable time from LOW level	Waveform 3, C_L = 5pF		25		12	ns

NOTE:
Per industry convention, f_{MAX} is the worst case value of the maximum device operating frequency with no constraints on t_r, t_f, pulse width or duty cycle.

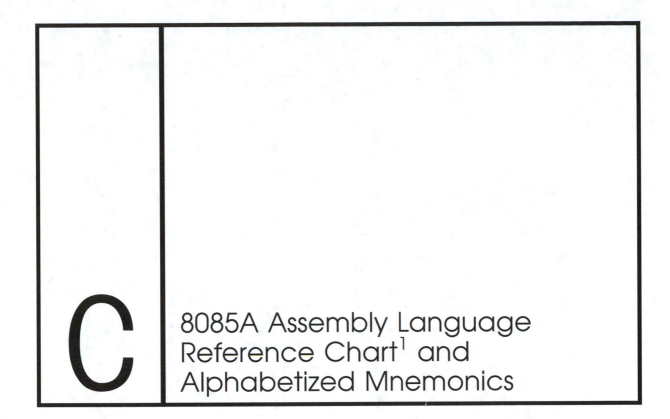

C

8085A Assembly Language Reference Chart[1] and Alphabetized Mnemonics

[1]Courtesy of Intel Corporation.

DATA TRANSFER GROUP

Move

	A,A	7F
	A,B	78
	A,C	79
MOV	A,D	7A
	A,E	7B
	A,H	7C
	A,L	7D
	A,M	7E

	B,A	47
	B,B	40
	B,C	41
MOV	B,D	42
	B,E	43
	B,H	44
	B,L	45
	B,M	46

	C,A	4F
	C,B	48
	C,C	49
MOV	C,D	4A
	C,E	4B
	C,H	4C
	C,L	4D
	C,M	4E

	D,A	57
	D,B	50
	D,C	51
MOV	D,D	52
	D,E	53
	D,H	54
	D,L	55
	D,M	56

Move (cont)

	E,A	5F
	E,B	58
	E,C	59
MOV	E,D	5A
	E,E	5B
	E,H	5C
	E,L	5D
	E,M	5E

	H,A	67
	H,B	60
	H,C	61
MOV	H,D	62
	H,E	63
	H,H	64
	H,L	65
	H,M	66

	L,A	6F
	L,B	68
	L,C	69
MOV	L,D	6A
	L,E	6B
	L,H	6C
	L,L	6D
	L,M	6E

	M,A	77
	M,B	70
	M,C	71
MOV	M,D	72
	M,E	73
	M,H	74
	M,L	75

XCHG   EB

Move Immediate

	A, byte	3E
	B, byte	06
	C, byte	0E
MVI	D, byte	16
	E, byte	1E
	H, byte	26
	L, byte	2E
	M, byte	36

Load Immediate

	B, dble	01
LXI	D, dble	11
	H, dble	21
	SP, dble	31

Load/Store

LDAX B	0A
LDAX D	1A
LHLD adr	2A
LDA adr	3A
STAX B	02
STAX D	12
SHLD adr	22
STA adr	32

byte = constant, or logical/arithmetic expression that evaluates to an 8-bit data quantity (Second byte of 2-byte instructions)
dble = constant, or logical/arithmetic expression that evaluates to a 16-bit data quantity (Second and Third bytes of 3-byte instructions)
adr = 16-bit address (Second and Third bytes of 3-byte instructions)
* = all flags (C, Z, S, P, AC) affected.
** = all flags except CARRY affected. (exception INX and DCX affect no flags)
† = only CARRY affected

ARITHMETIC AND LOGICAL GROUP

Add*

	A	87
	B	80
	C	81
ADD	D	82
	E	83
	H	84
	L	85
	M	86

	A	8F
	B	88
	C	89
ADC	D	8A
	E	8B
	H	8C
	L	8D
	M	8E

Subtract*

	A	97
	B	90
	C	91
SUB	D	92
	E	93
	H	94
	L	95
	M	96

	A	9F
	B	98
	C	99
SBB	D	9A
	E	9B
	H	9C
	L	9D
	M	9E

Double Add †

	B	09
DAD	D	19
	H	29
	SP	39

Increment**

	A	3C
	B	04
	C	0C
INR	D	14
	E	1C
	H	24
	L	2C
	M	34

	B	03
INX	D	13
	H	23
	SP	33

Decrement**

	A	3D
	B	05
	C	0D
DCR	D	15
	E	1D
	H	25
	L	2D
	M	35

	B	0B
DCX	D	1B
	H	2B
	SP	3B

Specials

DAA*	27
CMA	2F
STC†	37
CMC†	3F

Rotate †

RLC	07
RRC	0F
RAL	17
RAR	1F

Logical*

	A	A7
	B	A0
	C	A1
ANA	D	A2
	E	A3
	H	A4
	L	A5
	M	A6

	A	AF
	B	A8
	C	A9
XRA	D	AA
	E	AB
	H	AC
	L	AD
	M	AE

	A	B7
	B	B0
	C	B1
ORA	D	B2
	E	B3
	H	B4
	L	B5
	M	B6

	A	BF
	B	B8
	C	B9
CMP	D	BA
	E	BB
	H	BC
	L	BD
	M	BE

Arith & Logical Immediate

ADI byte	C6
ACI byte	CE
SUI byte	D6
SBI byte	DE
ANI byte	E6
XRI byte	EE
ORI byte	F6
CPI byte	FE

BRANCH CONTROL GROUP

Jump

JMP adr	C3
JNZ adr	C2
JZ adr	CA
JNC adr	D2
JC adr	DA
JPO adr	E2
JPE adr	EA
JP adr	F2
JM adr	FA
PCHL	E9

Call

CALL adr	CD
CNZ adr	C4
CZ adr	CC
CNC adr	D4
CC adr	DC
CPO adr	E4
CPE adr	EC
CP adr	F4
CM adr	FC

Return

RET	C9
RNZ	C0
RZ	C8
RNC	D0
RC	D8
RPO	E0
RPE	E8
RP	F0
RM	F8

Restart

	0	C7
	1	CF
	2	D7
RST	3	DF
	4	E7
	5	EF
	6	F7
	7	FF

I/O AND MACHINE CONTROL

Stack Ops

	B	C5
PUSH	D	D5
	H	E5
	PSW	F5

	B	C1
POP	D	D1
	H	E1
	PSW*	F1

XTHL	E3
SPHL	F9

Input/Output

OUT byte	D3
IN byte	DB

Control

DI	F3
EI	FB
NOP	00
HLT	76

New Instructions (8085 Only)

RIM	20
SIM	30

RESTART TABLE

Name	Code	Restart Address
RST 0	C7	0000_{16}
RST 1	CF	0008_{16}
RST 2	D7	0010_{16}
RST 3	DF	0018_{16}
RST 4	E7	0020_{16}
TRAP	Hardware* Function	0024_{16}
RST 5	EF	0028_{16}
RST 5 5	Hardware* Function	$002C_{16}$
RST 6	F7	0030_{16}
RST 6 5	Hardware* Function	0034_{16}
RST 7	FF	0038_{16}
RST 7 5	Hardware* Function	$003C_{16}$

*NOTE The hardware functions refer to the on-chip interrupt feature of the 8085 only

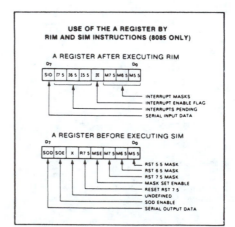

USE OF THE A REGISTER BY RIM AND SIM INSTRUCTIONS (8085 ONLY)

A REGISTER AFTER EXECUTING RIM

D7								D0
SID	I7 5	I6 5	I5 5	IE	M7 5	M6 5	M5 5

INTERRUPT MASKS
INTERRUPT ENABLE FLAG
INTERRUPTS PENDING
SERIAL INPUT DATA

A REGISTER BEFORE EXECUTING SIM

D7								D0
SOD	SOE	X	R7 5	MSE	M7 5	M6 5	M5 5

RST 5 5 MASK
RST 6 5 MASK
RST 7 5 MASK
MASK SET ENABLE
RESET RST 7 5
UNDEFINED
SOD ENABLE
SERIAL OUTPUT DATA

00	NOP		2B	DCX	H	56	MOV	D,M	81	ADD	C	AC	XRA	H	D7	RST	2
01	LXI	B,dble	2C	INR	L	57	MOV	D,A	82	ADD	D	AD	XRA	L	D8	RC	
02	STAX	B	2D	DCR	L	58	MOV	E,B	83	ADD	E	AE	XRA	M	D9	···	
03	INX	B	2E	MVI	L,byte	59	MOV	E,C	84	ADD	H	AF	XRA	A	DA	JC	adr
04	INR	B	2F	CMA		5A	MOV	E,D	85	ADD	L	B0	ORA	B	DB	IN	byte
05	DCR	B	30	SIM*		5B	MOV	E,E	86	ADD	M	B1	ORA	C	DC	CC	adr
06	MVI	B,byte	31	LXI	SP,dble	5C	MOV	E,H	87	ADD	A	B2	ORA	D	DD	···	
07	RLC		32	STA	adr	5D	MOV	E,L	88	ADC	B	B3	ORA	E	DE	SBI	byte
08	···		33	INX	SP	5E	MOV	E,M	89	ADC	C	B4	ORA	H	DF	RST	3
09	DAD	B	34	INR	M	5F	MOV	E,A	8A	ADC	D	B5	ORA	L	E0	RPO	
0A	LDAX	B	35	DCR	M	60	MOV	H,B	8B	ADC	E	B6	ORA	M	E1	POP	H
0B	DCX	B	36	MVI	M,byte	61	MOV	H,C	8C	ADC	H	B7	ORA	A	E2	JPO	adr
0C	INR	C	37	STC		62	MOV	H,D	8D	ADC	L	B8	CMP	B	E3	XTHL	
0D	DCR	C	38	···		63	MOV	H,E	8E	ADC	M	B9	CMP	C	E4	CPO	adr
0E	MVI	C,byte	39	DAD	SP	64	MOV	H,H	8F	ADC	A	BA	CMP	D	E5	PUSH	H
0F	RRC		3A	LDA	adr	65	MOV	H,L	90	SUB	B	BB	CMP	E	E6	ANI	byte
10	···		3B	DCX	SP	66	MOV	H,M	91	SUB	C	BC	CMP	H	E7	RST	4
11	LXI	D,dble	3C	INR	A	67	MOV	H,A	92	SUB	D	BD	CMP	L	E8	RPE	
12	STAX	D	3D	DCR	A	68	MOV	L,B	93	SUB	E	BE	CMP	M	E9	PCHL	
13	INX	D	3E	MVI	A,byte	69	MOV	L,C	94	SUB	H	BF	CMP	A	EA	JPE	adr
14	INR	D	3F	CMC		6A	MOV	L,D	95	SUB	L	C0	RNZ		EB	XCHG	
15	DCR	D	40	MOV	B,B	6B	MOV	L,E	96	SUB	M	C1	POP	B	EC	CPE	adr
16	MVI	D,byte	41	MOV	B,C	6C	MOV	L,H	97	SUB	A	C2	JNZ	adr	ED	···	
17	RAL		42	MOV	B,D	6D	MOV	L,L	98	SBB	B	C3	JMP	adr	EE	XRI	byte
18	···		43	MOV	B,E	6E	MOV	L,M	99	SBB	C	C4	CNZ	adr	EF	RST	5
19	DAD	D	44	MOV	B,H	6F	MOV	L,A	9A	SBB	D	C5	PUSH	B	F0	RP	
1A	LDAX	D	45	MOV	B,L	70	MOV	M,B	9B	SBB	E	C6	ADI	byte	F1	POP	PSW
1B	DCX	D	46	MOV	B,M	71	MOV	M,C	9C	SBB	H	C7	RST	0	F2	JP	adr
1C	INR	E	47	MOV	B,A	72	MOV	M,D	9D	SBB	L	C8	RZ		F3	DI	
1D	DCR	E	48	MOV	C,B	73	MOV	M,E	9E	SBB	M	C9	RET		F4	CP	adr
1E	MVI	E,byte	49	MOV	C,C	74	MOV	M,H	9F	SBB	A	CA	JZ	adr	F5	PUSH	PSW
1F	RAR		4A	MOV	C,D	75	MOV	M,L	A0	ANA	B	CB	···		F6	ORI	byte
20	RIM*		4B	MOV	C,E	76	HLT		A1	ANA	C	CC	CZ	adr	F7	RST	6
21	LXI	H,dble	4C	MOV	C,H	77	MOV	M,A	A2	ANA	D	CD	CALL	adr	F8	RM	
22	SHLD	adr	4D	MOV	C,L	78	MOV	A,B	A3	ANA	E	CE	ACI	byte	F9	SPHL	
23	INX	H	4E	MOV	C,M	79	MOV	A,C	A4	ANA	H	CF	RST	1	FA	JM	adr
24	INR	H	4F	MOV	C,A	7A	MOV	A,D	A5	ANA	L	D0	RNC		FB	EI	
25	DCR	H	50	MOV	D,B	7B	MOV	A,E	A6	ANA	M	D1	POP	D	FC	CM	adr
26	MVI	H,byte	51	MOV	D,C	7C	MOV	A,H	A7	ANA	A	D2	JNC	adr	FD	···	
27	DAA		52	MOV	D,D	7D	MOV	A,L	A8	XRA	B	D3	OUT	byte	FE	CPI	byte
28	···		53	MOV	D,E	7E	MOV	A,M	A9	XRA	C	D4	CNC	adr	FF	RST	7
29	DAD	H	54	MOV	D,H	7F	MOV	A,A	AA	XRA	D	D5	PUSH	D			
2A	LHLD	adr	55	MOV	D,L	80	ADD	B	AB	XRA	E	D6	SUI	byte			

*8085 Only

INTEL® 8080/8085 INSTRUCTION SET REFERENCE TABLES

INTERNAL REGISTER ORGANIZATION

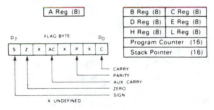

A Reg (8)	
B Reg (8)	C Reg (8)
D Reg (8)	E Reg (8)
H Reg (8)	L Reg (8)
Program Counter (16)	
Stack Pointer (16)	

FLAG BYTE

D7 ... D0

S	Z	X	AC	X	P	X	C

CARRY
PARITY
AUX CARRY
ZERO
SIGN

X UNDEFINED

REGISTER-PAIR ORGANIZATION

PSW

A (8)	FLAGS (8)

B	(B/C) (16)
D	(D/E) (16)
H	(H/L) (16)
Prog Ctr	(16)
Stack Ptr	(16)

NOTE: Leftmost Byte is high-order byte for arithmetic operations and addressing. Left byte is pushed on stack first. Right byte is popped first.

BRANCH CONTROL INSTRUCTIONS

Flag Condition	Jump		Call		Return	
Zero=True	JZ	CA	CZ	CC	RZ	C8
Zero=False	JNZ	C2	CNZ	C4	RNZ	C0
Carry=True	JC	DA	CC	DC	RC	D8
Carry=False	JNC	D2	CNC	D4	RNC	D0
Sign=Positive	JP	F2	CP	F4	RP	F0
Sign=Negative	JM	FA	CM	FC	RM	F8
Parity=Even	JPE	EA	CPE	EC	RPE	E8
Parity=Odd	JPO	E2	CPO	E4	RPO	E0
Unconditional	JMP	C3	CALL	CD	RET	C9

ACCUMULATOR OPERATIONS

	Code	Function
XRA A	AF	Clear A and Clear Carry
ORA A	B7	Clear Carry
CMC	3F	Complement Carry
CMA	2F	Complement Accumulator
STC	37	Set Carry
RLC	07	Rotate Left
RRC	0F	Rotate Right
RAL	17	Rotate Left Thru Carry
RAR	1F	Rotate Right Thru Carry
DAA	27	Decimal Adjust Accum

REGISTER PAIR AND STACK OPERATIONS

	PSW (A/F)	B (B/C)	D (D/E)	H (H/L)	SP	PC	Function
INX		03	13	23	33		Increment Register Pair
DCX		0B	1B	2B	3B		Decrement Register Pair
LDAX		0A	1A	7E(1)			Load A Indirect (Reg Pair holds Adrs)
STAX		02	12	77(2)			Store A Indirect (Reg Pair holds Adrs)
LHLD				2A			Load H L Direct (Bytes 2 and 3 hold Adrs)
SHLD				22			Store H L Direct (Bytes 2 and 3 hold Adrs)
LXI		01	11	21	31	C3(3)	Load Reg Pair Immediate (Bytes 2 and 3 hold immediate data)
PCHL						E9	Load PC with H L (Branch to Adrs in H L)
XCHG			EB				Exchange Reg Pairs D E and H L
DAD		09	19	29	39		Add Reg Pair to H L
PUSH	F5	C5	D5	E5			Push Reg Pair on Stack
POP	F1	C1	D1	E1			Pop Reg Pair off Stack
XTHL				E3			Exchange H L with Top of Stack
SPHL					F9		Load SP with H L

Notes: 1 This is MOV A,M　2 This is MOV M,A　3 This is JMP

Alphabetized 8085A Mnenomics with Hex Op-Codes

Hex	Mnemonic		Hex	Mnemonic		Hex	Mnemonic		Hex	Mnemonic	
CE	ACI	8-bit	2B	DCX	H	52	MOV	D,D	E5	PUSH	H
8F	ADC	A	3B	DCX	SP	53	MOV	D,E	F5	PUSH	PSW
88	ADC	B	F3	DI		54	MOV	D,H	17	RAL	
89	ADC	C	FB	EI		55	MOV	D,L	1F	RAR	
8A	ADC	D	76	HLT		56	MOV	D,M	D8	RC	
8B	ADC	E	DB	IN	8-bit	5F	MOV	E,A	C9	RET	
8C	ADC	H	3C	INR	A	58	MOV	E,B	20	RIM	
8D	ADC	L	04	INR	B	59	MOV	E,C	07	RLC	
8E	ADC	M	0C	INR	C	5A	MOV	E,D	F8	RM	
87	ADD	A	14	INR	D	5B	MOV	E,E	D0	RNC	
80	ADD	B	IC	INR	E	5C	MOV	E,H	C0	RNZ	
81	ADD	C	24	INR	H	5D	MOV	E,L	F0	RP	
82	ADD	D	2C	INR	L	5E	MOV	E,M	38	RPE	
83	ADD	E	34	INR	M	67	MOV	H,A	E0	RPO	
84	ADD	H	03	INX	B	60	MOV	H,B	0F	RRC	
85	ADD	L	13	INX	D	61	MOV	H,C	C7	RST	0
86	ADD	M	23	INX	H	62	MOV	H,D	CF	RST	1
C6	ADI	8-bit	33	INX	SP	63	MOV	H,E	D7	RST	2
A7	ANA	A	DA	JC	16-bit	64	MOV	H,H	DF	RST	3
A0	ANA	B	FA	JM	16-bit	65	MOV	H,L	E7	RST	4
A1	ANA	C	C3	JMP	16-bit	66	MOV	H,M	EF	RST	5
A2	ANA	D	D2	JNC	16-bit	6F	MOV	L,A	F7	RST	6
A3	ANA	E	C2	JNZ	16-bit	68	MOV	L,B	FF	RST	7
A4	ANA	H	F2	JP	16-bit	69	MOV	L,C	C8	RZ	
A5	ANA	L	EA	JPE	16-bit	6A	MOV	L,D	9F	SBB	A
A6	ANA	M	E2	JPO	16-bit	6B	MOV	L,E	98	SBB	B
E6	ANI	8-bit	CA	JZ	16-bit	6C	MOV	L,H	99	SBB	C
CD	CALL	16-bit	3A	LDA	16-bit	6D	MOV	L,L	9A	SBB	D
DC	CC	16-bit	0A	LDAX	B	6E	MOV	L,M	9B	SBB	E
FC	CM	16-bit	1A	LDAX	D	77	MOV	M,A	9C	SBB	H
2F	CMA		2A	LHLD	16-bit	70	MOV	M,B	9D	SBB	L
3F	CMC		01	LXI	B,16-bit	71	MOV	M,C	9E	SBB	M
BF	CMP	A	11	LXI	D,16-bit	72	MOV	M,D	DE	SBI	8-bit
B8	CMP	B	21	LXI	H,16-bit	73	MOV	M,E	22	SHLD,	16-bit
B9	CMP	C	31	LXI	SP,16-bit	74	MOV	M,H	30	SIM	
BA	CMP	D	7F	MOV	A,A	75	MOV	M,L	F9	SPHL	
BB	CMP	E	78	MOV	A,B	3E	MVI	A, 8-bit	32	STA	16-bit
BC	CMP	H	79	MOV	A,C	06	MVI	B, 8-bit	02	STAX	B
BD	CMP	L	7A	MOV	A,D	0E	MVI	C, 8-bit	12	STAX	D
BE	CMP	M	7B	MOV	A,E	16	MVI	D, 8-bit	37	STC	
D4	CNC	16-bit	7C	MOV	A,H	1E	MVI	E, 8-bit	97	SUB	A
C4	CNZ	16-bit	7D	MOV	A,L	26	MVI	H, 8-bit	90	SUB	B
F4	CP	16-bit	7E	MOV	A,M	2E	MVI	L, 8-bit	91	SUB	C
EC	CPE	16-bit	47	MOV	B,A	36	MVI	M, 8-bit	92	SUB	D
FE	CPI	8-bit	40	MOV	B,B	00	NOP		93	SUB	E
E4	CPO	16-bit	41	MOV	B,C	B7	ORA	A	94	SUB	H
CC	CZ	16-bit	42	MOV	B,D	B0	ORA	B	95	SUB	L
27	DAA		43	MOV	B,E	B1	ORA	C	96	SUB	M
09	DAD	B	44	MOV	B,H	B2	ORA	D	D6	SUI	8-bit
19	DAD	D	45	MOV	B,L	B3	ORA	E	EB	XCHG	
29	DAD	H	46	MOV	B,M	B4	ORA	H	AF	XRA	A
39	DAD	SP	4F	MOV	C,A	B5	ORA	L	A8	XRA	B
3D	DCR	A	48	MOV	C,B	B6	ORA	M	A9	XRA	C
05	DCR	B	49	MOV	C,C	F6	ORI	8-bit	AA	XRA	D
0D	DCR	C	4A	MOV	C,D	D3	OUT	8-bit	AB	XRA	E
15	DCR	D	4B	MOV	C,E	E9	PCHL		AC	XRA	H
1D	DCR	E	4C	MOV	C,H	C1	POP	B	AD	XRA	L
25	DCR	H	4D	MOV	C,L	D1	POP	D	AE	XRA	M
2D	DCR	L	4E	MOV	C,M	E1	POP	H	EE	XRI	8-bit
35	DCR	M	57	MOV	D,A	F1	POP	PSW	E3	XTHL	
0B	DCX	B	50	MOV	D,B	C5	PUSH	B			
1B	DCX	D	51	MOV	D,C	D5	PUSH	D			

D

8085A Instruction Set Reference Encyclopedia[1]

[1]Courtesy of Intel Corporation.

THE INSTRUCTION SET

INSTRUCTION SET ENCYCLOPEDIA

In the ensuing dozen pages, the complete 8085A instruction set is described, grouped in order under five different functional headings, as follows:

1. **Data Transfer Group** — Moves data between registers or between memory locations and registers. Includes moves, loads, stores, and exchanges.

2. **Arithmetic Group** — Adds, subtracts, increments, or decrements data in registers or memory.

3. **Logic Group** — ANDs, ORs, XORs, compares, rotates, or complements data in registers or between memory and a register.

4. **Branch Group** — Initiates conditional or unconditional jumps, calls, returns, and restarts.

5. **Stack, I/O, and Machine Control Group** — Includes instructions for maintaining the stack, reading from input ports, writing to output ports, setting and reading interrupt masks, and setting and clearing flags.

The formats described in the encyclopedia reflect the assembly language processed by Intel-supplied assembler, used with the Intellec® development systems.

Data Transfer Group

This group of instructions transfers data to and from registers and memory. **Condition flags are not affected by any instruction in this group.**

MOV r1, r2   (Move Register)
    (r1) ← (r2)
    The content of register r2 is moved to register r1.

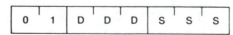

Cycles:	1
States:	4 (8085), 5 (8080)
Addressing:	register
Flags:	none

MOV r, M   (Move from memory)
    (r) ← ((H) (L))
    The content of the memory location, whose address is in registers H and L, is moved to register r.

Cycles:	2
States:	7
Addressing:	reg. indirect
Flags:	none

MOV M, r   (Move to memory)
    ((H) (L)) ← (r)
    The content of register r is moved to the memory location whose address is in registers H and L.

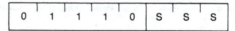

Cycles:	2
States:	7
Addressing:	reg. indirect
Flags:	none

MVI r, data   (Move Immediate)
    (r) ← (byte 2)
    The content of byte 2 of the instruction is moved to register r.

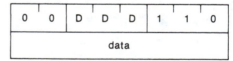

Cycles:	2
States:	7
Addressing:	immediate
Flags:	none

MVI M, data   (Move to memory immediate)
    ((H) (L)) ← (byte 2)
    The content of byte 2 of the instruction is moved to the memory location whose address is in registers H and L.

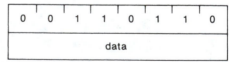

Cycles:	3
States:	10
Addressing:	immed./reg. indirect
Flags:	none

THE INSTRUCTION SET

LXI rp, data 16 (Load register pair immediate)
(rh) ← (byte 3),
(rl) ← (byte 2)
Byte 3 of the instruction is moved into the high-order register (rh) of the register pair rp. Byte 2 of the instruction is moved into the low-order register (rl) of the register pair rp.

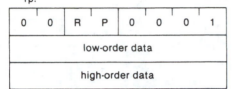

0	0	R	P	0	0	0	1

low-order data

high-order data

Cycles: 3
States: 10
Addressing: immediate
Flags: none

LDA addr (Load Accumulator direct)
(A) ← ((byte 3)(byte 2))
The content of the memory location, whose address is specified in byte 2 and byte 3 of the instruction, is moved to register A.

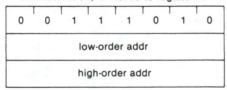

0	0	1	1	1	0	1	0

low-order addr

high-order addr

Cycles: 4
States: 13
Addressing: direct
Flags: none

STA addr (Store Accumulator direct)
((byte 3)(byte 2)) ← (A)
The content of the accumulator is moved to the memory location whose address is specified in byte 2 and byte 3 of the instruction.

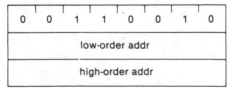

0	0	1	1	0	0	1	0

low-order addr

high-order addr

M~ Cycles: 4
1~ States: 13
Addressing: direct
Flags: none

LHLD addr (Load H and L direct)
(L) ← ((byte 3)(byte 2))
(H) ← ((byte 3)(byte 2) + 1)
The content of the memory location, whose address is specified in byte 2 and byte 3 of the instruction, is moved to register L. The content of the memory location at the succeeding address is moved to register H.

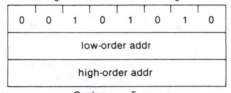

0	0	1	0	1	0	1	0

low-order addr

high-order addr

Cycles: 5
States: 16
Addressing: direct
Flags: none

SHLD addr (Store H and L direct)
((byte 3)(byte 2)) ← (L)
((byte 3)(byte 2) + 1) ← (H)
The content of register L is moved to the memory location whose address is specified in byte 2 and byte 3. The content of register H is moved to the succeeding memory location.

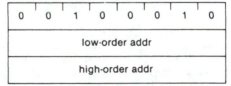

0	0	1	0	0	0	1	0

low-order addr

high-order addr

Cycles: 5
States: 16
Addressing: direct
Flags: none

LDAX rp (Load accumulator indirect)
(A) ← ((rp))
The content of the memory location, whose address is in the register pair rp, is moved to register A. Note: only register pairs rp = B (registers B and C) or rp = D (registers D and E) may be specified.

0	0	R	P	1	0	1	0

Cycles: 2
States: 7
Addressing: reg. indirect
Flags: none

THE INSTRUCTION SET

STAX rp   (Store accumulator indirect)
  ((rp)) ← (A)
  The content of register A is moved to the memory location whose address is in the register pair rp. Note: only register pairs rp = B (registers B and C) or rp = D (registers D and E) may be specified.

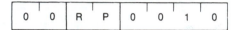

	Cycles:	2
	States:	7
	Addressing:	reg. indirect
	Flags:	none

XCHG   (Exchange H and L with D and E)
  (H) ↔ (D)
  (L) ↔ (E)
  The contents of registers H and L are exchanged with the contents of registers D and E.

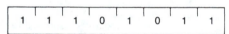

	Cycles:	1
	States:	4
	Addressing:	register
	Flags:	none

Arithmetic Group

This group of instructions performs arithmetic operations on data in registers and memory.

Unless indicated otherwise, all instructions in this group affect the Zero, Sign, Parity, Carry, and Auxiliary Carry flags according to the standard rules.

All subtraction operations are performed via two's complement arithmetic and set the carry flag to one to indicate a borrow and clear it to indicate no borrow.

ADD r   (Add Register)
  (A) ← (A) + (r)
  The content of register r is added to the content of the accumulator. The result is placed in the accumulator.

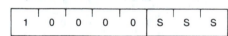

	Cycles:	1
	States:	4
	Addressing:	register
	Flags:	Z,S,P,CY,AC

ADD M   (Add memory)
  (A) ← (A) + ((H) (L))
  The content of the memory location whose address is contained in the H and L registers is added to the content of the accumulator. The result is placed in the accumulator.

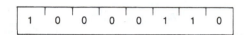

	Cycles:	2
	States:	7
	Addressing:	reg. indirect
	Flags:	Z,S,P,CY,AC

ADI data   (Add immediate)
  (A) ← (A) + (byte 2)
  The content of the second byte of the instruction is added to the content of the accumulator. The result is placed in the accumulator.

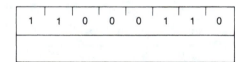

	Cycles:	2
	States:	7
	Addressing:	immediate
	Flags:	Z,S,P,CY,AC

ADC r   (Add Register with carry)
  (A) ← (A) + (r) + (CY)
  The content of register r and the content of the carry bit are added to the content of the accumulator. The result is placed in the accumulator.

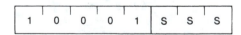

	Cycles:	1
	States:	4
	Addressing:	register
	Flags:	Z,S,P,CY,AC

*All mnemonics copyrighted ©Intel Corporation 1976.

THE INSTRUCTION SET

ADC M   (Add memory with carry)
(A) ← (A) + ((H) (L)) + (CY)
The content of the memory location whose address is contained in the H and L registers and the content of the CY flag are added to the accumulator. The result is placed in the accumulator.

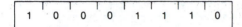

| | | | | | | | |
|1|0|0|0|1|1|1|0|

Cycles: 2
States: 7
Addressing: reg. indirect
Flags: Z,S,P,CY,AC

SUB M   (Subtract memory)
(A) ← (A) − ((H) (L))
The content of the memory location whose address is contained in the H and L registers is subtracted from the content of the accumulator. The result is placed in the accumulator.

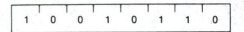

| | | | | | | | |
|1|0|0|1|0|1|1|0|

Cycles: 2
States: 7
Addressing: reg. indirect
Flags: Z,S,P,CY,AC

ACI data   (Add immediate with carry)
(A) ← (A) + (byte 2) + (CY)
The content of the second byte of the instruction and the content of the CY flag are added to the contents of the accumulator. The result is placed in the accumulator.

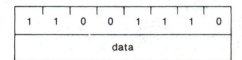

1	1	0	0	1	1	1	0
			data				

Cycles: 2
States: 7
Addressing: immediate
Flags: Z,S,P,CY,AC

SUI data   (Subtract immediate)
(A) ← (A) − (byte 2)
The content of the second byte of the instruction is subtracted from the content of the accumulator. The result is placed in the accumulator.

1	1	0	1	0	1	1	0
			data				

Cycles: 2
States: 7
Addressing: immediate
Flags: Z,S,P,CY,AC

SUB r   (Subtract Register)
(A) ← (A) − (r)
The content of register r is subtracted from the content of the accumulator. The result is placed in the accumulator.

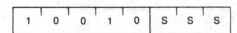

| | | | | | | | |
|1|0|0|1|0|S|S|S|

Cycles: 1
States: 4
Addressing: register
Flags: Z,S,P,CY,AC

SBB r   (Subtract Register with borrow)
(A) ← (A) − (r) − (CY)
The content of register r and the content of the CY flag are both subtracted from the accumulator. The result is placed in the accumulator.

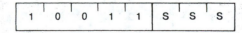

| | | | | | | | |
|1|0|0|1|1|S|S|S|

Cycles: 1
States: 4
Addressing: register
Flags: Z,S,P,CY,AC

THE INSTRUCTION SET

SBB M (Subtract memory with borrow)
(A) ← (A) − ((H) (L)) − (CY)
The content of the memory location whose address is contained in the H and L registers and the content of the CY flag are both subtracted from the accumulator. The result is placed in the accumulator.

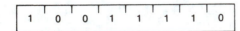

| 1 | 0 | 0 | 1 | 1 | 1 | 1 | 0 |

Cycles:	2
States:	7
Addressing:	reg. indirect
Flags:	Z,S,P,CY,AC

INR M (Increment memory)
((H) (L) ← ((H) (L)) + 1
The content of the memory location whose address is contained in the H and L registers is incremented by one. Note: All condition flags **except CY** are affected.

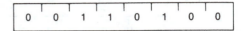

| 0 | 0 | 1 | 1 | 0 | 1 | 0 | 0 |

Cycles:	3
States:	10
Addressing:	reg. indirect
Flags:	Z,S,P,AC

SBI data (Subtract immediate with borrow)
(A) ← (A) − (byte 2) − (CY)
The contents of the second byte of the instruction and the contents of the CY flag are both subtracted from the accumulator. The result is placed in the accumulator.

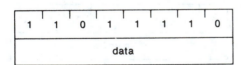

| 1 | 1 | 0 | 1 | 1 | 1 | 1 | 0 |
| | | | data | | | | |

Cycles:	2
States:	7
Addressing:	immediate
Flags:	Z,S,P,CY,AC

DCR r (Decrement Register)
(r) ← (r) − 1
The content of register r is decremented by one. Note: All condition flags **except CY** are affected.

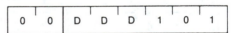

| 0 | 0 | D | D | D | 1 | 0 | 1 |

Cycles:	1
States:	4 (8085), 5 (8080)
Addressing:	register
Flags:	Z,S,P,AC

INR r (Increment Register)
(r) ← (r) + 1
The content of register r is incremented by one. Note: All condition flags **except CY** are affected.

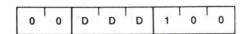

| 0 | 0 | D | D | D | 1 | 0 | 0 |

Cycles:	1
States:	4 (8085), 5 (8080)
Addressing:	register
Flags:	Z,S,P,AC

DCR M (Decrement memory)
((H) (L)) ← ((H) (L)) − 1
The content of the memory location whose address is contained in the H and L registers is decremented by one. Note: All condition flags **except CY** are affected.

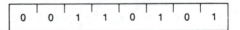

| 0 | 0 | 1 | 1 | 0 | 1 | 0 | 1 |

Cycles:	3
States:	10
Addressing:	reg. indirect
Flags:	Z,S,P,AC

THE INSTRUCTION SET

INX rp   (Increment register pair)
(rh) (rl) ← (rh) (rl) + 1
The content of the register pair rp is incremented by one. Note: **No condition flags are affected.**

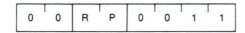

0	0	R	P	0	0	1	1

Cycles: 1
States: 6 (8085), 5 (8080)
Addressing: register
Flags: none

DCX rp   (Decrement register pair)
(rh) (rl) ← (rh) (rl) − 1
The content of the register pair rp is decremented by one. Note: **No condition flags are affected.**

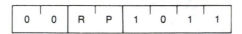

0	0	R	P	1	0	1	1

Cycles: 1
States: 6 (8085), 5 (8080)
Addressing: register
Flags: none

DAD rp   (Add register pair to H and L)
(H) (L) ← (H) (L) + (rh) (rl)
The content of the register pair rp is added to the content of the register pair H and L. The result is placed in the register pair H and L. Note: **Only the CY flag is affected.** It is set if there is a carry out of the double precision add; otherwise it is reset.

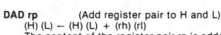

0	0	R	P	1	0	0	1

Cycles: 3
States: 10
Addressing: register
Flags: CY

DAA   (Decimal Adjust Accumulator)
The eight-bit number in the accumulator is adjusted to form two four-bit Binary-Coded-Decimal digits by the following process:

1. If the value of the least significant 4 bits of the accumulator is greater than 9 **or** if the AC flag is set, 6 is added to the accumulator.

2. If the value of the most significant 4 bits of the accumulator is now greater than 9, **or** if the CY flag is set, 6 is added to the most significant 4 bits of the accumulator.

NOTE: All flags are affected.

0	0	1	0	0	1	1	1

Cycles: 1
States: 4
Flags: Z,S,P,CY,AC

Logical Group

This group of instructions performs logical (Boolean) operations on data in registers and memory and on condition flags.

Unless indicated otherwise, all instructions in this group affect the Zero, Sign, Parity, Auxiliary Carry, and Carry flags according to the standard rules.

ANA r   (AND Register)
(A) ← (A) ∧ (r)
The content of register r is logically ANDed with the content of the accumulator. The result is placed in the accumulator. **The CY flag is cleared and AC is set (8085). The CY flag is cleared and AC is set to the OR'ing of bits 3 of the operands (8080).**

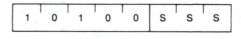

1	0	1	0	0	S	S	S

Cycles: 1
States: 4
Addressing: register
Flags: Z,S,P,CY,AC

THE INSTRUCTION SET

ANA M   (AND memory)

(A) ← (A) ∧ ((H) (L))

The contents of the memory location whose address is contained in the H and L registers is logically ANDed with the content of the accumulator. The result is placed in the accumulator. **The CY flag is cleared and AC is set (8085). The CY flag is cleared and AC is set to the OR'ing of bits 3 of the operands (8080).**

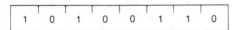

1	0	1	0	0	1	1	0

Cycles: 2
States: 7
Addressing: reg. indirect
Flags: Z,S,P,CY,AC

ANI data   (AND immediate)

(A) ← (A) ∧ (byte 2)

The content of the second byte of the instruction is logically ANDed with the contents of the accumulator. The result is placed in the accumulator. **The CY flag is cleared and AC is set (8085). The CY flag is cleared and AC is set to the OR'ing of bits 3 of the operands (8080).**

1	1	1	0	0	1	1	0
data

Cycles: 2
States: 7
Addressing: immediate
Flags: Z,S,P,CY,AC

XRA r   (Exclusive OR Register)

(A) ← (A) ⊻ (r)

The content of register r is exclusive-OR'd with the content of the accumulator. The result is placed in the accumulator. **The CY and AC flags are cleared.**

1	0	1	0	1	S	S	S

Cycles: 1
States: 4
Addressing: register
Flags: Z,S,P,CY,AC

XRA M   (Exclusive OR Memory)

(A) ← (A) ⊻ ((H) (L))

The content of the memory location whose address is contained in the H and L registers is exclusive-OR'd with the content of the accumulator. The result is placed in the accumulator. **The CY and AC flags are cleared.**

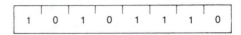

1	0	1	0	1	1	1	0

Cycles: 2
States: 7
Addressing: reg. indirect
Flags: Z,S,P,CY,AC

XRI data   (Exclusive OR immediate)

(A) ← (A) ⊻ (byte 2)

The content of the second byte of the instruction is exclusive-OR'd with the content of the accumulator. The result is placed in the accumulator. **The CY and AC flags are cleared.**

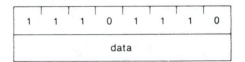

1	1	1	0	1	1	1	0
data

Cycles: 2
States: 7
Addressing: immediate
Flags: Z,S,P,CY,AC

ORA r   (OR Register)

(A) ← (A) V (r)

The content of register r is inclusive-OR'd with the content of the accumulator. The result is placed in the accumulator. **The CY and AC flags are cleared.**

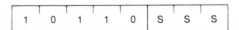

1	0	1	1	0	S	S	S

Cycles: 1
States: 4
Addressing: register
Flags: Z,S,P,CY,AC

*All mnemonics copyrighted © Intel Corporation 1976.

THE INSTRUCTION SET

ORA M   (OR memory)

$(A) \leftarrow (A) \vee ((H) (L))$

The content of the memory location whose address is contained in the H and L registers is inclusive-OR'd with the content of the accumulator. The result is placed in the accumulator. **The CY and AC flags are cleared.**

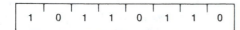

1	0	1	1	0	1	1	0

Cycles: 2
States: 7
Addressing: reg. indirect
Flags: Z,S,P,CY,AC

ORI data   (OR Immediate)

$(A) \leftarrow (A) \vee (byte\ 2)$

The content of the second byte of the instruction is inclusive-OR'd with the content of the accumulator. The result is placed in the accumulator. **The CY and AC flags are cleared..**

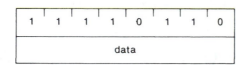

1	1	1	1	0	1	1	0
data							

Cycles: 2
States: 7
Addressing: immediate
Flags: Z,S,P,CY,AC

CMP r   (Compare Register)

$(A) - (r)$

The content of register r is subtracted from the accumulator. The accumulator remains unchanged. The condition flags are set as a result of the subtraction. **The Z flag is set to 1 if (A) = (r). The CY flag is set to 1 if (A) < (r).**

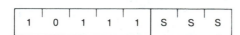

1	0	1	1	1	S	S	S

Cycles: 1
States: 4
Addressing: register
Flags: Z,S,P,CY,AC

CMP M   (Compare memory)

$(A) - ((H) (L))$

The content of the memory location whose address is contained in the H and L registers is subtracted from the accumulator. The accumulator remains unchanged. The condition flags are set as a result of the subtraction. **The Z flag is set to 1 if (A)=((H) (L)). The CY flag is set to 1 if (A)< ((H) (L)).**

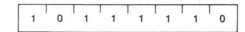

1	0	1	1	1	1	1	0

Cycles: 2
States: 7
Addressing: reg. indirect
Flags: Z,S,P,CY,AC

CPI data   (Compare immediate)

$(A) - (byte\ 2)$

The content of the second byte of the instruction is subtracted from the accumulator. The condition flags are set by the result of the subtraction. **The Z flag is set to 1 if (A)=(byte 2). The CY flag is set to 1 if (A)< (byte 2).**

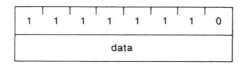

1	1	1	1	1	1	1	0
data							

Cycles: 2
States: 7
Addressing: immediate
Flags: Z,S,P,CY,AC

RLC   (Rotate left)

$(A_{n+1}) \leftarrow (A_n) ; (A_0) \leftarrow (A_7)$

$(CY) \leftarrow (A_7)$

The content of the accumulator is rotated left one position. The low order bit and the CY flag are both set to the value shifted out of the high order bit position. **Only the CY flag is affected.**

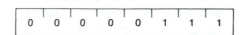

0	0	0	0	0	1	1	1

Cycles: 1
States: 4
Flags: CY

THE INSTRUCTION SET

RRC   (Rotate right)
$(A_n) \leftarrow (A_{n+1}); (A_7) \leftarrow (A_0)$
$(CY) \leftarrow (A_0)$
The content of the accumulator is rotated right one position. The high order bit and the CY flag are both set to the value shifted out of the low order bit position. **Only the CY flag is affected.**

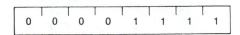

0	0	0	0	1	1	1	1

Cycles: 1
States: 4
Flags: CY

RAL   (Rotate left through carry)
$(A_{n+1}) \leftarrow (A_n); (CY) \leftarrow (A_7)$
$(A_0) \leftarrow (CY)$
The content of the accumulator is rotated left one position through the CY flag. The low order bit is set equal to the CY flag and the CY flag is set to the value shifted out of the high order bit. **Only the CY flag is affected.**

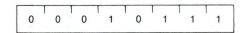

0	0	0	1	0	1	1	1

Cycles: 1
States: 4
Flags: CY

RAR   (Rotate right through carry)
$(A_n) \leftarrow (A_{n+1}); (CY) \leftarrow (A_0)$
$(A_7) \leftarrow (CY)$
The content of the accumulator is rotated right one position through the CY flag. The high order bit is set to the CY flag and the CY flag is set to the value shifted out of the low order bit. **Only the CY flag is affected.**

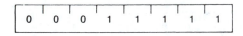

0	0	0	1	1	1	1	1

Cycles: 1
States: 4
Flags: CY

*All mnemonics copyrighted ©Intel Corporation 1976.

CMA   (Complement accumulator)
$(A) \leftarrow (\overline{A})$
The contents of the accumulator are complemented (zero bits become 1, one bits become 0). **No flags are affected.**

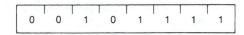

0	0	1	0	1	1	1	1

Cycles: 1
States: 4
Flags: none

CMC   (Complement carry)
$(CY) \leftarrow (\overline{CY})$
The CY flag is complemented. **No other flags are affected.**

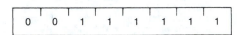

0	0	1	1	1	1	1	1

Cycles: 1
States: 4
Flags: CY

STC   (Set carry)
$(CY) \leftarrow 1$
The CY flag is set to 1. **No other flags are affected.**

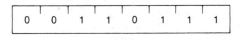

0	0	1	1	0	1	1	1

Cycles: 1
States: 4
Flags: CY

THE INSTRUCTION SET

Branch Group

This group of instructions alter normal sequential program flow.

Condition flags are not affected by any instruction in this group.

The two types of branch instructions are unconditional and conditional. Unconditional transfers simply perform the specified operation on register PC (the program counter). Conditional transfers examine the status of one of the four processor flags to determine if the specified branch is to be executed. The conditions that may be specified are as follows:

CONDITION		CCC
NZ —	not zero (Z = 0)	000
Z —	zero (Z = 1)	001
NC —	no carry (CY = 0)	010
C —	carry (CY = 1)	011
PO —	parity odd (P = 0)	100
PE —	parity even (P = 1)	101
P —	plus (S = 0)	110
M —	minus (S = 1)	111

JMP addr (Jump)
(PC) ← (byte 3) (byte 2)
Control is transferred to the instruction whose address is specified in byte 3 and byte 2 of the current instruction.

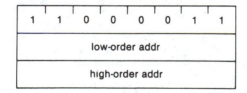

1	1	0	0	0	0	1	1

low-order addr

high-order addr

Cycles: 3
States: 10
Addressing: immediate
Flags: none

Jcondition addr (Conditional jump)
If (CCC),
(PC) ← (byte 3) (byte 2)
If the specified condition is true, control is transferred to the instruction whose address is specified in byte 3 and byte 2 of the current instruction; otherwise, control continues sequentially.

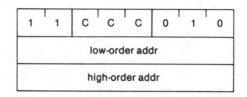

1	1	C	C	C	0	1	0

low-order addr

high-order addr

Cycles: 2/3 (8085), 3 (8080)
States: 7/10 (8085), 10 (8080)
Addressing: immediate
Flags: none

CALL addr (Call)
((SP) − 1) ← (PCH)
((SP) − 2) ← (PCL)
(SP) ← (SP) − 2
(PC) ← (byte 3) (byte 2)
The high-order eight bits of the next instruction address are moved to the memory location whose address is one less than the content of register SP. The low-order eight bits of the next instruction address are moved to the memory location whose address is two less than the content of register SP. The content of register SP is decremented by 2. Control is transferred to the instruction whose address is specified in byte 3 and byte 2 of the current instruction.

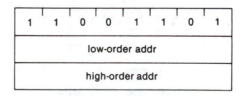

1	1	0	0	1	1	0	1

low-order addr

high-order addr

Cycles: 5
States: 18 (8085), 17 (8080)
Addressing: immediate/ reg. indirect
Flags: none

THE INSTRUCTION SET

Ccondition addr (Condition call)
If (CCC),
   ((SP) − 1) ← (PCH)
   ((SP) − 2) ← (PCL)
   (SP) ← (SP) − 2
   (PC) ← (byte 3) (byte 2)
If the specified condition is true, the actions specified in the CALL instruction (see above) are performed; otherwise, control continues sequentially.

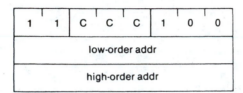

1	1	C	C	C	1	0	0
low-order addr							
high-order addr							

Cycles: 2/5 (8085), 3/5 (8080)
States: 9/18 (8085), 11/17 (8080)
Addressing: immediate/
         reg. indirect
Flags: none

RET   (Return)
   (PCL) ← ((SP));
   (PCH) ← ((SP) + 1);
   (SP) ← (SP) + 2;
The content of the memory location whose address is specified in register SP is moved to the low-order eight bits of register PC. The content of the memory location whose address is one more than the content of register SP is moved to the high-order eight bits of register PC. The content of register SP is incremented by 2.

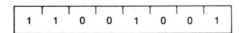

1	1	0	0	1	0	0	1

Cycles: 3
States: 10
Addressing: reg. indirect
Flags: none

Rcondition   (Conditional return)
If (CCC),
   (PCL) ← ((SP))
   (PCH) ← ((SP) + 1)
   (SP) ← (SP) + 2
If the specified condition is true, the actions specified in the RET instruction (see above) are performed; otherwise, control continues sequentially.

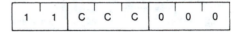

1	1	C	C	C	0	0	0

Cycles: 1/3
States: 6/12 (8085), 5/11 (8080)
Addressing: reg. indirect
Flags: none

RST n   (Restart)
   ((SP) − 1) ← (PCH)
   ((SP) − 2) ← (PCL)
   (SP) ← (SP) − 2
   (PC) ← 8 * (NNN)
The high-order eight bits of the next instruction address are moved to the memory location whose address is one less than the content of register SP. The low-order eight bits of the next instruction address are moved to the memory location whose address is two less than the content of register SP. The content of register SP is decremented by two. Control is transferred to the instruction whose address is eight times the content of NNN.

1	1	N	N	N	1	1	1

Cycles: 3
States: 12 (8085), 11 (8080)
Addressing: reg. indirect
Flags: none

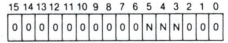

15	14	13	12	11	10	9	8	7	6	5	4	3	2	1	0
0	0	0	0	0	0	0	0	0	0	N	N	N	0	0	0

Program Counter After Restart

THE INSTRUCTION SET

PCHL   (Jump H and L indirect —
move H and L to PC)

(PCH) ← (H)
(PCL) ← (L)
The content of register H is moved to the high-order eight bits of register PC. The content of register L is moved to the low-order eight bits of register PC.

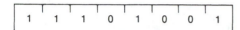

Cycles: 1
States: 6 (8085), 5 (8080)
Addressing: register
Flags: none

Stack, I/O, and Machine Control Group

This group of instructions performs I/O, manipulates the Stack, and alters internal control flags.

Unless otherwise specified, **condition flags are not affected by any instructions in this group.**

PUSH rp   (Push)

((SP) − 1) ← (rh)
((SP) − 2) ← (rl)
((SP) ← (SP) − 2

The content of the high-order register of register pair rp is moved to the memory location whose address is one less than the content of register SP. The content of the low-order register of register pair rp is moved to the memory location whose address is two less than the content of register SP. The content of register SP is decremented by 2. **Note: Register pair rp = SP may not be specified.**

Cycles: 3
States: 12 (8085), 11 (8080)
Addressing: reg. indirect
Flags: none

PUSH PSW   (Push processor status word)

((SP) − 1) ← (A)
((SP) − 2)$_0$ ← (CY) , ((SP) − 2)$_1$ ← X
((SP) − 2)$_2$ ← (P) , ((SP) − 2)$_3$ ← X
((SP) − 2)$_4$ ← (AC) , ((SP) − 2)$_5$ ← X
((SP) − 2)$_6$ ← (Z) , ((SP) − 2)$_7$ ← (S)
(SP) ← (SP) − 2   X: Undefined.

The content of register A is moved to the memory location whose address is one less than register SP. The contents of the condition flags are assembled into a processor status word and the word is moved to the memory location whose address is two less than the content of register SP. The content of register SP is decremented by two.

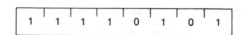

Cycles: 3
States: 12 (8085), 11 (8080)
Addressing: reg. indirect
Flags: none

FLAG WORD

D$_7$	D$_6$	D$_5$	D$_4$	D$_3$	D$_2$	D$_1$	D$_0$
S	Z	X	AC	X	P	X	CY

X: undefined

POP rp   (Pop)

(rl) ← ((SP))
(rh) ← ((SP) + 1)
(SP) ← (SP) + 2

The content of the memory location, whose address is specified by the content of register SP, is moved to the low-order register of register pair rp. The content of the memory location, whose address is one more than the content of register SP, is moved to the high-order register of register rp. The content of register SP is incremented by 2. **Note: Register pair rp = SP may not be specified.**

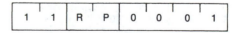

Cycles: 3
States: 10
Addressing: reg.indirect
Flags: none

THE INSTRUCTION SET

POP PSW   (Pop processor status word)

$(CY) \leftarrow ((SP))_0$
$(P) \leftarrow ((SP))_2$
$(AC) \leftarrow ((SP))_4$
$(Z) \leftarrow ((SP))_6$
$(S) \leftarrow ((SP))_7$
$(A) \leftarrow ((SP) + 1)$
$(SP) \leftarrow (SP) + 2$

The content of the memory location whose address is specified by the content of register SP is used to restore the condition flags. The content of the memory location whose address is one more than the content of register SP is moved to register A. The content of register SP is incremented by 2.

1	1	1	1	0	0	0	1

```
     Cycles:   3
     States:   10
Addressing:    reg. indirect
     Flags:    Z,S,P,CY,AC
```

XTHL   (Exchange stack top with H and L)

$(L) \leftrightarrow ((SP))$
$(H) \leftrightarrow ((SP) + 1)$

The content of the L register is exchanged with the content of the memory location whose address is specified by the content of register SP. The content of the H register is exchanged with the content of the memory location whose address is one more than the content of register SP.

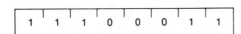

```
     Cycles:   5
     States:   16 (8085), 18 (8080)
Addressing:    reg. indirect
     Flags:    none
```

SPHL   (Move HL to SP)

$(SP) \leftarrow (H) (L)$
The contents of registers H and L (16 bits) are moved to register SP.

1	1	1	1	1	0	0	1

```
     Cycles:   1
     States:   6 (8085), 5 (8080)
Addressing:    register
     Flags:    none
```

IN port   (Input)

$(A) \leftarrow (data)$
The data placed on the eight bit bi-directional data bus by the specified port is moved to register A.

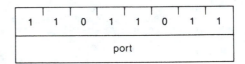

```
     Cycles:   3
     States:   10
Addressing:    direct
     Flags:    none
```

OUT port   (Output)

$(data) \leftarrow (A)$
The content of register A is placed on the eight bit bi-directional data bus for transmission to the specified port.

```
     Cycles:   3
     States:   10
Addressing:    direct
     Flags:    none
```

THE INSTRUCTION SET

EI   (Enable interrupts)
The interrupt system is enabled **following the execution of the next instruction. Interrupts are not recognized during the EI instruction.**

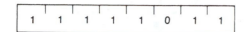

Cycles: 1
States: 4
Flags: none

NOTE: Placing an EI instruction on the bus in response to INTA during an INA cycle is prohibited. (8085)

DI   (Disable interrupts)
The interrupt system is disabled **immediately following the execution of the DI instruction. Interrupts are not recognized during the DI instruction.**

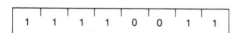

Cycles: 1
States: 4
Flags: none

NOTE: Placing a DI instruction on the bus in response to INTA during an INA cycle is prohibited. (8085)

HLT   (Halt)
The processor is stopped. The registers and flags are unaffected. (8080) A second ALE is generated during the execution of HLT to strobe out the Halt cycle status information. (8085)

Cycles: 1+ (8085), 1 (8080)
States: 5 (8085), 7 (8080)
Flags: none

NOP   (No op)
No operation is performed. The registers and flags are unaffected.

*All mnemonics copyrighted © Intel Corporation 1976.

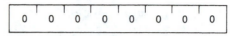

Cycles: 1
States: 4
Flags: none

RIM   (Read Interrupt Masks) (8085 only)
The RIM instruction loads data into the accumulator relating to interrupts and the serial input. This data contains the following information:

- Current interrupt mask status for the RST 5.5, 6.5, and 7.5 hardware interrupts (1 = mask disabled)
- Current interrupt enable flag status (1 = interrupts enabled) except immediately following a TRAP interrupt. (See below.)
- Hardware interrupts pending (i.e., signal received but not yet serviced), on the RST 5.5, 6.5, and 7.5 lines.
- Serial input data.

Immediately following a TRAP interrupt, the RIM instruction must be executed as a part of the service routine if you need to retrieve current interrupt status later. Bit 3 of the accumulator is (in this special case only) loaded with the interrupt enable (IE) flag status that existed prior to the TRAP interrupt. Following an RST 5.5, 6.5, 7.5, or INTR interrupt, the interrupt flag flip-flop reflects the current interrupt enable status. Bit 6 of the accumulator (I7.5) is loaded with the status of the RST 7.5 flip-flop, which is always set (edge-triggered) by an input on the RST 7.5 input line, even when that interrupt has been previously masked. (See SIM Instruction.)

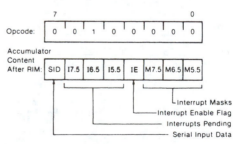

Cycles: 1
States: 4
Flags: none

THE INSTRUCTION SET

SIM   (Set Interrupt Masks) (8085 only)

The execution of the SIM instruction uses the contents of the accumulator (which must be previously loaded) to perform the following functions:

- Program the interrupt mask for the RST 5.5, 6.5, and 7.5 hardware interrupts.
- Reset the edge-triggered RST 7.5 input latch.
- Load the SOD output latch.

To program the interrupt masks, first set accumulator bit 3 to 1 and set to 1 any bits 0, 1, and 2, which disable interrupts RST 5.5, 6.5, and 7.5, respectively. Then do a SIM instruction. If accumulator bit 3 is 0 when the SIM instruction is executed, the interrupt mask register will not change. If accumulator bit 4 is 1 when the SIM instruction is executed, the RST 7.5 latch is then reset. RST 7.5 is distinguished by the fact that its latch is always set by a rising edge on the RST 7.5 input pin, even if the jump to service routine is inhibited by masking. This latch remains high until cleared by a RESET IN, by a SIM Instruction with accumulator bit 4 high, or by an internal processor acknowledge to an RST 7.5 interrupt subsequent to the removal of the mask (by a SIM instruction). The RESET IN signal always sets all three RST mask bits.

If accumulator bit 6 is at the 1 level when the SIM instruction is executed, the state of accumulator bit 7 is loaded into the SOD latch and thus becomes available for interface to an external device. The SOD latch is unaffected by the SIM instruction if bit 6 is 0. SOD is always reset by the RESET IN signal.

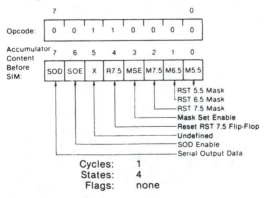

Cycles: 1
States: 4
Flags: none

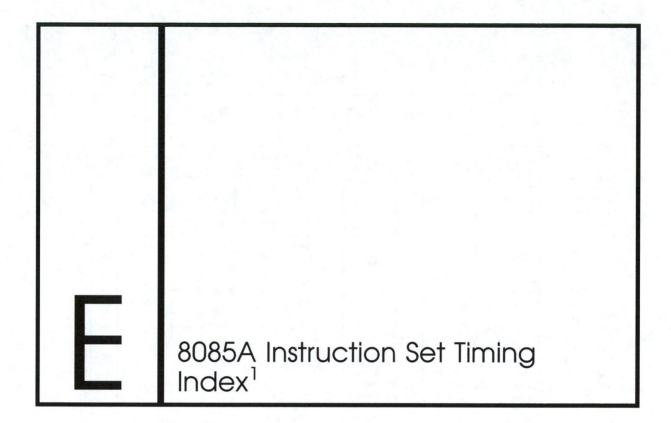

E

8085A Instruction Set Timing Index[1]

[1]Courtesy of Intel Corporation.

8085A

8080A/8085A INSTRUCTION SET INDEX

Instruction		Code	Bytes	T States 8085A	T States 8080A	Machine Cycles
ACI	DATA	CE data	2	7	7	F R
ADC	REG	1000 1SSS	1	4	4	F
ADC	M	8E	1	7	7	F R
ADD	REG	1000 0SSS	1	4	4	F
ADD	M	86	1	7	7	F R
ADI	DATA	C6 data	2	7	7	F R
ANA	REG	1010 0SSS	1	4	4	F
ANA	M	A6	1	7	7	F R
ANI	DATA	E6 data	2	7	7	F R
CALL	LABEL	CD addr	3	18	17	S R R W W*
CC	LABEL	DC addr	3	9/18	11/17	S R•/S R R W W*
CM	LABEL	FC addr	3	9/18	11/17	S R•/S R R W W*
CMA		2F	1	4	4	F
CMC		3F	1	4	4	F
CMP	REG	1011 1SSS	1	4	4	F
CMP	M	BE	1	7	7	F R
CNC	LABEL	D4 addr	3	9/18	11/17	S R•/S R R W W*
CNZ	LABEL	C4 addr	3	9/18	11/17	S R•/S R R W W*
CP	LABEL	F4 addr	3	9/18	11/17	S R•/S R R W W*
CPE	LABEL	EC addr	3	9/18	11/17	S R•/S R R W W*
CPI	DATA	FE data	2	7	7	F R
CPO	LABEL	E4 addr	3	9/18	11/17	S R•/S R R W W*
CZ	LABEL	CC addr	3	9/18	11/17	S R•/S R R W W*
DAA		27	1	4	4	F
DAD	RP	00RP 1001	1	10	10	F B B
DCR	REG	00SS S101	1	4	5	F*
DCR	M	35	1	10	10	F R W
DCX	RP	00RP 1011	1	6	5	S*
DI		F3	1	4	4	F
EI		FB	1	4	4	F
HLT		76	1	5	7	F B
IN	PORT	DB data	2	10	10	F R I
INR	REG	00SS S100	1	4	5	F*
INR	M	34	1	10	10	F R W
INX	RP	00RP 0011	1	6	5	S*
JC	LABEL	DA addr	3	7/10	10	F R/F R R†
JM	LABEL	FA addr	3	7/10	10	F R/F R R†
JMP	LABEL	C3 addr	3	10	10	F R R
JNC	LABEL	D2 addr	3	7/10	10	F R/F R R†
JNZ	LABEL	C2 addr	3	7/10	10	F R/F R R†
JP	LABEL	F2 addr	3	7/10	10	F R/F R R†
JPE	LABEL	EA addr	3	7/10	10	F R/F R R†
JPO	LABEL	E2 addr	3	7/10	10	F R/F R R†
JZ	LABEL	CA addr	3	7/10	10	F R/F R R†
LDA	ADDR	3A addr	3	13	13	F R R R
LDAX	RP	000X 1010	1	7	7	F R
LHLD	ADDR	2A addr	3	16	16	F R R R R
LXI	RP,DATA16	00RP 0001 data16	3	10	10	F R R
MOV	REG,REG	01DD DSSS	1	4	5	F*
MOV	M,REG	0111 0SSS	1	7	7	F W
MOV	REG,M	01DD D110	1	7	7	F R
MVI	REG,DATA	00DD D110 data	2	7	7	F R
MVI	M,DATA	36 data	2	10	10	F R W
NOP		00	1	4	4	F
ORA	REG	1011 0SSS	1	4	4	F
ORA	M	B6	1	7	7	F R
ORI	DATA	F6 data	2	7	7	F R
OUT	PORT	D3 data	2	10	10	F R O
PCHL		E9	1	6	5	S*
POP	RP	11RP 0001	1	10	10	F R R
PUSH	RP	11RP 0101	1	12	11	S W W*
RAL		17	1	4	4	F
RAR		1F	1	4	4	F
RC		D8	1	6/12	5/11	S/S R R*
RET		C9	1	10	10	F R R
RIM (8085A only)		20	1	4	–	F
RLC		07	1	4	4	F
RM		F8	1	6/12	5/11	S/S R R*
RNC		D0	1	6/12	5/11	S/S R R*
RNZ		C0	1	6/12	5/11	S/S R R*
RP		F0	1	6/12	5/11	S/S R R*
RPE		E8	1	6/12	5/11	S/S R R*
RPO		E0	1	6/12	5/11	S/S R R*
RRC		0F	1	4	4	F
RST	N	11XX X111	1	12	11	S W W*
RZ		C8	1	6/12	5/11	S/S R R*
SBB	REG	1001 1SSS	1	4	4	F
SBB	M	9E	1	7	7	F R
SBI	DATA	DE data	2	7	7	F R
SHLD	ADDR	22 addr	3	16	16	F R R W W
SIM (8085A only)		30	1	4	–	F
SPHL		F9	1	6	5	S*
STA	ADDR	32 addr	3	13	13	F R R W
STAX	RP	000X 0010	1	7	7	F W
STC		37	1	4	4	F
SUB	REG	1001 0SSS	1	4	4	F
SUB	M	96	1	7	7	F R
SUI	DATA	D6 data	2	7	7	F R
XCHG		EB	1	4	4	F
XRA	REG	1010 1SSS	1	4	4	F
XRA	M	AE	1	7	7	F R
XRI	DATA	EE data	2	7	7	F R
XTHL		E3	1	16	18	F R R W W

Machine cycle types

F	Four clock period instr fetch
S	Six clock period instr fetch
R	Memory read
I	I/O read
W	Memory write
O	I/O write
B	Bus idle
X	Variable or optional binary digit
DDD	Binary digits identifying a destination register
SSS	Binary digits identifying a source register
RP	Register Pair

B = 000, C = 001, D = 010 Memory = 110
E = 011, H = 100, L = 101 A = 111

BC = 00, HL = 10
DE = 01, SP = 11

*Five clock period instruction fetch with 8080A.

†The longer machine cycle sequence applies regardless of condition evaluation with 8080A.

•An extra READ cycle (R) will occur for this condition with 8080A.

*All mnemonics copyrighted Intel Corporation 1976.

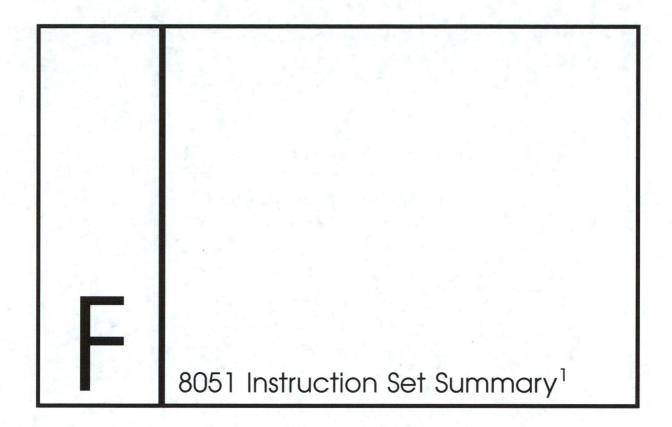

F

8051 Instruction Set Summary[1]

[1]Courtesy of Intel Corporation.

MCS®-51 PROGRAMMER'S GUIDE AND INSTRUCTION SET

MCS®-51 INSTRUCTION SET

8051 Instruction Set Summary

Interrupt Response Time: Refer to Hardware Description Chapter.

Instructions that Affect Flag Settings[1]

Instruction	Flag			Instruction	Flag		
	C	OV	AC		C	OV	AC
ADD	X	X	X	CLR C	O		
ADDC	X	X	X	CPL C	X		
SUBB	X	X	X	ANL C,bit	X		
MUL	O	X		ANL C,/bit	X		
DIV	O	X		ORL C,bit	X		
DA	X			ORL C,bit	X		
RRC	X			MOV C,bit	X		
RLC	X			CJNE	X		
SETB C	1						

[1]Note that operations on SFR byte address 208 or bit addresses 209-215 (i.e., the PSW or bits in the PSW) will also affect flag settings.

Note on instruction set and addressing modes:

Rn   — Register R7–R0 of the currently selected Register Bank.

direct — 8-bit internal data location's address. This could be an Internal Data RAM location (0–127) or a SFR [i.e., I/O port, control register, status register, etc. (128–255)].

@Ri   — 8-bit internal data RAM location (0–255) addressed indirectly through register R1 or R0.

#data   — 8-bit constant included in instruction.

#data 16 — 16-bit constant included in instruction.

addr 16 — 16-bit destination address. Used by LCALL & LJMP. A branch can be anywhere within the 64K-byte Program Memory address space.

addr 11 — 11-bit destination address. Used by ACALL & AJMP. The branch will be within the same 2K-byte page of program memory as the first byte of the following instruction.

rel   — Signed (two's complement) 8-bit offset byte. Used by SJMP and all conditional jumps. Range is −128 to +127 bytes relative to first byte of the following instruction.

bit   — Direct Addressed bit in Internal Data RAM or Special Function Register.

•   — New operation not provided by 8048AH/8049AH.

Mnemonic		Description	Byte	Oscillator Period
ARITHMETIC OPERATIONS				
ADD	A,Rn	Add register to Accumulator	1	12
ADD	A,direct	Add direct byte to Accumulator	2	12
ADD	A,@Ri	Add indirect RAM to Accumulator	1	12
ADD	A,#data	Add immediate data to Accumulator	2	12
ADDC	A,Rn	Add register to Accumulator with Carry	1	12
ADDC	A,direct	Add direct byte to Accumulator with Carry	2	12
ADDC	A,@Ri	Add indirect RAM to Accumulator with Carry	1	12
ADDC	A,#data	Add immediate data to Acc with Carry	2	12
SUBB	A,Rn	Subtract Register from Acc with borrow	1	12
SUBB	A,direct	Subtract direct byte from Acc with borrow	2	12
SUBB	A,@Ri	Subtract indirect RAM from ACC with borrow	1	12
SUBB	A,#data	Subtract immediate data from Acc with borrow	2	12
INC	A	Increment Accumulator	1	12
INC	Rn	Increment register	1	12
INC	direct	Increment direct byte	2	12
INC	@Ri	Increment direct RAM	1	12
DEC	A	Decrement Accumulator	1	12
DEC	Rn	Decrement Register	1	12
DEC	direct	Decrement direct byte	2	12
DEC	@Ri	Decrement indirect RAM	1	12

MCS®-51 PROGRAMMER'S GUIDE AND INSTRUCTION SET

8051 Instruction Set Summary (Continued)

Mnemonic		Description	Byte	Oscillator Period
ARITHMETIC OPERATIONS (Continued)				
INC	DPTR	Increment Data Pointer	1	24
MUL	AB	Multiply A & B	1	48
DIV	AB	Divide A by B	1	48
DA	A	Decimal Adjust Accumulator	1	12
LOGICAL OPERATIONS				
ANL	A,Rn	AND Register to Accumulator	1	12
ANL	A,direct	AND direct byte to Accumulator	2	12
ANL	A,@Ri	AND indirect RAM to Accumulator	1	12
ANL	A,#data	AND immediate data to Accumulator	2	12
ANL	direct,A	AND Accumulator to direct byte	2	12
ANL	direct,#data	AND immediate data to direct byte	3	24
ORL	A,Rn	OR register to Accumulator	1	12
ORL	A,direct	OR direct byte to Accumulator	2	12
ORL	A,@Ri	OR indirect RAM to Accumulator	1	12
ORL	A,#data	OR immediate data to Accumulator	2	12
ORL	direct,A	OR Accumulator to direct byte	2	12
ORL	direct,#data	OR immediate data to direct byte	3	24
XRL	A,Rn	Exclusive-OR register to Accumulator	1	12
XRL	A,direct	Exclusive-OR direct byte to Accumulator	2	12
XRL	A,@Ri	Exclusive-OR indirect RAM to Accumulator	1	12
XRL	A,#data	Exclusive-OR immediate data to Accumulator	2	12
XRL	direct,A	Exclusive-OR Accumulator to direct byte	2	12
XRL	direct,#data	Exclusive-OR immediate data to direct byte	3	24
CLR	A	Clear Accumulator	1	12
CPL	A	Complement Accumulator	1	12

Mnemonic		Description	Byte	Oscillator Period
LOGICAL OPERATIONS (Continued)				
RL	A	Rotate Accumulator Left	1	12
RLC	A	Rotate Accumulator Left through the Carry	1	12
RR	A	Rotate Accumulator Right	1	12
RRC	A	Rotate Accumulator Right through the Carry	1	12
SWAP	A	Swap nibbles within the Accumulator	1	12
DATA TRANSFER				
MOV	A,Rn	Move register to Accumulator	1	12
MOV	A,direct	Move direct byte to Accumulator	2	12
MOV	A,@Ri	Move indirect RAM to Accumulator	1	12
MOV	A,#data	Move immediate data to Accumulator	2	12
MOV	Rn,A	Move Accumulator to register	1	12
MOV	Rn,direct	Move direct byte to register	2	24
MOV	Rn,#data	Move immediate data to register	2	12
MOV	direct,A	Move Accumulator to direct byte	2	12
MOV	direct,Rn	Move register to direct byte	2	24
MOV	direct,direct	Move direct byte to direct	3	24
MOV	direct,@Ri	Move indirect RAM to direct byte	2	24
MOV	direct,#data	Move immediate data to direct byte	3	24
MOV	@Ri,A	Move Accumulator to indirect RAM	1	12

All mnemonics copyrighted © Intel Corporation 1980

MCS®-51 PROGRAMMER'S GUIDE AND INSTRUCTION SET

8051 Instruction Set Summary (Continued)

	Mnemonic	Description	Byte	Oscillator Period
DATA TRANSFER (Continued)				
MOV	@Ri,direct	Move direct byte to indirect RAM	2	24
MOV	@Ri, #data	Move immediate data to indirect RAM	2	12
MOV	DPTR, #data16	Load Data Pointer with a 16-bit constant	3	24
MOVC	A,@A + DPTR	Move Code byte relative to DPTR to Acc	1	24
MOVC	A,@A + PC	Move Code byte relative to PC to Acc	1	24
MOVX	A,@Ri	Move External RAM (8-bit addr) to Acc	1	24
MOVX	A,@DPTR	Move External RAM (16-bit addr) to Acc	1	24
MOVX	@Ri,A	Move Acc to External RAM (8-bit addr)	1	24
MOVX	@DPTR,A	Move Acc to External RAM (16-bit addr)	1	24
PUSH	direct	Push direct byte onto stack	2	24
POP	direct	Pop direct byte from stack	2	24
XCH	A,Rn	Exchange register with Accumulator	1	12
XCH	A,direct	Exchange direct byte with Accumulator	2	12
XCH	A,@Ri	Exchange indirect RAM with Accumulator	1	12
XCHD	A,@Ri	Exchange low-order Digit indirect RAM with Acc	1	12

	Mnemonic	Description	Byte	Oscillator Period
BOOLEAN VARIABLE MANIPULATION				
CLR	C	Clear Carry	1	12
CLR	bit	Clear direct bit	2	12
SETB	C	Set Carry	1	12
SETB	bit	Set direct bit	2	12
CPL	C	Complement Carry	1	12
CPL	bit	Complement direct bit	2	12
ANL	C,bit	AND direct bit to CARRY	2	24
ANL	C,/bit	AND complement of direct bit to Carry	2	24
ORL	C,bit	OR direct bit to Carry	2	24
ORL	C,/bit	OR complement of direct bit to Carry	2	24
MOV	C,bit	Move direct bit to Carry	2	12
MOV	bit,C	Move Carry to direct bit	2	24
JC	rel	Jump if Carry is set	2	24
JNC	rel	Jump if Carry not set	2	24
JB	bit,rel	Jump if direct Bit is set	3	24
JNB	bit,rel	Jump if direct Bit is Not set	3	24
JBC	bit,rel	Jump if direct Bit is set & clear bit	3	24
PROGRAM BRANCHING				
ACALL	addr11	Absolute Subroutine Call	2	24
LCALL	addr16	Long Subroutine Call	3	24
RET		Return from Subroutine	1	24
RETI		Return from interrupt	1	24
AJMP	addr11	Absolute Jump	2	24
LJMP	addr16	Long Jump	3	24
SJMP	rel	Short Jump (relative addr)	2	24

MCS®-51 PROGRAMMER'S GUIDE AND INSTRUCTION SET

8051 Instruction Set Summary (Continued)

Mnemonic		Description	Byte	Oscillator Period
PROGRAM BRANCHING (Continued)				
JMP	@A + DPTR	Jump indirect relative to the DPTR	1	24
JZ	rel	Jump if Accumulator is Zero	2	24
JNZ	rel	Jump if Accumulator is Not Zero	2	24
CJNE	A,direct,rel	Compare direct byte to Acc and Jump if Not Equal	3	24
CJNE	A, # data,rel	Compare immediate to Acc and Jump if Not Equal	3	24

Mnemonic		Description	Byte	Oscillator Period
PROGRAM BRANCHING (Continued)				
CJNE	Rn, # data,rel	Compare immediate to register and Jump if Not Equal	3	24
CJNE	@Ri, # data,rel	Compare immediate to indirect and Jump if Not Equal	3	24
DJNZ	Rn,rel	Decrement register and Jump if Not Zero	2	24
DJNZ	direct,rel	Decrement direct byte and Jump if Not Zero	3	24
NOP		No Operation	1	12

All mnemonics copyrighted ©Intel Corporation 1980

G Answers to Selected Problems

CHAPTER ONE

1. A microprocessor-based system would be used whenever: calculations are to be made; decisions based on inputs are to be made; a memory of events is needed; a modifiable system is needed.

3. The address bus is used to select a particular location or device within the system.

7. The input port has three-stated outputs so that it can be disabled when it is not being read.

9. 2^{16} (65,536)

11. It stores the contents of the accumulator out to address 6000H.

13. Instruction decoder and register: register and circuitry inside the μP, which receives the machine language code and produces the internal control signals required to execute the instruction.

15. First pulse: Read memory location 2000 (LDA)

Second and third pulses: Read address bytes @ 2001, 2002 (4000H)

Fourth pulse: Read data @ address 4000H.

CHAPTER TWO

1. A high-level language (e.g., Fortran or Basic) has the advantage of being easier to write and understand. Its disadvantage is that the programs are not memory efficient.

3. (a) LDA *Addr* IO/$\overline{\text{M}}$ is LOW
   (c) IN *Port* IO/$\overline{\text{M}}$ is HIGH
   (b) STA *Addr* IO/$\overline{\text{M}}$ is LOW
   (d) OUT *Port* IO/$\overline{\text{M}}$ is HIGH

5. U6a and U6b are drawn as inverted-input NAND gates to make the logical flow of the schematic easier to understand.

7. (a) IN instruction, $\overline{\text{RD}}$ is pulsed LOW.
   (b) OUT instruction, $\overline{\text{WR}}$ is pulsed LOW.

9. (1) A_8–A_{15} = FEH
   (2) IO/$\overline{\text{M}}$ = HIGH
   (3) $\overline{\text{WR}}$ is pulsed LOW/HIGH

11. MVI A,4FH

13. (a) MVI D,*data* = 16   (b) INR C = 0C
       (c) JNZ *Addr* = C2   (d) DCR B = 05

15. (a) 2010   3E   INIT: MVI A,04H   ;A ← 04H
             2011   04
             2012   3D   X1:   DCR A   ;A ← A-1
             2013   CA   JZ INIT   ;Jump on zero → 2010
             2014   10
             2015   20
             2016   C3   JMP X1   ;Jump → 2012
             2017   12
             2018   20

       (b) 2010   3E   INIT: MVI A,04H   ;A ← 04
             2011   04
             2012   3D   X1:   DCR A   ;A ← A-1___
             2013   C2   JNZ X1   ;Jump on zero to 2012
             2014   12
             2015   20
             2016   C3   JMP INIT   ;Jump to 2010
             2017   10
             2018   20

17. CPI 0DH compares the number in the accumulator with 0DH. If A = 0D, the zero flag is set. If A < 0D, the carry flag is set.

19. The first CMA is used because the output LEDs are active LOW. The second CMA is used to restore the accumulator for the count.

21. (a) B, C, D, E, H, L   (b) BC, DE, HL

23. B; destination   D; source

25. (a) D = 00   E = FF   (b) D = 40E = 51
       (c) D = 41   E = 00   (d) D = 40E = 00
       (e) D = 9F   E = FF   (f) D = DFE = 00

27. MVI D,38H (56_{10})

29. 204E   26   DELAY: MVI H,04H   ;H ← 04H
             204F   04
             2050   16   LOOP3:   MVI D,8CH   ;D ← 8CH
               :
             205C   25   DCR H   ;H ← H-1
             205D   C2   JNZ LOOP3   ;Jump to LOOP3
             205E   50   ;   4 times
             205F   20
             2060   C9   RET

31. FLASH: MOV B,A
       LOOP: CMA
                  OUT FE
                  CALL DELAY
                  MVI A,FF
                  OUT FE
                  CALL DELAY
                  MOV A,B
                  JUMP LOOP

33. 2000   DB   READCD: IN FFH   ;Read code
             2001   FF
             2002   FE   CPI 00H   ;No trouble,
             2003   00   ;   keep reading
             2004   CA   JZ READCD   ;   code
             2005   00   ;on zero go to 2000
             2006   20
             2007   47   MOV B,A   ;etc.
             2008

CHAPTER THREE

1. Serial data input and output
3. **(a)** LOW   **(b)** LOW   **(c)** HIGH
5. Multiplexed bus: Advantage, reduced pin count. Disadvantage, external demultiplexing is needed.
7. Address
9. Positive edge
13. 74LS138 is enabled:
    (1) $\overline{RD}$ or $\overline{WR}$ is LOW
    (2) $IO/\overline{M}$ is LOW
    (3) $A_{14} + A_{15}$ are both LOW
15. 1024; 4 bits
17. 2400–27FF; it exists because the RAMs are still enabled by the address decoder during these addresses.
19. **(a)** 10 T-states * .5 μs = 5 μs   **(b)** 10 T-states * .5 μs = 5 μs
    (c) 7 T-states * .5 μs = 3.5 μs   **(d)** 10 T-states * .5 μs = 5 μs
21. F → Opcode Fetch decoded as LDA
    R → Memory Read, Low order 8 bits of address
    R → Memory Read, High order 8 bits of address
    R → Memory Read, Data at address (byte2+byte3) is loaded into accumulator.
25. The 8755A should be used during the early stages of system development because it has 2K of EPROM.
27. 0800H–08FFH
29. 20H
31. MVI A,03H   7 6 5 4 3 2 1 0
    OUT 20H   Command Reg 0 0 0 0 0 0 1 1
33. 1/10KHz = 100 μs   MVI A,40H ;(MSB,TM)
                                          OUT 25H
    100 μs = .5 μs * Count Length MVI A,C8H ;(LSB)
    Count Length = 200 = C8H   OUT 24H
                                          MVI A,C0H ;Command Reg
                                          OUT 20H
                                          HLT

CHAPTER FOUR

1. LXI H,20B0H
   MOV A,M
   INX H
   MOV M,A
3. LXI H,20C5H
   MOV A,M
   INX H
   MOV M,A
5.

2000	3E	START:	MVI A,00H	;Port A → Inputs
2001	00			
2002	D3		OUT 02H	;Program DDR A
2003	02			
2004	3E		MVI A,FFH	;Port B → Outputs
2005	FF			
2006	DE		OUT 03H	;Program DDR B
2007	03			
2008	26		MVI H,20H	;H ← 20 (HL = 20XX)
2009	20			
200A	DB	READEM:	IN 00H	;Read input switches
200B	00			

200C	6F	MOV L,A	;A (switch settings) → L
			(HL now has 20XX)
200D	7E	MOV A,M	;M(HL) → A
200E	D3	OUT 01H	;M(20XX) → LEDs(Port B)
200F	01		
2010	CD	CALL DELAY;1/4 sec delay	
2011	50		
2012	20		
2013	C3	JMP READEM	
2014	0A		
2015	20		
⋮			
2050		DELAY	Delay subroutine

7. 200E   MVI A,E0H

9. START: LXI B,20A0H ;BC ← 20A0 (source)
         LXI D,20B0H ;DE ← 20B0 (destination)
    LOOP: LDAX B   ;A ← M(BC)
         STAX D   ;M(DE) ← A
         INX B   ;BC ← BC+1
         INX D   ;DE ← DE+1
         MOV A,E   ;A ← E
         CPI C0H   ;Does A = C0?
         JNZ LOOP: ;Jump not zero to loop
         HLT

11. (a) S, Z, AC, P (b) S, Z, AC, P, C (c) None (d) None (e) C (f) C (g) None
    (h) S, Z, AC, P, C

13. (a) A = 7FH   (d) A = 67H
        B = 77H   F = 00H
        F = 00H   (e) A = 39H
    (b) A = 69H   F = 05H (P,C)
        F = 14H
    (c) A = 8DH
        F = 84H

15. ANI F0H after reading the input port.

17. (a) CY = 1   (b) CY = 0   (c) CY = 1
        A = 83H   A = 00H   A = EBH

19.

2000 3E	START:	MVI A,FFH	;DDR B → outputs
2001 FF			
2002 D3		OUT 03H	
2003 03			
2004 3E		MVI A,80H	;A ← 1000 0000
2005 80			
2006 D3		OUT 01H	;Turn on leftmost LED
2007 01			
2008 CD		CALL DELAY	;Call 1/4 sec delay
2009 50			
200A 20			
200B 3E	RIGHT:	MVI A,40H	;A ← 0100 0000
200C 40			
200D D3	LOOP1:	OUT 01H	;Turn LED on
200E 01			
200F CD		CALL DELAY	;Call 1/4 sec delay
2010 50			
2011 20			
2012 0F		RRC	;Rotate right
2013 DA		JC LEFT	;Jump on carry to LEFT
2014 19			

```
2015 20
2016 C3              JMP LOOP1      ;Jump to LOOP1
2017 0D
2018 20
2019 3E   LEFT:      MVI A,02H      ;A ← 0000 0010
201A 02
201B D3   LOOP2:     OUT 01H        ;Turn LED on
201C 01
201D CD              CALL DELAY     ;Call 1/4 sec delay
201E 50
201F 20
2020 07              RLC            ;Rotate left
2021 DA              JC RIGHT       ;Jump on carry to RIGHT
2022 0B
2023 20
2024 C3              JMP LOOP2      ;Jump to LOOP2
2025 1B
2026 20
  ⋮
2050 DELAY:                         ;1/4 sec delay
```

21. end

23. False; Last on, first off

25.
```
DELAY:     PUSH D        ;Save DE rp
           MVI D,8CH
LOOP2:     MVI E,FFH
LOOP1:     DCR E
           JNZ LOOP1
           DCR D
           JNZ LOOP2
           POP D         ;Restore DE
           RET
```

27. It is like a subroutine because it branches to a specific address, but unlike a subroutine, it can occur at any time during program execution.

29.
```
MVI A,0CH   ;A ← 0000 1100
SIM         ;Set interrupt mask
EI          ;Enable interrupts
```

31.
```
003C C3    RST 7.5:  JMP 20CEH      ;Jump to ISR
003D CE
003E 20
  ⋮
2000 31    MAIN:     LXI SP,20A0H   ;Initial SP
2001 A0
2002 20
2003 3E              MVI A,00H      ;DDR A = inputs
2004 00
2005 D3              OUT 02H
2006 02
2007 3E              MVI A,FFH      ;DDR B = outputs
2008 FF
2009 D3              OUT 03H
200A 03
200B 3E              MVI A,0BH      ;RST 7.5 to be enabled
200C 0B
200D 30              SIM            ;Set interrupt mask
200E FB              EI             ;Enable interrupt
200F 00    LOOP:     NOP            ;Do nothing loop
2010 C3              JMP LOOP
2011 0F
```

```
2012 20

2050              DELAY:                        ;1/4 sec delay

2080 DB          ISR:        IN 00H            ;Read switches
2081 00
2082 D3                      OUT 01H           ;Turn on LEDs
2083 01
2084 CD                      CALL DELAY        ;1/4 sec delay
2085 50
2086 20
2087 FB                      EI                ;Re-enable interrupts
2088 C9                      RET               ;Return
20CE C3                      JMP ISR           ;Jump to different RAM area
20CF 80
20D0 20
```

CHAPTER FIVE

1. (a) $I_{out} = 2mA (1/256) = 7.81\mu A$ $V_{out} = 7.81\mu A * 5k\Omega = 39.1mV$
   (b) $I_{out} = 2mA (1/2) = 1mA$ $V_{out} = 1mA * 5k\Omega = 5V$
   (c) $I_{out} = 2mA (1/2 + 1/4 + etc.) = 1.99mA$ $V_{out} = 1.99mA * 5k\Omega = 9.96V$

3. $V_{out}(40H) = (2mA[1/4] * 5k\Omega) = 2.50V$ T-states $= 7 + 10 = 17$
   $V_{out}(04H) = (2mA[1/64] * 5k\Omega) = .156V$ T-states $= 10 + 7 + 10 = 27$
   Time (40H) $= 17 * .326 \mu s = 5.53 \mu s$
   Time (04H) $= 27 * .326 \mu s = 8.79 \mu s$

5.
```
   START:   MVI A,FFH    ;DDR B = output
            OUT 03H      ;
            CMA          ;A ← 00
   UP:      OUT 01H      ;Output to DAC
            INR A        ;A ← A + 1
            JNZ UP       ;Count up until zero
            CMA          ; A ← FF
   DOWN:    OUT 01H      ;Output to DAC
            DCR A        ;A ←A − 1
            JNZ DOWN     ;Count down until zero
            JMP UP       ;Up again
```

7.
```
   SC:  MVI A,00H
        OUT 01H
        MVI A,01H
        OUT 01H
```

9. Binary-to-BCD

11. Port A is used to drive the segments via transistor current buffers. Port B is used to drive one digit at a time. Port A outputs the segments to be turned on for a digit while it is enabled by Port B. This is done for each of the six digits (one at a time). The μP cycles through each digit fast enough so that they appear to be all on at the same time.

13. Because the segment bus is driven next, and the next digit to be turned on is not known.

15.
```
   MAIN:  LXI SP,20C0H   ;Initialize stack pointer
          MVI A,FFH      ;Program Ports A + B
          OUT 02H        ;DDR A = output
          OUT 03H        ;DDR B = output
   LOOP:  MVI B,89H      :B ← H segments
          MVI C,F7H      ;C ← 4th digit
          CALL DISP      ;Display H
          MVI B,86H      ;B← E segments
          MVI C,FBH      ;C ← 3rd digit
          CALL DISP      ;Display E
```

```
                MVI B,C7H        ;B ← L segments
                MVI C,FDH        ;C ← 2nd digit
                CALL DISPLAY     ;Display L
                MVI B,8CH        ;B ← P segments
                MVI C,FEH        ;C ← 1st digit
                CALL DISP        ;Display P
                JMP LOOP         ;Repeat
        DISP:   Same as Ex. 5–4
```

17. A zero is output on one row (only). The μP then reads the columns. If a key in the active LOW row is depressed, then the data read in will have a zero in bit 0, 1, 2, or 3. The program will pinpoint which key. If none of the columns' bits is LOW, then the next row is made LOW.

19.
```
        INIT:   MVI A,FFH
                OUT 02H
                CMA
                OUT 03H
        ROW:    MVI A,FDH        ;Row 1 active
                OUT 00H
        COL:    IN 01H
                CMP FBH          ;Check for Col 2 Active
                JMZ COL
        LED:    MVI A,7FH
                OUT 00H
                JMP LED
```

21. A stepper motor rotates in steps instead of with the continuous motion of conventional motors.

23. HIGH

25. (a) Because the A register is used in the delay subroutine.
   (b) Yes;
```
        DELAY:  Push PSW
                IN 01H
                etc.
        LOOP:
                JNZ LOOP
                POP PSW
                RET
```

CHAPTER SIX

1. Because it has RAM, ROM, I/O ports, and a timer/counter on it.

3. Extra 4K ROM, 128 bytes RAM, 16-bit timer/counter, 1 interrupt.

5. High

7. 80H–FFH

9. By reading the two bank-select bits (D0H.3, D0H.4) in the PSW.

11. (a) A = 40H   (b) A = 88H   (c) A = 88H   (d) A = 40H

13. (a) MOV P3,#0C7H   (b) MOV R7,P1   (c) MOV A,#55H   (d) MOV A,@R0
   (e) MOV P0,R1

15.
```
        START:  MOV A,#20H
        LOOP:   MOV P1,A
                INC A
                CJNE A,#91H,LOOP
                JMP START
```

17. (a) A = 75H   (b) A = F5H   (c) A = EBH

19.
```
        MOV A,P0
        ADD A,#05H
        MOV P1,A
```

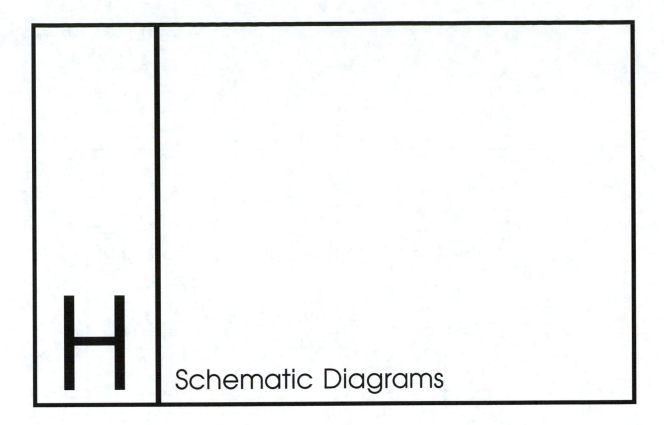

H

Schematic Diagrams

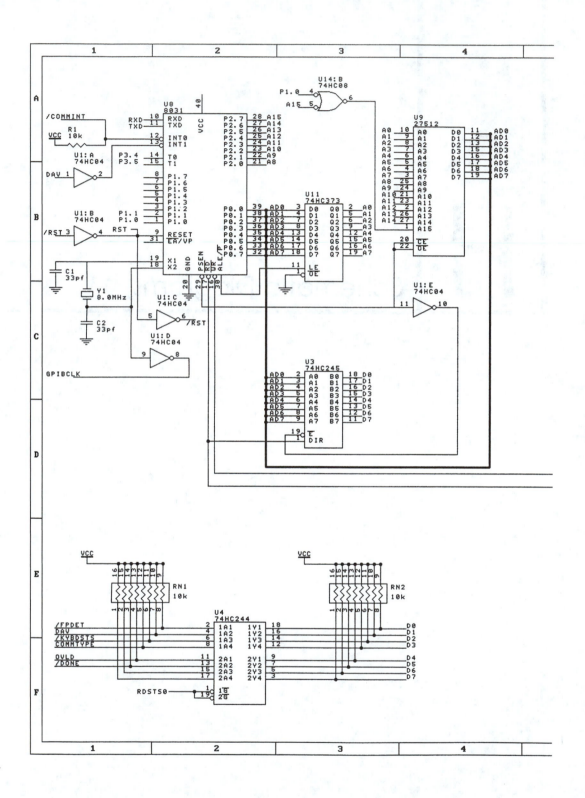

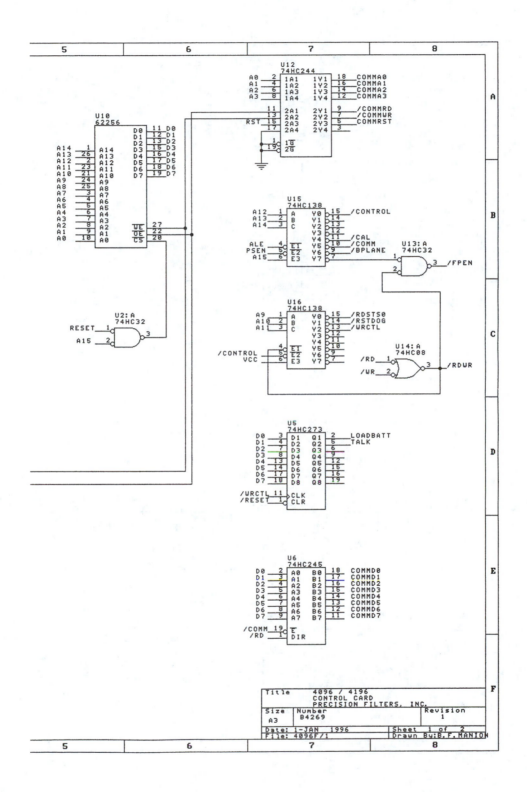

Title   4096 / 4196
         CONTROL CARD
         PRECISION FILTERS, INC.
Size   Number   Revision
A3   B4269   1
Date: 1-JAN 1996   Sheet 1 of 2
File: 4096F/1   Drawn By:B.F.MANION

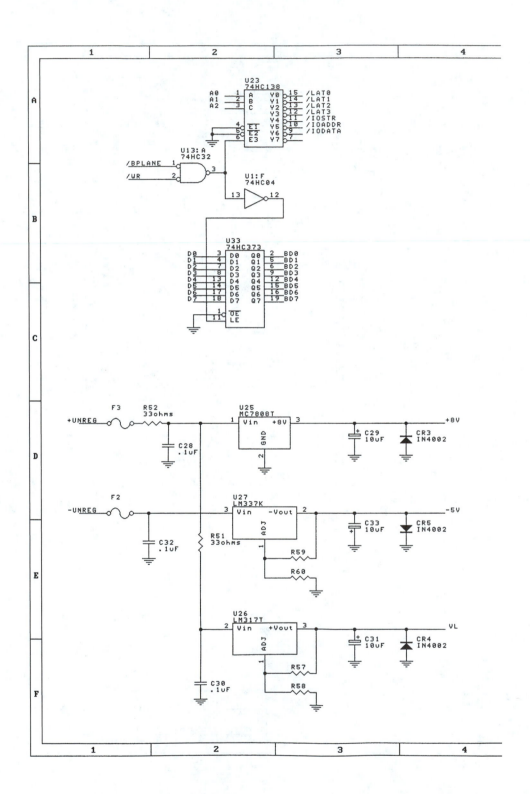

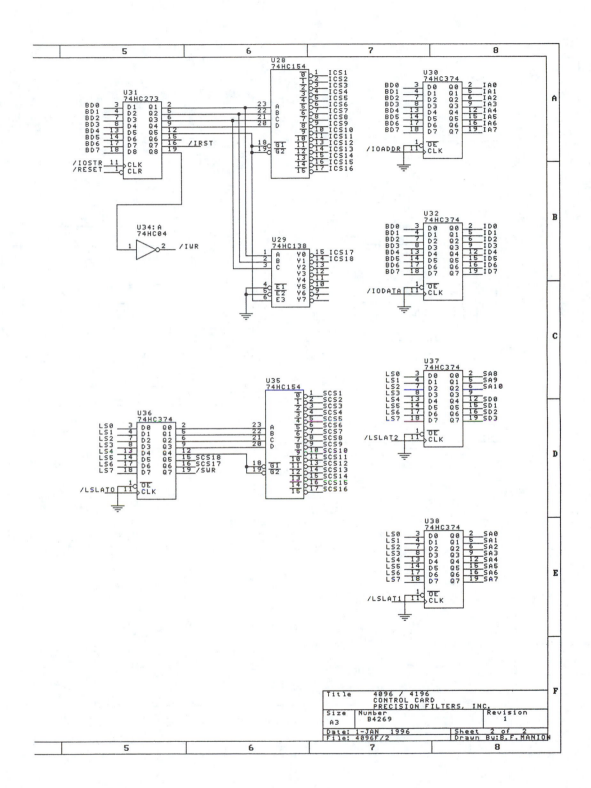

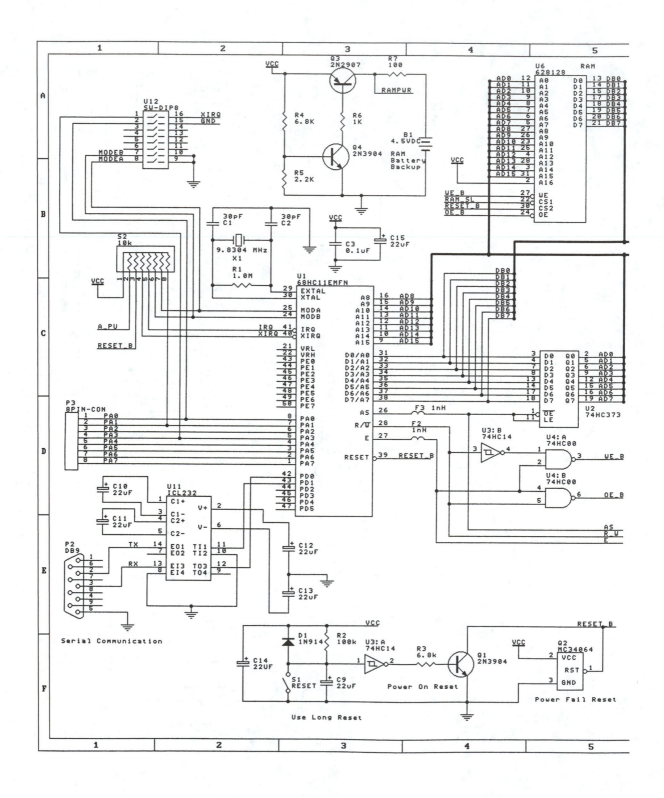

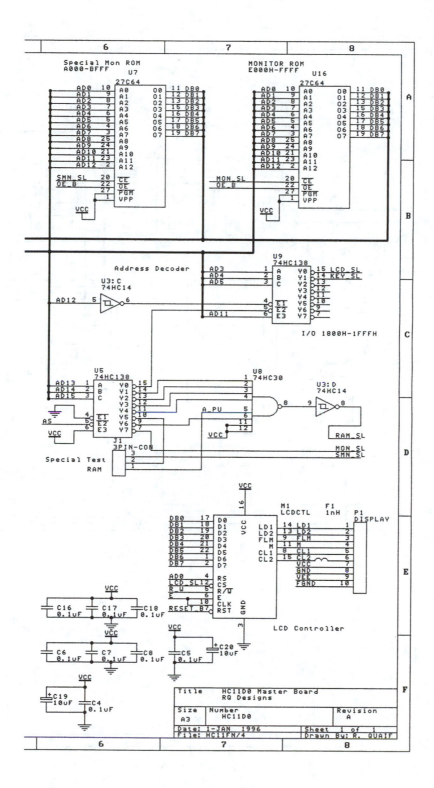

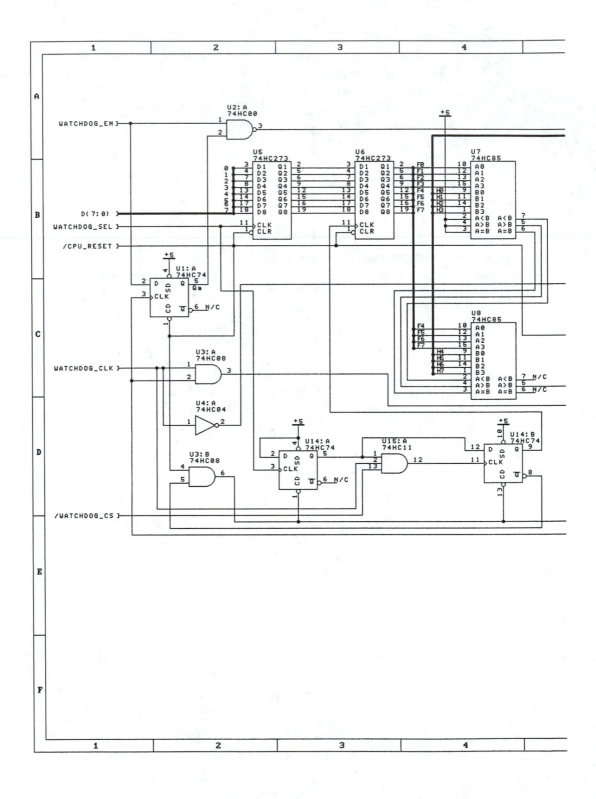

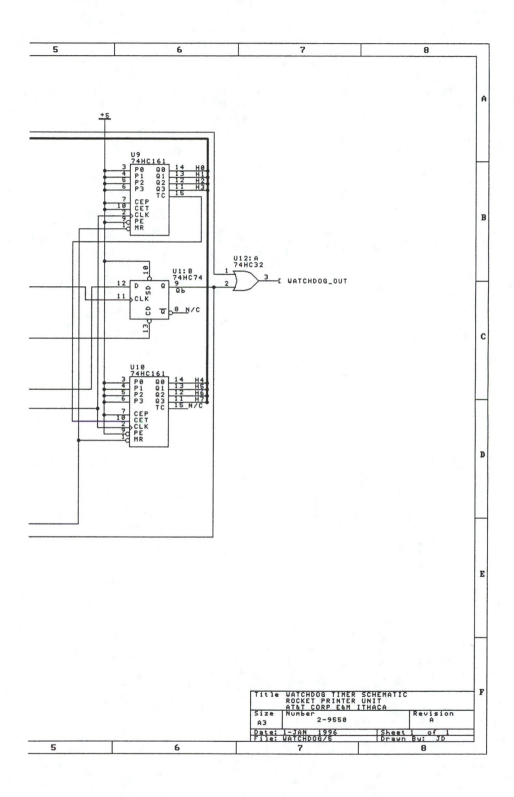

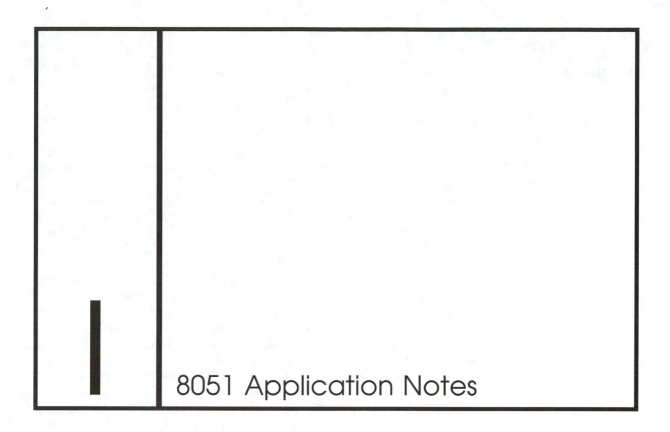

8051 Application Notes

AN 8051-BASED DATA ACQUISITION AND CONTROL APPLICATION

The object of this appendix is to implement the 8051-based data acquisition and control system shown in Figure I–1. Three modules will be discussed using several external transducers and instruments:

1. ADC module with hex display of the output.
2. DAC module with hex display of the input.
3. 8051 microcontroller module with connection points for numbers 1 and 2.

Assembly-language software will be written and stored on an EPROM connected to the 8051. This software will exercise the ADC/DAC modules and perform other I/O functions.

One of the outcomes of these designs is their use in colleges for teaching the concepts of data acquisition and control, so careful attention will be paid to the cost, durability, and ease of reproduction of each module.

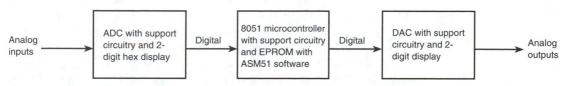

Figure I–1   Modular 8051-based data acquisition and control application.

HARDWARE

The 8051 Microcontroller Module

The 8051 microcontroller module is shown in Figure I–2. The heart of this module is the 8051 microcontroller. Also on the module are input and output buffers, an address latch, and an EPROM interface.

In Figure I–2, the microcontroller used is the 8031, which is a subset of the 8051. The 8031 differs because it is the ROMless part. Instead of using the 8051, which has an internal mask-programmable ROM, we will use the 8031 and interface an EPROM to it to supply our program statements.

The 8031 will be run with a 12MHz crystal. This crystal was chosen because most of the instructions take 12 clock periods to execute. This way, accurate timing can be developed based on one microsecond instruction execution time.

The EPROM is interfaced to the 8031 via port 0 and port 2. The 12-bit address required to access the EPROM comes from the 8 bits provided from port 0 and the 4 bits provided from port 2. The data output from the EPROM is sent back into the microcontroller via port 0. Since port 0 is dual purpose (i.e., address and data), a control signal from the ALE line is used to tell the address latch when port 0 has valid addresses and when it has data. Also, the $\overline{EA}$ signal is grounded, which signifies that all instructions will be fetched from an external ROM. The PSEN line goes LOW when the microcontroller is ready to read data from the EPROM. This LOW control signal is attached to the $\overline{OE}$ line of the 2732 EPROM, which changes the outputs at D_0 through D_7 from their float condition to an active condition. At that point the microcontroller reads the data.

Hardware reset is provided at pin 9 via the R-C circuit of R1–C3. At power-up the capacitor is initially discharged and the large inrush current through R1 provides a HIGH-to-LOW level for pin 9 to be reset. Resetting can also be accomplished with the push-button, which shorts the 5 volt supply directly to pin 9 any time you want to have a user reset.

Two eight-bit I/Os are provided via port 1 and port 3. In this circuit, port 1 is used as an output port capable of sinking or sourcing up to four LSTTL loads. This is equivalent to a sink current of approximately 1.6mA, which is normally not enough to drive loads such as LED indicators. Because of this, the 74LS244 (U1) is used as an output buffer. The 74LS244 can sink 24mA and source 15mA. The outputs of this buffer are always enabled by grounding pins 1 and 19. This way, whatever appears at port 1 will immediately be available to the LEDs. The LEDs are connected as active-LOW by providing a series 270-ohm resistor to the +5 volt supply. When any of the outputs of U1 go LOW, the corresponding LED will become active. The output socket is also provided on this module so that other devices can be driven from this port at the same time that the LEDs are being activated.

In this circuit, port 3 is used for input. The 8-bit DIP switch is connected to port 3 in conjunction with the 10k DIP pack. Therefore, each of the bits of port 3 is normally HIGH via a 10k pullup. They are made LOW any time one of the DIP switches is closed. An input socket is also provided at this port so that external digital inputs can be input to port 3. To use the input socket, all eight of the DIP switches must be in their open position so that the devices driving the input socket can drive the appropriate line LOW or HIGH without a conflict with the LOW from the DIP switch.

The 74LS373 is an octal transparent latch used as an address demultiplexer. Data entered at the D inputs are transferred into the Q outputs whenever the LE input is HIGH. The data at the D inputs are latched when the LE goes LOW. This address latch is used to demultiplex port 0's address/data information. When port 0 has valid address information, the ALE line is pulsed HIGH. This causes the address latch to grab hold of the information on port 0 and pass it through to the Qs and latch onto it. After the addresses

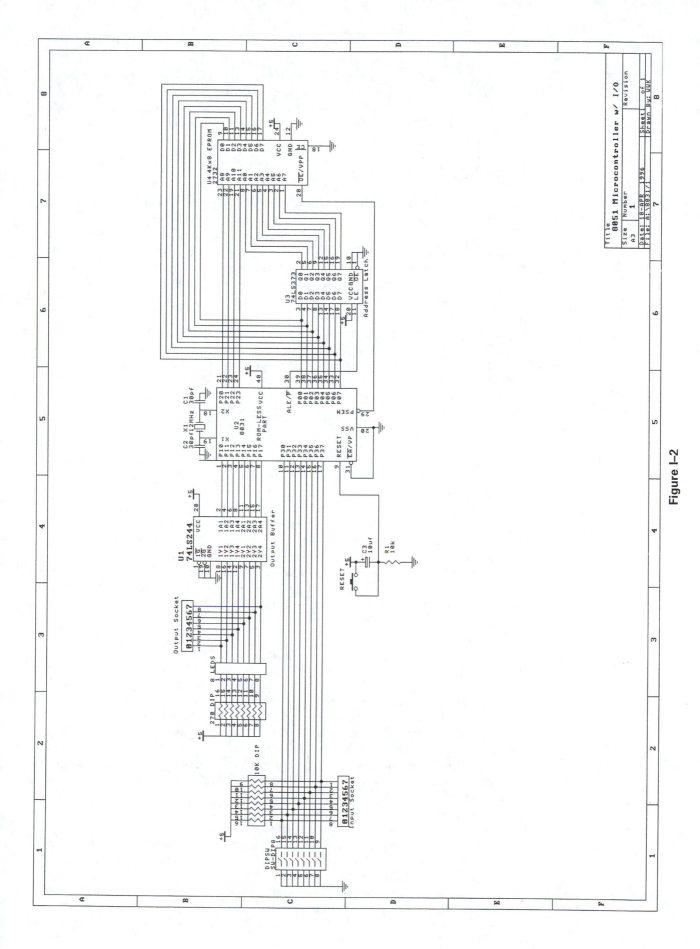

Figure I-2

211

from port 0 are latched, the port is then placed in the float condition so that it can be used to receive the data from the EPROM as the PSEN line is pulsed LOW. The LOW pulse on the PSEN line activates the active-LOW OE on the EPROM, which causes its outputs to become active. This data is routed back into port 0 of the microcontroller, where it is used as program instructions.

The ADC Interface Module

The heart of the ADC interface module (Figure I–3) is the ADC0804 IC. This analog-to-digital converter provides 8-bit output resolution and can be directly interfaced to a microcontroller. The object of this interface module is to convert analog quantities brought into $V_{in(+)}$ into 8-bit digital outputs. The digital outputs will be routed to an I/O connector that can be interfaced to other devices or the microcontroller module. It will also be connected to the 2-digit hex display so that you can constantly monitor the 8-bit values that were converted.

The clock oscillator for the ADC is provided via R1–C1. The frequency of oscillation can be calculated by taking the reciprocal of $(1.1 \times 10k\Omega \times 150$ picofarads), which equals approximately 606KHz. Since this is a successive approximation ADC, we can assume that the conversion will take place in 10 to 12 clock periods, which provides a conversion time of about 20 ms.

The chip select (CS) pin on U1 is connected to ground so that the chip is always activated. The RD pin is an active-LOW output enable. This is connected to ground also, so that the outputs are always active. To start a conversion, the WR line, which is also known as the start-conversion (SC), is pulsed LOW-then-HIGH. After the SAR has completed its conversion, it issues a LOW pulse on the INTR line [also known as end-of-conversion (EOC)], which will be read by the microcontroller to determine if the conversion is complete.

The $V_{ref/2}$ pin is connected to a reference voltage that overrides the normal reference of 5 volts provided by V_{cc}. By setting the $V_{ref/2}$ at 1.28 volts, the actual V_{ref} will be 2.56 volts. This way, with a V_{ref} of 2.56 volts, and an ADC that has a maximum number of steps of 256, the change in the output will be 1 bit change or 1 binary step for every 10 millivolts of input change. This provides a convenient conversion for the linear temperature sensor (T1) because T1 provides a 10mV change for every degree C. It also makes the calculations for the linear phototransistor sensor much simpler.

The DAC Interface Module

The heart of the DAC interface module (Figure I–4) is the MC1408 (U1). This is an 8-bit digital-to-analog converter. The 8 bits to be converted are brought into the A_8–A_1 digital input side, with A_1 receiving the MSB. The DAC provides an analog output current proportional to that digital input string. The amount of full scale output current is dictated by the R1–R2 reference resistors. With a 15-volt supply and a $10k\Omega$ resistor, the maximum output current will be 1.5 milliamps.

The analog output current must be converted into a usable voltage. To perform this current-to-voltage conversion, a 741 op amp is used. The current at I_o is drawn through the 10-kΩ feedback resistor of U2. This way, the analog V_{out} will be equal to I_o times 10kΩ. The analog output voltage can be predicted by using a ratio method. The ratio of the analog V_{out} to the binary input is proportional to the ratio of the maximum analog V_{out} to the maximum binary input (15 V maximum divided by 256 maximum). (Since the supply on the op amp is plus and minus 15 volts, we will never be able to achieve 15 volts at V_{out} but instead will be limited to about 13.5.)

A two-digit hexadecimal display is connected directly to the input to the DAC chip. This provides a way to monitor the binary input at any time.

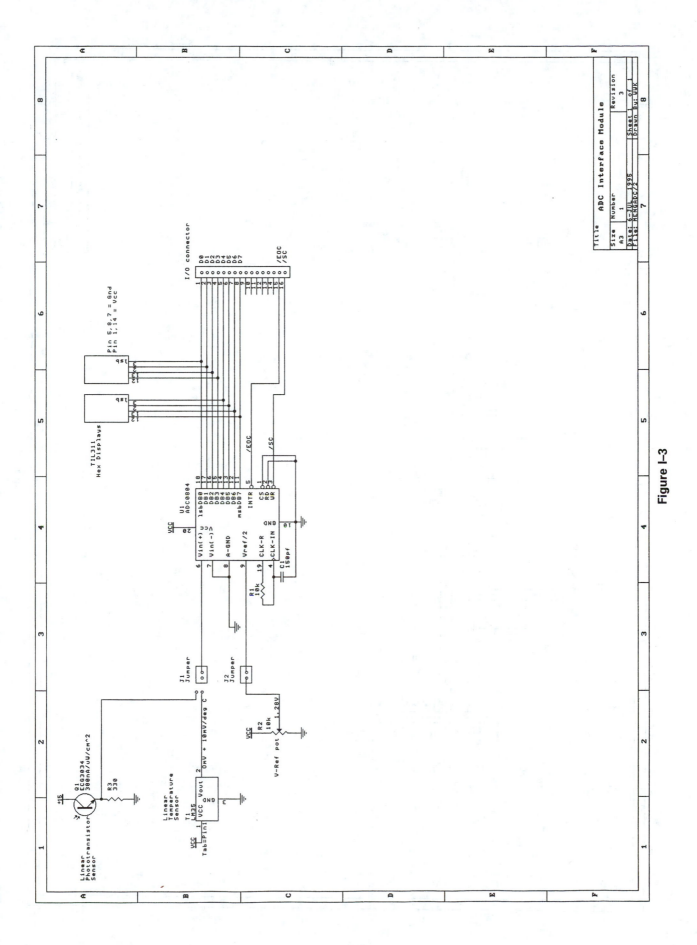

Figure I-3

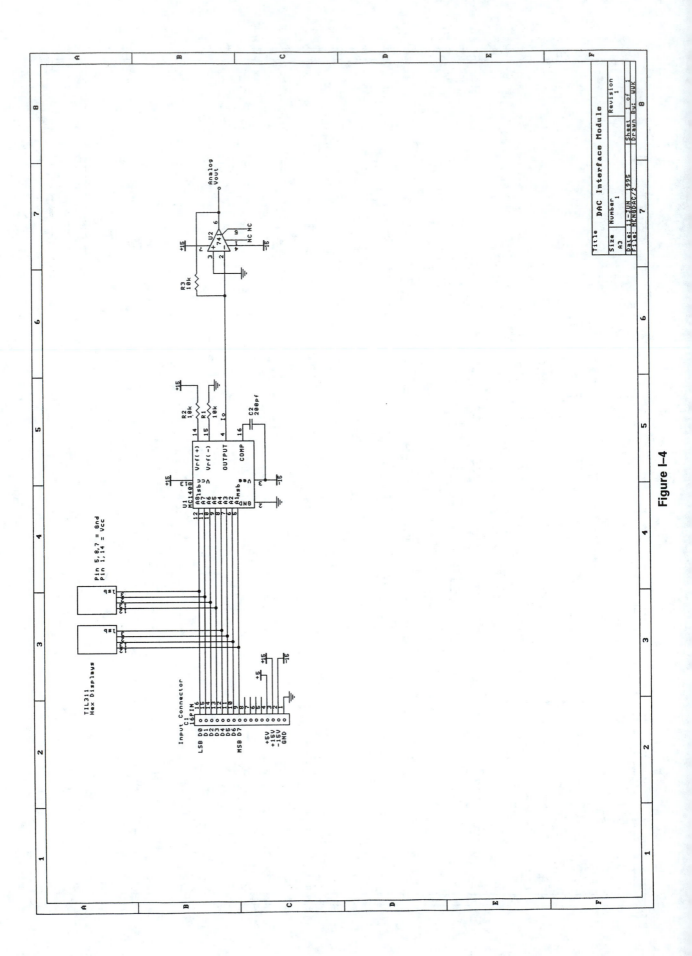

Figure I-4

214

APPLICATIONS

Three separate applications were used to exercise the three modules. Each of these applications are controlled by the microcontroller and will read analog input values with the ADC and output analog values with the DAC.

Centigrade Thermometer

The centigrade thermometer application is shown in Figure I–5. Software is written for the 8051 microcontroller to read the temperature input to the ADC and display a binary coded decimal (BCD) output of the temperature. The LM35 linear temperature sensor is used to measure the temperature. It outputs 10mV for every degree C. This millivolt value is converted by the ADC into an 8-bit binary string, which is displayed on the hex display and also input to the microcontroller. Since the V_{ref} on the ADC is set at 2.56 volts, then the output of the ADC is an actual hexadecimal display of the degrees C.

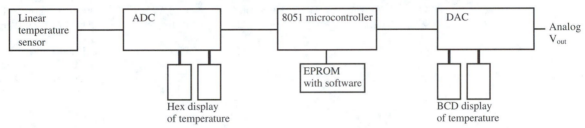

Figure I–5 Centigrade thermometer.

The microcontroller is used to start the ADC conversion and then monitor the end-of-conversion ($\overline{EOC}$) line to wait for the conversion to be complete. Once the conversion is complete, the microcontroller then has to read the digital string and convert the hexadecimal value into a BCD value so that it can be read by the user on the display of the DAC module. The analog output value of the DAC is not used.

The ASM51 software used by this application is given in Table I–1. This listing basically has four columns. The first lists the memory locations 0000–0062 that are programmed in the EPROM. The next shows the actual hex contents of the memory locations, starting with 802E and continuing down through 22. The third shows the assembly language programming, starting with the ORG 0008H and ending with the RET statement. In the extreme right-hand column is the comments section for the program.

As you read through the comments section, you will see that three subroutines are used to call the three different operations that are going to take place. The first subroutine, ADC, is used to float the buses on port 3 and port 1 and then issue the start conversion ($\overline{SC}$) signal. The "wait" part of that subroutine is necessary to wait until $\overline{EOC}$ goes LOW before reading the data from port 3 into register 0.

After the ADC routine is complete and the digital value is stored in register 0, that value in register 0 must be converted from hex to BCD. To do this, a counter routine is used to count up in BCD until the hex value is reached. At that point, the accumulator will have in it the correct BCD value that was achieved by using the decimal adjust instruction (DA A). After the DAC displays the BCD result, a delay is used for approximately 4 seconds so that there will be a 4-second delay before the temperature is refreshed.

TABLE I–1

Centigrade Thermometer Software

ADDR	HEX	LABEL	ASM51		COMMENTS
0000			ORG	0000H	; START OF EPROM
0000	802E		SJMP	START	; SKIP OVER 8051 RESTART ; LINK AREA
0030			ORG	0030H	; START OF PGM
0030	1138	START:	ACALL	ADC	; PERFORM AN A-TO-D CON- ; VERSION
0032	1159		ACALL	DAC	; DISPLAY RESULT AND PER- ; FORM D-TO-A ; CONVERSION
0034	114C		ACALL	DELAY	; DELAY 4 SECOND
0036	80F8		SJMP	START	; REPEAT ;
0038	75B0FF	ADC:	MOV	P3,#0FFH	; FLOAT THE BUS
003B	7590FF		MOV	P1,#0FFH	; FLOAT THE BUS
003E	C2B7	SC:	CLR	P3.7	; DROP SC LINE LOW
0040	D2B7		SETB	P3.7	; THEN RAISE HIGH
0042	20B6FD	WAIT:	JB	P3.6, WAIT	; WAIT TILL EOC GOES LOW
0045	C2B6		CLR	P3.6	; CLEAR P3.6 WHICH WAS ; USED FOR EOC
0047	C2B7		CLR	P3.7	; CLEAR P3.7 WHICH WAS ; USED FOR SC
0049	A8B0		MOV	R0,P3	; STORE FINAL ADC RESULT ; INTO R0
004B	22		RET		;
004C	7F20	DELAY:	MOV	R7,#20H	; OUTERMOST LOOP (32X)
004E	7D00		MOV	R5,#00H	; INNERMOST LOOP (256X)
0050	7EF3	LOOP2:	MOV	R6,#0F3H	; MIDDLE LOOP (243X)
0052	DDFE	LOOP1:	DJNZ	R5,LOOP1	;
0054	DEFC		DJNZ	R6,LOOP1	;
0056	DFF8		DJNZ	R7,LOOP2	;
0058	22		RET		; CONVERT HEX TO BCD ; AND DISPLAY ON DAC ; MODULE
0059	7400	DAC:	MOV	A,#00H	; ZERO OUT ACCUMULATOR
005B	2401	LOOP3:	ADD	A,#01H	; Acc WILL HAVE VALID BCD, ; R0 = ADC HEX ; RESULT
005D	D4		DA	A	; DECIMAL ADJUST Acc IF ; INVALID BCD
005E	D8FB		DJNZ	R0,LOOP3	; DECR R0 WHILE INCR AND ; ADJSTNG Acc TILL ; R0 = 0
0060	F590		MOV	P1,A	; MOV CORRECTED BCD TO ; DAC DISPLAY
0062	22		RET		;
0000			END		;

Temperature-Dependent PWM Speed Control

This application is shown in Figure I–6. It uses most of the same hardware as the centigrade thermometer. The object of this application is to monitor the temperature and produce a pulse-width-modulated (PWM) square wave whose duty cycle is proportional to the temperature. This PWM square wave can be used to drive a DC motor. The effective DC value

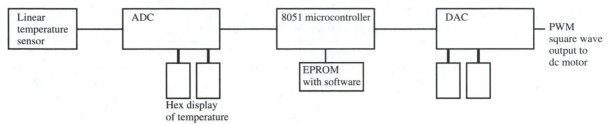

Figure I–6   Temperature-dependent PWM speed control.

will increase as the duty cycle increases. Because the duty cycle increases with increasing temperature, the speed of the motor will also increase with increasing temperature.

The ASM51 software used to drive this application is given in Table I–2. Basically, this software has two subroutines that will be called. The first one is the ADC subroutine. This subroutine starts the conversion, waits until the conversion is complete, and moves the ADC result into register 0. The next subroutine, the PWM, is used to produce the PWM square wave. To produce a PWM square wave, the output of the DAC will first be held LOW (0 volts) for a delay multiple equivalent to 10 hexadecimal. Then the DAC will be sent HIGH, which in this case is one half of the full scale output (80 hex). This HIGH is held for a delay multiple equivalent to the temperature value received from the ADC conversion. This way, as the ADC result increases with increasing temperature, the duty cycle of the PWM will increase, thus increasing the effective DC value sent to the motor.

Integrating Solar Radiometer

The block diagram for the integrating solar radiometer is given in Figure I–7. The object of this application is to measure sunlight intensity and produce a real time display of the irradiation from the sunlight and then accumulate the irradiation, the same as taking the integral, and display the integrated output as an analog voltage and also on a hex display. To measure the irradiation, an ECG 3034 phototransistor is used. It produces 300 nanoamps per microwatt per centimeter squared. The current is changed to a voltage by the 330-ohm resistor. This analog voltage is converted with the ADC and is then integrated using an ASM51 software program. The integrated output of the ADC will be proportional to the amount of sunlight that struck the measured surface over a certain length of time. This length of time could be one hour, one day, one week, or whatever time is desired.

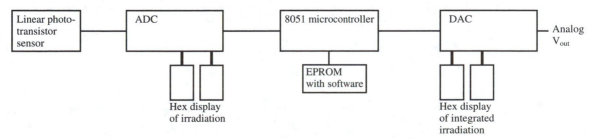

Figure I–7   Integrating solar radiometer.

TABLE I–2

Temperature-Dependent PWM Speed Control Software

ADDR	HEX	LABEL	ASM51		COMMENTS
0000			ORG	0000H	; START OF EPROM
0000	8030		SJMP	START	; SKIP OVER 8051 RESTART ; LINK AREA
0030			ORG	0030H	; START OF PGM
0030	7F01	START:	MOV	R7,#01H	; TO ENABLE ADC READ ON ; 1st LOOP
0032	1138	LOOP:	ACALL	ADC	; PERFORM AN A-TO-D CON- ; VERSION
0034	114C		ACALL	PWM	; DRIVE DC MOTOR WITH ; PWM SIGNAL
0036	80FA		SJMP	LOOP:	; REPEAT
0038	DF11	ADC:	DJNZ	R7,ERET	; TAKE AN ADC READ EVERY ; 256th TIME FOR ; STABILITY
003A	75B0FF		MOV	P3,#0FFH	; FLOAT THE BUS
003D	C2B7	SC:	CLR	P3.7	; DROP SC LINE LOW
003F	D2B7		SETB	P3.7	; THEN RAISE HIGH (PRO- ; VIDES POSITIVE EDGE)
0041	20B6FD	WAIT:	JB	P3.6,WAIT	; WAIT TILL EOC GOES LOW
0044	E5B0		MOV	A,P3	; STORE ADC RESULT INTO ; Acc
0046	547F		ANL	A,#01111111B	; CLEAR BIT 7 WHICH WAS ; USED FOR SC
0048	F8		MOV	R0,A	; MOVE ADC RESULT TO ; REG 0
0049	AF40		MOV	R7,40H	; RESET REG 7 TO 64 DECI- ; MAL
004B	22	ERET:	RET		
				;	
004C	759000	PWM:	MOV	P1,#00H	; OUTPUT A LOW
004F	743F		MOV	A,#3FH	; 3FH IS HIGHEST ASSUMED ; ADC OUTPUT VALUE
0051	98		SUBB	A,R0	; SUBTRACT THE ADC ; VALUE FROM 3FH
0052	F9		MOV	R1,A	; R1 (DELAY VALUE) FOR ; LOW OUT (DEC W/ INC ; TEMP)
0053	115D		ACALL	DELAY	; CALL DELAY TO HOLD LOW
0055	7590FF		MOV	P1,#0FFH	; OUTPUT FULL SCALE OUT- ; PUT FOR A HIGH
0058	A900		MOV	R1,R0	; USE TEMPERATURE AS DE- ; LAY MULTIPLIER ; FOR HIGH
005A	115D		ACALL	DELAY	; CALL DELAY TO HOLD ; HIGH
005C	22		RET		; RETURN
					;
005D	7D80	DELAY:	MOV	R5,#80H	; START COUNT OF R5
005F	DDFE	LOOP1:	DJNZ	R5,LOOP1	; R5 = INNERLOOP COUNT ; DOWN TO ZERO
0061	D9FA		DJNZ	R1,DELAY	; R1 = MULTIPLIER FROM ; PWM ROUTINE
0063	22		RET		
0000			END		

The software used to execute this application is given in Table I–3. The first subroutine is the ADC subroutine, which is used to convert the irradiation into a digital value. After the microcontroller has this digital value, the DAC routine performs the integration simply by accumulating the ADC result over each period of time. The DAC provides both the hexadecimal equivalent of the integrated irradiation as well as an analog output voltage proportional to the integrated irradiation.

TABLE I–3

Integrating Solar Radiometer Software

ADDR	HEX	LABEL	ASM51		COMMENTS
0000		ORG	0000H		; START OF EPROM
0000	8030		SJMP	START	; SKIP OVER 8051 RESTART ; LINK AREA
0030			ORG	0030H	; START OF PGM
0030	7400	START:	MOV	A,#00H	; RESET ACCUMULATOR
0032	113A	LOOP:	ACALL	ADC	; PERFORM AN A-TO-D CON- ; VERSION
0034	1158		ACALL	DAC	; DISPLAY RESULT AND PER- ; FORM D-TO-A ; CONVERSION
0036	114B		ACALL	DELAY	; DELAY 4 SECOND
0038	80F8		SJMP	LOOP:	; REPEAT
003A	75B0FF	ADC:	MOV	P3,#0FFH	; FLOAT THE BUS
003D	C2B7	SC:	CLR	P3.7	; DROP $\overline{SC}$ LINE LOW
003F	D2B7		SETB	P3.7	; THEN RAISE HIGH
0041	20B6FD	WAIT:	JB	P3.6,WAIT	; WAIT TILL EOC GOES LOW
0044	C2B6		CLR	P3.6	; CLEAR P3.6 WHICH WAS ; USED FOR EOC
0046	C2B7		CLR	P3.7	; CLEAR P3.7 WHICH WAS ; USED FOR $\overline{SC}$
0048	A8B0		MOV	R0,P3	; STORE FINAL ADC RESULT ; INTO R0
004A	22		RET		
					; ** DELAY 4 SECONDS**
004B	7F20	DELAY:	MOV	R7,#20H	; OUTERMOST LOOP (32X)
004D	7D00		MOV	R5,#00H	; INNERMOST LOOP (256X)
004F	7EF3	LOOP2:	MOV	R6,#0F3H	; MIDDLE LOOP (243X)
0051	DDFE	LOOP1:	DJNZ	R5,LOOP1	;
0053	DEFC		DJNZ	R6,LOOP1	;
0055	DFF8		DJNZ	R7,LOOP2	;
0057	22		RET		
					; INTEGRATE BY ACCUMU- ; LATING ADC RESULT
0058	8840	DAC:	MOV	40H,R0	; MOVE ADC RESULT TO ; RAM LOCATION 40H
005A	53403F		ANL	40H,#00111111B	; MASK OFF UNWANTED ; DATA
005D	2540		ADD	A,40H	; ACCUMULATE NEW ADC ; VALUE TO PREVIOUS ; TOTAL
005F	F590		MOV	P1,A	; MOVE TO DAC DISPLAY
0061	22		RET		;
0000			END		
					;

This three-module method for data acquisition and control proves to be a very inexpensive and simple way to input both analog and digital quantities and to output both digital and analog quantities. Having the hex displays connected to the input and output modules is an effective way of monitoring the real time activity of the DAC and the ADC. The entire three-module data acquisition setup is very portable because it requires only a bipolar power supply to operate it. The software used to exercise these modules is very straightforward and is effectively written using the ASM51 assembler on a personal computer and downloaded to an EPROM using a standard EPROM programming software package. Once you have the programmed EPROM, all that is required for a stand-alone data acquisition system is a power supply.

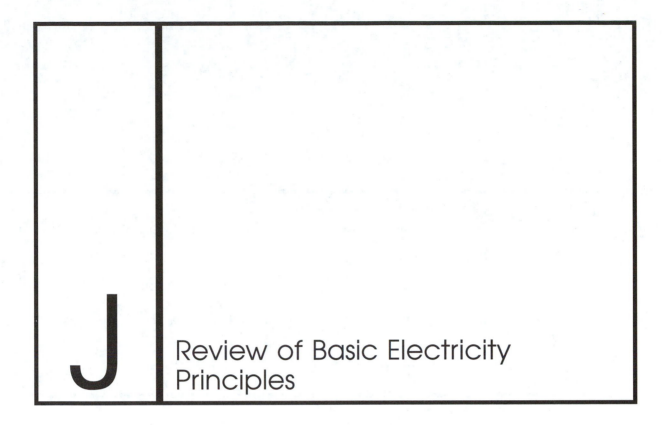

J | Review of Basic Electricity Principles

DEFINITIONS FOR FIGURE J–1

$V \equiv$ voltage source that pushes the current
(I) through the circuit, like water through a pipe

$I \equiv$ current that flows through the circuit

$R \equiv$ resistance to the flow of current

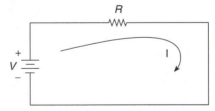

Figure J–1

UNITS

voltage = volts (V), for example, 12 V, 6 mV

current = amperes (A), for example 2 A, 2.5 mA

resistance = ohms (Ω), for example, 100 Ω, 4.7 kΩ

OHM'S LAW

The current (I) in a complete circuit is proportional to the applied voltage (V) and inversely proportional to the resistance (R) of the circuit.

FORMULAS

$$I = \frac{V}{R}$$

$$V = I \times R$$

$$R = \frac{V}{I}$$

EXAMPLE J–1

Determine the current (I) in the circuit of Figure J–1 if $V = 10$ V and $R = 1$ kΩ.

Solution:

$$I = \frac{V}{R}$$

$$= \frac{10 \text{ V}}{1 \text{ k}\Omega}$$

$$= 10 \times 10^{-3} \text{ A}$$

$$= 10 \text{ mA}$$

EXAMPLE J–2

A *series circuit* has two or more resistors end to end. The total resistance is equal to the sum of the individual resistances ($R_T = R_1 + R_2$). Also, the sum of the voltage drops across all resistors will equal the total applied voltage ($V_T = V_{R1} + V_{R2}$).

Find the current in the circuit (I), the voltage across R_1 (V_{R1}), and the voltage across R_2 (V_{R2}) in Figure J–2.

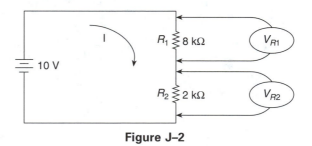

Figure J–2

Solution:

$$R_T = 8 \text{ k}\Omega + 2 \text{ k}\Omega = 10 \text{ k}\Omega$$

$$I = \frac{10 \text{ V}}{10 \text{ k}\Omega} = 1 \text{ mA}$$

$$V_{R1} = 1 \text{ mA} \times 8 \text{ k}\Omega = 8 \text{ V}$$

$$V_R = 1 \text{ mA} \times 2 \text{ k}\Omega = 2 \text{ V}$$

Check:

$$V_T = 8 \text{ V} + 2 \text{ V} = 10 \text{ V}$$

Notice that the voltage across any resistor in the series circuit is proportional to the size of the resistor. This fact is used in developing the *voltage-divider equation*:

$$V_{R1} = V_T \times \frac{R_1}{R_1 + R_2}$$

$$= 10 \text{ V} \times \frac{8 \text{ k}\Omega}{2 \text{ k}\Omega + 8 \text{ k}\Omega}$$

$$= 8 \text{ V}$$

EXAMPLE J–3

Use the voltage-divider equation to find V_{out} in Figure J–3. (V_{out} is the voltage from the point labeled V_{out} to the ground symbol.)

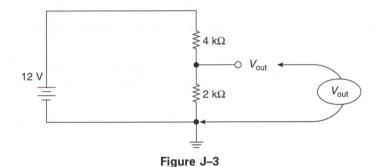

Figure J–3

Solution:

$$V_{out} = 12 \text{ V} \times \frac{2 \text{ k}\Omega}{2 \text{ k}\Omega + 4 \text{ k}\Omega}$$

$$= 4 \text{ V}$$

EXAMPLE J–4

A *short circuit* occurs when an electrical conductor is purposely or inadvertently placed across a circuit component. The short causes the current to bypass the shorted component. Calculate V_{out} in Figure J–4.

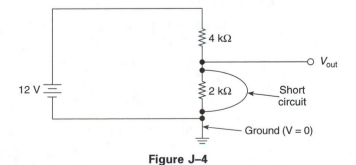

Figure J–4

Solution: V_{out} is connected directly to ground; therefore, $V_{out} = 0$ V.

EXAMPLE J–5

Find V_{out} in Figure J–5.

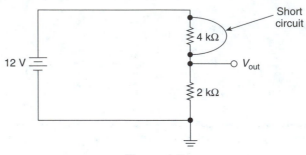

Figure J–5

Solution: V_{out} is connected directly to the top of the 12-V source battery. Therefore, $V_{out} = 12$ V.

EXAMPLE J–6

An *open circuit* is a break in a circuit. This break will cause the current to stop flowing to all components fed from that point. Calculate V_{out} in Figure J–6.

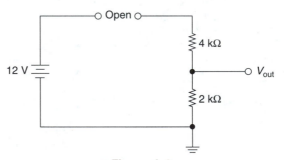

Figure J–6

Solution: Because $I = 0$ A,

$$V_{2\,k\Omega} = 0\ A \times 2\ k\Omega = 0\ V$$

$$V_{out} = V_{2\,k\Omega} = 0\ V$$

EXAMPLE J–7

Calculate V_{out} in Figure J–7.

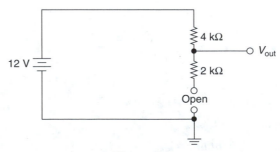

Figure J–7

Solution: Because $I = 0$ A,

$$V_{\text{drop (4 k}\Omega)} = 0\,\text{A} \times 4\,\text{k}\Omega = 0\,\text{V}$$

$$V_{\text{out}} = 12\,\text{V} - V_{\text{drop}} = 12\,\text{V}$$

EXAMPLE J–8

The symbol for a battery is seldom drawn in schematic diagrams. Figure J–8 is an alternative schematic for a series circuit. Solve for V_{out}.

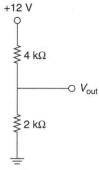

Figure J–8

Solution:

V_{out}

$$= 12\,\text{V} \times \frac{2\,\text{k}\Omega}{2\,\text{k}\Omega + 4\,\text{k}\Omega}$$

$$= 4\,\text{V}$$

EXAMPLE J–9

A relay's contacts or a transistor's collector-emitter can be used to create opens and shorts. Figure J–9(a) uses a relay to short one resistor in a series circuit. Sketch the waveform at V_{out} in Figure J–9(a).

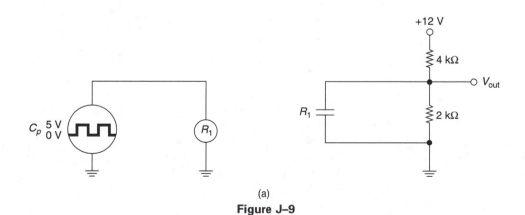

(a)

Figure J–9

Solution: When the R_1 coil energizes, the R_1 contacts close, shorting the 2-kΩ resistor and making $V_{\text{out}} = 0$ V. When the coil is deenergized, the contacts are open and V_{out} is found using the voltage-divider equation.

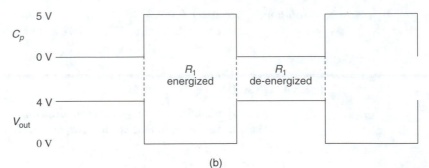

(b)

Figure J–9 *(Continued)*

$$V_{out} = 12 \text{ V} \times \frac{2 \text{ k}\Omega}{2 \text{ k}\Omega + 4 \text{ k}\Omega}$$
$$= 4 \text{ V}$$

The clock oscillator (C_p) and V_{out} waveforms are given in Figure J–9(b).

REVIEW QUESTIONS

J–1. What value of voltage will cause 6 mA to flow in Figure J–1 if $R = 2$ kΩ (3 V, 0.333 V, or 12 V)?

J–2. To increase the current in Figure J–1, the resistor value should be _____ (increased, decreased).

J–3. In a series voltage-divider circuit like Figure J–2, the larger resistor will have the larger voltage across it. True or false?

J–4. In Figure J–2, if R_1 is changed to 8 MΩ and R_2 is changed to 2 Ω, V_{R2} will be close to _____ (0 V, 10 V).

J–5. If the supply voltage in Figure J–3 is increased to 18 V, V_{out} becomes _____ (6 V, 12 V).

J–6. A short circuit causes current to stop flowing in the part of the circuit not being shorted. True or false?

J–7. The current leaving the battery in Figure J–4 _____ (increases, decreases) if the short circuit is removed.

J–8. The short circuit in Figure J–5 causes V_{out} to become 12 V because the current through the 2-kΩ resistor becomes 0 A. True or false?

J–9. In Figure J–6, the voltage across the 2-kΩ resistor is the same as that across the 4-kΩ resistor. True or false?

J–10. If the 4-kΩ resistor in Figure J–7 is doubled, V_{out} will _____ (increase, decrease, remain the same)?

ANSWERS TO REVIEW QUESTIONS

J–1. 12 V
J–2. Decreased
J–3. True
J–4. 0 V
J–5. 6 V
J–6. False
J–7. Decreases
J–8. False
J–9. True
J–10. Remain the same

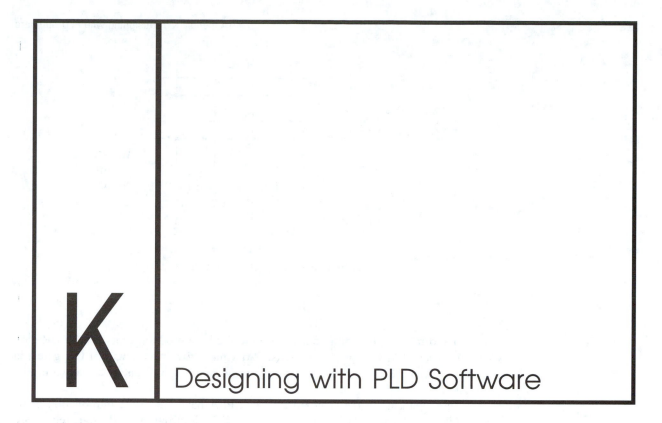

K

Designing with PLD Software

Complex combinational logic circuits can be reduced to their simplest sum-of-products (SOP) form using DeMorgan's theorem and Karnaugh mapping. An example of an SOP expression is $X = A\overline{B}\overline{C} + \overline{A}\overline{B}C + \overline{A}B\overline{C}$. To implement that expression using conventional logic would require three different ICs: a hex inverter, a triple three-input AND gate, and a three-input OR gate. As the SOP logic complexity increases, the number of SSI or MSI ICs becomes excessive.

An increasingly popular solution used today is to implement the logic function using programmable logic devices (PLDs). PLD ICs can be selected from the TTL, CMOS, or ECL families, depending on your requirements for high-speed, low-power, and logic function availability. The three basic forms of PLDs are the programmable read-only memory (PROM), programmable array logic (PAL), and programmable logic array (PLA). The PROM is most commonly used as a memory device and is not well suited for implementing complex logic equations.

The standard PAL has several multi-input AND gates connected to the input of an OR gate and inverter. The inputs are set up as a fusible-link programmable multi-variable array. The user, by burning specific fuses in the array, can program the IC to solve a multitude of various combinational logic problems. Hard array logic (HAL), requiring custom mask design by the manufacturer, is also available (a HAL is to a PAL as a ROM is to a PROM).

The standard PLA (or field-programmable logic array, FPLA) also has multi-input programmable AND gates, but has the additional flexibility of having its AND gates connected to several *programmable OR gates*. Because of the additional flexibility, the PLA is slightly more difficult to program than the PAL and the additional level of logic gates increases the overall propagation delay times.

To keep the logic diagrams for PLDs easy to read, a one-line convention has been adopted, as illustrated in Figure K–1. There is a fused link at each intersection of the straight lines. The programmer selects which fuses are to be left intact and which fuses will be blown. A dot signifies which fuses are left intact. All other fuses are blown, breaking their connection. Figure K–1 shows four *product terms: W, X, Y,* and *Z.*

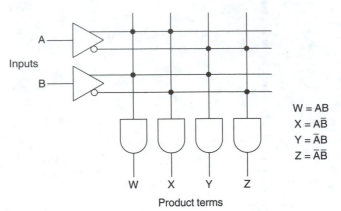

W = AB
X = A$\overline{\text{B}}$
Y = $\overline{\text{A}}$B
Z = $\overline{\text{A}}\overline{\text{B}}$

Product terms

Figure K–1   One-line convention for PLDs.

To form an SOP expression, we need to feed the product terms into an OR gate. This is where PALs differ from PLAs. PALs have *fixed* (hard wired) OR gates, as shown in Figure K–2, whereas PLAs have *programmable* OR gates, as shown in Figure K–3.

Improvements in the standard PAL and PLA have led to the introduction of *sequential logic* (*D* and *S-R* flip-flops) within the IC. Field-programmable logic sequencers (FPLS) and sequential PALs provide the additional capability to allow the user to program in *sequential operations,* such as those required for counter and shift register operations. Electrically erasable PLDs (EEPLDs) are also available. EEPLDs allow the user to erase a previous design and program in a new one, saving the cost of buying a new PLD.

Programmable arrays are sometimes called *semicustom logic.* They are provided as a standard IC part with programmable links that allow users to develop their own custom parts. These programmable arrays bridge the gap between random combinational logic gates and expensive manufacturer-designed, mask-type custom ICs. Programmable arrays reduce the chip count on a typical PC board and allow a design engineer to create a desired logic circuit from a family of blank programmable ICs, instead of stocking a full line of TTL and CMOS chips.

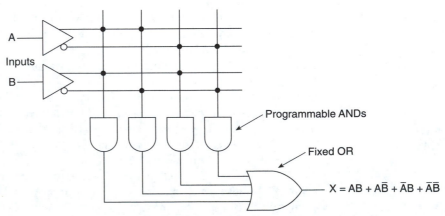

Programmable ANDs

Fixed OR

X = AB + A$\overline{\text{B}}$ + $\overline{\text{A}}$B + $\overline{\text{A}}\overline{\text{B}}$

Figure K–2   PAL architecture.

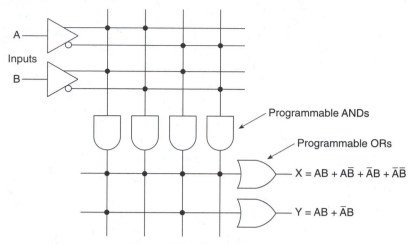

Figure K-3 PLA architecture.

PLD designs are solved using PLD computer software. The manufacturers of PLDs offer this programming software at a slight fee or free of charge to encourage designers to use their PLDs.

The software prompts the user to input the logic operations to be performed and automatically determines which fuses are to be blown. The logic operations are usually input as Boolean equations or truth tables, but in some cases they can even be entered as timing waveforms or schematic diagrams. The software then reduces the input logic to its simplest form and determines if the resultant equations can be implemented on the PLD that you have chosen. It then determines which fuses are to be blown and produces a *fuse map,* which is output to a computer file that conforms to the JEDEC format. JEDEC stands for Joint Electronic Device Engineering Council. The council developed the standard so that the hardware that programs the PLD ICs (blows fuses) will use the same fuse-map configuration regardless of the PLD vendor or software.

After the JEDEC file has been created, the designer uses a hardware device called a PLD programmer to program the actual PLD IC. The device programmer is usually connected to a personal computer so that it can access the JEDEC file created by the PLD design software. The device programmer also has software associated with it that runs on the PC. This software basically asks the user what the name of the JEDEC file is and what the target PLD IC is.

Before you actually program the PLD IC, some PLD design software packages allow you to *simulate* the operation of the logic on a model of the PLD that you have chosen. To perform a simulation, you tell the simulator the timing and levels that you want to inject into the PLD model. The simulator output shows the resultant truth table and timing waveforms so that you can see if the PLD is responding as you wanted. Figure K–4 shows the flow of the development cycle for PLD programming.

Several versions of PLD design software are marketed today. Most PLD IC manufacturers want to encourage colleges and industries to use their product, so they offer evaluation versions of their design software free or at a reduced charge. Table K–1 lists the names of companies that provide logic design software. The software comes on computer disks, which usually have to be loaded onto a hard disk drive before use. The documentation included gives step-by-step procedures to lead you through several software design examples.

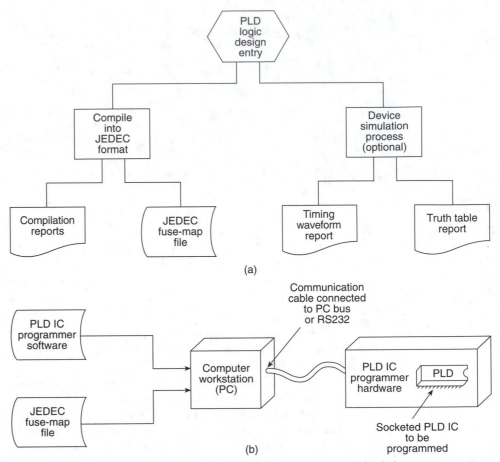

Figure K–4 The PLD programming cycle: (a) design and simulation operations; (b) hardware for programming the PLD IC.

The software by itself gives you a good experience in PLD design, but to actually program a PLD you need to purchase PLD programming hardware. Depending on the level of sophistication and features that you need, the cost of this hardware ranges from $200 to $2000, or more. Table K–2 lists some of the companies commonly recommended by PLD IC manufacturers. (Usually, these companies will also offer a PLD design software package for sale.)

TABLE K–1

Sample of Companies That Produce PLD ICs and/or Software

Company	Phone Number
Advanced Micro Devices	(512) 462-4360
Altera	(800) 925-8372
Cypress	(408) 943-2600
Intel	(800) 468-8118
Lattice Semiconductor	(800) 327-8425
National Semiconductor	(800) 272-9959
Orcad	(800) 671-9505
Philips (Signetics)	(408) 991-2000
Texas Instruments	(800) 477-8924
Xilinx	(800) 291-3381

TABLE K–2

Sample of Companies That Provide PLD Programming Hardware

Company	Phone Number
Actel	(800) 228-3532
Advin Systems	(800) 627-2456
Altera	(408) 894-7000
Data I/O	(800) 426-1045
Emulation Technology	(408) 982-0660
Logical Devices	(800) 315-7766
Needhams Electronics	(916) 924-8037

USING ADVANCED MICRO DEVICE'S PALASM 4 SOFTWARE

Programmable array logic was invented at Monolithic Memories, Inc., now a part of Advanced Micro Devices (AMD), in the late 1970s. AMD's line of programmable logic ICs, design software, and programming hardware is commonly used in electronic designs. In the following pages we will use AMD's design software PALASM 4 to solve three circuit design problems. The problems to be solved and the PLD used to implement the design are given in Table K–3.

TABLE K–3

Circuit Designs to Be Solved with PALASM 4

Circuit Design	PLD Used
Combinational logic circuit	PAL16H2
74138 octal decoder	PAL16L8
Johnson shift counter	PAL16R8

The users manual provided with PALASM 4 describes everything that you need to know to design a PLD solution. It tells you to first run the INSTALL program, which copies the PALASM programs from the floppy disks provided over to the hard drive on your PC. After installation, you run the PALASM program. The program is completely menu driven, which means there will be prompts at the top of the computer screen that you respond to as you proceed through the design stages. There are several good examples in the documentation that lead you through the design process. The design solutions that follow are not intended to explain all the details of running the software, but instead they show you some of the capabilities that are most pertinent to our basic understanding of PLD software.

Each of the following design solutions will illustrate the three most important files associated with the design process. The file names always start with the name that you have chosen and have one of the following extensions: .PDS, .XPT, or .HST (*example:* PROBLEM1.PDS).

The .PDS file is created by the user. It declares which PLD IC is to be used, defines its pins, defines the logic to be implemented, and gives the simulation criteria.

The .XPT file shows each node within the PLD as having the fuse blown or left intact. By comparing this output with the logic diagram, you can see exactly what logic function has been created by the software.

The .HST file contains the output results of the simulation in the form of a truth table and/or timing waveforms. By studying it you can determine if the output response to your predefined input criteria is what it is supposed to be.

PAL SOLUTION TO COMBINATIONAL LOGIC

The goal of this design is to solve the equation $X = \bar{A} + \bar{C} + B$ using a PAL. This is a combinational logic problem that can be implemented with one of the basic PAL devices like the 16H2 shown in Figure K–5.

Figure K–6 shows the file EX3–12.PDS as it would be defined by the user. In the *Declaration Segment,* you name the design and PLD to be used. In the *PIN Declarations Segment,* you assign the inputs and outputs to specific pins. In the *Boolean Equation Segment,* you enter the original equation to be simplified and mapped into the PLD. In the *Simulation Segment,* you list the simulation activity that you want to occur.

Figure K–7 shows the file EX3–12.XPT as it would be output by the PALASM software. It is called a fuse map because it shows which fuses are to be blown ($-$) and which are to be left intact (X). This file is used by the PALASM compiler to create the JEDEC file.

To interpret the XPT file, you need to compare it to a logic diagram for a 16H2 (see Figure K–8). The 16H2 has 16 inputs (pins 1 to 9, 11 to 14, and 17 to 19) and two outputs (pins 15 and 16). Both true and complement inputs are connected to the 32 vertical lines. Each OR gate output can have up to eight product terms (AND gates), with each product term having up to 32 input variables (chosen from the vertical lines). In our design we have the *A*-variable input on pin 1. This makes the vertical line labeled 2 connect to *A* and 3 is connected to $\bar{A}$. *B* is input on pin 2, so vertical line 0 is *B* and line 1 is $\bar{B}$. *C* is input on pin 3, so vertical line 4 is *C* and line 5 is $\bar{C}$.

Now, by comparing Figure K–8 to Figure K–7, you should be able to determine that the output at *X* (pin 16) is the correctly *simplified equation* that we expected, $X = \bar{A} + \bar{C} + B$.

Figure K–9 is the simulator output showing the output at *X* for the eight possible input conditions at *A*, *B*, and *C* repeated three times. There are two ways to view the simulation. Figure K–9(a) shows the simulation in the form of a truth table, and Figure K–9(b) shows a photograph of the waveform output as it appears on a computer display.

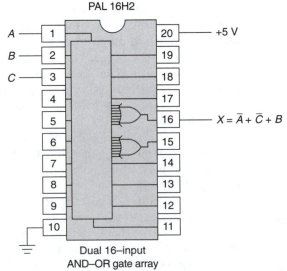

Figure K–5   Connections to a PAL16H2 to solve the equation $X = \bar{A} + \bar{C} + B$.

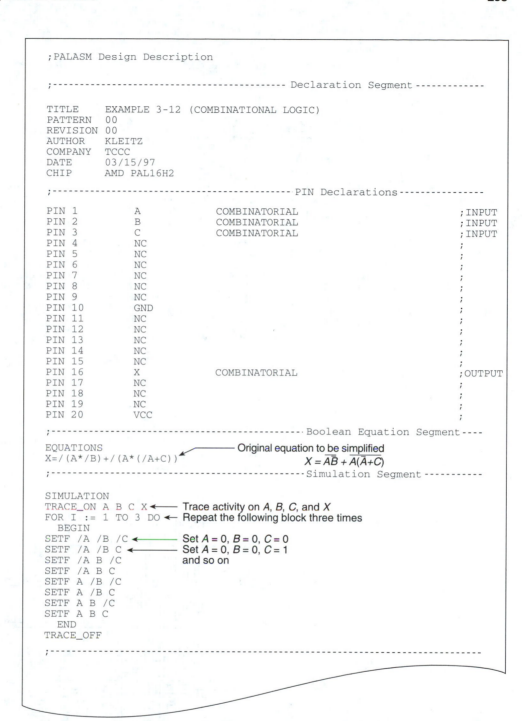

```
;PALASM Design Description

;------------------------------------------- Declaration Segment -------------

TITLE      EXAMPLE 3-12 (COMBINATIONAL LOGIC)
PATTERN    00
REVISION   00
AUTHOR     KLEITZ
COMPANY    TCCC
DATE       03/15/97
CHIP       AMD PAL16H2

;------------------------------------------- PIN Declarations ----------------

PIN 1          A              COMBINATORIAL                          ; INPUT
PIN 2          B              COMBINATORIAL                          ; INPUT
PIN 3          C              COMBINATORIAL                          ; INPUT
PIN 4          NC                                                    ;
PIN 5          NC                                                    ;
PIN 6          NC                                                    ;
PIN 7          NC                                                    ;
PIN 8          NC                                                    ;
PIN 9          NC                                                    ;
PIN 10         GND                                                   ;
PIN 11         NC                                                    ;
PIN 12         NC                                                    ;
PIN 13         NC                                                    ;
PIN 14         NC                                                    ;
PIN 15         NC                                                    ;
PIN 16         X              COMBINATORIAL                          ;OUTPUT
PIN 17         NC                                                    ;
PIN 18         NC                                                    ;
PIN 19         NC                                                    ;
PIN 20         VCC                                                   ;

;------------------------------------------- Boolean Equation Segment ----

EQUATIONS                              ── Original equation to be simplified
X=/(A*/B)+/(A*(/A+C))
                                            X = ĀB̄ + Ā(Ā+C)
;------------------------------------------- Simulation Segment -----------

SIMULATION
TRACE_ON A B C X  ◄─── Trace activity on A, B, C, and X
FOR I := 1 TO 3 DO  ◄─ Repeat the following block three times
  BEGIN
SETF /A /B /C  ◄───── Set A = 0, B = 0, C = 0
SETF /A /B C   ◄───── Set A = 0, B = 0, C = 1
SETF /A B /C          and so on
SETF /A B C
SETF A /B /C
SETF A /B C
SETF A B /C
SETF A B C
  END
TRACE_OFF

;-----------------------------------------------------------------------
```

Figure K–6   EX3–12.PDS file (design definitions). (Copyright © Advanced Micro Devices, Inc. 1991. Reprinted with permission of copyright owner. All rights reserved.)

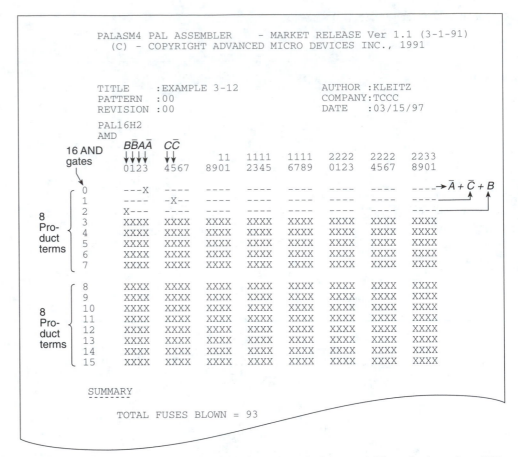

```
PALASM4 PAL ASSEMBLER     - MARKET RELEASE Ver 1.1 (3-1-91)
    (C) - COPYRIGHT ADVANCED MICRO DEVICES INC., 1991


      TITLE    :EXAMPLE 3-12          AUTHOR :KLEITZ
      PATTERN  :00                    COMPANY:TCCC
      REVISION :00                    DATE   :03/15/97

      PAL16H2
      AMD
            B̄B̄ĀĀ   CC̄
16 AND      ↓↓↓↓   ↓↓
gates       ↓↓↓↓   ↓↓        11   1111   1111   2222   2222   2233
            0123   4567   8901   2345   6789   0123   4567   8901

        0   ---X   ----   ----   ----   ----   ----   ----   ----→Ā + C̄ + B
        1   ----   -X--   ----   ----   ----   ----   ----   ----      ↑        ↑
        2   X---   ----   ----   ----   ----   ----   ----   ----─────────────┘
 8      3   XXXX   XXXX   XXXX   XXXX   XXXX   XXXX   XXXX   XXXX
Pro-    4   XXXX   XXXX   XXXX   XXXX   XXXX   XXXX   XXXX   XXXX
duct    5   XXXX   XXXX   XXXX   XXXX   XXXX   XXXX   XXXX   XXXX
terms   6   XXXX   XXXX   XXXX   XXXX   XXXX   XXXX   XXXX   XXXX
        7   XXXX   XXXX   XXXX   XXXX   XXXX   XXXX   XXXX   XXXX

        8   XXXX   XXXX   XXXX   XXXX   XXXX   XXXX   XXXX   XXXX
        9   XXXX   XXXX   XXXX   XXXX   XXXX   XXXX   XXXX   XXXX
 8     10   XXXX   XXXX   XXXX   XXXX   XXXX   XXXX   XXXX   XXXX
Pro-   11   XXXX   XXXX   XXXX   XXXX   XXXX   XXXX   XXXX   XXXX
duct   12   XXXX   XXXX   XXXX   XXXX   XXXX   XXXX   XXXX   XXXX
terms  13   XXXX   XXXX   XXXX   XXXX   XXXX   XXXX   XXXX   XXXX
       14   XXXX   XXXX   XXXX   XXXX   XXXX   XXXX   XXXX   XXXX
       15   XXXX   XXXX   XXXX   XXXX   XXXX   XXXX   XXXX   XXXX


      SUMMARY
      -------
            TOTAL FUSES BLOWN = 93
```

Figure K–7 EX3–12.XPT file (fuse map). (Copyright © Advanced Micro Devices, Inc. 1991. Reprinted with permission of copyright owner. All rights reserved.)

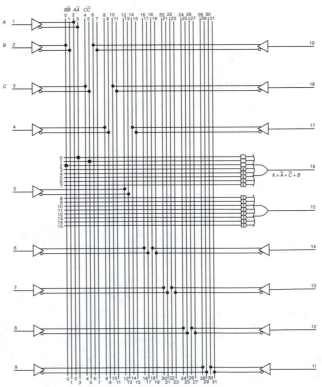

Figure K–8 Logic diagram for a PAL16H2.

```
PALASM4 PLDSIM    - MARKET RELEASE Ver 1.1 (3-1-91)
  (C) - COPYRIGHT ADVANCED MICRO DEVICES INC., 1991

PALASM SIMULATION HISTORY LISTING

TITLE    :EXAMPLE 3-12                    AUTHOR :KLEITZ
PATTERN  :00                              COMPANY:TCCC
REVISION :00                              DATE   :03/15/97

PAL16H2
Page: 1
```

	ggggggggggggggggggggggggg	→ g represents SETF
A	LLLLHHHHLLLLHHHHLLLLHHHH	⎫
B	LLHHLLHHLLHHLLHHLLHHLLHH	⎬ The eight combinations of A, B, C repeated three times
C	LHLHLHLHLHLHLHLHLHLHLHLH	⎭
GND	LLLLLLLLLLLLLLLLLLLLLLLL	
X	HHHHHLHHHHHHHLHHHHHHHLHH	→ X = HIGH for $\bar{A} + \bar{C} + B$
VCC	HHHHHHHHHHHHHHHHHHHHHHHH	

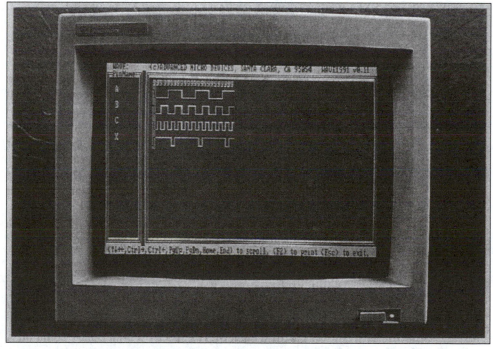

Figure K–9 PALASM simulator output: (a) EX3–12.HST file (truth table format); (b) computer display showing waveform simulation at *A, B, C,* and *X.* (Copyright © Advanced Micro Devices, Inc. 1991. Reprinted with permission of copyright owner. All rights reserved.)

DESIGNING AN OCTAL DECODER (74138) USING A PAL16L8

A common use of programmable logic devices is to implement customized data conversion functions like decoding and encoding. To illustrate this application, we will design an octal decoder to function exactly like the 74138.

By reviewing the 74138, you can see that we need to provide eight active-LOW outputs (O_7 to O_0). The output to be made active is selected by a 3-bit binary code (A_0 to A_2) as long as the three enable inputs (E_1 to E_3) are satisfied.

A good choice to implement the circuit is the 16L8 PAL IC. It has eight active-LOW outputs (that is what the L8 stands for) and 16 true and complemented inputs avail-

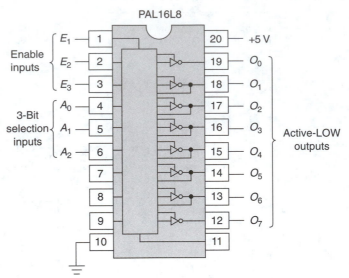

Figure K–10 Pin connections to a 16L8 PAL to function as a 74138 octal decoder.

able as product terms. Figure K–10 shows the inputs and outputs that we will define on the PAL16L8.

Figure K–11 shows the FIG4–5.PDS design definition file. The pin declaration variable names are all listed in their true (not complemented) form. The equations section forms an active-LOW input or output by using a slash (/) in front of the variable name.

The simulation segment is set up to trace the activity on all inputs and outputs for 12 different input conditions. The first SETF sets E_1 HIGH. Because the other five inputs are not specified, they will be don't-cares. The first column in the simulation listing (Figure K–12) shows this condition. Notice that all outputs are HIGH, as they should be, because E_1 must be LOW to enable the decoder.

The next SETF sets E_1 LOW and E_2 HIGH. This is also a disable condition because E_1 and E_2 must both be LOW. The second column in Figure K–12 shows all outputs are still HIGH.

The third SETF is still a disable condition, and the outputs are still HIGH. The fourth SETF satisfies all three enables (E_1 = LOW, E_2 = LOW, E_3 = HIGH). Now the eight outputs are undetermined (X) because the 3-bit binary input has not been specified yet.

The next eight SETFs specify a 3-bit binary count on A_0 to A_2. The last specification given for E_1 to E_3 remains in effect unless specified otherwise, so the decoder remains enabled. Notice that as the inputs are counting, the last eight columns in the simulation listing (Figure K–12) show the active-LOW output moving from O_0 to O_1 to O_2, and so on, just as it's supposed to!

IMPLEMENTING A JOHNSON SHIFT COUNTER USING THE REGISTERED OUTPUTS OF THE PAL16R8

The two previous PAL solutions were strictly combinational logic circuits. Sequential logic circuits, such as counters and shift registers, can be implemented only by using PAL devices that have *registered* outputs. The registered outputs are usually D flip-flops.

The PAL that we will use to solve the sequential logic requirements of a Johnson shift counter is the 16R8. The R8 in the part number signifies that it has 8 registered outputs. The abbreviated logic diagram in Figure K–13 shows that the eight D flip-flops are driven by a common buffered clock on pin 1 (CLK). The Q outputs are available on pins 12 through 19 via three-stated inverting buffers controlled by an active-LOW output enable on pin 11 (OE).

```
;PALASM Design Description


;------------------------------------------- Declaration Segment -------------
TITLE     Fig. 4-5 (74138 Octal Decoder)
PATTERN   00
REVISION  00
AUTHOR    Kleitz
COMPANY   TCCC
DATE      03/15/97

CHIP      AMD PAL16L8
;----------------------------------------------- PIN Declarations ----------------

PIN 1          E1              COMBINATORIAL                              ;ENABLE
PIN 2          E2              COMBINATORIAL                              ;ENABLE
PIN 3          E3              COMBINATORIAL                              ;ENABLE
PIN 4          A0              COMBINATORIAL                              ;INPUT
PIN 5          A1              COMBINATORIAL                              ;INPUT
PIN 6          A2              COMBINATORIAL                              ;INPUT
PIN 7          NC                                                        ;
PIN 8          NC                                                        ;
PIN 9          NC                                                        ;
PIN 10         GND                                                       ;
PIN 11         NC                                                        ;
PIN 12         O7              COMBINATORIAL                             ;OUTPUT
PIN 13         O6              COMBINATORIAL                             ;OUTPUT
PIN 14         O5              COMBINATORIAL                             ;OUTPUT
PIN 15         O4              COMBINATORIAL                             ;OUTPUT
PIN 16         O3              COMBINATORIAL                             ;OUTPUT
PIN 17         O2              COMBINATORIAL                             ;OUTPUT
PIN 18         O1              COMBINATORIAL                             ;OUTPUT
PIN 19         O0              COMBINATORIAL                             ;OUTPUT
PIN 20         VCC                                                       ;
;--------------------------------------------Boolean Equation Segment----
EQUATIONS
/O0=/E1*/E2*E3*/A0*/A1*/A2  ←— Read as O0 is LOW for 001000
/O1=/E1*/E2*E3* A0*/A1*/A2  ←— Read as O1 is LOW for 001100
/O2=/E1*/E2*E3*/A0* A1*/A2      and so on
/O3=/E1*/E2*E3* A0* A1*/A2
/O4=/E1*/E2*E3*/A0*/A1* A2
/O5=/E1*/E2*E3* A0*/A1* A2
/O6=/E1*/E2*E3*/A0* A1* A2
/O7=/E1*/E2*E3* A0* A1* A2

;------------------------------------------------Simulation Segment -----------
SIMULATION
TRACE_ON E1 E2 E3 A0 A1 A2 O1 O2 O3 O4 O5 O6 O7 ←—— Trace activity on
 SETF   E1                                            all inputs and outputs
 SETF  /E1   E2
 SETF  /E1  /E2  /E3
 SETF  /E1  /E2   E3
 SETF  /A0  /A1  /A2
 SETF   A0  /A1  /A2     Simulate outputs for
 SETF  /A0   A1  /A2     these twelve input conditions
 SETF   A0   A1  /A2
 SETF  /A0  /A1   A2
 SETF   A0  /A1   A2
 SETF  /A0   A1   A2
 SETF   A0   A1   A2
TRACE_OFF
;-------------------------------------------------------------------
```

Figure K–11 FIG4–5.PDS design definition file. (Copyright © Advanced Micro Devices, Inc. 1991. Reprinted with permission of copyright owner. All rights reserved.)

```
PALASM4 PLDSIM    - MARKET RELEASE Ver 1.1 (3-1-91)
   (C) - COPYRIGHT ADVANCED MICRO DEVICES INC., 1991

PALASM SIMULATION HISTORY LISTING

Title    :FIG. 4-5 (74138)              Author :KLEITZ
Pattern  :00                            Company:TCCC
Revision :00                            Date   :03/30/97

PAL16L8
Page: 1

        ggggggggggg
  E1    HLLLLLLLLLLL
  E2    XHLLLLLLLLLL  } 0 0 1 Enables decoder
  E3    XXLHHHHHHHHH
  A0    XXXXLHLHLHLH
  A1    XXXXLLHHLLHH  } Output selection bits
  A2    XXXXLLLLHHHH
  GND   LLLLLLLLLLLL
  O7    HHHXHHHHHHHL
  O6    HHHXHHHHHHLH
  O5    HHHXHHHHHLHH
  O4    HHHXHHHHLHHH  } Output goes LOW when selected by A0 to A2
  O3    HHHXHHHLHHHH
  O2    HHHXHHLHHHHH
  O1    HHHXHLHHHHHH
  00    HHHXLHHHHHHH
  VCC   HHHHHHHHHHHH
         |←Enabled→|
       →|  |←Disabled
```

Figure K–12   FIG4–5.HST simulation truth table listing. (Copyright © Advanced Micro Devices, Inc. 1991. Reprinted with permission of copyright owner. All rights reserved.)

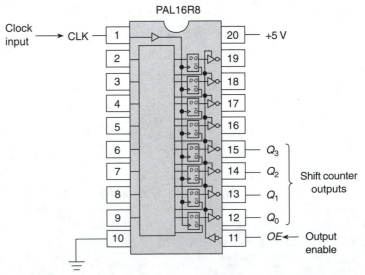

Figure K–13   Circuit connections to a registered-output PAL16R8 to be used as the Johnson shift counter.

The design description file in Figure K–14 defines the eight pins used on the chip to implement the function. As before, all variable names are given in their true form. The *Q*s are declared as "registered" because they are flip-flop outputs. The common clock (CLK) and output enable (OE) are declared as "combinatorial."

The equations section defines the necessary connections from flip-flop to flip-flop. The cross connection from the last flip-flop back to the first (which is required for the Johnson configuration) is defined by the first equation: /Q0 = Q3. The next three equations define the other three flip-flop connections. Because the *Q*s are registered outputs, they change states only after a LOW-to-HIGH clock transition. Therefore, the first equation should *not* be interpreted as "/*Q*0 *equals Q*3," but instead it should be interpreted as "/*Q*0 receives the level of *Q*3 after the active clock transition."

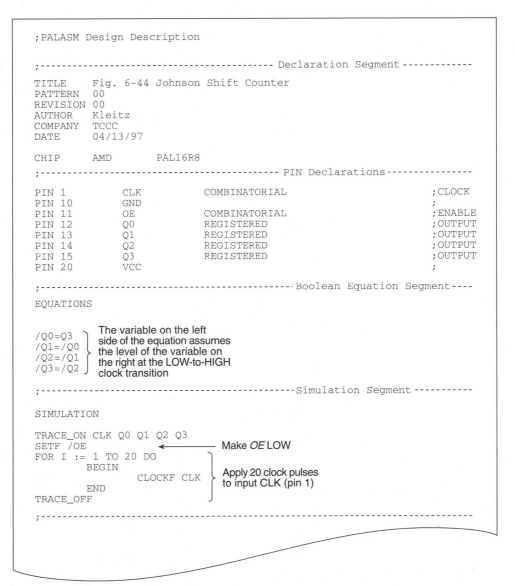

```
;PALASM Design Description


;----------------------------------------------- Declaration Segment -------------

TITLE     Fig. 6-44 Johnson Shift Counter
PATTERN   00
REVISION  00
AUTHOR    Kleitz
COMPANY   TCCC
DATE      04/13/97


CHIP      AMD         PAL16R8
;---------------------------------------------- PIN Declarations ----------------

PIN 1         CLK           COMBINATORIAL                       ;CLOCK
PIN 10        GND                                               ;
PIN 11        OE            COMBINATORIAL                       ;ENABLE
PIN 12        Q0            REGISTERED                          ;OUTPUT
PIN 13        Q1            REGISTERED                          ;OUTPUT
PIN 14        Q2            REGISTERED                          ;OUTPUT
PIN 15        Q3            REGISTERED                          ;OUTPUT
PIN 20        VCC                                               ;

;-------------------------------------------------Boolean Equation Segment----

EQUATIONS


/Q0=Q3            The variable on the left
/Q1=/Q0           side of the equation assumes
/Q2=/Q1           the level of the variable on
/Q3=/Q2           the right at the LOW-to-HIGH
                  clock transition

;-----------------------------------------------Simulation Segment -----------

SIMULATION

TRACE_ON CLK Q0 Q1 Q2 Q3
SETF /OE                          ←—— Make OE LOW
FOR I := 1 TO 20 DO
        BEGIN
                 CLOCKF CLK       Apply 20 clock pulses
        END                       to input CLK (pin 1)
TRACE_OFF

;-----------------------------------------------------------------------------
```

Figure K–14 FIG6–44.PDS design description file for a PAL16R8. (Copyright © Advanced Micro Devices, Inc. 1991. Reprinted with permission of copyright owner. All rights reserved.)

```
PALASM4 PLDSIM      - MARKET RELEASE Ver 1.1 (3-1-91)
  (C) - COPYRIGHT ADVANCED MICRO DEVICES INC., 1991

PALASM SIMULATION HISTORY LISTING

Title    :FIG. 6-44 Johnson Shift          Author :KLEITZ
Pattern  :00                               Company:TCCC
Revision :00                               Date   :04/13/97

PAL16L8                                          c represents LOW-to-HIGH
Page: 1                                          clock edge

      gc c  c  c  c  c  c  c  c  c  c  c  c  c  c  c  c  c  c  c  c
CLK   LHHLHHLHHLHHLHHLHHLHHLHHLHHLHHLHHLHHLHHLHHLHHLHHLHHLHHLHHLHH
GND   LLLLLLLLLLLLLLLLLLLLLLLLLLLLLLLLLLLLLLLLLLLLLLLLLLLLLLLLLLLL
OE    LLLLLLLLLLLLLLLLLLLLLLLLLLLLLLLLLLLLLLLLLLLLLLLLLLLLLLLLLLLL
Q0    HHLLLLLLLLLLLLLHHHHHHHHHHHHLLLLLLLLLLLLLHHHHHHHHHHHHLLLLLLLLLLLL ⌐ Shift
Q1    HHHHLLLLLLLLLLLLLHHHHHHHHHHHHLLLLLLLLLLLLLHHHHHHHHHHHHLLLLLLLL | counter
Q2    HHHHHHLLLLLLLLLLLLLHHHHHHHHHHHHLLLLLLLLLLLLLHHHHHHHHHHHHLLLLL > output
Q3    HHHHHHHHLLLLLLLLLLLLLHHHHHHHHHHHHLLLLLLLLLLLLLHHHHHHHHHHHHL ⌐ pattern
VCC   HHHHHHHHHHHHHHHHHHHHHHHHHHHHHHHHHHHHHHHHHHHHHHHHHHHHHHHHHHHH
```

Figure K–15   FIG6–44.HST simulator truth table listing for a Johnson shift counter. (Copyright © Advanced Micro Devices, Inc. 1991. Reprinted with permission of copyright owner. All rights reserved.)

To simulate the circuit operation, we need to make *OE* LOW (SETF /OE) and apply clock pulses to the CLK input (CLOCKF CLK). The simulation history listing is given in Figure K–15. The letter c is used across the top of the listing to indicate each occurrence of a LOW-to-HIGH transition of CLK. By scanning across the output listing, you can see that the *Q* outputs are performing the shift counter operation correctly.

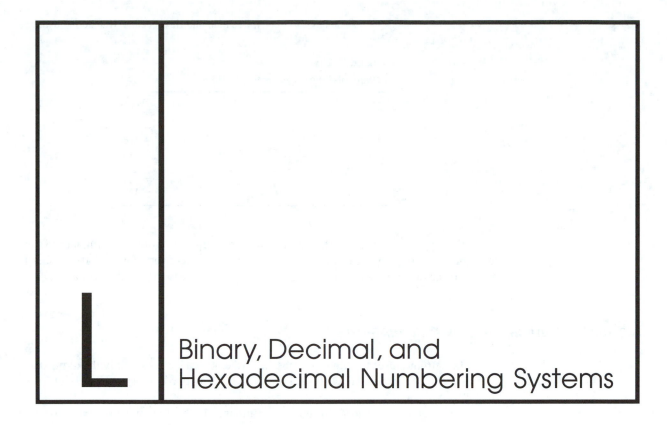

L
Binary, Decimal, and Hexadecimal Numbering Systems

L–1 DECIMAL NUMBERING SYSTEM (BASE 10)

In the decimal numbering system, each position will contain 10 different possible digits. These digits are 0, 1, 2, 3, 4, 5, 6, 7, 8, and 9. Each position in a multidigit number will have a weighting factor based on a power of 10.

EXAMPLE L–1

In a four-digit decimal number, the least significant position (rightmost) will have a weighting factor of 10^0; the most significant position (leftmost) will have a weighting factor of 10^3:

$$10^3 \quad 10^2 \quad 10^1 \quad 10^0$$

where
$$10^3 = 1000$$
$$10^2 = 100$$
$$10^1 = 10$$
$$10^0 = 1$$

To evaluate the decimal number 4623, the digit in each position is multiplied by the appropriate weighting factor:

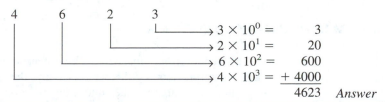

$$
\begin{array}{rr}
3 \times 10^0 = & 3 \\
2 \times 10^1 = & 20 \\
6 \times 10^2 = & 600 \\
4 \times 10^3 = & +\ 4000 \\
\hline
& 4623 \quad \textit{Answer}
\end{array}
$$

TABLE L–1

Powers-of-2 Binary Weighting Factors

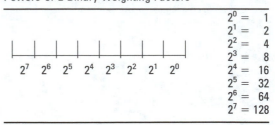

$$2^0 = 1$$
$$2^1 = 2$$
$$2^2 = 4$$
$$2^3 = 8$$
$$2^4 = 16$$
$$2^5 = 32$$
$$2^6 = 64$$
$$2^7 = 128$$

Example L–1 illustrates the procedure used to convert from some number system to its decimal (base 10) equivalent. (In that example, we converted a base 10 number to a base 10 answer.) Now let's look at base 2 (binary) and base 16 (hexadecimal).

L–2 BINARY NUMBERING SYSTEM (BASE 2)

Digital electronics uses the binary numbering system because it uses only the digits 0 and 1, which can be represented easily in a digital system by two distinct voltage levels, such as +5 V = 1 and 0 V = 0.

The weighting factors for binary positions will be the powers of 2 shown in Table L–1.

EXAMPLE L–2

Convert the binary number 01010110_2 to decimal. (Notice the subscript 2 used to indicate that 01010110 is a base 2 number.)

Solution: Multiply each binary digit by the appropriate weighting factor and total the results.

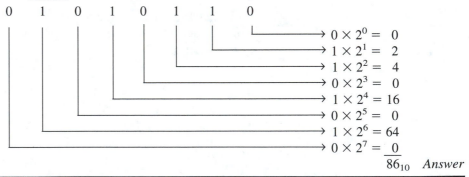

$$0 \times 2^0 = 0$$
$$1 \times 2^1 = 2$$
$$1 \times 2^2 = 4$$
$$0 \times 2^3 = 0$$
$$1 \times 2^4 = 16$$
$$0 \times 2^5 = 0$$
$$1 \times 2^6 = 64$$
$$0 \times 2^7 = \underline{0}$$
$$86_{10} \quad Answer$$

L–3 DECIMAL-TO-BINARY CONVERSION

The conversion from binary to decimal is usually performed by the digital computer for ease of interpretation by the person reading the number. On the other hand, when a person enters a decimal number into a digital computer, that number must be converted to binary before it can be operated on. Let's look at decimal-to-binary conversion.

EXAMPLE L–3

Convert 133_{10} to binary.

Solution: Referring to Table L–1, we can see that the largest power of 2 that will fit into 133 is 2^7 ($2^7 = 128$). But that will still leave the value 5 ($133 - 128 = 5$) to be accounted for. Five can be taken care of by 2^2 and 2^0 ($2^2 = 4$, $2^0 = 1$). So the process looks like this:

$$
\begin{array}{r}
133 \\
- 128 \rightarrow 2^7 \\
\hline
5 \\
- 4 \rightarrow 2^2 \\
\hline
1 \\
- 1 \rightarrow 2^0 \\
\hline
0
\end{array}
\qquad
\begin{array}{|c|c|c|c|c|c|c|c|}
\hline
1 & 0 & 0 & 0 & 0 & 1 & 0 & 1 \\
\hline
2^7 & 2^6 & 2^5 & 2^4 & 2^3 & 2^2 & 2^1 & 2^0 \\
\end{array}
$$

Answer: 10000101_2.

Note: The powers of 2 that fit into the number 133 were first determined. Then all other positions were filled with zeros.

EXAMPLE L–4

Convert 122_{10} to binary.

Solution:

$$
\begin{array}{r}
122 \\
- 64 \rightarrow 2^6 \\
\hline
58 \\
- 32 \rightarrow 2^5 \\
\hline
26 \\
- 16 \rightarrow 2^4 \\
\hline
10 \\
- 8 \rightarrow 2^3 \\
\hline
2 \\
- 2 \rightarrow 2^1 \\
\hline
0
\end{array}
\qquad
\begin{array}{cccccccc}
0 & 1 & 1 & 1 & 1 & 0 & 1 & 0 \\
2^7 & 2^6 & 2^5 & 2^4 & 2^3 & 2^2 & 2^1 & 2^0 \\
\end{array}
$$

Answer: 01111010_2.

Another method of converting decimal to binary is by *successive division*. Successive division is done by repeated division by the number of the base to which you are converting. For example, to convert 122_{10} to base 2, use the following procedure:

$$122 \div 2 = 61 \quad \text{with a remainder of} \quad 0 \quad \text{(LSB)}$$

$$61 \div 2 = 30 \quad \text{with a remainder of} \quad 1$$

$$30 \div 2 = 15 \quad \text{with a remainder of} \quad 0$$

$$15 \div 2 = 7 \quad \text{with a remainder of} \quad 1$$

$$7 \div 2 = 3 \quad \text{with a remainder of} \quad 1$$

$$3 \div 2 = 1 \quad \text{with a remainder of} \quad 1$$

$$1 \div 2 = 0 \quad \text{with a remainder of} \quad 1 \quad \text{(MSB)}$$

The first remainder, 0, is the *least significant bit* (LSB) of the answer; the last remainder, 1, is the *most significant bit* (MSB) of the answer; therefore, the answer is

$$1 \quad 1 \quad 1 \quad 1 \quad 0 \quad 1 \quad 0_2$$

However, because most computers or digital systems deal with groups of 4, 8, 16, or 32 *bits* (binary digits), we should keep all our answers in that form. Adding a leading zero to the number $1\ 1\ 1\ 1\ 0\ 1\ 0_2$ will not change its numeric value; therefore, the 8-bit answer is

$$1\ 1\ 1\ 1\ 0\ 1\ 0_2 = 0\ 1\ 1\ 1\ 1\ 0\ 1\ 0_2$$

EXAMPLE L–5

Convert 152_{10} to binary using successive division.

Solution:

$$152 \div 2 = 76 \quad \text{remainder} \quad 0 \quad \text{(LSB)}$$
$$76 \div 2 = 38 \quad \text{remainder} \quad 0$$
$$38 \div 2 = 19 \quad \text{remainder} \quad 0$$
$$19 \div 2 = 9 \quad \text{remainder} \quad 1$$
$$9 \div 2 = 4 \quad \text{remainder} \quad 1$$
$$4 \div 2 = 2 \quad \text{remainder} \quad 0$$
$$2 \div 2 = 1 \quad \text{remainder} \quad 0$$
$$1 \div 2 = 0 \quad \text{remainder} \quad 1 \quad \text{(MSB)}$$

Answer: 10011000_2.

L–4 HEXADECIMAL NUMBERING SYSTEM (BASE 16)

The hexadecimal numbering system is a method of grouping bits to simplify entering and reading instructions or data present in digital computer systems. Hexadecimal uses 4-bit groupings; therefore, instructions or data used in 8-, 16-, or 32-bit computer systems can be represented as a two-, four-, or eight-digit hexadecimal code instead of as a long string of binary digits (see Table L–2).

Hexadecimal (hex) uses 16 different digits and is a method of grouping binary numbers in groups of four. The 16 allowable hex digits are 0, 1, 2, 3, 4, 5, 6, 7, 8, 9, A, B, C, D, E, and F.

L–5 HEXADECIMAL CONVERSIONS

To convert from binary to hexadecimal, group the binary number in groups of four (starting in the least significant position) and write down the equivalent hex digit.

EXAMPLE L–6

Convert $0\ 1\ 1\ 0\ 1\ 1\ 0\ 1_2$ to hex.

Solution:

$$\underbrace{0\ 1\ 1\ 0}_{6} \quad \underbrace{1\ 1\ 0\ 1_2}_{D} \quad = 6D_{16} \quad \textit{Answer}$$

TABLE L–2

Hexadecimal Numbering System

Decimal	Binary	Hexadecimal
0	0000 0000	0 0
1	0000 0001	0 1
2	0000 0010	0 2
3	0000 0011	0 3
4	0000 0100	0 4
5	0000 0101	0 5
6	0000 0110	0 6
7	0000 0111	0 7
8	0000 1000	0 8
9	0000 1001	0 9
10	0000 1010	0 A
11	0000 1011	0 B
12	0000 1100	0 C
13	0000 1101	0 D
14	0000 1110	0 E
15	0000 1111	0 F
16	0001 0000	1 0
17	0001 0001	1 1
18	0001 0010	1 2
19	0001 0011	1 3
20	0001 0100	1 4

To convert *hexadecimal to binary,* use the reverse process.

EXAMPLE L–7

Convert $A9_{16}$ to binary.

Solution:

$$\begin{matrix} A & \quad & 9 \end{matrix}$$

$$1\ 0\ 1\ 0 \quad 1\ 0\ 0\ 1 = 1\ 0\ 1\ 0\ 1\ 0\ 0\ 1_2 \quad \textit{Answer}$$

To convert *hexadecimal to decimal,* multiply each hex digit by its appropriate weighting factor (powers of 16).

EXAMPLE L–8

Convert $2A6_{16}$ to decimal.

Solution:

$$\begin{matrix} 2 & A & 6 \end{matrix}$$

$$6 \times 16^0 = 6 \times 1 = 6$$
$$A \times 16^1 = 10 \times 16 = 160$$
$$2 \times 16^2 = 2 \times 256 = 512$$

$$678_{10} \quad \textit{Answer}$$

To convert from *decimal to hexadecimal,* use successive division.

EXAMPLE L–9

Convert 151_{10} to hex.

Solution:

$$151 \div 16 = 9 \quad \text{remainder } 7 \quad \text{(LSD)}$$
$$9 \div 16 = 0 \quad \text{remainder } 9 \quad \text{(MSD)}$$
$$151_{10} = 97_{16} \quad \textit{Answer}$$

Check:

97_{16}

$$\longrightarrow 7 \times 16^0 = \quad 7$$
$$\longrightarrow 9 \times 16^1 = \underline{144}$$
$$\overline{151} \; \sqrt{}$$

EXAMPLE L–10

Convert 498_{10} to hex.

Solution:

$$498 \div 16 = 31 \quad \text{remainder} \quad 2 \quad\quad \text{(LSD)}$$
$$31 \div 16 = \;\; 1 \quad \text{remainder} \quad 15 \, (= F)$$
$$1 \div 16 = \;\; 0 \quad \text{remainder} \quad 1 \quad\quad \text{(MSD)}$$
$$498_{10} = 1F2_{16}$$

Check:

$$1F2_{16} \quad 2 \times 16^0 = \;\; 2 \times \;\; 1 = \;\; 2$$
$$F \times 16^1 = 15 \times \;\; 16 = 240$$
$$1 \times 16^2 = \;\; 1 \times 256 = \underline{256}$$
$$\overline{498} \; \sqrt{}$$

L–6 BINARY-CODED-DECIMAL SYSTEM

The binary-coded-decimal system is used to represent each of the 10 decimal digits as a 4-bit binary code. This code is useful for outputting to displays that are always numeric (0 to 9), such as those found in digital clocks or digital voltmeters. To form a BCD number, simply convert each decimal digit to its 4-bit binary code.

EXAMPLE L–11

Convert 496_{10} to BCD.

Solution:

$$\begin{array}{ccc} 4 & 9 & 6 \\ \overbrace{0100} & \overbrace{1001} & \overbrace{0110} \end{array} = 0100 \quad 1001 \quad 0110_{BCD} \quad \textit{Answer}$$

To convert BCD to decimal, just reverse the process.

EXAMPLE L–12

Convert 0111 0101 1000$_{BCD}$ to decimal.

Solution:

$$\underbrace{0111}_{7} \quad \underbrace{0101}_{5} \quad \underbrace{1000}_{8} \quad = 758_{10} \quad \textit{Answer}$$

EXAMPLE L–13

Convert 0110 0100 1011$_{BCD}$ to decimal.

Solution:

$$0110 \quad 0100 \quad 1011$$

$$6 \qquad 4 \qquad *$$

*This conversion is impossible because 1011 is not a valid binary-boded decimal. It is not in the range 0 to 9.

L–7 COMPARISON OF NUMBERING SYSTEMS

Table L–3 shows a comparison of the four number systems commonly used in digital electronics and computer systems.

TABLE L–3

Comparison of Numbering Systems

Decimal	Binary		Hexadecimal		BCD	
0	0000	0000	0	0	0000	0000
1	0000	0001	0	1	0000	0001
2	0000	0010	0	2	0000	0010
3	0000	0011	0	3	0000	0011
4	0000	0100	0	4	0000	0100
5	0000	0101	0	5	0000	0101
6	0000	0110	0	6	0000	0110
7	0000	0111	0	7	0000	0111
8	0000	1000	0	8	0000	1000
9	0000	1001	0	9	0000	1001
10	0000	1010	0	A	0001	0000
11	0000	1011	0	B	0001	0001
12	0000	1100	0	C	0001	0010
13	0000	1101	0	D	0001	0011
14	0000	1110	0	E	0001	0100
15	0000	1111	0	F	0001	0101
16	0001	0000	1	0	0001	0110
17	0001	0001	1	1	0001	0111
18	0001	0010	1	2	0001	1000
19	0001	0011	1	3	0001	1001
20	0001	0100	1	4	0010	0000

M

Octal Three-State Buffers, Latches, and Transceivers

When we start studying microprocessor hardware, we'll see a need for transmitting a number of bits simultaneously as a group. A single flip-flop will not do. What we need is a group of flip-flops, called a *register,* to facilitate the movement and temporary storage of binary information. The most commonly used registers are 8 bits wide and function as either a buffer, a latch, or a transceiver.

THREE-STATE BUFFERS

In microprocessor systems several input and output devices have to share the same data lines going into the microprocessor IC. (These "shared" data lines are called the *data bus.*) For example, if an 8-bit microprocessor has to interface with four separate 8-bit input devices, we must provide a way to enable just one of the devices to place its data on the data bus at a time while the other three are disabled. One way to accomplish this is to use three-state octal buffers.

In Figure M–1 the second buffer is enabled, which allows the eight data bits from input device 2 to reach the data bus. The other three buffers are disabled, keeping their outputs in the "float" condition.

A buffer is simply a device that, when enabled, passes a digital level from its input to its output, unchanged. It provides isolation, or a "buffer," between the input device and the data bus. A buffer also provides the sink or source current required by any devices connected to its output without loading down the input device. An octal buffer IC has eight individual buffers within a single package.

The term *three-state* refers to the fact that the output can have one of three levels: HIGH, LOW, or float. The symbol and function table for an individual three-state buffer are shown in Figure M–2.

From Figure M–2 we can see that the circuit acts like a straight buffer (output = input) when $\overline{OE}$ is LOW (active-LOW output enable). When the output is disabled ($\overline{OE}$ = HIGH), the output level is placed in the "float" or "high-impedance" state. In the

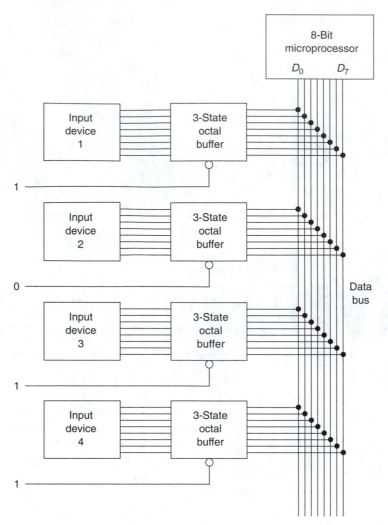

Figure M–1   Using a three-state octal buffer to pass eight data bits from input device 2 to the data bus.

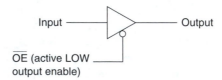

Input	$\overline{OE}$	Output
1	0	1
0	0	0
1	1	Float
0	1	Float

Figure M–2   Three-state buffer symbol and function table.

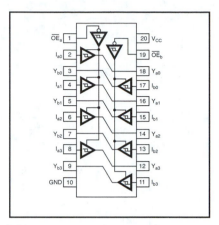

Figure M–3 Pin configuration for the 74LS244 three-state octal buffer.

high-impedance state the output looks like an open circuit to anything else connected to it. In other words, in the float state the output is neither HIGH nor LOW and cannot sink or source current.

A popular three-state octal buffer is the 74LS244 shown in Figure M–3. The buffers are configured in two groups of four. The first group (group *a*) is controlled by $\overline{OE}_a$ and the second group (group *b*) is controlled by $\overline{OE}_b$. Here also $\overline{OE}$ is active-LOW, meaning that it takes a LOW to allow data to pass from the inputs (*I*) to the outputs (*Y*). Other features of the 74LS244 are that it has Schmitt trigger hysteresis and very high sink and source current capabilities (24 and 15 mA, respectively).

OCTAL LATCHES/FLIP-FLOPS

In microprocessor systems, we need latches and flip-flops to "remember" digital states that the microprocessor issues before it goes on to other tasks. Take, for example, a microprocessor system used to drive two separate 8-bit output devices, as shown in Figure M–4.

To send information to output device 1, the microprocessor first sets up the data bus (D_0–D_7) with the appropriate data, then issues a LOW-to-HIGH pulse on line C_1. The positive edge of the pulse causes the data at D_0–D_7 of the flip-flop to be stored at Q_0–Q_7. Since $\overline{OE}$ is tied LOW, those data are sent on to output device 1. (The diagonal line with the number 8 above it is a shorthand method used to indicate eight separate lines or conductors.)

Next, the microprocessor sets up the data bus with data for output device 2 and issues a LOW-to-HIGH pulse on C_2. Now the second octal *D* flip-flop is loaded with valid data. The outputs of the *D* flip-flops will remain at those digital levels, allowing the microprocessor to perform other tasks.

In a digital electronics course, you may have studied the 7475 transparent latch and the 7474 *D* flip-flop. The 74LS373 and 74LS374 shown in Figure M–5 operate the same way, except they were developed to handle 8-bit data operations.

TRANSCEIVERS

Another way to connect devices to a shared data bus is to use a transceiver (transmitter/receiver). The transceiver differs from a buffer or latch because it is *bidirectional,* which

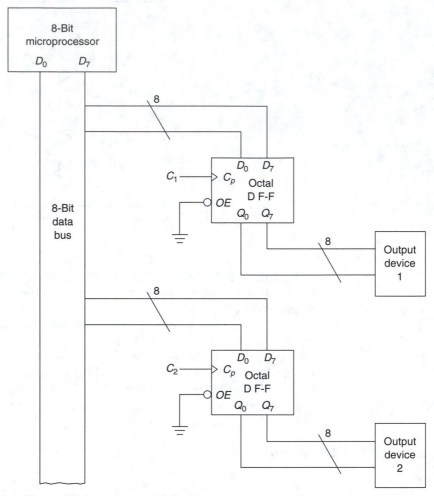

Figure M–4   Using octal *D* flip-flops to capture data that appear momentarily on a microprocessor data bus.

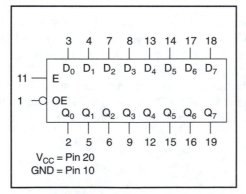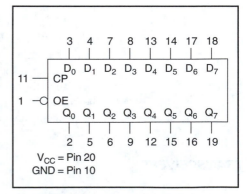

Figure M–5   Logic symbol for the 74LS373 octal latch and the 74LS374 octal *D* flip-flop.

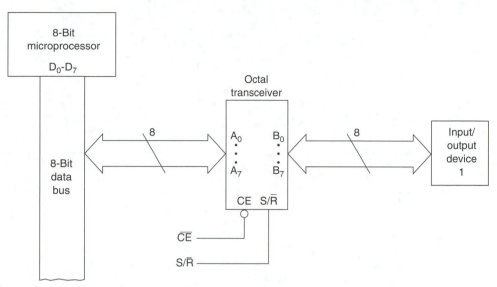

Figure M–6 Using an octal transceiver to interface an input/output device to an 8-bit data bus.

is a necessary characteristic for interfacing devices used for *both input and output* to the microprocessor. Figure M–6 shows a common way to connect an I/O device to a data bus via a transceiver.

To make input/output device 1 the active interface, the $\overline{CE}$ (chip enable) line must first be made LOW. If $\overline{CE}$ is HIGH, the transceiver disconnects the I/O device from the bus by making the connection float.

After making $\overline{CE}$ LOW, the microprocessor then issues the appropriate level on the $S/\overline{R}$ line, depending on whether it wants to *send data to* the I/O device or *receive data from* the I/O device. If $S/\overline{R}$ is made HIGH, the transceiver allows data to pass to the I/O device (from *A* to *B*). If $S/\overline{R}$ is made LOW, the transceiver allows data to pass to the microprocessor data bus (from *B* to *A*).

To see how the transceiver is able to both send and receive data, study the internal logic of the 74LS245 shown in Figure M–7.

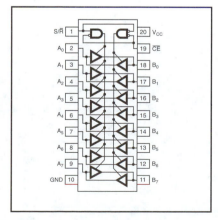

Figure M–7 Pin configuration and internal logic of the 74LS245 octal three-state transceiver.

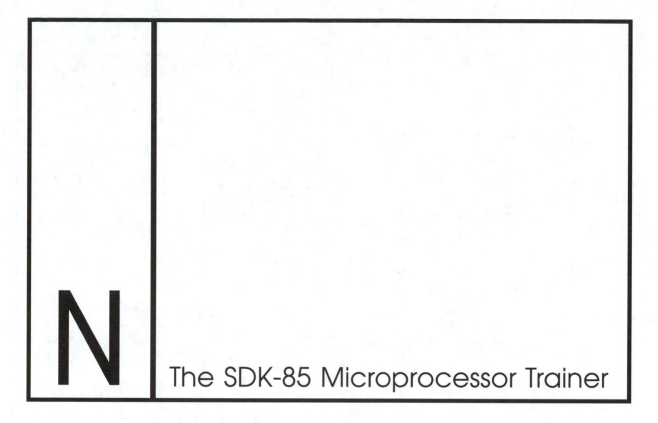

The SDK-85 Microprocessor Trainer

The SDK-85 is an 8085A-based microprocessor trainer used primarily in colleges for teaching the fundamentals of microprocessor hardware and software. The board layout given in Figure N–1 shows the physical layout of the trainer. As you can see, the 8085A is located near the center of the board and is driven by a 6.144-MHz crystal. User interface to the board is provided via the keypad located in the lower right or a computer terminal connected to the TTY interface expansion circuitry available in the upper right of the board. A 4-digit display for the addresses and a 2-digit display for the 8-bit data are located just above the keypad. Several bus expansion and I/O connectors (J1 through J5) are provided next to the blank prototyping area on the left side of the board. The prototyping area is provided for students to build custom circuitry of their own to interface to the SDK-85 board.

The functional block diagram in Figure N–2 shows the interconnection of the major parts of the trainer. As shown, the 8085 sends and receives signals from all three buses in the system. Chip enabling is controlled by the 8205 address decoder or its replacement, the 74LS138. This IC provides a chip enable for either the 8355, the 8155, or the 8279.

The 8355 (or its replacement, the 8755 EPROM) is a 2K ROM containing the monitor program (operating system) provided by the manufacturer for the SDK-85. It also provides 16 bits of I/O capability.

The 8155 is a 256-byte RAM used to hold the software programs entered by the student. The 8155 also provides hardware counter/timers and 22 bits of I/O.

The 8279 is a keyboard and display controller. The monitor program uses this IC to read the keyboard and drive the 6 LED displays.

Room is also provided on the board for 8212s and 8216s for bus expansion to the J1 to J5 connectors.

The layout of the keypad is given in Figure N–3. The keypad provides the means to enter hexadecimal digits for representing addresses and data values that make up the

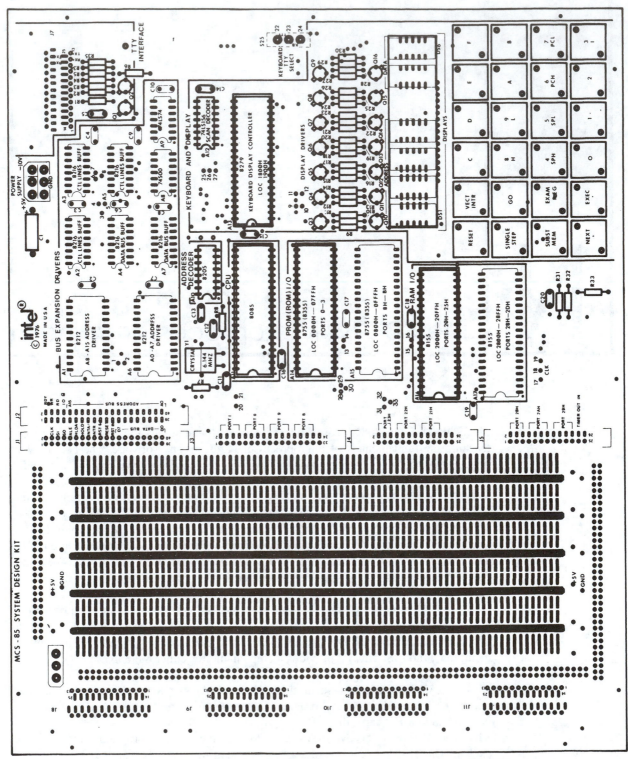

Figure N–1 The SDK-85 board layout. (Courtesy of URDA, Inc.)

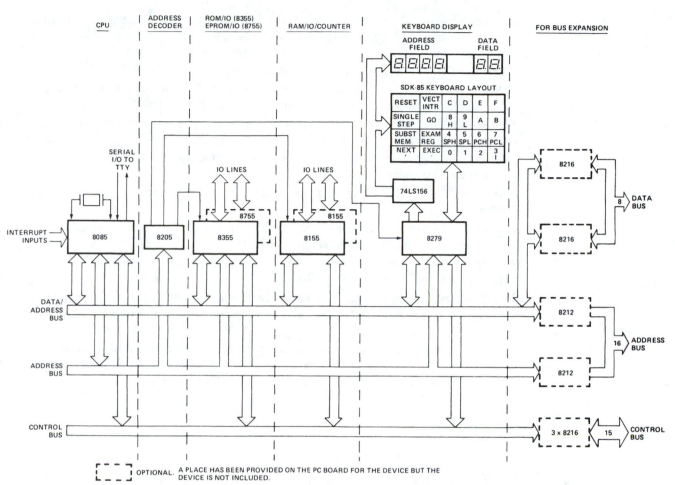

Figure N–2 The SDK-85 functional block diagram. (Courtesy of URDA, Inc.)

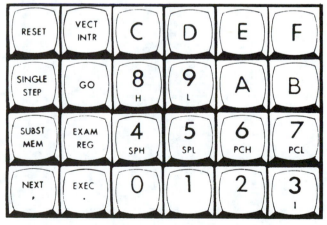

Figure N–3 The SDK-85 keypad. (Courtesy of URDA, Inc.)

student's program. The 8 keys on the left of the keypad are used to enter, execute, and troubleshoot programs. The function of each key is as follows:

RESET —This causes a hardware reset and starts the monitor.

SINGLE STEP —A powerful troubleshooting tool that allows the user to step through the program one statement at a time to watch the effect of each step.

SUBST MEM —Substitute Memory allows the user to read ROM memory and to read or write to RAM memory.

NEXT —This key stores the displayed data byte into the displayed address and increments to the next address location.

VECT INTR —The Vector Interrupt key initiates a hardware interrupt directly to the 8085A.

GO —This key displays the address contents of the program counter. It can then be changed to the starting address of the program to be executed.

EXAM REG —Examine Register is another troubleshooting tool used to look at the contents of any of the internal 8085A registers.

EXEC —Pressing the Execute key transfers control to the 8085A, which then executes the program starting at the address shown in the address field of the display.

Detailed instructions on the operation of the SDK-85 are provided by the manufacturer of the trainer. The SDK-85 is available from URDA Inc., 1811 Jancey Street, Suite 200, Pittsburgh, PA 15206, 1-800-338-0517 or (412) 363-0990.

Index

*Note: Page number in **boldface** indicates end-of-chapter glossary definition for the term.

Supplementary Index of ICs

This is an index of the integrated circuits (ICs) discussed in this book. The page numbers indicate where the IC is first discussed. Page numbers in **boldface** type indicate pages containing a data sheet for the device.

00	NOP		2B	DCX	H	56	MOV	D,M
01	LXI	B,dble	2C	INR	L	57	MOV	D,A
02	STAX	B	2D	DCR	L	58	MOV	E,B
03	INX	B	2E	MVI	L,byte	59	MOV	E,C
04	INR	B	2F	CMA		5A	MOV	E,D
05	DCR	B	30	SIM*		5B	MOV	E,E
06	MVI	B,byte	31	LXI	SP,dble	5C	MOV	E,H
07	RLC		32	STA	adr	5D	MOV	E,L
08	– – –		33	INX	SP	5E	MOV	E,M
09	DAD	B	34	INR	M	5F	MOV	E,A
0A	LDAX	B	35	DCR	M	60	MOV	H,B
0B	DCX	B	36	MVI	M,byte	61	MOV	H,C
0C	INR	C	37	STC		62	MOV	H,D
0D	DCR	C	38	– – –		63	MOV	H,E
0E	MVI	C,byte	39	DAD	SP	64	MOV	H,H
0F	RRC		3A	LDA	adr	65	MOV	H,L
10	– – –		3B	DCX	SP	66	MOV	H,M
11	LXI	D,dble	3C	INR	A	67	MOV	H,A
12	STAX	D	3D	DCR	A	68	MOV	L,B
13	INX	D	3E	MVI	A,byte	69	MOV	L,C
14	INR	D	3F	CMC		6A	MOV	L,D
15	DCR	D	40	MOV	B,B	6B	MOV	L,E
16	MVI	D,byte	41	MOV	B,C	6C	MOV	L,H
17	RAL		42	MOV	B,D	6D	MOV	L,L
18	– – –		43	MOV	B,E	6E	MOV	L,M
19	DAD	D	44	MOV	B,H	6F	MOV	L,A
1A	LDAX	D	45	MOV	B,L	70	MOV	M,B
1B	DCX	D	46	MOV	B,M	71	MOV	M,C
1C	INR	E	47	MOV	B,A	72	MOV	M,D
1D	DCR	E	48	MOV	C,B	73	MOV	M,E
1E	MVI	E,byte	49	MOV	C,C	74	MOV	M,H
1F	RAR		4A	MOV	C,D	75	MOV	M,L
20	RIM*		4B	MOV	C,E	76	HLT	
21	LXI	H,dble	4C	MOV	C,H	77	MOV	M,A
22	SHLD	adr	4D	MOV	C,L	78	MOV	A,B
23	INX	H	4E	MOV	C,M	79	MOV	A,C
24	INR	H	4F	MOV	C,A	7A	MOV	A,D
25	DCR	H	50	MOV	D,B	7B	MOV	A,E
26	MVI	H,byte	51	MOV	D,C	7C	MOV	A,H
27	DAA		52	MOV	D,D	7D	MOV	A,L
28	– – –		53	MOV	D,E	7E	MOV	A,M
29	DAD	H	54	MOV	D,H	7F	MOV	A,A
2A	LHLD	adr	55	MOV	D,L	80	ADD	B

*8085 Only.

81	ADD	C	AC	XRA	H	D7	RST	2
82	ADD	D	AD	XRA	L	D8	RC	
83	ADD	E	AE	XRA	M	D9	– – –	
84	ADD	H	AF	XRA	A	DA	JC	adr
85	ADD	L	B0	ORA	B	DB	IN	byte
86	ADD	M	B1	ORA	C	DC	CC	adr
87	ADD	A	B2	ORA	D	DD	– – –	
88	ADC	B	B3	ORA	E	DE	SBI	byte
89	ADC	C	B4	ORA	H	DF	RST	3
8A	ADC	D	B5	ORA	L	E0	RPO	
8B	ADC	E	B6	ORA	M	E1	POP	H
8C	ADC	H	B7	ORA	A	E2	JPO	adr
8D	ADC	L	B8	CMP	B	E3	XTHL	
8E	ADC	M	B9	CMP	C	E4	CPO	adr
8F	ADC	A	BA	CMP	D	E5	PUSH	H
90	SUB	B	BB	CMP	E	E6	ANI	byte
91	SUB	C	BC	CMP	H	E7	RST	4
92	SUB	D	BD	CMP	L	E8	RPE	
93	SUB	E	BE	CMP	M	E9	PCHL	
94	SUB	H	BF	CMP	A	EA	JPE	adr
95	SUB	L	C0	RNZ		EB	XCHG	
96	SUB	M	C1	POP	B	EC	CPE	adr
97	SUB	A	C2	JNZ	adr	ED	– – –	
98	SBB	B	C3	JMP	adr	EE	XRI	byte
99	SBB	C	C4	CNZ	adr	EF	RST	5
9A	SBB	D	C5	PUSH	B	F0	RP	
9B	SBB	E	C6	ADI	byte	F1	POP	PSW
9C	SBB	H	C7	RST	0	F2	JP	adr
9D	SBB	L	C8	RZ		F3	DI	
9E	SBB	M	C9	RET		F4	CP	adr
9F	SBB	A	CA	JZ	adr	F5	PUSH	PSW
A0	ANA	B	CB	– – –		F6	ORI	byte
A1	ANA	C	CC	CZ	adr	F7	RST	6
A2	ANA	D	CD	CALL	adr	F8	RM	
A3	ANA	E	CE	ACI	byte	F9	SPHL	
A4	ANA	H	CF	RST	1	FA	JM	adr
A5	ANA	L	D0	RNC		FB	EI	
A6	ANA	M	D1	POP	D	FC	CM	adr
A7	ANA	A	D2	JNC	adr	FD	– – –	
A8	XRA	B	D3	OUT	byte	FE	CPI	byte
A9	XRA	C	D4	CNC	adr	FF	RST	7
AA	XRA	D	D5	PUSH	D			
AB	XRA	E	D6	SUI	byte			